AMERICAN ECONOMIC POLICY

FROM THE REVOLUTION TO THE

NEW DEAL

AMERICAN ECONOMIC POLICY
FROM THE REVOLUTION TO THE NEW DEAL

WILLIAM LETWIN, EDITOR

Routledge
Taylor & Francis Group

LONDON AND NEW YORK

First published 1961 by Transaction Publishers

Published 2017 by Routledge
2 Park Square, Milton Park, Abingdon, Oxon OX14 4RN
711 Third Avenue, New York, NY 10017, USA

Routledge is an imprint of the Taylor & Francis Group, an informa business

Library of Congress Catalog Number: 2006041346

Library of Congress Cataloging-in-Publication Data

American economic policy from the revolution to the New Deal / William Letwin, editor.
    p. cm.
    Includes bibliographical references.
    ISBN 978-0-202-30924-8 (alk. paper)
    1. United States—Economic policy. 2. United States—Economic conditions. I. Letwin, William.

HC103.A455   2007
338.973—dc22   2006041346

ISBN 13: 978-0-202-30924-8 (pbk)

Preface

A country's economic history is the record of all the economic actions of all its inhabitants. These actions are countless, and the records they leave behind are so numerous, fragmentary, and scattered that the historian can neither hope nor wish to examine more than a minute fraction of them. No small collection of these myriad scraps of evidence—old invoices, canceled checks and expired leases, faded blueprints and barely legible calculations on the backs of used envelopes—can reveal much about how people lived.

But economic history is also the record of deliberate efforts men have made to shape their country's economic life. And this aspect, the history of economic policy, is well documented. The documents, being efforts at persuasion, are coherent and self-contained. Usually addressed to a wide audience, they avoid technical jargon. They try to demonstrate that some proposed policy fits the structure and aims of the community. They therefore present clear and vivid evidence of what men have desired and hoped to achieve, and explain not only much that is crucial about how men lived in the past but much also about the inheritance of the present.

No collection of these documents can, in any final sense, be representative. But the task of selection is lightened by recognizing that certain questions of economic policy constantly recur. In fact, some of those questions are continuous. For instance, in every community sophisticated enough to use money, there are always issues of monetary policy. The forms of money may change, the specific monetary problems that the community regards as pressing may change very quickly, and at times the monetary mechanism may function so well that the public is not conscious of a monetary problem—but the problem is always there. The same is true of taxation, import and export control, public investment in industry, banking, regulation of public utilities, public control of natural resources, and other general questions of economic policy.

These problems become clearest when one of them erupts, for the moment, as a major political issue. The question, for instance, of how banks and credit should be regulated, became a matter of great public excitement when the second Bank of the United States applied for renewal of its charter. At such moments, some statesmen, experts, or journalists issue statements that are perhaps impassioned yet nevertheless careful and comprehensive treatments of the central subject in its relations to the whole of political and social life. Great cases may, as Holmes said, make bad law; but great debates make great and classic documents.

Although space does not permit me to trace any single policy through its whole career in American history, I have wanted to include a fairly wide (though necessarily incomplete) variety of economic problems. I have therefore chosen to show how each of a number of problems was treated, at one of the moments when it was politically urgent. The central control of banking is, for instance, presented in the context of the debate on renewing the charter of the second Bank of the United States. In making this choice, I do not mean to assert that the central banking problem was the single most serious question of economic policy during the 1830s, or that this episode was the most important moment in the history of central bank policy in the United States. My choice implies instead that control of banking is a basic problem of policy, that it was an important political issue during the 1830s, and that the documents offered here deal in an especially illuminating way not only with certain permanent problems of banking but with other issues as well that were peculiar to the time and place. I have therefore used a dual system of classification. The documents are presented in roughly chronological order, and are grouped as well according to the policy problems they deal with.

I have made no effort, in choosing the documents, to balance one view with another, as though every opinion necessarily brought forth an equal and opposite opinion. There are often many conflicting views, and sometimes an opinion is opposed by little but apathy, habit, or malice; to arrange documents in a neatly counterpoised pattern would suggest a picture infinitely more symmetrical than ever exists in reality. To deny that history is tidy is not however to assert that it is random. I have sketched in the introductory essay the historical pattern into which I believe these documents fall.

In editing the documents I have tried to omit little except formal technicalities. In some instances, the portion printed is part of a larger whole but always as far as possible a self-contained part. Spelling and punctuation have been modernized only when it seemed essential. The citation for each document is a guide to an accessible and authoritative edition of its full text. Further guides to the literature can be found in the Dictionary of American Biography and the Harvard Guide to American History.

Miss Bettina Cleveland and Mr. Thomas K. Glennan, Jr., have given invaluable help, which I gratefully acknowledge, in preparing the documents for publication.

Contents

Part II: 1862–1912

PART III: 1912–1935

Introduction

To study a nation's economic policy, one must take notice of what people said they would like to do, what they said they did, and what they *in fact* did. No one of these alone is economic policy. Intentions often go unrealized, especially if they can be realized only within a political process. It is no safer to observe actions alone, rather than words, for the action cannot be understood apart from the actors' intentions and motives. The history of economic policy necessarily becomes a history of all the vague facts and sentiments, ideas and feelings that have influenced the nation's government.

The path that economic policy follows in its historical development is sinuous and obscure. To trace all its convolutions is an immensely difficult task. Faced with it, historians fall back, as they must, on simplifying notions. Instead of mapping all the meanderings of the real path, scholars try to match it, however roughly, with ready-made patterns. The professional tool kit of economists and historians contains a few basic patterns that are thought to be generally useful for dealing with economic policy. They bear such names as *laissez-faire*, socialism, mercantilism, communism, and welfare state.

From this none too ample selection, the pattern usually chosen to describe American economic policy is the one labeled *laissez-faire*. The United States developed as it did, historians say, because its government governed little. The nation grew rich because its governors suffered robber barons gladly.

The exponents of this view differ on the desirability of the outcome. One group holds that the enrichment of the few was the necessary and natural way to accomplish the welfare, albeit unequal welfare, of all. Others maintain that the policy of negative government gave rise to inequities and abuses so disturbing that eventually, during the Great Depression and through the efforts of the New Deal, a welfare state was grudgingly installed as the alternative to utter collapse and revolution. While historians disagree about the merits of traditional economic policy in the United States, they accept without question the view that American economic policy was long *laissez-faire* and only very lately anything else.

So neat a formulation should invite disbelief. There is something too tidy and too implausible in the notion that a government of many different, changing men could for two centuries remain so faithfully and consistently attached to a single set of means and ends. And once one turns from the ready-made pattern to the details, it becomes evident that the formula of a long reign of *laissez-faire* has persisted only because historians have preferred to make neat maps that leave out difficult irregularities, to deduce decisions on economic policy too exclusively from economic theories, and to ignore non-economic motives and desires.

I

In reviewing the history of American economic policy, I shall find it convenient to separate it into three eras, 1789 to 1862, 1862 to 1912, and 1912 to 1935. The first of these periods, from the foundation of the Republic to the Civil War, offers the happiest ground for those who deduce economic policy from the theoretical remarks of statesmen. Never since that time have so many American statesmen spoken so well, and never since have so many of them spoken the language of economic liberalism.

Nowhere is this language more clearly to be heard than in the voice of Thomas Jefferson. In his first inaugural address, delivered in 1801, after enumerating the rich opportunities available to Americans, he said:

> With all these blessings, what more is necessary to make us a happy and prosperous people? Still one thing more, fellow-citizens—a wise and frugal government, which shall restrain men from injuring one another, which shall leave them otherwise free to regulate their own pursuits of industry and improvement, and shall not take from the mouth of labor the bread it has earned. This is the sum of good government, and this is necessary to close the circle of our felicities.

This statement of creed, much as it reflected the hopes of Jefferson and many other Americans then and since, is a poor guide to what government actually did during Jefferson's tenure of office, or at any other time.

The government, according to Jefferson, was to act seldom and tax little. In accordance with this view, he went far toward disarming the United States, resting his diplomacy on the estimate that foreign nations would not attack a nation much more valuable to them as a customer than as a vassal. During his first administration, federal revenues were applied in large part to reducing the public debt incurred during the War of Independence. Once the public debt had been paid off, taxes were to be reduced still further—or so Jefferson must have planned. But nothing of the sort happened.

Four years later Jefferson made his second inaugural address. Revenues, largely obtained from tariff duties, had been rising; the debt was being reduced. Jefferson might have been expected to announce the near prospect that the tariff, doubly repugnant because it was a tax and because it was in part deliberately protective, would be reduced. He announced instead: "Redemption once effected, the revenue thereby liberated may, by a just repartition among the States and a corresponding amendment of the Constitution, be applied, in time of peace, to rivers, canals, roads, arts, manufactures, education, and other great objects within each State."

Government would, in short, become an encourager and promoter of industry. No longer would it leave men "free to regulate their own pursuits of industry and improvement"; instead it would tax the citizens in order to benefit them, in order to finance the improvements—build the canals and stimulate the manufactures—which private enterprise could not be depended on to undertake. The system of "internal improvements" that Jefferson in office now advocated was no kin to the doctrines of minimal government that Jefferson, the political philosopher, had often espoused.

The expenditures of the federal government during Jefferson's presidential terms do not show much spending on internal improvements. The annual average was under $100,000, a very small figure even then. But this does not mean that the antipathy to government spending prevailed after all. The complete record of a government's economic activity is not to be found in its budget—certainly not, especially during the first decades of the nineteenth century, in the budget of the federal government, then perhaps the feeblest and certainly the youngest government within the United States.

The chief authors of economic policy at this time were the state governments themselves. In ratifying the Constitution, they had handed over to the central government sole power to control and tax interstate and foreign commerce and sole power to coin money. The states retained almost all other powers to rule economic life and these they exercised vigorously at first.

The activities of Massachusetts are a fair sample of the whole. The state inherited from the colonial government that it succeeded a full armory of economic measures, for the colonial government had practiced a policy that can be labeled mercantilist with fewer qualms than one often feels in using that term. How surprising would it have been had this well-established policy suddenly been abandoned merely because Massachusetts had become a sovereign commonwealth.

During the first half of the nineteenth century, the state of Massachusetts—or local bodies acting on its authority—regulated and inspected the production of lumber, flaxseed, potash, tobacco, and various foodstuffs. The inspection system was managed by projectors and fee-farmers and financed by producers and merchants. Innkeepers, confectioners, and victualers could do business only under license. Bridge-keepers, ferrymen, and millowners might charge only such fees as were prescribed by law. Banks must maintain minimum reserve ratios. The whole of early corporation law had a regulatory character. The charter was granted by a special act of incorporation, which created the body and authorized it to do certain business; at the same time the charter imposed limits and required certain services.

At the other end of the scale was a widespread system of economic encouragement. Massachusetts subsidized fisheries, awarded bounties for the growing of hemp and the manufacture of sailcloth. Such subsidies were, as usual, justified by the benefits they presumably bestowed on others than the recipients. Cultivation of hemp was encouraged on the ground that

its cheapness would help ropemakers and shipowners, manufacture of sailcloth on the argument that the subsidy would
"enable the manufacturer to give such a price for flax as will
induce the farmer to exert himself." The state advanced loans
to some entrepreneurs and exempted others from taxation—if,
for example, they did such signal service as brewing more than
a hundred barrels of beer annually. By 1812 the government
had invested one-eighth of all the capital of banks in the state.
It issued its scrip as security for loans by the Western Railroad,
lending between 1835 and 1841 $4 million of its credit, or
over half the capital invested in the railroad.

Nor was Massachusetts indifferent to welfare considerations.
The municipal authorities operated a system of poor relief, and
about 1850 the state supplemented the facilities by building
institutions under its immediate supervision. A weak child
labor law was passed in 1836; a more effective one in 1858,
setting standards of compulsory schooling for children who
worked in factories.

The total impact of government on the economy cannot be
read in the activities of the federal government alone; neither
can the whole effort of the state governments be traced in their
statute books. The legal status of trade unions and strikes,
which, in England and later in the United States, was defined
by the various combination acts, came into being in the United
States through the operation of common-law courts. The right
of unions to strike was established as early as 1842 by a decision of the Massachusetts supreme court in the case of *Commonwealth vs. Hunt.*

Other states did more and some did less than Massachusetts, but taken all together the states exercised a much
greater influence on economic life during the first fifty years
than did the federal government. Little by little, however,
functions were transferred from the local to the central government. The case of internal improvements is characteristic of
the transition.

At first it was the states which fostered canals, turnpike and
bridge companies, and the railroads. Often and more and more

they did so with resources handed over for the purpose by the federal government. This indirect method was dictated by constitutional interpretation: early in the nineteenth century it was accepted that the federal government could not build roads or schools within the states. The federal government could and did finance such undertakings by direct grants to the states. The importance of these aids, even in the early period, has often been overlooked because they were made in kind rather than cash and their value was accordingly not entered in the federal budget.

In 1802 and 1803, Congress provided that public lands should be given over to the new State of Ohio so that it should lay out roads leading to the Ohio River. Slowly this method of encouragement came into fashion. In 1828, Alabama was given 400,000 acres for the improvement of its river system. Large tracts of land were given to Indiana and Illinois to assist the construction of canals. After the invention of railroads the device began to be used in earnest. During the 1850s and 1860s massive grants were handed over, at first to the states, later directly to the railroad corporations themselves. All together, between 1823 and 1871, almost 150,000,000 acres of public land were ceded for the construction of railroads, canals, and roads. Over 100,000,000 acres more were given to the states for education, bridges, reservoirs, and other internal improvements. In short, about one-eighth of the present area of the United States went into such subsidies before 1871. This land alone, not to mention other forms of associated subsidies, may easily have been worth $500,000,000 when granted. This sum is more than what the federal government spent on all other civil functions (excluding the management and redemption of debt) between 1800 and 1850. A land budget of the federal government would give a more accurate account of its economic activities before the Civil War than can the fiscal budget.

Besides absorbing gradually the major responsibility for internal improvement, the federal government itself had meanwhile acquired a more elaborate and detailed economic policy than is often supposed. From the beginning it maintained a system of compulsory health insurance for seamen. It licensed fur traders, and established its own fur posts, which were intended to reduce the monopsonistic power of the private traders. It subsidized codfishing and merchant-marine construction, and regulated those industries in the interests of health and safety. Moreover, although there was no federal labor legislation before 1860, a ten-hour day was instituted for federal employees before 1840.

The most vital way, however, in which the federal government exercised its economic policy was through the tariff. In view of the fact that the United States maintained, except for brief intervals, a deliberately protective tariff, one is bound to wonder how its economic policy could ever have been described as "negative." To be sure, Hamilton appreciated Adam Smith's arguments so well that he based his support of protective tariffs on the infant industry plea. But the infant industries of 1789, which were supposed to need protection only until they learned to stand on their own feet, were not infants thirty or forty years later, and yet tariff protection was still requested and granted. The justification had been sketched in by Hamilton; Henry Clay, founding spokesman of the so-called American System, was its strongest advocate. He maintained that, if foreign commerce was dammed off, the full flow of goods produced within the United States would be forced to circulate there, scouring out new channels of domestic trade, extending and consolidating the national economy. No doubt many had more partisan and interested reasons for favoring protection; but, whatever the motives, a policy autarkic in character became the accepted American mode. It has remained, despite the long and impassioned efforts of its opponents, one of the more stable features of the American heritage.

Economic policy between the Revolutionary and Civil wars was, therefore, anything but negative. It seems so only if one ignores the action of state and municipal governments; if one restricts one's investigations to the statute books while overlooking the law reports; if, instead of recognizing that many subsidies took non-pecuniary forms and that the costs of much regulation are borne as private non-pecuniary costs, one measures the costs of policy only by the cash outlay of government. But if one includes all the activities of government, and takes into reckoning all the costs, one must conclude that an economic policy, aimed principally at encouraging the internal growth of the nation's economy, was pursued with great energy and at considerable expense.

II

The characteristic feature of economic policy changed, during the second period, 1862–1912, from subsidy to regulation. The change, irregular, and at first noticeable only as a change of emphasis, was closely connected with what may be described, imprecisely, as the maturing of the American economy.

One of the facts, for instance, that underlay the new attitude was that the facilities for internal transportation had by 1870 become reasonably ample. With the completion of the transcontinental railroads, the period of fastest railroad building was over. Those villages, those farmers and merchants, who had clamored for railroads, who had competed with one another for the privilege of having tracks pass their doors, and who had wildly bought the stocks and bonds of railroads, now had their railroads.

Also, they were confronted with the consequences of their frenzy, consequences that seemed to them appalling. A vast block of public land had been handed over to the railroads, which were now selling that land at much increased prices; this realization put an end to land grants after 1872. Between certain major centers, especially in the northeastern quarter of the country, there were enough railroads to provide extremely sharp competition. This led to bankruptcy of the weaker railroads, antagonizing many small investors who attributed their losses to frenzied and fraudulent financial practices.

In other areas, especially in the outlying rural sections of the country, railroads took advantage of their local monopoly powers to charge rates that seemed outrageously high. The contrast between service at the nodes in the railroad network, connected by several carriers, and between the many points connected by only a single carrier made for the short-haul long-haul anomaly. To ship a ton of wheat 1000 miles between Chicago and New York might cost less than to ship the same quantity between two intermediate points connected by one railroad only. Moreover, the threat of potential competition from large shippers—who might, if they were, for instance, oil refiners, build their own pipelines—together with economies in handling large shipments, made the carriers offer discriminatory rates. These practices offended the less-favored shippers and many disinterested bystanders.

During the 1870s, accordingly, a powerful movement—misnamed the Granger movement, for farmers organized in the Grange supplied only part of its force—quickly grew up and brought about statutory regulation of railroad rates and service. Granger laws were passed in many states, but before long they encountered a serious constitutional obstacle. No state law might directly interfere with interstate commerce, plenary power over which had been assigned to the federal government. This obstacle was overcome in 1887 with the passage by Congress of the Interstate Commerce Act, the foundation of all federal regulation of public services and utilities.

The attitude toward the mechanics of government regulation revealed by the construction of the Interstate Commerce Act is typically American in its utter indifference to economic doctrine. Bills on the subject were introduced into Congress for almost a decade. But the bills could not be passed because of a fundamental disagreement among the lawmakers. One group of congressmen maintained that the law should simply prohibit malpractice by the railroads, making such actions criminal offenses and grounds for civil suit at the same time. Another group proposed instead that a regulatory commission be given power to judge and decide each case on its merits.

The issue was resolved only by compromise of the happiest sort: each side got all it wanted. The act of 1887 accordingly opened with a universal prohibition of unjust and unreasonable rates; it went on to establish the Interstate Commerce Commission, which would decide in each case whether the discriminatory practice was or was not justifiable in view of all the surrounding circumstances.

That *all* price discrimination is undesirable and that *some* price discrimination is desirable are two views logicians might find difficult to reconcile. The Interstate Commerce Act reconciled them, or treated them as reconcilable. Congress was aware of the difficulty, but held it more important to establish some control over railroads than to insist on an intellectually rigorous attitude toward price discrimination. This preference for solving political problems with a solution that is economically dubious or vague, is not unknown in other countries, but it is so common in American history as to suggest that it satisfies some special need in American tradition and temperament.

The same traits are exhibited in another important field of economic policy during the period 1862 to 1912, namely antitrust regulation. Here again, the underlying fact was that manufacturing—which had developed slowly, despite protection—now suddenly seemed no longer to need subsidy and encouragement. This view became popular during the 1880s, when a great wave of industrial consolidation and integration began to take place. What made the public especially hostile to the change was that many of the large new firms were brash enough to call themselves trusts. Trusts, everyone knew, was a euphemism for monopolies. Monopolies have been steadily detested by Americans since the beginning of their history.

An early proposal was that trusts be denied tariff protection. As a stronger attack was preferred, the Sherman Antitrust Law of 1890 was passed. That law made it a penal offense and civil wrong to form a combination in restraint of trade or to monopolize any industry. The Sherman Act did not incorporate the suggestions of those who urged that a regulatory commission—quasi-legislative, quasi-judicial, on the model of the Interstate Commerce Commission—be created to supervise the industrial organization of the economy. A commission would have suited those congressmen who maintained that competition was good and combination was good and too much of either was bad.

However, the pressure for this very American solution continued to mount. A leading spokesman for a regulatory agency in the antitrust field was Theodore Roosevelt, who insisted that trusts should be chastised with a big stick, and also insisted, not quite in the same breath, that there were good trusts and bad trusts. Finally, in 1914, the Federal Trade Commission was established and given overlapping authority with the Justice Department to enforce the antitrust laws. Mr. Dooley, that folk figure whom every economic historian feels compelled to quote, described the state of mind that antitrust officials should have aimed at after the Federal Trade Commission went to work: "On the one hand," said Mr. Dooley, "all trusts are evil; on the other hand, not so fast!" This, broadly understood, can be taken as the keynote of economic regulation in the United States, to serve which a complex structure of administrative agencies has been elaborated, a structure supported by no foundation of economic doctrine.

One other aspect of economic policy illustrative of its prevailing tone during the second period deserves to be mentioned. This is the attitude toward land and natural resources. Government, as I have said, lavishly spent public land during the first period. Some reasons for this prodigality emerge from the report in 1845 of Robert Walker, Secretary of the Treasury. Walker bewailed the fact that public land was being sold so slowly that it would still be on the government's hands a century later; he recommended that the price be lowered.

In 1890 the Director of the Census announced that from then on there could "hardly be said to be a frontier line." Now as anyone might have known, the Director's remark meant no more than that the frontier had collided with the Pacific coast; one line had reached another. Between the Mississippi and the Pacific, however, lay millions of acres, barren and empty, yet capable of being settled, cultivated, and used. Nevertheless, the stunning fact that the frontier boundary was gone had many interesting psychic effects. It gave occasion for Turner's frontier thesis, which predicted momentous changes in American political outlook because of curtailed opportunity. More important for economic policy, this fact persuaded people that a land which they had thought offered everyone a surfeit of natural bounty had suddenly become a land of scarcity; Americans began to feel that they had exhausted the free fruits of their Eden.

The result of this view was a series of acts designed to conserve the land. Government set aside large areas as national parks and forests. It reserved to itself mineral and other resources in public lands. It began, with the passage of the Newlands Act in 1902, to "reclaim" land from arid regions by way of publicly financed irrigation schemes. It began to teach farmers how to use their land more efficiently. All these things and more the states did also. In short, a misunderstanding of a relatively inconsequential fact helped bring about an obsessive desire to preserve—without regard to cost—earth, water, plants and animals.

Thus the urgent desire of Americans to build up their nation as quickly as possible in the period before 1862 gave way in the period after to a slightly panicked sense that too much had happened. The consequence was a set of policies aimed to slow down the expansion of railroads, the consolidation of industry, the exploitation of natural resources. Fittingly enough, these moves were accompanied by a strong movement to restrict immigration. A country that had aimed to grow as quickly as possible found itself becoming too big for its taste.

III

Economic facts seldom explain economic policy. Certainly in the case of American policy, the explanation—insofar as one can hope for it—is to be found in moral ideas that cannot themselves be explained by economic facts.

The chief facets of economic policy adopted by American government during the period since 1914 show the influence of a vague general notion of economic equity far more than

that of any economic event. "Equality," as vague as that term
is, does not describe the notion as well. The idea, in any event,
is easier to see in its effects than to describe abstractly. Its legal
manifestations are familiar. Labor unions acquired statutory
exemptions and immunities that have made them, of all organizations known to the law, the least subject to law. Farmers
achieved, by the operation of price-support schemes, an im-
munity that only few others share from the operation of the
price system. The purchasers of foods and drugs were offered
protection against fraud, misrepresentation, and their own carelessness or errors of judgment. Buyers of shares and stocks were
insulated against the extreme risks of risk-taking. The young
and the aged, the unemployed and injured, widows and or-
phans were all taken under the protection of the social security
system. All those, in short, who might be designated as the
victims of economic inequity were afforded protection and
reparation by government.

It is not always easy to understand from the outside what
qualifies certain groups as authentic victims for the purposes
of this branch of economic policy. Farmers require support,
it is said, because agricultural prices have not risen as far since
1914 as the prices of non-agricultural goods. Parity—to name
the mystic sign of this faith—has not been maintained. Even
if it were demonstrated that the farmers who draw the largest
benefits from price supports are those who least need public
aid, many people would remain convinced that a price-support program is essential because government exists to diminish
or obliterate economic differences. Small businessmen have
been the protégés of the Small Business Administration and of
a special committee of Congress. Presumably they warrant special care because small businessmen are smaller than big
businessmen. Foreign aid seems sometimes to be propounded
on a similar logic, which says that anyone who has more owes
something to those with less.

Much of the impulse toward these policies has been furnished by pure generosity. It would be misrepresenting the
motives of many who support these policies to suggest that the
generosity they feel is often practiced with other people's

money. It might also be impertinent to suggest that even acts of generosity can be purchased at too high a price. Despite all that, the fact remains that the policies of security—which aim to mitigate all risks or alleviate all losses from risk—are characteristic of the present period.

Their source, as I have said, was a notion of economic equity that has been growing for a long while. Its first great manifestation in national economic policy was the abortive income-tax law of 1894. An amendment to the Constitution, ratified in 1913, made a federal income tax lawful.

The early date of progressive income taxation suggests that the policies of equity and security are not, as many would have it, a legacy of the Great Depression and the New Deal. Many aspects of the policy antedate the Depression. The privileged status of labor unions dates, in federal law, from the Clayton Act of 1914, and was reinforced between then and the New Deal. The Adamson Act, ordaining an eight-hour day for railroad workers, was passed in 1916. Four years earlier, Massachusetts had set minimum wages for women and children. The modern regulation of wages and hours stems from this period during and shortly after the World War. The Federal Farm Loan Act of 1916 provided for long-term, low-interest loans to farmers. Farm price-support programs were passed by large Congressional majorities during the 1920s and failed to become law only because of Presidential vetoes. The Pure Food and Drug Act and the Meat Inspection Act were passed in 1906. The fundamental policy of security was therefore well implanted long before the Depression.

The policy was not a reaction to economic facts but to noneconomic sentiments. It was not an inevitable response to extreme hardship. Quite the contrary; the groups that came under protection were often better off at the moment just before protection was first afforded than they had ever been before; their real incomes had been rising and the inequality of incomes had probably been declining. What changed was the public's perception of equity in economic relations.

This moral sense was, of course, much heightened during

the Great Depression, and the policy of security was undoubtedly expanded more rapidly than it might otherwise have been. It has, nevertheless, continued to expand quite regularly during the long and unexampled prosperity since.

IV

The economic policy of the United States today is an amalgam of the chief tendencies that were emphasized during each of the three periods. Economic development by hothouse methods still persists. American manufacturers are given preference over foreign suppliers in bidding for government contracts. Railroads, steamship lines and airlines continue to be aided, partly by lucrative mail contracts, partly by restraints that the regulatory commissions place on rate competition. In the transport industries the United States may be said to administer a set of approved cartels. The tariff is still frankly protective in certain of its branches. American bicycle manufacturers, for instance, are kept in business by a high wall that shuts out what are known as "cheap foreign goods." In many sectors of American economic policy, the notions that are appropriate, if ever, only in a very young economy still operate, as though by reflex.

The regulatory mechanisms established during the second period and the security and redistribution measures of the third period are very much in evidence. In short, the development of economic policy in the United States has not consisted of a neat progression in which new policies have replaced outworn policies. What has happened, rather, is that the new policies have been added on to the old ones. In this sense, the role of government has expanded, the variety of its economic activities has widened. The possibility of explaining the whole of economic policy as the outcome of a coherent theoretical program has correspondingly diminished. History, not logic, Justice Holmes said, is the life of the law; the same is true of the economic policy that has accumulated in the laws.

It would be convenient to know whether the economic role
of government has expanded also in the other sense, that government now exercises a greater influence on economic life
than it did in the past. The record of expenditures by the federal government would support this view and is often invoked
for this purpose. The expenditures of the United States government amounted in 1800 to about 2 per cent of national income; today they are about 20 per cent. A more telling comparison, and one based on better statistics, shows that as recently as 1930 the civil expenditures of the federal government
were about 2.5 per cent of personal income, as compared with
about 10 per cent now.

But these numbers do not tell the story they seem to. The
federal government's expenditures are only part of the whole
of government expenditure. More important, the real burden
of government intervention cannot be fully stated by the
budget. Two tax systems, for instance a universal sales tax and
a protective tariff, may cost the same to administer and may
yield the same public revenue, but their real effects on the
economy will be very different. Burdensome government need
not cost much: a harsh police state may operate cheaply because it can avoid the expensive services of appeals court
judges. This elementary distinction between cheap government
and free government is regularly disregarded by those who
draw conclusions about economic policy from mere fiscal
statistics. Nobody can say with any assurance how much a
complex system of government really costs the governed. How
the governed judge the cost depends in large measure on their
views of what government ought to be doing.

What then does the history of economic policy in the United
States reveal about the theory or theories of economic policy
that Americans have entertained? The answer one is forced to
is that economic doctrines have never as much influenced the
making of American economic policy as have political and constitutional considerations. The reason why the whole of American economic policy looks so incoherent—with mercantilist, so-
cialist, liberal, or autarkic elements all living happily side by

side—is that political balance rather than economic consistency has been the more powerful drive.

Those who speak of the American economy as "mixed" speak better than they know. Economic policy has consistently been subordinated in the United States to the needs of political stability. Considering the economic and social mobility of Americans, and the effects of great and rapid immigration, it is more surprising that the United States has remained stable and capable of being governed by law than that it has become wealthy. Americans have not, in economic or political matters, been inclined to confuse professions of faith with commitments to act. Thanks to this, the pattern of American economic policy is exceedingly confused and therefore very annoying to historians and economists. But what is bad for the scholar has been good for the country. The extremism and disorder potentially so great in the United States have in this way been reduced to remarkable moderation.

PART I

1789-1862

A. Tariffs

During the early period, the tariff had a twofold importance. It was the federal government's chief instrument of regulation. It also furnished most of the federal revenues: from 1789 to 1862—except for 1796 and the two brief intervals of 1814–1818 and 1835–1840—customs receipts yielded over four-fifths of the government's annual income.

Some of the debate over the tariff arose from a clash between its two objectives. When, for instance, high protective duties yielded more revenue than the government chose to spend, it was faced with the troublesome problem of disposing of the surplus. When protective rates became so high that sales fell off, whereupon revenues declined, the government then had to curtail expenditures, borrow, or enlarge the use of other sources of revenue.

Politically, tariff questions divided the country by party, region, and economic interest. It is often loosely said that protective duties were favored by Federalists, Whigs and Republicans, inhabitants of the Northeast, and manufacturers; and opposed by Democrats, Southerners and Westerners, and farmers. Such a summary oversimplifies the position of men—such as Southern Federalists and New England farmers—who fit into two or more categories supposed to have been mutually exclusive.

Much of the attitude toward tariffs was determined in fact by the theoretical arguments on the two sides. The merits of protection and free trade have continued to be debated throughout American history; but the case for each has never been stated more authoritatively than by Hamilton (1) and by Walker (2).

Hamilton's powers as a constitutional theorist and economic analyst appear to best advantage in a set of papers that he wrote while Secretary of the Treasury (1789–95). These outlined the economic policy of Washington's administration, and they have had a lasting effect on the whole structure of American economic life. The report on public credit (1790) set out the basic financial arrangements between the states and the federal government as to public debt. The report on a Bank of the U. S. (1791) led to the establishment of a central bank (D). The report on manufactures (1) helped fix the American attitude toward economic growth.

The position Hamilton criticizes in the opening of this report is the one associated with Jefferson. The authority whom he later quotes and sometimes amends is Adam Smith.

Walker, a prominent spokesman in the Senate for the Southwest, served as Secretary of the Treasury under Polk from 1845 to 1849. His first report (2) was quickly recognized as a classic statement of the objections to protective duties, and certain of its proposals were incorporated into the tariff bill of 1846. The report is valuable also for indicating some characteristic Democratic views on such questions as banking, public lands, and internal improvements, and the expansionist attitude toward Oregon and Texas.

In speaking of the "true maximum" rate—"the lowest rate which will yield the largest amount of revenue"—Walker assumes that a number of different rates may all yield the maximum revenue. For example, 100 units of an article priced at $1, imported when the tariff rate stood at 10 per cent, would yield a tariff revenue of $10. If the rate were raised to 12½ per cent and only 80 units were imported, the revenue yield would still be $10.

1

ALEXANDER HAMILTON (1755–1804)
Report on Manufactures (5 Dec. 1791)
[Hamilton, *Works* (ed. Lodge), III, 294]

The expediency of encouraging manufactures in the United
States, which was not long since deemed very questionable,
appears at this time to be pretty generally admitted. The embarrassments which have obstructed the progress of our external trade, have led to serious reflections on the necessity of
enlarging the sphere of our domestic commerce. The restrictive
regulations, which, in foreign markets, abridge the vent of the
increasing surplus of our agricultural produce, serve to beget
an earnest desire, that a more extensive demand for that surplus
may be created at home; and the complete success which has
rewarded manufacturing enterprise, in some valuable branches,
conspiring with the promising symptoms which attend some
less mature essays in others, justify a hope, that the obstacles
to the growth of this species of industry are less formidable than
they were apprehended to be; and that it is not difficult to
find, in its further extension, a full indemnification for any external disadvantages, which are or may be experienced, as well
as an accession of resources, favorable to national independence and safety.

There still are, nevertheless, respectable patrons of opinions
unfriendly to the encouragement of manufactures. The following are, substantially, the arguments by which these opinions
are defended.

"In every country (say those who entertain them) agriculture is the most beneficial and productive object of human industry. This position, generally, if not universally true, applies
with peculiar emphasis to the United States, on account of
their immense tracts of fertile territory, uninhabited and un-

improved. Nothing can afford so advantageous an employment for capital and labor, as the conversion of this extensive wilderness into cultivated farms. Nothing, equally with this, can contribute to the population, strength, and real riches of the country.

"To endeavor, by the extraordinary patronage of government, to accelerate the growth of manufactures, is, in fact, to endeavor, by force and art, to transfer the natural current of industry from a more to a less beneficial channel. Whatever has such a tendency, must necessarily be unwise; indeed, it can hardly ever be wise in a government to attempt to give a direction to the industry of its citizens. This, under the quick-sighted guidance of private interest, will, if left to itself, infallibly find its own way to the most profitable employment; and it is by such employment, that the public prosperity will be most effectually promoted. To leave industry to itself, therefore, is, in almost every case, the soundest as well as the simplest policy.

"This policy is not only recommended to the United States, by considerations which affect all nations; it is, in a manner, dictated to them by the imperious force of a very peculiar situation. The smallness of their population compared with their territory; the constant allurements to emigration from the settled to the unsettled parts of the country; the facility with which the less independent condition of an artisan can be exchanged for the more independent condition of a farmer; these, and similar causes, conspire to produce, and, for a length of time, must continue to occasion, a scarcity of hands for manufacturing occupation, and dearness of labor generally. To these disadvantages for the prosecution of manufactures, a deficiency of pecuniary capital being added, the prospect of a successful competition with the manufactures of Europe, must be regarded as little less than desperate. Extensive manufactures can only be the offspring of a redundant, at least of a full population. Till the latter shall characterize the situation of this country, 'tis vain to hope for the former.

"If, contrary to the natural course of things, an unseasonable and premature spring can be given to certain fabrics,* by heavy duties, prohibitions, bounties, or by other forced expedients, this will only be to sacrifice the interests of the community to those of particular classes. Besides the misdirection of labor, a virtual monopoly will be given to the persons employed on such fabrics; and an enhancement of price, the inevitable consequence of every monopoly, must be defrayed at the expense of the other parts of society. It is far preferable, that those persons should be engaged in the cultivation of the earth, and that we should procure, in exchange for its productions, the commodities with which foreigners are able to supply us in greater perfection, and upon better terms."

This mode of reasoning is founded upon facts and principles which have certainly respectable pretensions. If it had governed the conduct of nations more generally than it has done, there is room to suppose that it might have carried them faster to prosperity and greatness than they have attained by the pursuit of maxims too widely opposite. Most general theories, however, admit of numerous exceptions, and there are few, if any, of the political kind, which do not blend a considerable portion of error with the truths they inculcate.

In order to an accurate judgment how far that which has been just stated ought to be deemed liable to a similar imputation, it is necessary to advert carefully to the considerations which plead in favor of manufactures, and which appear to recommend the special and positive encouragement of them in certain cases, and under certain reasonable limitations.

It ought readily to be conceded that the cultivation of the earth, as the primary and most certain source of national supply; as the immediate and chief source of subsistence to man; as the principal source of those materials which constitute the nutriment of other kinds of labor; as including a state most favorable to the freedom and independence of the human mind—one, perhaps, most conducive to the multiplication of the human species; has intrinsically a strong claim to preeminence over every other kind of industry.

* [Fabrics = manufactures]

But, that it has a title to any thing like an exclusive predilection, in any country, ought to be admitted with great caution; that it is even more productive than every other branch of industry, requires more evidence than has yet been given in support of the position. That its real interests, precious and important as, without the help of exaggeration, they truly are, will be advanced, rather than injured, by the due encouragement of manufactures, may, it is believed, be satisfactorily demonstrated. And it is also believed, that the expediency of such encouragement, in a general view, may be shown to be recommended by the most cogent and persuasive motives of national policy.

It has been maintained, that agriculture is not only the most productive, but the only productive species of industry. The reality of this suggestion, in either respect, has, however, not been verified by any accurate detail of facts and calculations; and the general arguments which are adduced to prove it, are rather subtile and paradoxical, than solid or convincing.

Those which maintain its exclusive productiveness, are to this effect:

Labor bestowed upon the cultivation of land, produces enough not only to replace all the necessary expenses incurred in the business, and to maintain the persons who are employed in it, but to afford, together with the ordinary profit on the stock or capital of the farmer, a net surplus or rent for the landlord or proprietor of the soil. But the labor of artificers does nothing more than replace the stock which employs them (or which furnishes materials, tools, and wages), and yield the ordinary profit upon that stock. It yields nothing equivalent to the rent of land; neither does it add any thing to the total value of the whole annual produce of the land and labor of the country. The additional value given to those parts of the produce of land, which are wrought into manufactures, is counterbalanced by the value of those other parts of that produce which are consumed by the manufacturers. It can, therefore, only be by saving or parsimony, not by the positive productiveness of their labor, that the classes of artificers can, in any degree, augment the revenue of the society.

To this it has been answered:

1. "That, inasmuch as it is acknowledged that manufacturing labor re-produces a value equal to that which is expended or consumed in carrying it on, and continues in existence the original stock or capital employed, it ought, on that account, alone, to escape being considered as wholly unproductive. That, though it should be admitted, as alleged, that the consumption of the produce of the soil, by the classes of artificers or manufacturers, is exactly equal to the value added by their labor to the materials upon which it is exerted, yet, it would not thence follow, that it added nothing to the revenue of the society, or to the aggregate value of the annual produce of its land and labor. If the consumption, for any given period, amounted to a given sum, and the increased value of the produce manufactured, in the same period, to a like sum, the total amount of the consumption and production, during that period, would be equal to the two sums, and consequently double the value of the agricultural produce consumed; and, though the increment of value produced by the classes of artificers should, at no time, exceed the value of the produce of the land consumed by them, yet, there would be, at every moment, in consequence of their labor, a greater value of goods in the market than would exist independent of it."

2. "That the position, that artificers can augment the revenue of a society only by parsimony, is true in no other sense than in one which is equally applicable to husbandmen or cultivators. It may be alike affirmed of all these classes, that the fund acquired by their labor, and destined for their support, is not, in an ordinary way, more than equal to it. And hence, it will follow, that augmentations of the wealth or capital of the community (except in the instances of some extraordinary dexterity or skill), can only proceed, with respect to any of them, from the savings of the more thrifty and parsimonious."

3. "That the annual produce of the land and labor of a country can only be increased in two ways—by some improvement in the productive powers of the useful labor which actually exist within it, or by some increase in the quantity of such labor. That, with regard to the first, the labor of artificers

being capable of greater sub-division and simplicity of operation than that of cultivators, it is susceptible, in a proportion-
ably greater degree of improvement in its productive powers,
whether to be derived from an accession of skill or from the
application of ingenious machinery: in which particular, therefore, the labor employed in the culture of land can pretend
to no advantage over that engaged in manufactures. That,
with regard to an augmentation of the quantity of useful labor,
this, excluding adventitious circumstances, must depend essentially upon an increase of capital, which again must depend
upon the savings made out of the revenues of those who furnish or manage that which is at any time employed, whether
in agriculture or in manufactures, or in any other way."

But, while the exclusive productiveness of agricultural labor
has been thus denied and refuted, the superiority of its productiveness has been conceded without hesitation. As this concession involves a point of considerable magnitude, in relation to
maxims of public administration, the grounds on which it rests
are worthy of a distinct and particular examination.

One of the arguments made use of in support of the idea,
may be pronounced both quaint and superficial. It amounts
to this: That, in the productions of the soil, nature co-operates
with man; and that the effect of their joint labor must be
greater than that of the labor of man alone.

This, however, is far from being a necessary inference. It is
very conceivable, that the labor of man alone, laid out upon a
work requiring great skill and art to bring it to perfection, may
be more productive, in value, than the labor of nature and
man combined, when directed towards more simple operations
and objects; and when it is recollected to what an extent the
agency of nature, in the application of the mechanical powers,
is made auxiliary to the prosecution of manufactures, the suggestion which has been noticed loses even the appearance of
plausibility.

It might also be observed, with a contrary view, that the
labor employed in agriculture, is, in a great measure, periodical and occasional, depending on seasons, and liable to various
and long intermissions; while that occupied in many manufac-

tures is constant and regular, extending through the year, embracing, in some instances, night as well as day. It is also probable that there are, among the cultivators of land, more examples of remissness than among artificers. The farmer, from the peculiar fertility of his land, or some other favorable circumstance, may frequently obtain a livelihood, even with a considerable degree of carelessness in the mode of cultivation; but the artisan can with difficulty effect the same object, without exerting himself pretty equally with all those who are engaged in the same pursuit. And if it may likewise be assumed as a fact, that manufactures open a wider field to exertions of ingenuity than agriculture, it would not be a strained conjecture, that the labor employed in the former, being at once more constant, more uniform, and more ingenious, than that which is employed in the latter, will be found, at the same time, more productive.

But it is not meant to lay stress on observations of this nature; they ought only to serve as a counter-balance to those of a similar complexion. Circumstances so vague and general, as well as so abstract, can afford little instruction in a matter of this kind.

Another, and that which seems to be the principal argument offered for the superior productiveness of agricultural labor, turns upon the allegation, that labor employed on manufactures yields nothing equivalent to the rent of land; or to that net surplus, as it is called, which accrues to the proprietor of the soil.

But this distinction, important as it has been deemed, appears rather verbal than substantial.

It is easily discernible, that what, in the first instance, is divided into two parts, under the denominations of the ordinary profit of the stock of the farmer and rent to the landlord, is, in the second instance, united under the general appellation of the ordinary profit on the stock of the undertaker; and that this formal or verbal distribution constitutes the whole difference in the two cases. It seems to have been overlooked, that the land is itself a stock or capital, advanced or lent by its owner to the occupier or tenart, and that the rent he receives

is only the ordinary profit of a certain stock in land, not managed by the proprietor himself, but by another, to whom he
lends or lets it, and who, on his part, advances a second capital, to stock and improve the land, upon which he also receives
the usual profit. The rent of the landlord and the profit of the
farmer are, therefore, nothing more than the ordinary profits
of the two capitals belonging to two different persons, and
united in the cultivation of a farm: as, in the other case, the
surplus which arises upon any manufactory, after replacing the
expenses of carrying it on, answers to the ordinary profits of
one or more capitals engaged in the prosecution of such manufactory. It is said one or more capitals, because, in fact, the
same thing which is contemplated in the case of the farm,
sometimes happens in that of a manufactory. There is one,
who furnishes a part of the capital or lends a part of the money
by which it is carried on, and another, who carries it on with
the addition of his own capital. Out of the surplus which remains after defraying expenses, an interest is paid to the money
lender, for the portion of the capital furnished by him, which
exactly agrees with the rent paid to the landlord; and the
residue of that surplus constitutes the profit of the undertaker
or manufacturer, and agrees with what is denominated the ordinary profits on the stock of the farmer. Both together, make
the ordinary profits of two capitals employed in a manufactory; as, in the other case, the rent of the landlord and the
revenue of the farmer compose the ordinary profits of two capitals employed in the cultivation of a farm.

The rent, therefore, accruing to the proprietor of the land,
far from being a criterion of exclusive productiveness, as has
been argued, is no criterion even of superior productiveness.
The question must still be, whether the surplus, after defraying
expenses of a given capital, employed in the purchase and
improvement of a piece of land, is greater or less than that of
a like capital, employed in the prosecution of a manufactory;
or whether the whole value produced from a given capital and
a given quantity of labor, employed in one way, be greater or
less than the whole value produced from an equal capital and
an equal quantity of labor, employed in the other way; or

rather, perhaps, whether the business of agriculture, or that of manufactures, will yield the greatest product, according to a compound ratio of the quantity of the capital, and the quantity of labor, which are employed in the one or in the other.

The solution of either of these questions is not easy; it involves numerous and complicated details, depending on an accurate knowledge of the objects to be compared. It is not known that the comparison has ever yet been made upon sufficient data, properly ascertained and analyzed. To be able to make it on the present occasion, with satisfactory precision, would demand more previous inquiry and investigation, than there has been hitherto either leisure or opportunity to accomplish.

Some essays, however, have been made towards acquiring the requisite information; which have rather served to throw doubt upon, than to confirm the hypothesis under examination. But it ought to be acknowledged, that they have been too little diversified, and are too imperfect to authorize a definitive conclusion either way; leading rather to probable conjecture than to certain deduction. They render it probable that there are various branches of manufactures, in which a given capital will yield a greater total product, and a considerably greater net product, than an equal capital invested in the purchase and improvement of lands; and that there are also some branches, in which both the gross and the net produce will exceed that of agricultural industry, according to a compound ratio of capital and labor. But it is on this last point that there appears to be the greatest room for doubt. It is far less difficult to infer generally, that the net produce of capital engaged in manufacturing enterprises is greater than that of capital engaged in agriculture.

The foregoing suggestions are not designed to inculcate an opinion that manufacturing industry is more productive than that of agriculture. They are intended rather to show that the reverse of this proposition is not ascertained; that the general arguments, which are brought to establish it, are not satisfactory; and consequently, that a supposition of the superior productiveness of tillage ought to be no obstacle to listening to any substantial inducements to the encouragement of manufactures, which may be otherwise perceived to exist, through an apprehension that they may have a tendency to divert labor from a more to a less profitable employment.

It is extremely probable, that, on a full and accurate development of the matter, on the ground of fact and calculation, it would be discovered that there is no material difference between the aggregate productiveness of the one, and of the other kind of industry; and that the propriety of the encouragements, which may, in any case, be proposed to be given to either, ought to be determined upon considerations irrelative to any comparison of that nature. . . .

A full view having now been taken of the inducements to the promotion of manufactures in the United States, accompanied with an examination of the principal objections which are commonly urged in opposition, it is proper, in the next place, to consider the means by which it may be effected, as introductory to a specification of the objects, which, in the present state of things, appear the most fit to be encouraged, and of the particular measures which it may be advisable to adopt, in respect to each.

In order to a better judgment of the means proper to be resorted to by the United States, it will be of use to advert to those which have been employed with success in other countries. The principal of these are:

1. *Protecting duties—or duties on those foreign articles which are the rivals of the domestic ones intended to be encouraged.*

Duties of this nature evidently amount to a virtual bounty on the domestic fabrics; since, by enhancing the charges on foreign articles, they enable the national manufacturers to undersell all their foreign competitors. The propriety of this species of encouragement need not be dwelt upon, as it is not only a clear result from the numerous topics which have been suggested, but is sanctioned by the laws of the United States, in a variety of instances; it has the additional recommendation of being a resource of revenue. Indeed, all the duties imposed on imported articles, though with an exclusive view to revenue,

have the effect, in contemplation, and, except where they fall
on raw materials, wear a beneficent aspect towards the manufacturers of the country.

2. *Prohibitions of rival articles, or duties equivalent to
prohibitions.*

This is another and an efficacious mean of encouraging national manufactures; but, in general, it is only fit to be employed when a manufacture has made such progress, and is
in so many hands, as to insure a due competition, and an adequate supply on reasonable terms. Of duties equivalent to
prohibitions, there are examples in the laws of the United
States; and there are other cases, to which the principle may
be advantageously extended, but they are not numerous.

Considering a monopoly of the domestic market to its own
manufacturers as the reigning policy of manufacturing nations,
a similar policy, on the part of the United States, in every
proper instance, is dictated, it might almost be said, by the
principles of distributive justice; certainly, by the duty of en-
deavoring to secure to their own citizens a reciprocity of advantages.

3. *Prohibitions of the exportation of the materials of manufactures.*

The desire of securing a cheap and plentiful supply for the
national workmen, and where the article is either peculiar to
the country, or of peculiar quality there, the jealousy of enabling foreign workmen to rival those of the nation with its
own materials, are the leading motives to this species of regulation. It ought not to be affirmed, that it is in no instance
proper; but is, certainly, one which ought to be adopted with
great circumspection, and only in very plain cases. It is seen
at once, that its immediate operation is to abridge the demand,
and keep down the price of the produce of some other branch
of industry—generally speaking, of agriculture—to the prejudice
of those who carry it on; and though, if it be really essential
to the prosperity of any very important national manufacture,
it may happen that those who are injured, in the first instance,
may be, eventually indemnified by the superior steadiness of
an extensive domestic market, depending on that prosperity;

yet, in a matter in which there is so much room for nice and difficult combinations, in which such opposite considerations combat each other, prudence seems to dictate that the expedient in question ought to be indulged with a sparing hand.

4. *Pecuniary bounties.*

This has been found one of the most efficacious means of encouraging manufactures, and is, in some views, the best. Though it has not yet been practised upon by the Government of the United States (unless the allowance on the expiration of dried and pickled fish and salted meat could be considered as a bounty), and though it is less favored by public opinion than some other modes, its advantages are these:

1. It is a species of encouragement more positive and direct than any other, and, for that very reason, has a more immediate tendency to stimulate and uphold new enterprises, increasing the chances of profit, and diminishing the risks of loss, in the first attempts.

2. It avoids the inconvenience of a temporary augmentation of price, which is incident to some other modes; or it produces it to a less degree, either by making no addition to the charges on the rival foreign article, as in the case of protecting duties, or by making a smaller addition. The first happens when the fund for the bounty is derived from a different object (which may or may not increase the price of some other article, according to the nature of that object), the second, when the fund is derived from the same, or a similar object, of foreign manufacture. One per cent duty on the foreign article, converted into a bounty on the domestic, will have an equal effect with a duty of 2 per cent, exclusive of such bounty; and the price of the foreign commodity is liable to be raised, in the one case, in the proportion of 1 per cent; in the other in that of 2 per cent. Indeed the bounty, when drawn from another source, is calculated to promote a reduction of price; because, without laying any new charge on the foreign article, it serves to introduce a competition with it, and to increase the total quantity of the article in the market.

3. Bounties have not, like high protecting duties, a tendency to produce scarcity. An increase of price is not always the im-

mediate, though, where the progress of a domestic manufacture does not counteract a rise, it is, commonly, the ultimate effect of an additional duty. In the interval between the laying of the duty and the proportional increase of price, it may discourage importation, by interfering with the profits to be expected from the sale of the article.

4. Bounties are, sometimes, not only the best, but the only proper expedient for uniting the encouragement of a new object of agriculture with that of a new object of manufacture. It is the interest of the farmer to have the production of the raw material promoted by counteracting the interference of the foreign material of the same kind. It is the interest of the manufacturer to have the material abundant and cheap. If, prior to the domestic production of the material, in sufficient quantity to supply the manufacturer on good terms, a duty be laid upon the importation of it from abroad, with a view to promote the raising of it at home, the interest both of the farmer and manufacturer will be disserved. By either destroying the requisite supply, or raising the price of the article beyond what can be afforded to be given for it by the conductor of an infant manufacture, it is abandoned or fails, and there being no domestic manufactories to create a demand for the raw material, which is raised by the farmer, it is in vain that the competition of the like foreign article may have been destroyed.

It cannot escape notice, that a duty upon the importation of an article can no otherwise aid the domestic production of it, than by giving the latter greater advantages in the home market. It can have no influence upon the advantageous sale of the article produced in foreign markets—no tendency, therefore, to promote its exportation.

The true way to conciliate these two interests is to lay a duty on foreign manufactures of the material, the growth of which is desired to be encouraged, and to apply the produce of that duty, by way of bounty, either upon the production of the material itself, or upon its manufacture at home, or upon both. In this disposition of the thing, the manufacturer commences his enterprise under every advantage which is attainable, as to quantity or price of the raw material; and the farmer, if the bounty be immediately to him, is enabled by it to enter into a successful competition with the foreign material. If the bounty be to the manufacturer, on so much of the domestic material as he consumes, the operation is nearly the same; he has a motive of interest to prefer the domestic commodity, if of equal quality, even at a higher price than the foreign, so long as the difference of price is anything short of the bounty which is allowed upon the article.

Except the simple and ordinary kinds of household manufacture, or those for which there are very commanding local advantages, pecuniary bounties are, in most cases, indispensable to the introduction of a new branch. A stimulus and a support, not less powerful and direct, is, generally speaking, essential to the overcoming of the obstacles which arise from the competitions of superior skill and maturity elsewhere. Bounties are especially essential in regard to articles upon which those foreigners, who have been accustomed to supply a country, are in the practice of granting them.

The continuance of bounties on manufactures long established, must almost always be of questionable policy: because a presumption would arise, in every such case, that there were natural and inherent impediments to success. But, in new undertakings, they are as justifiable as they are oftentimes necessary.

There is a degree of prejudice against bounties, from an appearance of giving away the public money without an immediate consideration, and from a supposition that they serve to enrich particular classes, at the expense of the community.

But neither of these sources of dislike will bear a serious examination. There is no purpose to which public money can be more beneficially applied, than to the acquisition of a new and useful branch of industry; no consideration more valuable, than a permanent addition to the general stock of productive labor.

As to the second source of objection, it equally lies against other modes of encouragement, which are admitted to be eligible. As often as a duty upon a foreign article makes an addition to its price, it causes an extra expense to the community, for the benefit of the domestic manufacturer. A bounty does no more. But it is the interest of the society, in each case, to submit to the temporary expense—which is more than compensated by an increase of industry and wealth; by an augmentation of resources and independence; and by the circumstance of eventual cheapness, which has been noticed in another place.

It would deserve attention, however, in the employment of this species of encouragement in the United States, as a reason for moderating the degree of it in the instances in which it might be deemed eligible, that the great distance of this country from Europe imposes very heavy charges on all the fabrics which are brought from thence, amounting to from 15 to 30 per cent on their value, according to their bulk.

A question has been made concerning the constitutional right of the Government of the United States to apply this species of encouragement; but there is certainly no good foundation for such a question. The National Legislature has express authority "to lay and collect taxes, duties, imposts, and excises, to pay the debts, and provide for the common defence and general welfare," with no other qualifications than that "all duties, imposts and excises, shall be uniform throughout the United States; and that no capitation or other direct tax shall be laid, unless in proportion to numbers, ascertained by a census or enumeration, taken on the principles prescribed in the constitution," and that "no tax or duty shall be laid on articles exported from any State."

These three qualifications excepted, the power to raise money is plenary and indefinite, and the objects to which it may be appropriated, are no less comprehensive than the payment of the public debts, and the providing for the common defence and general welfare. The terms "general welfare" were doubtless intended to signify more than was expressed or imported in those which preceded; otherwise, numerous exigencies incident to the affairs of a nation would have been left without a provision. The phrase is as comprehensive as any that could have been used; because it was not fit that the constitutional authority of the Union to appropriate its revenues should have been restricted within narrower limits than the "general welfare;" and because this necessarily embraces a vast variety of particulars, which are susceptible neither of specification nor of definition.

It is, therefore, of necessity, left to the discretion of the National Legislature to pronounce upon the objects which concern the general welfare, and for which, under that description, an appropriation of money is requisite and proper. And there seems to be no room for a doubt, that whatever concerns the general interests of learning, of agriculture, of manufactures, and of commerce, are within the sphere of the national councils, as far as regards an application of money.

The only qualification of the generality of the phrase in question, which seems to be admissible, is this: That the object, to which an appropriation of money is to be made, be general, and not local; its operation extending, in fact, or by possibility, throughout the Union, and not being confined to a particular spot.

No objection ought to arise to this construction, from a supposition that it would imply a power to do whatever else should appear to Congress conducive to the general welfare. A power to appropriate money with this latitude, which is granted, too, in express terms, would not carry a power to do any other thing not authorized in the constitution, either expressly or by fair implication.

5. *Premiums.*

These are of a nature allied to bounties, though distinguishable from them in some important features.

Bounties are applicable to the whole quantity of an article produced, or manufactured, or exported, and involve a correspondent expense. Premiums serve to reward some particular excellence or superiority, some extraordinary exertion or skill, and are dispensed only in a small number of cases. But their effect is to stimulate general effort; contrived so as to be both honorary and lucrative, they address themselves to different passions—touching the chords, as well of emulation as of interest. They are, accordingly, a very economical mean of exciting the enterprise of a whole community.

There are various societies, in different countries, whose object is the dispensation of premiums for the encouragement of agriculture, arts, manufactures, and commerce; and though they are, for the most part, voluntary associations, with comparatively slender funds, their utility has been immense. Much has been done, by this means, in Great Britain. Scotland, in particular, owes, materially to it, a prodigious amelioration of condition. From a similar establishment in the United States, supplied and supported by the Government of the Union, vast benefits might, reasonably, be expected. Some further ideas, on this head, shall, accordingly, be submitted, in the conclusion of this report.

6. *The exemption of the materials of manufactures from duty.*

The policy of that exemption, as a general rule, particularly in reference to new establishments, is obvious. It can hardly ever be advisable to add the obstructions of fiscal burthens to the difficulties which naturally embarrass a new manufacture; and where it is matured, and in condition to become an object of revenue, it is, generally speaking, better that the fabric, than the material, should be the subject of taxation. Ideas of proportion between the quantum of the tax and the value of the article, can be more easily adjusted in the former than in the latter case. An argument for exemptions of this kind, in the United States, is to be derived from the practice, as far as their necessities have permitted, of those nations whom we are to meet as competitors in our own and in foreign markets.

There are, however, exceptions to it, of which some examples will be given under the next head.

The laws of the Union afford instances of the observance of the policy here recommended, but it will probably be found advisable to extend it to some other cases. Of a nature, bearing some affinity to that policy, is the regulation which exempts from duty the tools and implements, as well as the books, clothes, and household furniture, of foreign artists, who come to reside in the United States—an advantage already secured to them by the laws of the Union, and which it is, in every view, proper to continue.

7. *Drawbacks of the duties which are imposed on the materials of manufactures.*

It has already been observed, as a general rule, that duties on those materials ought, with certain exceptions, to be forborne. Of these exceptions, three cases occur, which may serve as examples. One, where the material is itself an object of general or extensive consumption, and a fit and productive source of revenue. Another, where a manufacture of a simpler kind, the competition of which, with a like domestic article, is desired to be restrained, partakes of the nature of a raw material, from being capable, by a farther process, to be converted into a manufacture of a different kind, the introduction or growth of which is desired to be encouraged. A third, where the material itself is a production of the country, and in sufficient abundance to furnish a cheap and plentiful supply to the national manufacturers.

Under the first description comes the article of molasses. It is not only a fair object of revenue, but, being a sweet, it is just that the consumers of it should pay a duty as well as the consumers of sugar.

Cottons and linens, in their white state, fall under the second description. A duty upon such as are imported is proper, to promote the domestic manufacture of similar articles, in the same state. A drawback of that duty is proper, to encourage the printing and staining, at home, of those which are brought from abroad. When the first of these manufactures has attained sufficient maturity in a country to furnish a full supply for the second, the utility of the drawback ceases.

The article of hemp either now does, or may be expected soon to, exemplify the third case in the United States.

Where duties on the materials of manufactures are not laid for the purpose of preventing a competition with some domestic production, the same reasons which recommend, as a general rule, the exemption of those materials from duties, would recommend, as a like general rule, the allowance of drawbacks in favor of the manufacturer. Accordingly, such drawbacks are familiar in countries which systematically pursue the business of manufactures; which furnishes an argument for the observance of a similar policy in the United States; and the idea has been adopted by the laws of the Union, in the instances of salt and molasses. It is believed that it will be found advantageous to extend it to some other articles.

8. *The encouragement of new inventions and discoveries at home, and of the introduction into the United States of such as may have been made in other countries; particularly, those which relate to machinery.*

This is among the most useful and unexceptionable of the aids which can be given to manufactures. The usual means of that encouragement are pecuniary rewards, and, for a time, exclusive privileges. The first must be employed, according to the occasion, and the utility of the invention or discovery. For the last, so far as respects "authors and inventors," provision has been made by law. But it is desirable, in regard to improvements, and secrets of extraordinary value, to be able to extend the same benefit to introducers, as well as authors and inventors; a policy which has been practised with advantage in other countries. Here, however, as in some other cases, there is cause to regret, that the competency of the authority of the National Government to the good which might be done, is not without a question. Many aids might be given to industry, many internal improvements of primary magnitude might be promoted, by an authority operating throughout the Union, which cannot be effected as well, if at all, by an authority confirmed within the limits of a single State.

But, if the Legislature of the Union cannot do all the good that might be wished, it is, at least, desirable that all may be done which is practicable. Means for promoting the introduction of foreign improvements, though less efficaciously than might be accomplished with more adequate authority, will form a part of the plan intended to be submitted in the close of this report.

It is customary with manufacturing nations to prohibit, under severe penalties, the exportation of implements and machines, which they have either invented or improved. There are already objects for a similar regulation in the United States; and others may be expected to occur, from time to time. The adoption of it seems to be dictated by the principle of reciprocity. Greater liberality, in such respects, might better comport with the general spirit of the country; but a selfish and exclusive policy, in other quarters, will not always permit the free indulgence of a spirit which would place us upon an unequal footing. As far as prohibitions tend to prevent foreign competitors from deriving the benefit of the improvements made at home, they tend to increase the advantages of those by whom they may have been introduced, and operate as an encouragement to exertion.

9. *Judicious regulations for the inspection of manufactured commodities.*

This is not among the least important of the means by which the prosperity of manufactures may be promoted. It is, indeed, in many cases, one of the most essential. Contributing to prevent frauds upon consumers at home, and exporters to foreign countries; to improve the quality, and preserve the character of the national manufactures; it cannot fail to aid the expeditious and advantageous sale of them, and to serve as a guard against successful competition from other quarters. The reputation of the flour and lumber of some States, and of the potash of others, has been established by an attention to this point. And the like good name might be procured for those articles, wheresoever produced, by a judicious and uniform system of inspection, throughout the ports of the United States. A like system might also be extended with advantage to other commodities.

10. *The facilitating of pecuniary remittances from place to place*

is a point of considerable moment to trade in general, and to manufactures in particular, by rendering more easy the purchase of raw materials and provisions, and the payment for manufactured supplies. A general circulation of bank paper, which is to be expected from the institution lately established, will be a most valuable mean to this end. But much good would also accrue from some additional provisions respecting inland bills of exchange. If those drawn in one State, payable in another, were made negotiable every where, and interest and damages allowed in case of protest, it would greatly promote negotiations between the citizens of different States, by rendering them more secure, and with it the convenience and advantage of the merchants and manufacturers of each.

11. *The facilitating of the transportation of commodities.* Improvements favoring this object intimately concern all the domestic interests of a community; but they may, without impropriety, be mentioned as having an important relation to manufactures. There is, perhaps, scarcely any thing, which has been better calculated to assist the manufacturers of Great Britain, than the melioration of the public roads of that kingdom, and the great progress which has been of late made in opening canals. Of the former, the United States stand much in need; for the latter, they present uncommon facilities.

The symptoms of attention to the improvement of inland navigation which have lately appeared in some quarters, must fill with pleasure every breast, warmed with a true zeal for the prosperity of the country. These examples, it is to be hoped, will stimulate the exertions of the Government and citizens of every State. There can certainly be no object more worthy of the cares of the local administrations; and it were to be wished that there was no doubt of the power of the National Government to lend its direct aid on a comprehensive plan. This is one of those improvements which could be prosecuted with more efficacy by the whole, than by any part or parts of the Union. There are cases in which the general interest will be in danger to be sacrificed to the collision of some supposed local interests. Jealousies, in matters of this kind, are as apt to exist, as they are apt to be erroneous.

The following remarks are sufficiently judicious and pertinent to deserve a literal quotation:

"Good roads, canals, and navigable rivers, by diminishing the expense of carriage, put the remote parts of a country more nearly upon a level with those in the neighborhood of the town. They are, upon that account, the greatest of all improvements. They encourage the cultivation of the remote, which must always be the most extensive circle of the country. They are advantageous to the town, by breaking down the monopoly of the country in its neighborhood. They are advantageous, even to that part of the country. Though they introduce some rival commodities into the old market, they open many new markets to its produce. Monopoly, besides, is a great enemy to good management, which can never be universally established, but in consequence of that free and universal competition, which forces every body to have recourse to it for the sake of self-defence. It is not more than fifty years ago that some of the counties in the neighborhood of London petitioned the parliament against the extension of the turnpike roads into the remoter counties. Those remoter counties, they pretended, from the cheapness of labor, would be able to sell their grass and corn cheaper in the London market than themselves, and they would thereby reduce their rents, and ruin their cultivation. Their rents, however, have risen, and their cultivation has been improved since that time."

Specimens of a spirit similar to that which governed the counties here spoken of, present themselves too frequently to the eye of an impartial observer, and render it a wish of patriotism, that the body in this country, in whose councils a local or partial spirit is at least likely to predominate, were at liberty to pursue and promote the general interest, in those instances in which there might be danger of the interference of such a spirit.

The foregoing are the principal of the means by which the growth of manufactures is ordinarily promoted. . . .

2

ROBERT J. WALKER (1801–1869)
Report of the Secretary of the Treasury (1845)
[29 Cong. 1 Sess., H. Rep. Doct. 6]

In suggesting improvements in the revenue laws, the following principles have been adopted:

1st. That no more money should be collected than is necessary for the wants of the Government, economically administered.

2d. That no duty be imposed on any article above the lowest rate which will yield the largest amount of revenue.

3d. That below such rate discrimination may be made descending, in the scale of duties; or, for imperative reasons, the article may be placed in the list of those free from all duty.

4th. That the maximum revenue duty should be imposed on luxuries.

5th. That all minimums, and all specific duties, should be abolished, and ad valorem duties substituted in their place—care being taken to guard against fraudulent invoices and undervaluation, and to assess the duty upon the actual market value.

6th. That the duty should be so imposed as to operate as equally as possible throughout the Union, discriminating neither for nor against any class or section.

No horizontal scale of duties is recommended; because such a scale would be a refusal to discriminate for revenue, and might sink that revenue below the wants of the Government. Some articles will yield the largest revenue at duties that would be wholly or partially prohibitory in other cases. Luxuries, as a general rule, will bear the highest revenue duties: but even some very costly luxuries, easily smuggled, will bear but a light duty for revenue, whilst other articles, of great bulk and weight, will bear a higher duty for revenue. There is no instance within the knowledge of this Department of any horizontal tariff ever having been enacted by any one of the nations of the world. There must be discrimination for revenue, or the burden of taxation must be augmented, in order to bring the same amount of money into the Treasury. It is difficult, also, to adopt any arbitrary maximum to which an inflexible adherence must be demanded in all cases. Thus, upon brandy and spirits, a specific duty, varying as an equivalent ad valorem from 180 to 261 per cent, yields a large revenue; yet no one would propose either of these rates as a maximum. These duties are too high for revenue, from the encouragement they present for smuggling these baneful luxuries; yet a duty of 20 per cent upon brandy and spirits would be far below the revenue standard, would greatly diminish the income on these imports, require increased burdens upon the necessaries of life, and would revolt the moral sense of the whole community. There are many other luxuries which will bear a much higher duty for revenue than 20 per cent; and the only true maximum is that which experience demonstrates will bring, in each case, the largest revenue at the lowest rate of duty. Nor should maximum revenue duties be imposed upon all articles; for this would yield too large an income, and would prevent all discrimination within the revenue standard, and require necessaries to be taxed as high as luxuries. But, whilst it is impossible to adopt any horizontal scale of duties, or even any arbitrary maximum, experience proves that, as a general rule, a duty of 20 per cent, ad valorem will yield the largest revenue. There are, however, a few exceptions above, as well as many below, this standard. Thus, whilst the lowest revenue duty on most luxuries exceeds 20 per cent, there are many costly articles of small bulk, easily smuggled, which would bring, perhaps, no revenue at a duty as high as 20 per cent, and even at the present rate of 7½ per cent, they yield, in most cases, a small revenue; whilst coal, iron, sugar, and molasses, articles of great bulk and weight, yielded last year six millions of revenue, at an average rate of duty exceeding 60 per cent ad valorem. These duties are far too high for revenue upon all these articles, and ought to be reduced to the revenue standard; but if Congress desire to obtain the largest revenue from duties on these articles, those duties, at the lowest rate for revenue, would exceed 20 per cent ad valorem.

There are appended to this report tables, prepared with great care and labor, showing the rates of duty each year on each of these four articles, and the equivalent ad valorem from the organization of the Government down to the present period, with the revenue collected every year upon each; from which tables Congress will be enabled to judge how far the present rates exceed the lowest revenue duties, and how much they must be reduced so as to yield a revenue equal to that now obtained from these articles.

It is believed that sufficient means can be obtained at the lowest revenue duties on the articles now subjected to duty; but if Congress desire a larger revenue, it should be procured by taxing the free articles rather than transcend, in any case, the lowest revenue duties. It is thought, however, that, without exceeding that limit in any case, an adequate revenue will still be produced, and permit the addition to the free list of salt and guano. In one of his annual messages Mr. Jefferson recommended to Congress "the suppression of the duties on salt." A large portion of this duty is exhausted in heavy expenses of measuring salt, and in large sums paid for fishing bounties and allowances in lieu of the drawback of the duty, both which expenditures would fall with a repeal of the duty; which repeal, therefore, can cause no considerable reduction of the revenue. Salt is a necessary of life, and should be as free from tax as air or water. It is used in large quantities by the farmer and planter; and to the poor this tax operates most oppressively, not only in the use of the article itself, but as combined with salted provisions. The salt made abroad by solar evaporation is also most pure and wholesome, and, as conservative of health, should be exempt from taxation.

The duty on cotton-bagging is equivalent to 55.20 per cent ad valorem on the Scotch bagging, and to 123.11 per cent on the gunny-bag; and yet the whole revenue from these duties has fallen to $66,064.50. Nearly the entire amount, therefore, of this enormous tax makes no addition to the revenue, but inures to the benefit of about thirty manufacturers. As five-sixths of the cotton crop is exported abroad, the same proportion of the bagging around the bale is exported, and sold abroad at a heavy loss, growing out of a deduction for tare. Now, as duties are designed to operate only on the domestic consumption, there ought to be a drawback of the whole duty on cotton-bagging re-exported around the bale, on the same principles on which drawbacks are allowed in other cases. The cotton planting is the great exporting interest, and suffers from the tariff in the double capacity of consumer and exporter. Cotton is the great basis of our foreign exchange, furnishing most of the means to purchase imports and supply the revenue. It is thus the source of two-thirds of the revenue, and of our foreign freight and commerce, upholding our commercial marine and maritime power. It is also a bond of peace with foreign nations, constituting a stronger preventive of war than armies or navies, forts or armaments. At present prices, our cotton crop will yield an annual product of $72,000,000, and the manufactured fabric $504,000,000, furnishing profits abroad to thousands of capitalists, and wages to hundreds of thousands of the working classes; all of whom would be deeply injured by any disturbance, growing out of a state of war, to the direct and adequate supply of the raw material. If our manufacturers consume four hundred thousand bales, it would cost them $12,000,000 whilst selling the manufactured fabric for $84,000,000; and they should be the last to unite in imposing heavy taxes upon that great interest which supplies them with the raw material out of which they realize such large profits. Accompanying the drawback of the duty on cotton-bagging should be the repeal of the duty on foreign cotton, which is inoperative and delusive, and not desired by the domestic producer.

The condition of our foreign relations, it is said, should suspend the reduction of the tariff. No American patriot can desire to arrest our onward career in peace and prosperity; but if, unhappily, such should be the result, it would create an increased necessity for reducing our present high duties in order to obtain sufficient revenue to meet increased expenditures. The duties for the quarter ending the 30th September, 1844, yielded $2,011,885.90 more of revenue than the quarter ending 30th September, 1845; showing a very considerable decline of the revenue, growing out of a diminished importation of the highly-protected articles and the progressive substitution of the domestic rivals. Indeed, many of the duties are becoming dead letters, except for the purpose of prohibition, and, if not reduced, will ultimately compel their advocates to resort to direct taxation to support the Government. In the event of war, nearly all the high duties would become prohibitory, from the increased risk and cost of importations; and if there be, indeed, in the opinion of any, a serious danger of such an occurrence, it appeals most strongly to their patriotism to impose the lowest revenue duties on all articles, as the only means of securing, at such a period, any considerable income from the tariff.

The whole power to collect taxes, whether direct or indirect, is conferred by the same clause of the Constitution. The words are, "The Congress shall have the power to lay and collect taxes, duties, imposts and excises." A direct tax or excise, not for revenue, but for protection, clearly would not be within the legitimate object of taxation; and yet it would be as much so as a duty imposed for a similar purpose. The power is "to lay and *collect* taxes, duties, imposts, and excises." A duty must be laid only that it may be *collected;* and if it is so imposed that it cannot be collected, in whole or in part, it violates the declared object of the granted power. To lay all duties so high that none of them could be collected would be a prohibitory tariff. To lay a duty on any one article so high that it could not be collected would be a prohibitory tariff upon that article. If a duty of 100 per cent were imposed upon all or upon a number of articles, so as to diminish the revenue upon all or any of them, it would operate as a partial prohibition. A partial and a total prohibition are alike in violation of the true object of the taxing power. They only differ in degree, and not in principle. If the revenue limit may be exceeded 1 per cent, it may be exceeded one hundred. If it may be exceeded upon any one article, it may be exceeded on all; and there is no escape from this conclusion, but in contending that Congress may lay duties on all articles so high as to collect no revenue, and operate as a total prohibition.

The Constitution declares that "all bills for raising revenue shall originate in the House of Representatives." A tariff bill, it is conceded, can only originate in the House, because it is a bill for *raising revenue*. That is the only proper object of such a bill. A tariff is a bill to "lay and collect taxes." It is a bill for "raising revenue"; and whenever it departs from that object, in whole or in part, either by total or partial prohibition, it violates the purpose of the granted power.

In arranging the details of the tariff, it is believed that the maximum revenue duties should be imposed upon luxuries. It is deemed just that taxation, whether direct or indirect, should be as nearly as practicable in proportion to property. If the whole revenue were raised by a tax upon property, the poor, and especially those who live by the wages of labor, would pay but a very small portion of such tax; whereas, by the tariff, the poor, by the consumption of various imports, or domestic articles enhanced in price by the duties, pay a much larger share of the taxes than if they were collected by an assessment in proportion to property. To counteract, as far as possible, this effect of the tariff—to equalize its operation, and make it approximate as nearly as may be to a system of taxes in proportion to property—the duties upon luxuries, used almost exclusively by the rich, should be fixed at the highest revenue standard. This would not be discriminating in favor of the poor, however just that might be within the revenue limit; but it would mitigate, as far as practicable, that discrimination against the poor which results from every tariff, by compelling them to pay a larger amount of taxes than if assessed and collected on all property in proportion to its value. In accordance with these principles, it is believed that the largest practicable portion of the aggregate revenue should be raised by maximum revenue duties upon luxuries, whether grown, produced, or manufactured at home or abroad.

An appeal has been made to the poor, by the friends of protection, on the ground that it augments the wages of labor. In reply, it is contended that the wages of labor have not augmented since the tariff of 1842, and that in some cases they have diminished.

When the number of manufactories is not great, the power of the system to regulate the wages of labor is inconsiderable; but as the profit of capital invested in manufactures is augmented by the protective tariff, there is a corresponding increase of power, until the control of such capital over the wages of labor becomes irresistible. As this power is exercised from time to time, we find it resisted by combinations among the working classes, by turning out for higher wages, or for shorter time; by trades-unions; and in some countries, unfortunately, by violence and bloodshed. But the Government, by protective duties, arrays itself on the side of the manufacturing system, and, by thus augmenting its wealth and power, soon terminates in its favor the struggle between man and money—between capital and labor. When the tariff of 1842 was enacted, the maximum duty was 20 per cent. By that act, the average of duties on the protected articles was more than double. But the wages of labor did not increase in a corresponding ratio, or in any ratio whatever. On the contrary, whilst wages in some cases have diminished, the prices of many articles used by the working classes have greatly appreciated.

A protective tariff is a question regarding the enhancement of the profits of capital. That is its object, and not to augment the wages of labor, which would reduce those profits. It is a question of percentage, and is to decide whether money vested in our manufactures shall, by special legislation, yield a profit of 10, 20, or 30 per cent, or whether it shall remain satisfied with a dividend equal to that accruing from the same capital invested in agriculture, commerce, or navigation.

The present tariff is unjust and unequal, as well in its details as in the principles upon which it is founded. On some articles the duties are entirely prohibitory, and on others there is a partial prohibition. It discriminates in favor of manufactures, and against agriculture, by imposing many higher duties upon the manufactured fabric than upon the agricultural product out of which it is made. It discriminates in favor of the manufacturer, and against the mechanic, by many higher duties upon the manufacture than upon the article made out of it by the mechanic. It discriminates in favor of the manufacturer, and against the merchant, by injurious restrictions upon trade and commerce; and against the ship-building and navigating interest, by heavy duties on almost every article used in building or navigating vessels. It discriminates in favor of manufactures, and against exports, which are as truly the product of American industry as manufactures. It discriminates in favor of the rich, and against the poor, by high duties upon nearly all the necessaries of life, and by minimums and specific duties, rendering the tax upon the real value much higher on the cheaper than upon the finer article.

Minimums are a fictitious value, assumed by law, instead of the real value; and the operation of all minimums may be illustrated by a single example. Thus, by the tariff of 1842, a duty of 30 per cent ad valorem is levied on all manufactures of cotton; but the law further provides that cotton goods "not died, colored, printed, or stained, not exceeding in value twenty cents per square yard, shall be valued at twenty cents per square yard." If, then, the real value of the cheapest cotton goods is but four cents a square yard, it is placed by the law at the false value of twenty cents per square yard, and the duty levied on the fictitious value—raising it five times higher on the cheap article consumed by the poor, than upon the fine article purchased by the more wealthy. Indeed, by House document No. 306, of the first session of the Twenty-eighth Congress, this difference, by actual importation, was 65 per cent between the cheaper and the finer article of the 20 per cent minimum, 131 per cent on the 30 per cent minimum, 48½ per cent on the 35 per cent minimum, 84 per cent on the 60 per cent minimum, and 84 per cent on the 75 per cent minimum. This difference is founded on actual importation, and shows an average discrimination against the poor on cotton imports of 82 per cent beyond what the tax would be if assessed upon the actual value. The operation of the specific duty presents a similar discrimination against the poor and in favor of the rich. Thus, upon salt: the duty is not upon the value, but it is eight cents a bushel, whether the article be coarse or fine—showing, by the same document, from actual importation, a discrimination of 64 per cent against the cheap and in favor of the finer article; and this, to a greater or less extent, is the effect of all specific duties. When we consider that $2,892,621.74 of the revenue last year was collected by minimum duties, and $13,311,085.46 by specific duties, the discrimination against the cheaper article must amount, by estimates founded on the same document, to a tax of $5,108,422 exacted by minimums and specific duties annually from the poorer classes, by raising thus the duties on the cheaper articles above what they would be if the duty were assessed upon the actual value. If direct taxes were made specific, they would be intolerable. Thus, if an annual tax of thirty dollars was assessed on all houses, without respect to their actual value, making the owner of the humble tenement or cabin pay a tax of thirty dollars and the owner of the costly mansion a tax of but thirty dollars on their respective houses, it would differ only in degree, but not in principle, from the same unvarying specific duty on cheap as on fine articles. If any discrimination should be made, it should be the reverse of the specific duty, and of the minimum principle, by establishing a maximum standard, above which value the duties on the finer article should be higher, and below which they should be lower on the cheaper article. The tax upon the actual value is the most equal, and can only be accomplished by ad valorem duties. As to fraudulent invoices and undervaluations, these dangers are believed to be arrested effectually by the stringent provisions and severe penalty of the 17th section of the tariff of 1842; and now, one-half the revenue is collected from ad valorem duties.

At least two-thirds of the taxes imposed by the present tariff are paid, not into the Treasury, but to the protected classes. The revenue from imports last year exceeded twenty-seven millions of dollars. This, in itself, is a heavy tax; but the whole tax imposed upon the people by the present tariff is not less than eighty-one millions of dollars—of which twenty-seven millions are paid to the Government upon the imports, and fifty-four millions to the protected classes, in enhanced prices of similar domestic articles.

This estimate is based upon the position that the duty is added to the price of the import, and also of its domestic rival. If the import is enhanced in price by the duty, so must be the domestic rival; for, being like articles, their price must be the same in the same market. The merchant advances in cash the duty on the import, and adds the duty, with a profit upon it, and other charges, to the price—which must therefore be enhanced to that extent, unless the foreign producer has first deducted the duty from the price. But this is impossible: for

such now is, and long has been, the superabundance of capital
and active competition in Europe, that a profit of 6 per cent
in any business is sufficient to produce large investments of
money in that business; and if, by our tariff, a duty of 40
per cent be exacted on the products of such business, and
the foreign producer deducts that duty from his previous price,
he must sustain a heavy loss. This loss would also soon extend
beyond the sales for our consumption to sales to our merchants
of articles to be re-exported by them from our ports with a
drawback of duty, which would bring down their price
throughout the markets of the world. But this the foreign
producer cannot afford. The duty, therefore, must be added
to the price, and paid by the consumer—the duty constituting
as much a part of the price as the cost of production.

If it be true that, when a duty of 40 per cent is imposed
by our tariff, the foreign producer first deducts the duty from
the previous price on the sale to our merchant, it must be
equally true with a duty of 100 per cent, which is exactly
equal to the previous price, and, when deducted, would reduce the price to nothing.

The occasional fall in price of some articles after a tariff
is no proof that this was the effect of the tariff; because, from
improved machinery, diminished prices of the raw material,
or other causes, prices may fall even after a tariff, but they
would in such cases have fallen much more but for the tariff.
The truest comparison is between the present price of the same
article at home and abroad; and to the extent that the price
is lower in the foreign market than in our own, the duty, if
equal to that difference, must to that extent enhance the price,
and in the same ratio with the lower duty. The difference in
price at home or abroad is generally about equal to the difference in the cost of production, and presents, in a series of
years, the surest measure of the effect of the duty: the enhancement in price being equal to that difference, if the duty
be higher than that difference or equal to it; or if the duty be
lower, then the enhancement is equal to the duty; and if the
article is produced, like cotton, more cheaply here than

abroad, the duty is inoperative. The great argument for the tariff is, that foreign labor being cheaper than our own, the cost of foreign productions, it is said, is lessened to that extent, and that we must make up this difference by an equivalent duty and a corresponding enhancement of price in our own market both on the foreign article and of its rival domestic product—thus rendering the duty a tax on all consumers for the benefit of the protected classes. If the marshal were sent by the Federal Government to collect a direct tax from the whole people, to be paid over to manufacturing capitalists, to enable them to sustain their business, or realize a larger profit, it would be the same in effect as the protective duty, which, when analyzed in its simplest elements, and reduced to actual results, is a mere subtraction of so much money from the people to increase the resources of the protected classes. Legislation for classes is against the doctrine of equal rights, repugnant to the spirit of our free institutions, and, it is apprehended by many, may become but another form for privileged orders, under the name of protection instead of privilege; indicated here not by rank or title, but by profits and dividends extracted from the many, by taxes upon them, for the benefit of the few.

No prejudice is felt by the Secretary of the Treasury against manufacturers. His opposition is to the protective system, and not to classes or individuals. He doubts not that the manufacturers are sincerely persuaded that the system which is a source of so much profit to them is beneficial also to the country. He entertains a contrary opinion, and claims for the opponents of the system a settled conviction of its injurious effects. Whilst a due regard to the just and equal rights of all classes forbids a discrimination in favor of the manufacturers, by duties above the lowest revenue limit, no disposition is felt to discriminate against them by reducing such duties as operate in their favor below that standard. Under revenue duties it is believed they would still receive a reasonable profit, equal to that realized by those engaged in other pursuits; and it is thought they should desire no more, at least through the agency of governmental power. Equal rights and profits, so far as laws are made, best conform to the principles upon which the Constitution was founded, and with an undeviating regard to which all its functions should be exercised, looking to the whole country and not to classes or sections.

Soil, climate, and other causes, vary very much in different countries the pursuits which are most profitable in each; and the prosperity of all of them will be best promoted by leaving them, unrestricted by legislation, to exchange with each other those fabrics and products which they severally raise most cheaply. This is clearly illustrated by the perfect free trade which exists among all the States of the Union; and by the acknowledged fact that any one of these States would be injured by imposing duties upon the products of the others. It is generally conceded that reciprocal free trade among nations would best advance the interest of all; but it is contended that we must meet the tariffs of other nations by countervailing restrictions. That duties upon our exports by foreign nations are prejudicial to us, is conceded; but whilst this injury is slightly felt by the manufacturers, its weight falls almost exclusively upon agriculture, commerce, and navigation. If those interests which sustain the loss do not ask countervailing restrictions, it should not be demanded by the manufacturers, who do not feel the injury, and whose fabrics, in fact, are not excluded by the foreign legislation of which they complain. That agriculture, commerce, and navigation are injured by foreign restrictions, constitutes no reason why they should be subject to still severer treatment by additional restrictions and countervailing tariffs enacted at home. Commerce, agriculture, and navigation, harassed as they may be by foreign restrictions, diminishing the amount of exchangeable products which they could otherwise purchase abroad, are burdened with heavier impositions at home. Nor will augmented duties here lead to a reduction of foreign tariffs, but the reverse, by furnishing the protected classes there with the identical argument used by the protected classes here against reduction. By countervailing restrictions we injure our own fellow-citizens much more than the foreign nations at whom we propose to aim their force; and in the conflict of opposing tariffs we sacrifice our own commerce, agriculture, and navigation. As well might we impose monarchical or aristocratic restrictions on our own Government or people, because that is the course of foreign legislation. Let our commerce be as free as our political institutions. Let us, with revenue duties only, open our ports to all the world, and nation after nation will soon follow our example. If we reduce our tariff, the party opposed to the corn laws of England would soon prevail, and admit all our agricultural products at all times freely into her ports, in exchange for her exports. And if England would now repeal her duties upon our wheat, flour, Indian corn, and other agricultural products, our own restrictive system would certainly be doomed to overthrow. If the question is asked, Who shall begin this work of reciprocal reduction? it is answered by the fact that England has already abated her duties upon most of our exports. She has repealed the duty upon cotton, and greatly reduced the duty upon our breadstuffs, provisions, and other articles; and her present bad harvest, if accompanied by a reduction of our tariff, would lead to the repeal of her corn laws, and the unrestricted admission, at all times, of our agricultural products. The manufacturing interest opposes reciprocal free trade with foreign nations; it opposes the Zoll-Verein treaty; and it is feared that no other treaty producing a reciprocal reduction of our own and foreign tariffs will receive its support. If that interest preferred a reciprocal exchange of our own for foreign fabrics at revenue duties, it would not have desired a tariff operating, without exception, against all nations that adopted low as well as high tariffs, nor would it have opposed every amendment proposing, when the tariff of 1842 was under consideration, a reduction of our duties upon the exports of such nations as would receive, free of duty, our flour and other agricultural products. If that interest desired reciprocal free trade with other nations, it would have desired a very different tariff from that of 1842. It would have sought to confine the high duties to those cases where the foreign importer would sell his imports for cash only, and admitted a drawback of one-half of the duty where American exports would be taken abroad in exchange—not an actual

barter of foreign imports for an equal amount in value of our
products, but without any barter where a sum equal to the
value of their exports was used in purchasing here an equal
amount in value of any of our products; and the shipment
made abroad of these products upon the same principle under
which a drawback of duties is now allowed on the re-exporta-
tion of foreign imports. This would be less simple, and is not
recommended in lieu of that absolute reduction of the duties
which will accomplish the same object of unrestricted exchange. But such a provision would be a self-executing reciprocity law, and should be desired by those believing in countervailing tariffs against foreign nations, but in reciprocal free
trade with all—thus enabling our farmers and planters to sell
their products for cheaper foreign manufactures, getting more
for what they sell, and paying less for what they purchase
in exchange. It seems strange that while the profit of agriculture varies from 1 to 8 per cent, that of manufactures is
more than double. The reason is, that whilst the high duties
secure nearly a monopoly of the home market to the manufacturer, the farmer and planter are deprived to a great extent
of the foreign market by these duties. The farmer and planter
are, to a great extent, forbidden to buy in the foreign market,
and confined to the domestic articles enhanced in price by the
duties. The tariff is thus a double benefit to the manufacturer,
and a double loss to the farmer and planter; a benefit to the
former in nearly a monopoly of the home market, and in enhanced prices of their fabrics; and a loss to the latter in the
payment of those high prices, and a total or partial exclusion
from the foreign market. The true question is, whether the
farmer and planter shall, to a great extent, supply our people
with cheap manufactures, purchased abroad with their agricultural products, or whether this exchange shall be forbidden
by high duties on such manufactures, and their supply thrown,
as a monopoly, at large prices, by high tariffs, into the hands
of our own manufacturers. The number of manufacturing
capitalists who derive the benefit from the heavy taxes extracted by the tariff from twenty millions of people does not
exceed ten thousand. The whole number (including the work-

ing classes engaged in our manufactures) deriving any benefit from the tariff, does not exceed four hundred thousand, of whom not more than forty thousand have been brought into this pursuit by the last tariff. But this small number of forty thousand would still have been in the country, consuming our agricultural products; and in the attempt to secure them as purchasers, so small in number and not consuming one-half the supply of many counties, the farmer and planter are asked to sacrifice the markets of the world, containing a population of eight hundred millions, disabled from purchasing our products by our high duties on all they would sell in exchange. The farmer and planter have the home market without a tariff, and they would have the foreign market also to a much greater extent but for the total or partial prohibition of the last tariff.

We have more fertile lands than any other nation, can raise a greater variety of products, and, it may be said, could feed and clothe the people of nearly all the world. The home market, of itself, is wholly inadequate for such products. They must have the foreign market, or a large surplus, accompanied by great depression in price, must be the result. The States of Ohio, Indiana, and Illinois, if cultivated to their fullest extent, could, of themselves, raise more than sufficient food to supply the entire home market. Missouri or Kentucky could more than supply it with hemp; already the State of Mississippi raises more cotton than is sufficient for all the home market; Louisiana is rapidly approaching the same point as to sugar; and there are lands enough adapted to that product in Louisiana, Texas, and Florida, to supply with sugar and molasses nearly all the markets of the world. If cotton is depressed in price by the tariff, the consequence must be a comparative diminution of the product, and the raising in its place, to a great extent, hemp, wheat, corn, stock, and provisions, which otherwise would be supplied by the teeming products of the West. The growing West in a series of years must be the greatest sufferers by the tariff, in depriving them of the foreign market and that of the cotton-growing States. We demand, in fact, for our agricultural products, specie from nearly all the world, by heavy taxes upon all their manufactures; and their purchases from us must therefore be limited, as well as their sales to us enhanced in price. Such a demand for specie, which we know in advance cannot be complied with, is nearly equivalent to a decree excluding most of our agricultural products from the foreign markets. Such is the rigor of our restrictions, that nothing short of a famine opens freely the ports of Europe for our breadstuffs. Agriculture is our chief employment; it is best adapted to our situation; and, if not depressed by the tariff, would be the most profitable. We can raise a larger surplus of agricultural products, and a greater variety, than almost any other nation, and at cheaper rates. Remove, then, from agriculture all our restrictions, and by its own unfettered power it will break down all foreign restrictions, and, ours being removed, would feed the hungry and clothe the poor of our fellow-men throughout all the densely-peopled nations of the world. But now we will take nothing in exchange for these products but specie, except at very high duties; and nothing but a famine breaks down all foreign restrictions, and opens for a time the ports of Europe to our breadstuffs. If, on a reduction of our duties, England repeals her corn laws, nearly all Europe must follow her example, or give to her manufacturers advantages which cannot be successfully encountered in most of the markets of the world. The tariff did not raise the price of our breadstuffs; but a bad harvest in England does—giving us for the time that foreign market which we would soon have at all times by that repeal of the corn laws which must follow the reduction of our duties. But whilst breadstuffs rise with a bad harvest in England, cotton almost invariably falls; because the increased sum which, in that event, England must pay for our breadstuffs, we will take, not in manufactures, but only in specie; and not having it to spare, she brings down, even to a greater extent, the price of our cotton. Hence the result that a bad harvest in England reduces the aggregate price of our exports, often turns the exchanges against us, carrying our specie abroad, and inflicting a serious blow on our prosperity. Foreign nations cannot for a series of years import more than they export; and if we close our markets against their imports by high duties, they must buy less of our exports, or give a lower price, or both.

Prior to the 30th of June, 1842, a credit was given for the payment of duties; since which date, they have been collected in cash. Before the cash duties and the tariff of 1842, our trade in foreign imports re-exported abroad afforded large and profitable employment to our merchants, and freight to our commercial marine, both for the inward and outward voyage; but since the last tariff, this trade is being lost to the country, as is proved by the tables hereto annexed. The total amount of foreign imports re-exported during the three years since the last tariff, both of free and dutiable goods, is $33,384,394— being far less than in any three years (except during the war) since 1793, and less than was re-exported in any one of eight several years. The highest aggregate of any three years was $173,108,813, and the lowest aggregate $41,315,705—being in the years 1794, 1795, and 1796. Before 1820, the free goods are not distinguished in this particular from the dutiable goods; but since that date the returns show the following result: During the three years since the tariff of 1842, the value of dutiable imports re-exported was $12,590,811—being less than in any one of seven years preceding since 1820, the lowest aggregate of any three years since that date being $14,-918,444, and the highest $57,727,293. Even before the cash duties, for five years preceding the high tariff of 1828, the value of dutiable goods re-exported was $94,796,241; and for the five years succeeding that tariff, $66,784,192—showing a loss of $28,012,049 of our trade in foreign exports after the tariff of 1828. The diminution of this most valuable branch of commerce has been the combined result of cash duties and of the high tariff of 1842. If the cash duties are retained, as it is believed they should be, the only sure method of restoring this trade is the adoption of the warehousing system, by which the foreign imports may be kept in store by the Government until they are required for re-exportation abroad, or consumption at home—in which latter contingency, and at the time when, for that purpose, they are taken out of these stores for consumption, the duties are paid, and, if re-exported, they pay no duty, but only the expense of storage. Under the present system, the merchant introduces foreign imports of the value of $100,000. He must now, besides the advance for the goods, make a further advance in cash, in many cases, of $50,000 for the duties. Under such a system, but a small amount of goods will be imported for drawbacks; and the higher the duty, the larger must be the advance, and the smaller the imports for re-exportation.

The imports, before payment of duties, under the same regulations now applied to our imports in transit to Canada, may be taken from warehouse to warehouse—from the east to the lakes, and to Pittsburgh, Cincinnati, and Louisville—from New Orleans to Natchez, Vicksburg, Memphis, and St. Louis—and warehoused in these and other interior ports, the duties remaining unpaid until the goods are taken out of the warehouse, and out of the original package, at such ports, for consumption; thus carrying our foreign commerce into the interior, with all the advantage of augmented business and cheaper supplies throughout the country. It will introduce into our large ports on or near the seaboard assorted cargoes of goods, to be re-exported with our own, to supply the markets of the world. It will cheapen prices to the consumer, by deducting the interest and profit that are now charged upon the advance of duty—building up the marts of our own commerce, and giving profitable employment to our own commercial marine. It will greatly increase our revenue, by augmenting our imports, together with our exports; and is respectfully recommended to Congress, as an important part of the whole system now proposed for their consideration.

The act of the 3d of March last, allowing a drawback on foreign imports exported from certain of our ports to Canada, and also to Santa Fe and Chihuahua, in Mexico, has gone to some extent into effect under regulations prescribed by this Department, and is beginning to produce the most happy results, especially in an augmented trade in the supply of foreign exports to Canada from our own ports. Indeed this law must soon give to us the whole of this valuable trade during the long period when the St. Lawrence is closed by ice, and a large proportion of it at all seasons. The result would be still more beneficial if Canada were allowed to carry all her exports to foreign nations *in transitu* through our own railroads, rivers, and canals, to be shipped from our own ports. Such a system, whilst it would secure to us this valuable trade, would greatly enlarge the business on our rivers, lakes, railroads, and canals, as well as augment our commerce, and would soon lead to the purchase, by Canada, not only of our foreign exports, but also, in many cases, of our domestic products and fabrics, to complete an assortment. In this manner our commercial relations with Canada would become more intimate, and more and more of her trade every year would be secured to our people.

Connected with this Department and the finances is the question of the sales of the public lands. The proceeds of these sales, it is believed, should continue to constitute a portion of the revenue, diminishing to that extent the amount required to be raised by the tariff. The net proceeds of these sales paid into the Treasury during the last fiscal year was $2,077,022.30; and from the first sales in 1787 up to the 30th of September last was $118,607,335.91. The average annual sales have been much less than two millions of acres; yet the aggregate net proceeds of the sales in 1834, 1835, 1836, and 1837, was $51,-268,617.82. Those large sales were almost exclusively for speculation; and this can only be obviated at all times by confining the sales to settlers and cultivators in limited quantities, sufficient for farms or plantations. The price at which the public lands should be sold is an important question to the whole country, but especially to the people of the new States, living mostly remote from the seaboard, and who have scarcely felt the presence of the Government in local expenditures, but chiefly in the exhaustion of their means for purchases of public lands and for customs. The public lands are not of the same value, yet they are all fixed at one unvarying price, which is far above the value of a large portion of these lands. The quantity now subject to entry at the minimum price of $1.25 per acre is 133,307,457 acres, and 109,035,345 in addition, to which the Indian title has been extinguished—being an aggregate of 242,342,802 acres, and requiring a century and a quarter to complete the sales at the rate they have progressed heretofore, without including any of the unsold lands of Texas or Oregon, or of the vast region besides to which the Indian title is not yet extinguished. It is clear, then, that there is a vast and annually-increasing surplus of public lands, very little of which will be sold within any reasonable period at the present price, and in regard to which the public interest would be promoted, and the revenue augmented, by reducing the price. The reduction of the price of the public lands in favor of settlers and cultivators would enhance the wages of labor. It is an argument urged in favor of the tariff that we ought to protect our labor against what is called the pauper labor of Europe. But whilst the tariff does not enhance the wages of labor, the sales of the public lands at low prices, and in limited quantities to settlers and cultivators, would accomplish this object. If those who live by the wages of labor could purchase 320 acres of land for $80, 160 acres for $40, or 80 acres for $20, or a 40 acre lot for $10, the power of the manufacturing capitalist in reducing the wages of labor would be greatly diminished; because when these lands were thus reduced in price, those who live by the wages of labor could purchase farms at these low rates, and cultivate the soil for themselves and families, instead of working for others twelve hours a day in the manufactories. Reduce the price which the laborer must pay for the public domain; bring thus the means of purchase within his power; prevent all speculation and monopoly in the public lands; confine the sales to settlers and cultivators in limited quantities; preserve these hundreds of millions of acres, for ages to come, as homes for the poor and oppressed; reduce the taxes by reducing the tariff and bringing down the prices which the poor are thus compelled to pay for all the necessaries and comforts of life, and more will be done for the benefit of American labor than if millions were added to the profits of manufacturing capital by the enactment of a protective tariff.

The Secretary of the Treasury, on coming into office, found the revenues deposited with banks. The law establishing the Independent Treasury was repealed, and the Secretary had no

power to re-establish that system. Congress had not only repealed that law, but, as a substitute, had adopted the present
system of deposit banks, and prohibited changing any one of
those for another bank except for specified reasons. No alternative was left but to continue the existing system until Congress should think proper to change it. That change, it is
hoped, will now be made by a return to the Treasury of the
Constitution. One of the great evils of banks is the constant
expansion and contraction of the currency; and this evil is augmented by the deposits of the revenue with banks, whether
State or national. The only proper course for the Government
is to keep its own money separate from all banks and bankers,
in its own Treasury—whether in the Mint, branch mints, or
other Government agencies—and to use only gold and silver
coin in all receipts and disbursements. The business of the
country will be more safe when an adequate supply of specie
is kept within our limits, and its circulation encouraged by all
the means within the power of the Government. If this Government and the States and the people unite in suppressing the
use of specie, an adequate supply, for want of a demand, cannot be kept within our limits, and the condition of the business
and currency of the country will be perilous and uncertain.
It will be completely within the power of the banks, whose
paper will constitute the exclusive circulation of the whole
community. Nor will it be useful to establish a constitutional
Treasury, if it is to receive or disburse the paper of banks.
Separation from banks in that case would only be nominal,
and no addition would be made to the circulation of gold and
silver.

Various forms of paper credit have been suggested, as connected with the operations of the constitutional Treasury; but
they are all considered as impairing one of the great objects
of such a Treasury—namely, an augmented circulation of
specie. If paper, in whatever form, or from whatever source it
may issue, should be introduced as a circulation by the constitutional Treasury, it would, precisely to that extent, diminish its use as a means of circulating gold and silver.

The constitutional Treasury could be rendered a most pow-

erful auxiliary of the Mint in augmenting the specie circulation. The amount of public money which can be placed in
the Mint is now limited by law to one million of dollars; and
to that extent it is now used as a depository, and as a means
of increasing our coinage. It is suggested that this limitation
may be modified as to permit the use of our Mint and branch
mints for a much larger sum, in connection with the constitutional Treasury. The amount of public money received at New
York greatly exceeds that collected at all other points, and
would of itself seem to call for a place of public deposit there;
in view of which the location of a branch of the Mint of the
United States at that city would be most convenient and useful. The argument used against a constitutional Treasury, of
the alleged insecurity of the public funds in the hands of individuals, and especially the vast amount collected at New
York, will be entirely obviated by such an establishment. The
Mint of the United States has now been in existence fifty-two
years. It has had the custody of upwards of $114,000,000,
and during this long period of time there never has been a loss
of any of its specie in the Mint by the Government. The Mint
at Philadelphia is now conducted with great efficiency by the
able and faithful officer at the head of that establishment,
whose general supervisory authority, without leaving the par-
ent Mint, might still be wisely extended to the branch at New
York. Besides the utility of such a branch as a place for keeping
safely and disbursing the public money, it is believed that the
coinage might be greatly augmented by the existence of a
branch of the Mint at that great city. It is there that two-
thirds of the revenue is annually collected—the whole of which,
under the operation of the constitutional Treasury, would be
received in specie. Of that amount, a very large sum would
be received in coin of other countries, and especially in foreign
gold coins—all which could be speedily converted, upon the
spot, into our own coins of gold and silver. The amount also
of such foreign coin brought by emigrants to the city of New
York is very considerable; a large portion of which would find
its way to the branch of the Mint for recoinage. The foreign
gold coins do not, and it is feared will not, circulate generally

as a currency, notwithstanding they are made a tender by law. The rate at which these coins are fixed by law is not familiar to the people; the denomination of such coin is in-convenient; the parts into which it is divided are not decimal; the rates at which it is taken vary in different parts of the Union. It is inconvenient in the way of ready transfer in count-ing; it is more difficult, in common use, to distinguish the gen-uine from the counterfeit foreign coin; and the stamp upon it is not familiar to the people—from all which causes, a foreign gold coin does not, and will not, circulate generally as a cur-rency among the people. In many of the banks, nearly the whole of their specie is kept in every variety of foreign gold coin; and when it is tendered by them in payment of their notes, the great body of the people, not being familiar with these coins, do not receive them; and thus the circulation of a gold currency is, to a great extent, defeated. If these coins were converted at our Mint, or branch mints, into the eagle, the half-eagle, and quarter-eagle, we should speedily have a large supply of American gold coin, and it would very soon be brought into common use as a currency, and thus give to it greater stability, and greater security to all the business of the country. A considerable amount of foreign gold coin has, dur-ing the present year, under the directions of this Department, been converted into American gold coin; but the process would be much more rapid if aided by the organization of the constitutional Treasury, and the establishment of a branch of the Mint at the great commercial emporium of the Union. With the Mint and branch mints as depositories, the sum re-maining in the hands of other receivers of public money, whether of lands or customs, would be inconsiderable, and the Government could be readily protected from all losses of such sums by adequate bonds, and the power by law to convict and punish as criminals all who embezzle the public moneys.

It is believed, under such a system, that no defaults would take place, and that the public moneys would be safely kept and disbursed in gold and silver. This Government is made, by the Constitution, the guardian of a specie currency. That currency can only be coined, and its value regulated, by this

Government. It is one of its first duties to supply such a currency, by an efficient mint, and by general regulations of the coinage; but in vain will it attempt to perform that duty, if, when coin is made or regulated in value, this Government dispenses with its use, and expels it from circulation, or drives it out of the country, by substituting the paper of banks in all the transactions of the Government.

There is nothing which will advance so surely the prosperity of the country as an adequate supply of specie, diffused throughout every portion of the Union, and constituting, to a great extent, the ordinary circulation everywhere among the people. It is a currency that will never break nor fail; it will neither expand nor contract beyond the legitimate business of the country; it will lead to no extravagant speculations at one time, to be followed by certain depression at another; nor will labor ever be robbed of its reward by the depreciation of such currency. There is no danger that we shall have too much gold and silver in actual circulation, or too small an amount of bank paper, or that any injury ever will be inflicted upon the business of the country, by a diminution of the circulation of the paper of banks, and the substitution in its place, to that extent, of gold and silver. Even their most ardent advocates must admit that banks are subject to periodical expansions and contractions, and that this evil would be increased by giving them the funds of the Government to loan, and by receiving and disbursing nothing but their paper.

It is believed that the permanent interest of every class of the people will be advanced by the establishment of the constitutional Treasury, and that the manufacturers especially will derive great benefit from its adoption. It will give stability to all their operations, and insure them, to a great extent, against those fluctuations, expansions, and contractions of the currency so prejudicial to their interests. By guarding against inflations of the currency, it will have a tendency to check periodical excesses of foreign importations purchased in fact upon credit; while loans from banks, or dangerous enlargements of their business, and excessive issues of their paper, will be greatly diminished. Whilst a sound and stable currency guards the manufacturer against excessive importations from abroad, it protects him from disasters at home, and from those ruinous revulsions in which so many thousands are reduced to bankruptcy. The tariff, if followed, as in the absence of adequate checks it certainly soon will be, by an inflated currency, whilst it thus enhances the expenses of manufacturing at home, will speedily and certainly raise prices up to the whole amount of the duty, so as to repeal the operation of that duty in favor of the manufacturer, and enable the foreign importer again to flood the market, at the enhanced prices arising from an inflated currency. But soon the revulsion comes, and all are overwhelmed in a common ruin. The currency is reduced below the wants of the country, by a sudden and ruinous contraction; and the labor and industry of years are required to repair the mischief. Stability, both in the tariff and the currency, is what the manufacturer should most desire. Let the tariff be permanently adjusted, by a return to reasonable and moderate revenue duties, which, even when imposed truly and in good faith for that purpose, will yield sufficient advantage to afford reasonable profits; and let this permanent system (and none other can be permanent) be established, and accompanied by a stable currency, and the manufacturer, in a series of years, will derive the greatest benefits from the system. The present system cannot be permanent. It is too unequal and unjust, too exorbitant and oppressive, and too clearly in conflict with the fundamental principles of the Constitution. If the manufacturer thinks that this system can be permanent, let him look to the constant changes which have attended all attempts to establish and continue a protective tariff. The first tariff was based in part upon the principle of very moderate protection to domestic manufactures; and the result has been, as appears by the table hereto annexed, that the tariff has been changed and modified thirty times since that period—being more than once, on an average, for every Congress since the Government was founded; and one of these tariffs was in itself a system of successive biennial changes, operating through a period of ten years. Of these changes, fourteen have been general, and sixteen special. From 1816 onward, these changes

have been most frequent; and it is vain to expect permanency
from anything but a revenue tariff. Stability is what the manufacturer should desire, and especially that the question should
be taken out of the arena of politics, by a just and permanent
settlement. . . .

B. *Internal Improvements*

The policy of using federal funds to build roads, canals, and waterways and encourage education and science was at first regarded as a distinctively Federalist policy, but came to be supported more or less enthusiastically by all parties. The chief differences arose over the constitutional question of federal authority to build and supervise facilities that lay entirely within single states. Debate over this policy, as of many other problems of economic policy in the United States, was dominated by constitutional rather than purely economic considerations.

The economic issue, in its pure form, was why such facilities, however useful, should be supplied by government at all, whether local or national. If enough persons wanted a road between two places and were willing to pay for its use, then private investors would presumably build it to enjoy the profits. If no private investor did build the road, this meant there was insufficient demand for it, or so at least the potential private investors must have judged.

Opponents of government enterprise asked why public officials were thought better able to judge the road's commercial prospects than private investors; or why alternatively, taxpayers should be required to support roads that the users themselves could not or would not support. Although these questions were sometimes dealt with, as by Clay (3), most advocates of internal improvements simply assumed that to provide such facilities was a natural function of government.

Although Henry Clay is best known for his efforts to forestall a Civil War by such arrangements as the Missouri Compromise, his proposals in the sphere of economic policy were equally striking, and are summed up in what he called the American System, a plan to close and strengthen the economy by combining tariff protection with internal improvements. The system was first sketched out in an address to the House of Representatives (3). In March 1817, Madison had vetoed a bill that would have assigned profits of the second Bank of the United States to a fund for internal improvements. President Monroe, who took office a few days later, reiterated the view that internal improvements, desirable as they might be, could not be undertaken by the federal government without a constitutional amendment. A resolution was then introduced in the House asserting the contrary interpretation of the Constitution, and it was in its support that Clay spoke.

With the election of John Quincy Adams in 1824, a strong advocate of internal improvement succeeded to the presidency. His first annual message (4) outlined the program he had in view, while illustrating, as well, the general organization of public finance at the time. But Adams could not marshal the support needed to enact the widespread program of improvements to which he gave so much effort, and consequently regarded himself as a tragic failure.

3

HENRY CLAY (1777–1852)

Address on Internal Improvements (13 Mar. 1818)

[Clay, *Life and Works* (Colton ed., 1864), V, 115]

. . . It was the opinion of Mr. Jefferson, that, although there was no general power vested by the constitution in congress, to construct roads and canals, without the consent of the states, yet such a power might be exercised with their assent. Mr. Jefferson not only held this opinion in the abstract, but he practically executed it in the instance of the Cumberland road; and how? First, by a compact made with the state of Ohio, for the application of a specified fund, and then by compacts with Virginia, Pennsylvania, and Maryland, to apply the fund so set apart within their respective limits. If, however, I rightly understood my honorable friend the other day, he expressly denied (and in that I concur with him) that the power could be acquired by the mere consent of the state. Yet he defended the act of Mr. Jefferson, in the case referred to. . . .

It is far from my intention to misstate the gentleman. I certainly understood him to say, that, as the road was first stipulated for, in the compact with Ohio, it was competent afterwards to carry it through the states mentioned, with their assent. Now, if we have not the right to make a road in virtue of one compact made with a single state, can we obtain it by two contracts made with several states? The character of the fund cannot affect the question. It is totally immaterial whether it arises from the sales of the public lands, or from the general revenue. Suppose a contract made with Massachusetts, that a certain portion of the revenue, collected at the port of Boston, from foreign trade, should be expended in making roads and canals leading to that state, and that a subsequent compact should be made with Connecticut or New Hampshire, for the expenditure of the fund on these objects, within their limits. Can we acquire the power, in this manner, over internal improvements, if we do not possess it independently of such compacts? I conceive, clearly not. And I am entirely at a loss to comprehend how gentlemen, consistently with their own principles, can justify the erection of the Cumberland road. No man is prouder than I am of that noble monument of the provident care of the nation, and of the public spirit of its projectors; and I trust that, in spite of all constitutional and other scruples, here or elsewhere, an appropriation will be made to complete that road. I confess, however, freely, that I am entirely unable to conceive of any principle on which that road can be supported, that would not uphold the general power contended for.

I will now examine the opinion of Mr. Madison. Of all the acts of that pure, virtuous, and illustrious statesman, whose administration has so powerfully tended to advance the glory, honor, and prosperity of this country, I most regret, for his sake and for the sake of the country, the rejection of the bill of the last session. I think it irreconcilable with Mr. Madison's own principles—those great, broad, and liberal principles, on which he so ably administered the government. And, sir, when I appeal to the members of the last congress, who are now in my hearing, I am authorized to say, with regard to the majority of them, that no circumstance, not even an earthquake, that should have swallowed up one half of this city, could have excited more surprise than when it was first communicated to this house, that Mr. Madison had rejected his own bill—I say his own bill, for his message at the opening of the session meant nothing, if it did not recommend such an exercise of power as was contained in that bill. My friend, who is near me, the operations of whose vigorous and independent mind depend upon his own internal perceptions, has expressed himself with becoming manliness, and thrown aside the authority of names, as having no bearing with him on the question. But their authority has been referred to, and will have influence with others. It is impossible, moreover, to disguise the fact, that the question is now a question between the executive on the one side, and the representatives of the people on the other. So it is understood in the country, and such is the fact. Mr. Madison enjoys, in his retreat at Montpellier, the repose and the honors due to his eminent and laborious services; and I would be among the last to disturb it. However painful it is to me to animadvert upon any of his opinions, I feel perfectly sure that the circumstance can only be viewed by him with an enlightened liberality. What are the opinions which have been expressed by Mr. Madison on this subject? I will not refer to all the messages wherein he has recommended internal improvements; but to that alone which he addressed to congress, at the commencement of the last session, which contains this passage:

"I particularly invite *again* the attention of congress to the expediency of exercising their *existing powers,* and where necessary, of resorting to the prescribed mode of enlarging them, in order to *effectuate a comprehensive system of roads and canals,* such as will have the effect of drawing more closely together every part of our country, by promoting intercourse and improvements, and by increasing the share of every part in the common stock of national prosperity."

In the examination of this passage, two positions force themselves upon our attention. The first is, the assertion that there are existing powers in congress to effectuate a comprehensive system of roads and canals, the effect of which would be to draw the different parts of the country more closely together. And I would candidly admit, in the second place, that it was intimated, that, in the exercise of those existing powers, some defect might be discovered which would render an amendment of the constitution necessary. Nothing could be more clearly affirmed than the first position; but in the message of Mr. Madison returning the bill, passed in consequence of his recommendation, he has not specified a solitary case to which those existing powers are applicable; he has not told us what he meant by those existing powers; and the general scope of his reasoning, in that message, if well founded, proves that there are no existing powers whatever. It is apparent, that Mr. Madison himself has not examined some of those principal sources of the constitution from which, during this debate, the power has been derived. I deeply regret, and I know that Mr. Madison regretted, that the circumstances under which the bill was presented to him (the last day but one of a most busy session) deprived him of an opportunity of that thorough investigation of which no man is more capable. It is certain, that, taking his two messages at the same session together, they are perfectly irreconcilable. What, moreover, was the nature of that bill? It did not apply the money to any specific object of internal improvement, nor designate any particular mode in which it should be applied; but merely set apart and pledged the fund to the general purpose, subject to the future disposition of congress. If, then, there were any supposable case whatever, to which congress might apply money in the erection of a road, or cutting a canal, the bill did not violate the constitution. And it ought not to have been anticipated, that money constitutionally appropriated by one congress would be unconstitutionally expended by another.

I come now to the message of Mr. Monroe; and if, by the communication of his opinion to congress, he intended to prevent discussion, he has most woefully failed. I know that, according to a most venerable and excellent usage, the opinion, neither of the president nor of the senate, upon any proposition depending in this house, ought to be adverted to. Even in the parliament of Great Britain, a member who would refer to the opinion of the sovereign, in such a case, would be instantly called to order; but under the extraordinary circumstances of the president having, with, I have no doubt, the best motives, volunteered his opinion on this head, and inverted the order of legislation by beginning where it should end, I am compelled, most reluctantly, to refer to that opinion. I cannot but deprecate the practice of which the president has, in this instance, set the example to his successors. The constitutional order of legislation supposes that every bill originating in one house, shall be there deliberately investigated, without influence from any other branch of the legislature; and then remitted to the other house for a like free and unbiased consideration. Having passed both houses, it is to be laid before the president; signed if approved, and if disapproved, to be returned, with his objections, to the originating house. In this manner, entire freedom of thought and of action is secured, and the president finally sees the proposition in the most matured form which congress can give to it. The practical effect, to say no more, of forestalling the legislative opinion, and telling us what we may or may not do, will be to deprive the president himself of the opportunity of considering a proposition so matured, and us of the benefit of his reasoning applied specifically to such proposition. For the constitution further enjoins it upon him, to state his objections upon returning the bill. The originating house is then to reconsider it, and deliberately to weigh those objections; and it is further required, when the question is again taken, shall the bill pass, those objections notwithstanding? that the votes shall be solemnly spread, by ayes and noes, upon the record. Of this opportunity of thus recording our opinions, in matters of great public concern, we are deprived, if we submit to the innovation of the president. I will not press this part of the subject further. I repeat, again and again, that I have no doubt but that the president was actuated by the purest motives. I am compelled, however, in the exercise of that freedom of opinion which, so long as I exist, I will maintain, to say, that the proceeding is irregular and unconstitutional. Let us, however, examine the reasoning and opinion of the president.

"A difference of opinion has existed from the first formation of our constitution to the present time, among our most enlightened and virtuous citizens, respecting the right of congress to establish a system of internal improvement. Taking into view the trust with which I am now honored, it would be improper, after what has passed, that this discussion should be revived, with an uncertainty of my opinion respecting the right. Disregarding early impressions, I have bestowed on the subject all the deliberation which its great importance and a just sense of my duty required, and the result is, a settled conviction in my mind, that congress does not possess the right. It is not contained in any of the specified powers granted to congress; nor can I consider it incidental to, or a necessary mean, viewed on the most liberal scale, for carrying into effect any of the powers which are specifically granted. In communicating this result, I cannot resist the obligation which I feel, to suggest to congress the propriety of recommending to the states the adoption of an amendment to the constitution, which shall give the right in question. In cases of doubtful construction, especially of such vital interest, it comports with the nature and origin of our institutions, and will contribute much to preserve them, to apply to our constituents for an explicit grant of power. We may confidently rely, that, if it appears to their satisfaction that the power is necessary, it will always be granted."

In this passage, the president has furnished us with no reasoning, no argument in support of his opinion—nothing addressed to the understanding. He gives us, indeed, an historical account of the operations of his own mind, and he asserts that he has made a laborious effort to conquer his early impressions, but that the result is a settled conviction against the power, without a single reason. In his position, that the power must be specifically granted, or incident to a power so granted, it has been seen, that I have the honor to entirely concur with him; but, he says, the power is not among the specified powers. Has he taken into consideration the clause respecting post-roads, and told us how and why that does not convey the power? If he had acted within what I conceive to be his constitutional sphere of rejecting the bill, after it had passed both houses, he must have learned that great stress was placed on that clause, and we should have been enlightened by his comments upon it. As to his denial of the power, as an incident to any of the express grants, I would have thought that we might have safely appealed to the experience of the president, during the late war, when the country derived so much benefit from his judicious administration of the duties of the war department, whether roads and canals for military purposes were not essential to celerity and successful result in the operations of armies. This part of the message is all assertion, and contains no argument which I can comprehend, or which meet the points contended for during this debate. Allow me here to say, and I do it without the least disrespect to that branch of the government, on whose opinions and acts it has been rendered my painful duty to comment; let me say, in reference to any man, however elevated his station, even if he be endowed with the power and prerogatives of a sovereign, that his acts are worth infinitely more, and are more intelligible, than mere paper sentiments or declarations. And what have been the acts of the president? During his tour of the last summer, did he not order a road to be cut or repaired from near Plattsburgh to the St. Lawrence? My honorable friend will excuse me, if my comprehension is too dull to perceive the force of that argument, which seeks to draw a distinction between repairing an old and making a new road. . . .

Certainly no such distinction is to be found in the constitution, or exists in reason. Grant, however, the power of reparation, and we will make it do. We will take the post-roads, sinuous as they are, and put them in a condition to enable the mails to pass, without those mortifying delays and disappointments, to which we, at least in the West, are so often liable. The president, then, ordered a road of considerable extent to be constructed or repaired, on his sole authority, in a time of profound peace, when no enemy threatened the country, and when, in relation to the power as to which alone that road could be useful in time of war, there exists the best understanding, and a prospect of lasting friendship, greater than at any other period. On his sole authority the president acted, and we are already called upon by the chairman of the committee of ways and means to sanction the act by an appropriation. This measure has been taken, too, without the consent of the state of New York; and what is wonderful, when we consider the magnitude of the state rights which are said to be violated, without even a protest on the part of that state against it. On the contrary, I understand, from some of the military officers who are charged with the execution of the work, what is very extraordinary, that the people through whose quarter of the country the road passes, do not view it as a national calamity; that they would be very glad that the president would visit them often, and that he would order a road to be cut and improved, at the national expense, every time he should visit them. Other roads, in other parts of the union, have, it seems, been likewise ordered, or their execution, at the public expense, sanctioned by the executive, without the concurrence of congress. If the president has the power to cause these public improvements to be executed at his pleasure, whence is it derived? If any member will stand up in this place and say the president is clothed with this authority, and that it is denied to congress, let us hear from him; and let him point to the clause of the constitution which vests it in the executive and withholds it from the legislative branch.

There is no such clause; there is no such exclusive executive power. The power is derivable by the executive only from those provisions of the constitution which charge him with the duties of commanding the physical force of the country, and the employment of that force in war, and the preservation of the pub-

lic tranquillity, and in the execution of the laws. But congress
has paramount powers to the president. It alone can declare
war, can raise armies, can provide for calling out the militia,
in the specified instances, and can raise and appropriate the
ways and means necessary to those objects. Or is it come to
this, that there are to be two rules of construction for the constitution—one, an enlarged rule, for the executive, and another, a restricted rule, for the legislature? Is it already to be
held, that, according to the genius and nature of our constitution, powers of this kind may be safely intrusted to the executive, but, when attempted to be exercised by the legislature,
are so alarming and dangerous, that a war with all the allied
powers would be less terrible, and that the nation should clothe
itself straightway in sackcloth and ashes! No, sir; if the power
belongs only by implication to the chief magistrate, it is placed
both by implication and express grant in the hands of congress.
I am so far from condemning the act of the president, to which
I have referred, that I think it deserving of high approbation.
That it was within the scope of his constitutional authority, I
have no doubt; and I sincerely trust, that the secretary at war
will, in time of peace, constantly employ in that way the military force. It will at the same time guard that force against the
vices incident to indolence and inaction, and correct the evil of
subtracting from the mass of the labor of society, where labor
is more valuable than in any other country, that portion of it
which enters into the composition of the army. But I most
solemnly protest against any exercise of powers of this kind
by the president, which are denied to congress. And, if the
opinions expressed by him, in his message, were communicated, or are to be used here, to influence the judgment of
the house, their authority is more than countervailed by the
authority of his deliberate acts.

Some principles drawn from political economists have been
alluded to, and we are advised to leave things to themselves,
upon the ground that, when the condition of society is ripe for
internal improvements—that is, when capital can be so invested
with a fair prospect of adequate remuneration, they will be
executed by associations of individuals, unaided by govern-

ment. With my friend from South Carolina I concur in this as a general maxim; and I also concur with him that there are exceptions to it. The foreign policy which I think this country ought to adopt, presents one of those exceptions. It would perhaps be better for mankind, if, in the intercourse between nations, all would leave skill and industry to their unstimulated exertions. But this is not done; and if other powers will incite the industry of their subjects, and depress that of our citizens, in instances where they may come into competition, we must imitate their selfish example. Hence the necessity to protect our manufactures. In regard to internal improvements, it does not follow, that they will always be constructed whenever they will afford a competent dividend upon the capital invested. It may be true generally that, in old countries, where there is a great accumulation of surplus capital, and a consequent low rate of interest, they will be made. But, in a new country, the condition of society may be ripe for public works long before there is, in the hands of individuals, the necessary accumulation of capital to effect them; and, besides, there is generally, in such a country, not only a scarcity of capital, but such a multiplicity of profitable objects presenting themselves as to distract the judgment. Further; the aggregate benefit resulting to the whole society, from a public improvement, may be such as to amply justify the investment of capital in its execution, and yet that benefit may be so distributed among different and distant persons, that they can never be got to act in concert. The turnpike roads wanted to pass the Allegheny mountains, and the Delaware and Chesapeake canal, are objects of this description. Those who will be most benefited by these improvements, reside at a considerable distance from the sites of them; many of those persons never have seen and never will see them. How is it possible to regulate the contributions, or to present to individuals so situated a sufficiently lively picture of their real interests, to get them to make exertions in effectuating the object, commensurate with their respective abilities? I think it very possible that the capitalist, who should invest his money in one of these objects, might not be reimbursed three per centum annually upon it; and yet society, in various forms, might actually reap fifteen or twenty per centum. The benefit resulting from a turnpike road, made by private associations, is divided between the capitalist who receives his tolls, the lands through which it passes, and which are augmented in their value, and the commodities whose value is enhanced by the diminished expense of transportation. A combination, upon any terms, much less a just combination, of all those interests, to effect the improvement, is impracticable. And if you await the arrival of the period when the tolls alone can produce a competent dividend, it is evident that you will have to suspend its execution long after the general interests of society would have authorized it.

Again, improvements, made by private associations, are generally made by local capital. But ages must elapse before there will be concentrated in certain places, where the interests of the whole community may call for improvements, sufficient capital to make them. The place of the improvement, too, is not always the most interested in its accomplishment. Other parts of the union—the whole line of the seaboard—are quite as much, if not more interested, in the Delaware and Chesapeake canal, as the small tract of country through which it is proposed to pass. The same observation will apply to turnpike roads passing through the Allegheny mountain. Sometimes the interest of the place of the improvement is adverse to the improvement and to the general interest. I would cite Louisville, at the rapids of the Ohio, as an example, whose interest will probably be more promoted by the continuance, than the removal of the obstruction. Of all the modes in which a government can employ its surplus revenue, none is more permanently beneficial than that of internal improvement. Fixed to the soil, it becomes a durable part of the land itself, diffusing comfort, and activity, and animation, on all sides. The first direct effect is on the agricultural community, into whose pockets comes the difference in the expense of transportation between good and bad ways. Thus, if the price of transporting a barrel of flour by the erection of the Cumberland turnpike should be lessened two dollars, the producer of the article would receive that two dollars more now than formerly.

But, putting aside all pecuniary considerations, there may be political motives sufficiently powerful alone to justify certain internal improvements. Does not our country present such? How are they to be effected, if things are left to themselves? I will not press the subject further. I am but too sensible how much I have abused the patience of the committee by trespassing so long upon its attention. The magnitude of the question, and the deep interest I feel in its rightful decision, must be my apology. We are now making the last effort to establish our power, and I call on the friends of congress, of this house, or the true friends of state rights, (not charging others with intending to oppose them,) to rally round the constitution, and to support by their votes, on this occasion, the legitimate powers of the legislature. If we do nothing this session but pass an abstract resolution on the subject, I shall, under all circumstances, consider it a triumph for the best interests of the country, of which posterity will, if we do not, reap the benefit. I trust, that by the decision which shall be given, we shall assert, uphold, and maintain, the authority of congress, notwithstanding all that has been or may be said against it.

4

JOHN QUINCY ADAMS (1767–1848)
First Annual Message to Congress (1825)
[Richardson, *Messages and Papers of the Presidents,* II, 303]

. . . Among the unequivocal indications of our national prosperity is the flourishing state of our finances. The revenues of the present year, from all their principal sources, will exceed the anticipations of the last. The balance in the Treasury on the 1st of January last was a little short of $2,000,000, exclusive of two millions and a half, being the moiety of the loan of five millions authorized by the act of 26th of May, 1824. The receipts into the Treasury from the 1st of January to the 30th of September, exclusive of the other moiety of the same loan, are estimated at $16,500,000, and it is expected that those of the current quarter will exceed $5,000,000, forming an aggregate of receipts of nearly twenty-two millions, independent of the loan. The expenditures of the year will not exceed that sum more than two millions. By those expenditures nearly eight millions of the principal of the public debt have been discharged. More than a million and a half has been devoted to the debt of gratitude to the warriors of the Revolution; a nearly equal sum to the construction of fortifications and the acquisition of ordnance and other permanent preparations of national defense; half a million to the gradual increase of the Navy; an equal sum for purchases of territory from the Indians and payment of annuities to them; and upward of a million for objects of internal improvement authorized by special acts of the last Congress. If we add to these $4,000,000 for payment of interest upon the public debt, there remains a sum of about seven millions, which have defrayed the whole expense of the administration of Government in its legislative, executive, and judiciary departments, including the support of the military and naval establishments and all the occasional contingencies of a government coextensive with the Union.

The amount of duties secured on merchandise imported since the commencement of the year is about twenty-five millions and a half, and that which will accrue during the current quarter is estimated at five millions and a half; from these thirty-one millions, deducting the drawbacks, estimated at less than seven millions, a sum exceeding twenty-four millions will constitute the revenue of the year, and will exceed the whole expenditures of the year. The entire amount of the public debt remaining due on the 1st of January next will be short of $81,000,000.

By an act of Congress of the 3d of March last a loan of $12,000,000 was authorized at 4½ per cent, or an exchange of stock to that amount of 4½ per cent for a stock of 6 per cent, to create a fund for extinguishing an equal amount of the public debt, bearing an interest of 6 per cent, redeemable in 1826.

An account of the measures taken to give effect to this act will be laid before you by the Secretary of the Treasury. As the object which it had in view has been but partially accomplished, it will be for the consideration of Congress whether the power with which it clothed the Executive should not be renewed at an early day of the present session, and under what modifications.

The act of Congress of the 3d of March last, directing the Secretary of the Treasury to subscribe, in the name and for the use of the United States, for 1,500 shares of the capital stock of the Chesapeake and Delaware Canal Company, has been executed by the actual subscription for the amount specified; and such other measures have been adopted by that officer, under the act, as the fulfillment of its intentions requires. The latest accounts received of this important undertaking authorize the belief that it is in successful progress.

The payments into the Treasury from the proceeds of the sales of the public lands during the present year were estimated at $1,000,000. The actual receipts of the first two quarters have fallen very little short of that sum; it is not expected that the second half of the year will be equally productive, but the income of the year from that source may now be safely estimated at a million and a half. The act of Congress of 18th May, 1824, to provide for the extinguishment of the debt due to the United States by the purchasers of public lands, was limited in its operation of relief to the purchaser to the 10th of April last. Its effect at the end of the quarter during which it expired was to reduce that debt from ten to seven millions. By the operation of similar prior laws of relief, from and since that of 2d March, 1821, the debt had been reduced from upward of twenty-two millions to ten. It is exceedingly desirable that it should be extinguished altogether; and to facilitate that consummation I recommend to Congress the revival for one year more of the act of 18th May, 1824, with such provisional modification as may be necessary to guard the public interests against fraudulent practices in the resale of the relinquished land. The purchasers of public lands are among the most useful of our fellow-citizens, and since the system of sales for cash alone has been introduced great indulgence has been justly extended to those who had previously purchased upon credit. The debt which had been contracted under the credit sales had become unwieldy, and its extinction was alike advantageous to the purchaser and to the public. Under the system of sales, matured as it has been by experience, and adapted to the exigencies of the times, the lands will continue as they have become, an abundant source of revenue; and when the pledge of them to the public creditor shall have been redeemed by the entire discharge of the national debt, the swelling tide of wealth with which they replenish the common Treasury may be made to reflow in unfailing streams of improvement from the Atlantic to the Pacific Ocean.

The condition of the various branches of the public service resorting from the Department of War, and their administration during the current year, will be exhibited in the report of the Secretary of War and the accompanying documents herewith communicated. The organization and discipline of the Army are effective and satisfactory. To counteract the prevalence of desertion among the troops it has been suggested to withhold from the men a small portion of their monthly pay until the period of their discharge; and some expedient appears to be necessary to preserve and maintain among the officers so much of the art of horsemanship as could scarcely fail to be found wanting on the possible sudden eruption of a war, which should take us unprovided with a single corps of cavalry. The Military Academy at West Point, under the restrictions of a severe but paternal superintendence, recommends itself more and more to the patronage of the nation, and the numbers of meritorious officers which it forms and introduces to the public service furnishes the means of multiplying the undertakings of public improvements to which their acquirements at that institution are peculiarly adapted. The school of artillery practice established at Fortress Monroe is well suited to the same purpose, and may need the aid of further legislative provision to the same end. The reports of the various officers at the head of the administrative branches of the military service, connected with the quartering, clothing, subsistence, health, and pay of the Army, exhibit the assiduous vigilance of those officers in the performance of their respective duties, and the faithful accountability which has pervaded every part of the system.

Our relations with the numerous tribes of aboriginal natives of this country, scattered over its extensive surface and so dependent even for their existence upon our power, have been during the present year highly interesting. An act of Congress of 25th of May, 1824, made an appropriation to defray the expenses of making treaties of trade and friendship with the Indian tribes beyond the Mississippi. An act of 3d of March, 1825, authorized treaties to be made with the Indians for their consent to the making of a road from the frontier of Missouri to that of New Mexico, and another act of the same date provided for defraying the expenses of holding treaties with the Sioux, Chippeways, Menomenees, Sauks, Foxes, etc., for the purpose of establishing boundaries and promoting peace between said tribes. The first and the last objects of these acts have been accomplished, and the second is yet in a process of execution. The treaties which since the last session of Congress have been concluded with the several tribes will be laid before the Senate for their consideration conformably to the Constitution. They comprise large and valuable acquisitions of territory, and they secure an adjustment of boundaries and give pledges of permanent peace between several tribes which had been long waging bloody wars against each other.

On the 12th of February last a treaty was signed at the Indian Springs between commissioners appointed on the part of the United States and certain chiefs and individuals of the Creek Nation of Indians, which was received at the seat of Government only a very few days before the close of the last session of Congress and of the late Administration. The advice and consent of the Senate was given to it on the 3d of March, too late for it to receive the ratification of the then President of the United States; it was ratified on the 7th of March, under the unsuspecting impression that it had been negotiated in good faith and in the confidence inspired by the recommendation of the Senate. The subsequent transactions in relation to this treaty will form the subject of a separate communication.

The appropriations made by Congress for public works, as well in the construction of fortifications as for purposes of internal improvement, so far as they have been expended, have been faithfully applied. Their progress has been delayed by the want of suitable officers for superintending them. An increase of both the corps of engineers, military and topographical, was recommended by my predecessor at the last session of Congress. The reasons upon which that recommendation was founded subsist in all their force and have acquired additional urgency since that time. It may also be expedient to organize the topographical engineers into a corps similar to the present establishment of the Corps of Engineers. The Military Academy at West Point will furnish from the cadets annually graduated there officers well qualified for carrying this measure into effect.

The Board of Engineers for Internal Improvement, appointed for carrying into execution the act of Congress of 30th of April, 1824, "to procure the necessary surveys, plans, and estimates on the subject of roads and canals," have been actively engaged in that service from the close of the last session of Congress. They have completed the surveys necessary for ascertaining the practicability of a canal from the Chesapeake Bay to the Ohio River, and are preparing a full report on that subject, which, when completed, will be laid before you. The same observation is to be made with regard to the two other objects of national importance upon which the Board have been occupied, namely, the accomplishment of a national road from this city to New Orleans, and the practicability of uniting the waters of Lake Memphramagog with Connecticut River and the improvement of the navigation of that river. The surveys have been made and are nearly completed. The report may be expected at an early period during the present session of Congress.

The acts of Congress of the last session relative to the surveying, marking, or laying out roads in the Territories of Florida, Arkansas, and Michigan, from Missouri to Mexico, and for the continuation of the Cumberland road, are, some of them, fully executed, and others in the process of execution. Those for completing or commencing fortifications have been delayed only so far as the Corps of Engineers has been inadequate to furnish officers for the necessary superintendence of the works. Under the act confirming the statutes of Virginia and Maryland incorporating the Chesapeake and Ohio Canal Company, three commissioners on the part of the United States have been appointed for opening books and receiving subscriptions, in concert with a like number of commissioners appointed on the part of each of those States. A meeting of the commissioners has been postponed, to await the definitive report of the board of engineers. The light-houses and monuments for the safety of our commerce and mariners, the works for the security of Plymouth Beach and for the preservation of the islands in Boston Harbor, have received the attention required by the laws relating to those objects respectively. The continuation of the Cumberland road, the most important of them all, after surmounting no inconsiderable difficulty in fixing upon the direction of the road, has commenced under the most promising auspices, with the improvements of recent invention in the mode of construction, and with the advantage of a great reduction in the comparative cost of the work.

The operation of the laws relating to the Revolutionary pensioners may deserve the renewed consideration of Congress. The act of the 18th of March, 1818, while it made provision for many meritorious and indigent citizens who had served in the War of Independence, opened a door to numerous abuses and impositions. To remedy this the act of 1st May, 1820, exacted proofs of absolute indigence, which many really in want were unable and all susceptible of that delicacy which is allied to many virtues must be deeply reluctant to give. The result has been that some among the least deserving have been retained, and some in whom the requisites both of worth and want were combined have been stricken from the list. As the numbers of these venerable relics of an age gone by diminish; as the decays of body, mind, and estate of those that survive must in the common course of nature increase, should not a more liberal portion of indulgence be dealt out to them? May not the want in most instances be inferred from the demand when the service can be proved, and may not the last days of human infirmity be spared the mortification of purchasing a pittance of relief only by the exposure of its own necessities? I submit to Congress the expediency of providing for individual cases of this description by special enactment, or of revising the act of the 1st of May, 1820, with a view to mitigate the rigor of its exclusions in favor of persons to whom charity now bestowed can scarcely discharge the debt of justice.

The portion of the naval force of the Union in actual service has been chiefly employed on three stations—the Mediterranean, the coasts of South America bordering on the Pacific Ocean, and the West Indies. An occasional cruiser has been sent to range along the African shores most polluted by the traffic of slaves; one armed vessel has been stationed on the coast of our eastern boundary, to cruise along the fishing grounds in Hudsons Bay and on the coast of Labrador, and the first service of a new frigate has been performed in restoring to his native soil and domestic enjoyments the veteran hero whose youthful blood and treasure had freely flowed in the cause of our country's independence, and whose whole life has been a series of services and sacrifices to the improvement of his fellow-men. The visit of General Lafayette, alike honorable to himself and to our country, closed, as it had commenced, with the most affecting testimonials of devoted attachment on his part, and of unbounded gratitude of this people to him in return. It will form hereafter a pleasing incident in the annals of our Union, giving to real history the intense interest of romance and signally marking the unpurchasable tribute of a great nation's social affections to the disinterested champion of the liberties of human-kind.

The constant maintenance of a small squadron in the Mediterranean is a necessary substitute for the humiliating alternative of paying tribute for the security of our commerce in that sea, and for a precarious peace, at the mercy of every caprice of four Barbary States, by whom it was liable to be violated. An additional motive for keeping a respectable force stationed there at this time is found in the maritime war raging between the Greeks and the Turks, and in which the neutral navigation of this Union is always in danger of outrage and depredation. A few instances have occurred of such depredations upon our merchant vessels by privateers or pirates wearing the Grecian flag, but without real authority from the Greek or any other Government. The heroic struggles of the Greeks themselves, in which our warmest sympathies as freemen and Christians have been engaged, have continued to be maintained with vicissitudes of success adverse and favorable.

Similar motives have rendered expedient the keeping of a like force on the coasts of Peru and Chile on the Pacific. The irregular and convulsive character of the war upon the shores has been extended to the conflicts upon the ocean. An active warfare has been kept up for years with alternate success, though generally to the advantage of the American patriots. But their naval forces have not always been under the control of their own Governments. Blockades, unjustifiable upon any acknowledged principles of international law, have been proclaimed by officers in command, and though disavowed by the supreme authorities, the protection of our own commerce against them has been made cause of complaint and erroneous imputations against some of the most gallant officers of our Navy. Complaints equally groundless have been made by the commanders of the Spanish royal forces in those seas; but the most effective protection to our commerce has been the flag and the firmness of our own commanding officers. The cessation of the war by the complete triumph of the patriot cause has removed, it is hoped, all cause of dissension with one party and all vestige of force of the other. But an unsettled coast of many degrees of latitude forming a part of our own territory and a flourishing commerce and fishery extending to the islands of the Pacific and to China still require that the protecting power of the Union should be displayed under its flag as well upon the ocean as upon the land.

The objects of the West India Squadron have been to carry into execution the laws for the suppression of the African slave trade; for the protection of our commerce against vessels of

piratical character, though bearing commissions from either of
the belligerent parties; for its protection against open and unequivocal pirates. These objects during the present year have
been accomplished more effectually than at any former period.
The African slave trade has long been excluded from the use
of our flag, and if some few citizens of our country have continued to set the laws of the Union as well as those of nature
and humanity at defiance by persevering in that abominable
traffic, it has been only by sheltering themselves under the
banners of other nations less earnest for the total extinction of
the trade than ours. The irregular privateers have within the
last year been in a great measure banished from those seas,
and the pirates for months past appear to have been almost
entirely swept away from the borders and the shores of the
two Spanish islands in those regions. The active, persevering,
and unremitted energy of Captain Warrington and of the officers and men under his command on that trying and perilous
service have been crowned with signal success, and are entitled
to the approbation of their country. But experience has shown
that not even a temporary suspension or relaxation from as-
siduity can be indulged on that station without reproducing
piracy and murder in all their horrors; nor is it probable that
for years to come our immensely valuable commerce in those
seas can navigate in security without the steady continuance
of an armed force devoted to its protection.

   It were, indeed, a vain and dangerous illusion to believe that
in the present or probable condition of human society a commerce so extensive and so rich as ours could exist and be pursued in safety without the continual support of a military marine—the only arm by which the power of this Confederacy can
be estimated or felt by foreign nations, and the only standing
military force which can never be dangerous to our own liberties at home. A permanent naval peace establishment, therefore, adapted to our present condition, and adaptable to that
gigantic growth with which the nation is advancing in its
career, is among the subjects which have already occupied the
foresight of the last Congress, and which will deserve your
serious deliberations. Our Navy, commenced at an early period

of our present political organization upon a scale commensurate with the incipient energies, the scanty resources, and the comparative indigence of our infancy, was even then found adequate to cope with all the powers of Barbary, save the first, and with one of the principal maritime powers of Europe.

At a period of further advancement, but with little accession of strength, it not only sustained with honor the most unequal of conflicts, but covered itself and our country with unfading glory. But it is only since the close of the late war that by the numbers and force of the ships of which it was composed it could deserve the name of a navy. Yet it retains nearly the same organization as when it consisted only of five frigates. The rules and regulations by which it is governed earnestly call for revision, and the want of a naval school of instruction, corresponding with the Military Academy at West Point, for the formation of scientific and accomplished officers, is felt with daily increasing aggravation.

The act of Congress of 26th of May, 1824, authorizing an examination and survey of the harbor of Charleston, in South Carolina, of St. Marys, in Georgia, and of the coast of Florida, and for other purposes, has been executed so far as the appropriation would admit. Those of the 3d of March last, authorizing the establishment of a navy-yard and depot on the coast of Florida, in the Gulf of Mexico, and authorizing the building of ten sloops of war, and for other purposes, are in the course of execution, for the particulars of which and other objects connected with this Department I refer to the report of the Secretary of the Navy, herewith communicated.

A report from the Postmaster-General is also submitted, exhibiting the present flourishing condition of that Department. For the first time for many years the receipts for the year ending on the 1st of July last exceeded the expenditures during the same period to the amount of more than $45,000. Other facts equally creditable to the administration of this Department are that in two years from the 1st of July, 1823, an improvement of more than $185,000 in its pecuniary affairs has been realized; that in the same interval the increase of the transportation of the mail has exceeded 1,500,000 miles annually, and that 1,040 new post-offices have been established. It hence appears that under judicious management the income from this establishment may be relied on as fully adequate to defray its expenses, and that by the discontinuance of post-roads altogether unproductive others of more useful character may be opened, till the circulation of the mail shall keep pace with the spread of our population, and the comforts of friendly correspondence, the exchanges of internal traffic, and the lights of the periodical press shall be distributed to the remotest corners of the Union, at a charge scarcely perceptible to any individual, and without the cost of a dollar to the public Treasury.

Upon this first occasion of addressing the Legislature of the Union, with which I have been honored, in presenting to their view the execution so far as it has been effected of the measures sanctioned by them for promoting the internal improvement of our country, I can not close the communication without recommending to their calm and persevering consideration the general principle in a more enlarged extent. The great object of the institution of civil government is the improvement of the condition of those who are parties to the social compact, and no government, in whatever form constituted, can accomplish the lawful ends of its institution but in proportion as it improves the condition of those over whom it is established. Roads and canals, by multiplying and facilitating the communications and intercourse between distant regions and multitudes of men, are among the most important means of improvement. But moral, political, intellectual improvement are duties assigned by the Author of Our Existence to social no less than to individual man. For the fulfillment of those duties governments are invested with power, and to the attainment of the end— the progressive improvement of the condition of the governed —the exercise of delegated powers is a duty as sacred and indispensable as the usurpation of powers not granted is criminal and odious. Among the first, perhaps the very first, instrument for the improvement of the condition of men is knowledge, and to the acquisition of much of the knowledge adapted to the wants, the comforts, and enjoyments of human life public institutions and seminaries of learning are essential. So convinced of this was the first of my predecessors in this office, now first in the memory, as, living, he was first in the hearts, of our countrymen, that once and again in his addresses to the Congresses with whom he cooperated in the public service he earnestly recommended the establishment of seminaries of learning, to prepare for all the emergencies of peace and war—a national university and a military academy. With respect to the latter, had he lived to the present day, in turning his eyes to the institution at West Point he would have enjoyed the gratification of his most earnest wishes; but in surveying the city which has been honored with his name he would have seen the spot of earth which he had destined and bequeathed to the use and benefit of his country as the site for an university still bare and barren.

In assuming her station among the civilized nations of the earth it would seem that our country had contracted the engagement to contribute her share of mind, of labor, and of expense to the improvement of those parts of knowledge which lie beyond the reach of individual acquisition, and particularly to geographical and astronomical science. Looking back to the history only of the half century since the declaration of our independence, and observing the generous emulation with which the Governments of France, Great Britain, and Russia have devoted the genius, the intelligence, the treasures of their respective nations to the common improvement of the species in these branches of science, is it not incumbent upon us to inquire whether we are not bound by obligations of a high and honorable character to contribute our portion of energy and exertion to the common stock? The voyages of discovery prosecuted in the course of that time at the expense of those nations have not only redounded to their glory, but to the improvement of human knowledge. We have been partakers of that improvement and owe for it a sacred debt, not only of gratitude, but of equal or proportional exertion in the same common cause. Of the cost of these undertakings, if the mere expenditures of outfit, equipment, and completion of the expeditions were to be considered the only charges, it would be unworthy of a great and generous nation to take a second thought. One hundred expeditions of circumnavigation like those of Cook and La Pérouse would not burden the exchequer of the nation fitting them out so much as the ways and means of defraying a single campaign in war. But if we take into the account the lives of those benefactors of mankind of which their services in the cause of their species were the purchase, how shall the cost of those heroic enterprises be estimated, and what compensation can be made to them or to their countries for them? Is it not by bearing them in affectionate remembrance? Is it not still more by imitating their example—by enabling countrymen of our own to pursue the same career and to hazard their lives in the same cause?

In inviting the attention of Congress to the subject of internal improvements upon a view thus enlarged it is not my design to recommend the equipment of an expedition for circumnavigating the globe for purposes of scientific research and inquiry. We have objects of useful investigation nearer home, and to which our cares may be more beneficially applied. The interior of our own territories has yet been very imperfectly explored. Our coasts along many degrees of latitude upon the shores of the Pacific Ocean, though much frequented by our spirited commercial navigators, have been barely visited by our public ships. The River of the West, first fully discovered and navigated by a countryman of our own, still bears the name of the ship in which he ascended its waters, and claims the protection of our armed national flag at its mouth. With the establishment of a military post there or at some other point of that coast, recommended by my predecessor and already matured in the deliberations of the last Congress, I would suggest the expediency of connecting the equipment of a public ship for the exploration of the whole northwest coast of this continent.

The establishment of an uniform standard of weights and measures was one of the specific objects contemplated in the formation of our Constitution, and to fix that standard was one of the powers delegated by express terms in that instrument to Congress. The Governments of Great Britain and France have scarcely ceased to be occupied with inquiries and speculations on the same subject since the existence of our Constitution, and with them it has expanded into profound, laborious, and expensive researches into the figure of the earth and the comparative length of the pendulum vibrating seconds in various latitudes from the equator to the pole. These researches have resulted in the composition and publication of several works highly interesting to the cause of science. The experiments are yet in the process of performance. Some of them have recently been made on our own shores, within the walls of one of our own colleges, and partly by one of our own fellow-citizens. It would be honorable to our country if the sequel of the same experiments should be countenanced by the patronage of our Government, as they have hitherto been by those of France and Britain.

Connected with the establishment of an university, or separate from it, might be undertaken the erection of an astronomical observatory, with provision for the support of an astronomer, to be in constant attendance of observation upon the phenomena of the heavens, and for the periodical publication of his observations. It is with no feeling of pride as an American that the remark may be made that on the comparatively small territorial surface of Europe there are existing upward of 130 of these light-houses of the skies, while throughout the whole American hemisphere there is not one. If we reflect a moment upon the discoveries which in the last four centuries have been made in the physical constitution of the universe by the means of these buildings and of observers stationed in them, shall we doubt of their usefulness to every nation? And while scarcely a year passes over our heads without bringing some new astronomical discovery to light, which we must fain receive at second hand from Europe, are we not cutting ourselves off from the means of returning light for light while we have neither observatory nor observer upon our half of the globe and the earth revolves in perpetual darkness to our unsearching eyes?

When, on the 25th of October, 1791, the first President of the United States announced to Congress the result of the first enumeration of the inhabitants of this Union, he informed them that the returns gave the pleasing assurance that the population of the United States bordered on 4,000,000 persons. At the distance of thirty years from that time the last enumeration, five years since completed, presented a population bordering upon 10,000,000. Perhaps of all the evidences of a prosperous and happy condition of human society the rapidity of the increase of population is the most unequivocal. But the demonstration of our prosperity rests not alone upon this indication. Our commerce, our wealth, and the extent of our territories have increased in corresponding proportions, and the number of independent communities associated in our Federal Union has since that time nearly doubled. The legislative representation of the States and people in the two Houses of Congress has grown with the growth of their constituent bodies. The House, which then consisted of 65 members, now numbers upward of 200. The Senate, which consisted of 26 members, has now 48. But the executive and, still more, the judiciary departments are yet in a great measure confined to their primitive organization, and are now not adequate to the urgent wants of a still growing community.

The naval armaments, which at an early period forced themselves upon the necessities of the Union, soon led to the establishment of a Department of the Navy. But the Departments of Foreign Affairs and of the Interior, which early after the formation of the Government had been united in one, continue so united to this time, to the unquestionable detriment of the public service. The multiplication of our relations with the nations and Governments of the Old World has kept pace with that of our population and commerce, while within the last ten years a new family of nations in our own hemisphere has arisen among the inhabitants of the earth, with whom our intercourse, commercial and political, would of itself furnish occupation to an active and industrious department. The constitution of the judiciary, experimental and imperfect as it was even in the infancy of our existing Government, is yet more inadequate to the administration of national justice at our present maturity. Nine years have elapsed since a predecessor in this office, now not the last, the citizen who, perhaps, of all others throughout the Union contributed most to the formation and establishment of our Constitution, in his valedictory address to Congress, immediately preceding his retirement from public life, urgently recommended the revision of the judiciary and the establishment of an additional executive department. The exigencies of the public service and its unavoidable deficiencies, as now in exercise, have added yearly cumulative weight to the considerations presented by him as persuasive to the measure, and in recommending it to your deliberations I am happy to have the influence of his high authority in aid of the undoubting convictions of my own experience.

The laws relating to the administration of the Patent Office are deserving of much consideration and perhaps susceptible of some improvement. The grant of power to regulate the action of Congress upon this subject has specified both the end to be obtained and the means by which it is to be effected, "to promote the progress of science and useful arts by securing for limited times to authors and inventors the exclusive right to their respective writings and discoveries." If an honest pride might be indulged in the reflection that on the records of that office are already found inventions the usefulness of which has scarcely been transcended in the annals of human ingenuity, would not its exultation be allayed by the inquiry whether the laws have effectively insured to the inventors the reward destined to them by the Constitution—even a limited term of exclusive right to their discoveries?

On the 24th of December, 1799, it was resolved by Congress that a marble monument should be erected by the United States in the Capitol at the city of Washington; that the family of General Washington should be requested to permit his body to be deposited under it, and that the monument be so designed as to commemorate the great events of his military and political life. In reminding Congress of this resolution and that the monument contemplated by it remains yet without execution, I shall indulge only the remarks that the works at the Capitol are approaching to completion; that the consent of the family, desired by the resolution, was requested and obtained; that a monument has been recently erected in this city over the remains of another distinguished patriot of the Revolution, and that a spot has been reserved within the walls where you are deliberating for the benefit of this and future ages, in which the mortal remains may be deposited of him whose spirit hovers over you and listens with delight to every act of the representatives of his nation which can tend to exalt and adorn his and their country.

The Constitution under which you are assembled is a charter of limited powers. After full and solemn deliberation upon all or any of the objects which, urged by an irresistible sense of my own duty, I have recommended to your attention should you come to the conclusion that, however desirable in themselves, the enactment of laws for effecting them would transcend the powers committed to you by that venerable instrument which we are all bound to support, let no consideration induce you to assume the exercise of powers not granted to you by the people. But if the power to exercise exclusive legislation in all cases whatsoever over the District of Columbia; if the power to lay and collect taxes, duties, imposts, and excises, to pay the debts and provide for the common defense and general welfare of the United States; if the power to regulate commerce with foreign nations and among the several States and with the Indian tribes, to fix the standard of weights and measures, to establish post-offices and post-roads, to declare war, to raise and support armies, to provide and maintain a navy, to dispose of and make all needful rules and regulations respecting the territory or other property belonging to the United States, and to make all laws which shall be necessary and proper for carrying these powers into execution—if these powers and others enumerated in the Constitution may be effectually brought into action by laws promoting the improvement of agriculture, commerce, and manufactures, the cultivation and encouragement of the mechanic and of the elegant arts, the advancement of literature, and the progress of the sciences, ornamental and profound, to refrain from exercising them for the benefit of the people themselves would be to hide in the earth the talent committed to our charge—would be treachery to the most sacred of trusts.

The spirit of improvement is abroad upon the earth. It stimulates the hearts and sharpens the faculties not of our fellow-citizens alone, but of the nations of Europe and of their rulers. While dwelling with pleasing satisfaction upon the superior excellence of our political institutions, let us not be unmindful that liberty is power; that the nation blessed with the largest portion of liberty must in proportion to its numbers be the most powerful nation upon earth, and that the tenure of power by man is, in the moral purposes of his Creator, upon condition that it shall be exercised to ends of beneficence, to improve the condition of himself and his fellow-men. While foreign nations less blessed with that freedom which is power than ourselves are advancing with gigantic strides in the career of public improvement, were we to slumber in indolence or fold up our arms and proclaim to the world that we are palsied by the will of our constituents, would it not be to cast away the bounties of Providence and doom ourselves to perpetual inferiority? In the course of the year now drawing to its close we have beheld, under the auspices and at the expense of one State of this Union, a new university unfolding its portals to the sons of science and holding up the torch of human improvement to eyes that seek the light. We have seen under the persevering and enlightened enterprise of another State the waters of our Western lakes mingle with those of the ocean. If undertakings like these have been accomplished in the compass of a few years by the authority of single members of our Confederation, can we, the representative authorities of the whole Union, fall behind our fellow-servants in the exercise of the trust committed to us for the benefit of our common sovereign by the accomplishment of works important to the whole and to which neither the authority nor the resources of any one State can be adequate?

Finally, fellow-citizens, I shall await with cheering hope and faithful cooperation the result of your deliberations, assured that, without encroaching upon the powers reserved to the authorities of the respective States or to the people, you will, with a due sense of your obligations to your country and of the high responsibilities weighing upon yourselves, give effi-

cacy to the means committed to you for the common good.
And may He who searches the hearts of the children of men
prosper your exertions to secure the blessings of peace and promote the highest welfare of our country.

C. Corporation Law

More than any other actors on the economic scene except government itself, corporations are creatures of policy since, being artificial, they derive their powers from the laws that create and limit them.

It is often said that the corporation, though not natural, was necessary, for rapid industrial development could not have taken place without this means of organizing the funds of many investors into large blocks of capital. But there is no reason why a similar agglomeration of capital could not have been organized otherwise, why savings banks, for instance, could not have amalgamated large numbers of small deposits into a few large loans to unincorporated businesses. In any event, the chief attributes that now define a corporation—its indefinite life and the limited liability of its owners—could have been grafted onto the partnership form, and in some places have been. Besides, early corporations usually lacked these privileges; their charters were valued for the specific subsidies and occasional monopoly powers they granted.

At first, in the United States, the privilege of forming a corporation was conferred by state legislatures in special statutes drawn up to suit individual circumstances. Because enacting these private laws was a long and cumbersome business, and because the number of applicants for corporate status was increasing rapidly, the states began after 1830 to pass general incorporation laws, which gave an executive officer power to issue a charter to any group that met certain statutory conditions.

The corporate charter has always had some semblance of a bargain between the state, which endows certain people with special powers, and the incorporators, who promise to use those powers to the benefit of the public. The state has always exacted certain returns for its initial gift of life; corporations have always tended to use their powers to the fullest. How far either party might go, the one in restricting, the other in exploiting, has been the central problem of this branch of policy.

The state's power to regulate a corporation, once it had its charter, was somewhat limited by the decision in the *Dartmouth College* case (5). The College held a charter that predated the Revolution; in 1816 the legislature of New Hampshire passed laws enabling the Governor to appoint certain officers to the College. The trustees appointed under the original charter argued that the new statutes were unconstitutional, a view that the Supreme Court of the United States supported. The doctrine laid down by Chief Justice Marshall—that, as a corporate charter contains a contract, the state may not arbitrarily revoke or alter it—did not give corporations a free hand, but narrowed the means by which public regulation might take place. The charter might not be interfered with, but Marshall's doctrine left the states free to regulate the activities of corporations by general laws, and this they did.

The opposite limit of corporate power was defined by the *Charles River Bridge* decision (6). In that case, the corporation maintained that Massachusetts had unlawfully interfered with its charter by establishing a competing bridge. The Supreme Court held, however, that as its charter did not explicitly award the corporation a monopoly, the corporation could not claim one. The general rule of the decision, that a corporation could go no further than its charter clearly allowed, was by no means novel, but took on additional force by contrast with the *Dartmouth College* opinion. Later developments in corporation law are indicated by the case of *Munn vs. Illinois* (9) and many of the federal statutes enacted after 1861.

5
U. S. SUPREME COURT
Dartmouth College vs. Woodward (2 Feb. 1819)
[4 L. Ed. 624, 4 Wheat. 518]

(The opinion of the Court was delivered by Mr. Chief Justice Marshall:)

This is an action of trover, brought by the Trustees of Dartmouth College against William H. Woodward, in the State Court of New-Hampshire, for the book of records, corporate seal, and other corporate property, to which the plaintiffs allege themselves to be entitled.

A special verdict, after setting out the rights of the parties, finds for the defendant, if certain acts of the legislature of New-Hampshire, passed on the 27th of June, and on the 18th of December, 1816, be valid, and binding on the trustees without their assent, and not repugnant to the constitution of the United States; otherwise, it finds for the plaintiffs.

The Superior Court of Judicature of New-Hampshire rendered a judgment upon this verdict for the defendant, which judgment has been brought before this Court by writ of error. The single question now to be considered is, do the acts to which the verdict refers violate the constitution of the United States?

This Court can be insensible neither to the magnitude nor delicacy of this question. The validity of a legislative act is to be examined; and the opinion of the highest law tribunal of a State is to be revised: an opinion which carries with it intrinsic evidence of the diligence, of the ability, and the integrity, with which it was formed. On more than one occasion, this Court has expressed the cautious circumspection with which it approaches the consideration of such questions; and has declared, that, in no doubtful case, would it pronounce a legislative act to be contrary to the constitution. But the American people

have said, in the constitution of the United States, that "no
State shall pass any bill of attainder, *ex post facto* law, or law
impairing the obligation of contracts." In the same instrument
they have also said, "that the judicial power shall extend to all
cases in law and equity arising under the constitution." On the
judges of this Court, then, is imposed the high and solemn
duty of protecting, from even legislative violation, those contracts which the constitution of our country has placed beyond
legislative control; and, however irksome the task may be, this
is a duty from which we dare not shrink.

The title of the plaintiffs originates in a charter dated the
13th day of December, in the year 1769, incorporating twelve
persons therein mentioned, by the name of "The Trustees of
Dartmouth College," granting to them and their successors the
usual corporate privileges and powers, and authorizing the
trustees, who are to govern the college, to fill up all vacancies
which may be created in their own body.

The defendant claims under three acts of the legislature of
New-Hampshire, the most material of which was passed on the
27th of June, 1816, and is entitled, "an act to amend the
charter, and enlarge and improve the corporation of Dartmouth
College." Among other alterations in the charter, this act increases the number of trustees to twenty-one, gives the appointment of the additional members to the executive of the
State, and creates a board of overseers, with power to inspect
and control the most important acts of the trustees. This board
consists of twenty-five persons. The president of the senate, the
speaker of the house of representatives, of New-Hampshire,
and the governor and lieutenant governor of Vermont, for the
time being, are to be members *ex officio*. The board is to be
completed by the governor and council of New-Hampshire,
who are also empowered to fill all vacancies which may occur.
The acts of the 18th and 26th of December are supplemental
to that of the 27th of June, and are principally intended to
carry that act into effect.

The majority of the trustees of the college have refused to
accept this amended charter, and have brought this suit for

the corporate property, which is in possession of a person holding by virtue of the acts which have been stated.

It can require no argument to prove, that the circumstances of this case constitute a contract. An application is made to the crown for a charter to incorporate a religious and literary institution. In the application, it is stated that large contributions have been made for the object, which will be conferred on the corporation, as soon as it shall be created. The charter is granted, and on its faith the property is conveyed. Surely in this transaction every ingredient of a complete and legitimate contract is to be found.

The points for consideration are,

1. Is this contract protected by the constitution of the United States?

2. Is it impaired by the acts under which the defendant holds?

1. On the first point it has been argued, that the word "contract," in its broadest sense, would comprehend the political relations between the government and its citizens, would extend to offices held within a State for State purposes, and to many of those laws concerning civil institutions, which must change with circumstances, and be modified by ordinary legislation; which deeply concern the public, and which, to preserve good government, the public judgment must control. That even marriage is a contract, and its obligations are affected by the laws respecting divorces. That the clause in the constitution, if construed in its greatest latitude, would prohibit these laws. Taken in its broad unlimited sense, the clause would be an unprofitable and vexatious interference with the internal concerns of a State, would unnecessarily and unwisely embarrass its legislation, and render immutable those civil institutions, which are established for purposes of internal government, and which, to subserve those purposes, ought to vary with varying circumstances. That as the framers of the constitution could never have intended to insert in that instrument a provision so unnecessary, so mischievous, and so repugnant to its general spirit, the term *"contract"* must be understood in a more limited sense. That it must be understood as intended

to guard against a power of at least doubtful utility, the abuse of which had been extensively felt; and to restrain the legislature in future from violating the right to property. That anterior to the formation of the constitution, a course of legislation had prevailed in many, if not in all of the States, which weakened the confidence of man in man, and embarrassed all transactions between individuals, by dispensing with a faithful performance of engagements. To correct this mischief, by restraining the power which produced it, the State legislatures were forbidden "to pass any law impairing the obligation of contracts," that is, of contracts respecting property, under which some individual could claim a right to something beneficial to himself; and that since the clause in the constitution must in construction receive some limitation, it may be confined, and ought to be confined, to cases of this description; to cases within the mischief it was intended to remedy.

The general correctness of these observations cannot be controverted. That the framers of the constitution did not intend to restrain the States in the regulation of their civil institutions, adopted for internal government, and that the instrument they have given us, is not to be so construed, may be admitted. The provision of the constitution never has been understood to embrace other contracts, than those which respect property, or some object of value, and confer rights which may be asserted in a court of justice. It never has been understood to restrict the general right of the legislature to legislate on the subject of divorces. Those acts enable some tribunal, not to impair a marriage contract, but to liberate one of the parties because it has been broken by the other. When any State legislature shall pass an act annulling all marriage contracts, or allowing either party to annul it without the consent of the other, it will be time enough to inquire, whether such an act be constitutional.

The parties in this case differ less on general principles, less on the true construction of the constitution in the abstract, than on the application of those principles to this case, and on the true construction of the charter of 1769. This is the point on which the cause essentially depends. If the act of incorporation be a grant of political power, if it create a civil institution to be employed in the administration of the government, or if the funds of the college be public property, or if the State of New-Hampshire, as a government, be alone interested in its transactions, the subject is one in which the legislature of the State may act according to its own judgment, unrestrained by any limitation of its power imposed by the constitution of the United States.

But if this be a private eleemosynary institution, endowed with a capacity to take property for objects unconnected with government, whose funds are bestowed by individuals on the faith of the charter; if the donors have stipulated for the future disposition and management of those funds in the manner prescribed by themselves; there may be more difficulty in the case, although neither the persons who have made these stipulations, nor those for whose benefit they were made, should be parties to the cause. Those who are no longer interested in the property, may yet retain such an interest in the preservation of their own arrangements, as to have a right to insist, that those arrangements shall be held sacred. Or, if they have themselves disappeared, it becomes a subject of serious and anxious inquiry, whether those whom they have legally empowered to represent them forever, may not assert all the rights which they possessed, while in being; whether, if they be without personal representatives who may feel injured by a violation of the compact, the trustees be not so completely their representatives in the eye of the law, as to stand in their place, not only as respects the government of the college, but also as respects the maintenance of the college charter.

It becomes then the duty of the Court most seriously to examine this charter, and to ascertain its true character.

From the instrument itself, it appears, that about the year 1754, the Rev. Eleazer Wheelock established at his own expense, and on his own estate, a charity school for the instruction of Indians in the christian religion. The success of this institution inspired him with the design of soliciting contributions in England for carrying on, and extending, his undertaking. In this pious work he employed the Rev. Nathaniel Whitaker, who, by virtue of a power of attorney from Dr. Wheelock, appointed the Earl of Dartmouth and others, trustees of the money, which had been, and should be, contributed; which appointment Dr. Wheelock confirmed by a deed of trust authorizing the trustees to fix on a site for the college. They determined to establish the school on Connecticut river, in the western part of New-Hampshire; that situation being supposed favourable for carrying on the original design among the Indians, and also for promoting learning among the English; and the proprietors in the neighbourhood having made large offers of land, on condition, that the college should there be placed. Dr. Wheelock then applied to the crown for an act of incorporation; and represented the expediency of appointing those whom he had, by his last will, named as trustees in America, to be members of the proposed corporation. "In consideration of the premises," "for the education and instruction of the youth of the Indian tribes," &c. "and also of English youth, and any others," the charter was granted, and the trustees of Dartmouth College were by that name created a body corporate, with power, *for the use of the said college,* to acquire real and personal property, and to pay the president, tutors, and other officers of the college, such salaries as they shall allow.

The charter proceeds to appoint Eleazer Wheelock, "the founder of said college," president thereof, with power by his last will to appoint a successor, who is to continue in office until disapproved by the trustees. In case of vacancy, the trustees may appoint a president, and in case of the ceasing of a president, the senior professor or tutor, *being one of the trustees,* shall exercise the office, until an appointment shall be made. The trustees have power to appoint and displace professors, tutors, and other officers, and to supply any vacancies which may be created in their own body, by death, resignation, removal, or disability; and also to make orders, ordinances, and laws, for the government of the college, the same not being repugnant to the laws of Great Britain, or of New-Hampshire, and not excluding any person on account of his speculative sentiments in religion, or his being of a religious profession different from that of the trustees.

This charter was accepted, and the property, both real and personal, which had been contributed for the benefit of the college, was conveyed to, and vested in, the corporate body.

From this brief review of the most essential parts of the charter, it is apparent, that the funds of the college consisted entirely of private donations. . . .

From these funds the salaries of the tutors are drawn; and these salaries lessen the expense of education to the students. It is then an eleemosynary, and, as far as respects its funds, a private corporation.

Do its objects stamp on it a different character? Are the trustees and professors public officers, invested with any portion of political power, partaking in any degree in the administration of civil government, and performing duties which flow from the sovereign authority?

That education is an object of national concern, and a proper subject of legislation, all admit. That there may be an institution founded by government, and placed entirely under its immediate control, the officers of which would be public officers, amenable exclusively to government, none will deny. But is Dartmouth College such an institution? Is education altogether in the hands of the government? Does every teacher of youth become a public officer, and do donations for the purpose of education necessarily become public property, so far that the will of the legislature, not the will of the donor, becomes the law of the donation? These questions are of serious moment to society, and deserve to be well considered.

Doctor Wheelock, as the keeper of his charity school, instructing the Indians in the art of reading, and in our holy religion; sustaining them at his own expense, and on the voluntary contributions of the charitable, could scarcely be considered as a public officer, exercising any portion of those duties which belong to government; nor could the legislature have supposed, that his private funds, or those given by others, were subject to legislative management, because they were applied to the purposes of education. When, afterwards, his school was enlarged, and the liberal contributions made in England, and in America, enabled him to extend his cares to the education of the youth of his own country, no change was wrought in his own character, or in the nature of his duties. Had he employed assistant tutors with the funds contributed by others, or had the trustees in England established a school with Dr. Wheelock at its head, and paid salaries to him and his assistants, they would still have been private tutors; and the fact, that they were employed in the education of youth, could not have converted them into public officers, concerned in the administration of public duties, or have given the legislature a right to interfere in the management of the fund. The trustees, in whose care that fund was placed by the contributors, would have been permitted to execute their trust uncontrolled by legislative authority.

Whence, then, can be derived the idea, that Dartmouth College has become a public institution, and its trustees public officers, exercising powers conferred by the public for public objects? Not from the source whence its funds were drawn; for its foundation is purely private and eleemosynary—Not from the application of those funds; for money may be given for education, and the persons receiving it do not, by being employed in the education of youth, become members of the civil government. Is it from the act of incorporation? Let this subject be considered.

A corporation is an artificial being, invisible, intangible, and existing only in contemplation of law. Being the mere creature of law, it possesses only those properties which the charter of its creation confers upon it, either expressly, or as incidental to its very existence. These are such as are supposed best calculated to effect the object for which it was created. Among the most important are immortality, and, if the expression may be allowed, individuality; properties, by which a perpetual succession of many persons are considered as the same, and may act as a single individual. They enable a corporation to manage its own affairs, and to hold property without the perplexing intricacies, the hazardous and endless necessity, of perpetual conveyances for the purpose of transmitting it from hand to hand. It is chiefly for the purpose of clothing bodies of men, in succession, with these qualities and capacities, that corporations were invented, and are in use. By these means, a perpetual succession of individuals are capable of acting for the promotion of the particular object, like one immortal being. But this being does not share in the civil government of the country, unless that be the purpose for which it was created. Its immortality no more confers on it political power, or a political character, than immortality would confer such power or character on a natural person. It is no more a State instrument, than a natural person exercising the same powers would be. If, then, a natural person, employed by individuals in the education of youth, or for the government of a seminary in which youth is educated, would not become a public officer, or be considered as a member of the civil government, how is it, that this artificial being, created by law, for the purpose of being employed by the same individuals for the same purposes, should become a part of the civil government of the country? Is it because its existence, its capacities, its powers, are given by law? Because the government has given it the power to take and to hold property in a particular form, and for particular purposes, has the government a consequent right substantially to change that form, or to vary the purposes to which the property is to be applied? This principle has never been asserted or recognized, and is supported by no authority. Can it derive aid from reason?

The objects for which a corporation is created are universally such as the government wishes to promote. They are deemed beneficial to the country; and this benefit constitutes the consideration, and, in most cases, the sole consideration of the grant. In most eleemosynary institutions, the object would be difficult, perhaps unattainable, without the aid of a charter of incorporation. Charitable, or public spirited individuals, desirous of making permanent appropriations for charitable or other useful purposes, find it impossible to effect their design securely, and certainly, without an incorporating act. They apply to the government, state their beneficent object, and offer to advance the money necessary for its accomplishment, provided the government will confer on the instrument which is to execute their designs the capacity to execute them. The proposition is considered and approved. The benefit to the public is considered as an ample compensation for the faculty it confers, and the corporation is created. If the advantages to the public constitute a full compensation for the faculty it gives, there can be no reason for exacting a further compensation, by claiming a right to exercise over this artificial being a power which changes its nature, and touches the fund, for the security and application of which it was created. There can be no reason for implying in a charter, given for a valuable consideration, a power which is not only not expressed, but is in direct contradiction to its express stipulations.

From the fact, then, that a charter of incorporation has been granted, nothing can be inferred which changes the character of the institution, or transfers to the government any new power over it. The character of civil institutions does not grow out of their incorporation, but out of the manner in which they are formed, and the objects for which they are created. The right to change them is not founded on their being incorporated, but on their being the instruments of government, created for its purposes. The same institutions, created for the same objects, though not incorporated, would be public institutions, and of course, be controllable by the legislature. The incorporating act neither gives nor prevents this control. Neither, in reason, can the incorporating act change the character of a private eleemosynary institution.

We are next led to the inquiry, for whose benefit the property given to Dartmouth College was secured? The counsel for the defendant have insisted, that the beneficial interest is in the people of New-Hampshire. The charter, after reciting the preliminary measures which had been taken, and the application for an act of incorporation, proceeds thus: "Know ye, therefore, that we, considering the premises, and being willing to encourage the laudable and charitable design of spreading christian knowledge among the savages of our American wilderness, and, also, that the best means of education be established, in our province of New-Hampshire, for the benefit of said province, do, of our special grace," &c. Do these expressions bestow on New-Hampshire any exclusive right to the property of the college, any exclusive interest in the labours of the professors? Or do they merely indicate a willingness that New-Hampshire should enjoy those advantages which result to all from the establishment of a seminary of learning in the neighbourhood? On this point we think it impossible to entertain a serious doubt. The words themselves, unexplained by the context, indicate, that the "benefit intended for the province" is that which is derived from "establishing the best means of education therein;" that is, from establishing in the province Dartmouth College, as constituted by the charter. But, if these words, considered alone, could admit of doubt, that doubt is completely removed by an inspection of the entire instrument.

The particular interests of New-Hampshire never entered into the mind of the donors, never constituted a motive for their donation. The propagation of the christian religion among the savages, and the dissemination of useful knowledge among the youth of the country, were the avowed and the sole objects of their contributions. In these, New-Hampshire would participate; but nothing particular or exclusive was intended for her. Even the site of the college was selected, not for the sake of New-Hampshire, but because it was "most subservient to the great ends in view," and because liberal donations of land were offered by the proprietors, on condition that the institution should be there established. The real advantages from the location of the college, are, perhaps, not less considerable to those on the west, than to those on the east side of Connecticut river. The clause which constitutes the incorporation, and expresses the objects for which it was made, declares those objects to be the instruction of the Indians, "and also of English youth, and any others." So that the objects of the contributors, and the incorporating act, were the same; the promotion of christianity, and of education generally, not the interests of New-Hampshire particularly.

From this review of the charter, it appears, that Dartmouth College is an eleemosynary institution, incorporated for the purpose of perpetuating the application of the bounty of the donors, to the specified objects of that bounty; that its trustees or governors were originally named by the founder, and invested with the power of perpetuating themselves; that they are not public officers, nor is it a civil institution, participating in the administration of government; but a charity school, or a seminary of education, incorporated for the preservation of its property, and the perpetual application of that property to the objects of its creation.

Yet a question remains to be considered, of more real difficulty, on which more doubt has been entertained than on all that have been discussed. The founders of the college, at least those whose contributions were in money, have parted with the property bestowed upon it, and their representatives have no interest in that property. The donors of land are equally without interest, so long as the corporation shall exist. Could they be found, they are unaffected by any alteration in its constitution, and probably regardless of its form, or even of its existence. The students are fluctuating, and no individual among our youth has a vested interest in the institution, which can be asserted in a Court of justice. Neither the founders of the college, nor the youth for whose benefit it was founded, complain of the alteration made in its charter, or think themselves injured by it. The trustees alone complain, and the trustees have no beneficial interest to be protected. Can this be such a contract, as the constitution intended to withdraw from the power of State legislation? Contracts, the parties to which have a vested beneficial interest, and those only, it has been said, are the objects about which the constitution is solicitous, and to which protection is extended.

The Court has bestowed on this argument the most deliberate consideration, and the result will be stated. Dr. Wheelock, acting for himself, and for those who, at his solicitation, had made contributions to his school, applied for this charter, as the instrument which should enable him, and them, to perpetuate their beneficent intention. It was granted. An artificial, immortal being, was created by the crown, capable of receiving and distributing forever, according to the will of the donors, the donations which should be made to it. On this being, the contributions which had been collected were immediately bestowed. These gifts were made, not indeed to make a profit for the donors, or their posterity, but for something in their opinion of inestimable value; for something which they deemed a full equivalent for the money with which it was purchased. The consideration for which they stipulated, is the perpetual application of the fund to its object, in the mode prescribed by themselves. Their descendants may take no interest in the preservation of this consideration. But in this respect their descendants are not their representatives. They are represented by the corporation. The corporation is the assignee of their rights, stands in their place, and distributes their bounty, as they would themselves have distributed it, had they been immortal. So with respect to the students who are to derive learning from this source. The corporation is a trustee for them also. Their potential rights, which, taken distributively, are imperceptible, amount collectively to a most important interest. These are, in the aggregate, to be exercised, asserted and protected, by the corporation. They were as completely out of the donors, at the instant of their being vested in the corporation, and as incapable of being asserted by the students, as at present.

According to the theory of the British constitution, their parliament is omnipotent. To annul corporate rights might give a shock to public opinion, which that government has chosen to avoid; but its power is not questioned. Had parliament, immediately after the emanation of this charter, and the execution of those conveyances which followed it, annulled the instrument, so that the living donors would have witnessed the disappointment of their hopes, the perfidy of the transaction would have been universally acknowledged. Yet then, as now, the donors would have had no interest in the property; then, as now, those who might be students would have had no rights to be violated; then, as now, it might be said, that the trustees, in whom the rights of all were combined, possessed no private, individual, beneficial interest in the property confided to their protection. Yet the contract would at that time have been deemed sacred by all. What has since occurred to strip it of its inviolability? Circumstances have not changed it. In reason, in justice, and in law, it is now what it was in 1769.

This is plainly a contract to which the donors, the trustees, and the crown, (to whose rights and obligations New-Hampshire succeeds,) were the original parties. It is a contract made on a valuable consideration. It is a contract for the security and disposition of property. It is a contract, on the faith of which, real and personal estate has been conveyed to the corporation. It is then a contract within the letter of the constitution, and within its spirit also, unless the fact, that the property is invested by the donors in trustees for the promotion of religion and education, for the benefit of persons who are perpetually changing, though the objects remain the same, shall create a particular exception, taking this case out of the prohibition contained in the constitution.

It is more than possible, that the preservation of rights of this description was not particularly in the view of the framers of the constitution, when the clause under consideration was introduced into that instrument. It is probable, that interferences of more frequent recurrence, to which the temptation was stronger, and of which the mischief was more extensive, constituted the great motive for imposing this restriction on the State legislatures. But although a particular and a rare case may not, in itself, be of sufficient magnitude to induce a rule, yet it must be governed by the rule, when established, unless some plain and strong reason for excluding it can be given. It is not enough to say, that this particular case was not in the mind of the Convention, when the article was framed, nor of the American people, when it was adopted. It is necessary to go farther, and to say that, had this particular case been suggested, the language would have been so varied, as to exclude it, or it would have been made a special exception. The case being within the words of the rule, must be within its operation likewise, unless there be something in the literal construction so obviously absurd, or mischievous, or repugnant to the general spirit of the instrument, as to justify those who expound the constitution in making it an exception.

On what safe and intelligible ground can this exception

stand. There is no expression in the constitution, no sentiment delivered by its contemporaneous expounders, which would justify us in making it. In the absence of all authority of this kind, is there, in the nature and reason of the case itself, that which would sustain a construction of the constitution, not warranted by its words? Are contracts of this description of a character to excite so little interest, that we must exclude them from the provisions of the constitution, as being unworthy of the attention of those who framed the instrument? Or does public policy so imperiously demand their remaining exposed to legislative alteration, as to compel us, or rather permit us to say, that these words, which were introduced to give stability to contracts, and which in their plain import comprehend this contract, must yet be so construed, as to exclude it?

Almost all eleemosynary corporations, those which are created for the promotion of religion, of charity, or of education, are of the same character. The law of this case is the law of all. In every literary or charitable institution, unless the objects of the bounty be themselves incorporated, the whole legal interest is in trustees, and can be asserted only by them. The donors, or claimants of the bounty, if they can appear in Court at all, can appear only to complain of the trustees. In all other situations, they are identified with, and personated by, the trustees; and their rights are to be defended and maintained by them. Religion, Charity, and Education, are, in the law of England, legatees or donees, capable of receiving bequests or donations in this form. They appear in Court, and claim or defend by the corporation. Are they of so little estimation in the United States that contracts for their benefit must be excluded from the protection of words, which in their natural import include them? Or do such contracts so necessarily require new modelling by the authority of the legislature, that the ordinary rules of construction must be disregarded in order to leave them exposed to legislative alteration?

All feel that these objects are not deemed unimportant in the United States. The interest which this case has excited, proves that they are not. The framers of the constitution did not deem them unworthy of its care and protection. They have, though in a different mode, manifested their respect for science, by reserving to the government of the Union the power "to promote the progress of science and useful arts, by securing for limited times, to authors and inventors, the exclusive right to their respective writings and discoveries." They have so far withdrawn science, and the useful arts, from the action of the State governments. Why then should they be supposed so regardless of contracts made for the advancement of literature, as to intend to exclude them from provisions, made for the security of ordinary contracts between man and man? No reason for making this supposition is perceived.

If the insignificance of the object does not require that we should exclude contracts respecting it from the protection of the constitution; neither, as we conceive, is the policy of leaving them subject to legislative alteration so apparent, as to require a forced construction of that instrument in order to effect it. These eleemosynary institutions do not fill the place, which would otherwise be occupied by government, but that which would otherwise remain vacant. They are complete acquisitions to literature. They are donations to education; donations, which any government must be disposed rather to encourage than to discountenance. It requires no very critical examination of the human mind to enable us to determine, that one great inducement to these gifts is the conviction felt by the giver, that the disposition he makes of them is immutable. It is probable, that no man ever was, and that no man ever will be, the founder of a college, believing at the time, that an act of incorporation constitutes no security for the institution; believing, that it is immediately to be deemed a public institution, whose funds are to be governed and applied, not by the will of the donor, but by the will of the legislature. All such gifts are made in the pleasing, perhaps delusive hope, that the charity will flow forever in the channel which the givers have marked out for it. If every man finds in his own bosom strong evidence of the universality of this sentiment, there can be but little reason to imagine, that the framers of our constitution were strangers to it, and that, feeling the necessity and policy of giving permanence and security to contracts, of withdrawing them from the influence of legislative bodies, whose fluctuating policy, and repeated interferences, produced the most perplexing and injurious embarrassments, they still deemed it necessary to leave these contracts subject to those interferences. The motives for such an exception must be very powerful, to justify the construction which makes it.

The motives suggested at the bar grow out of the original appointment of the trustees, which is supposed to have been in a spirit hostile to the genius of our government, and the presumption, that, if allowed to continue themselves, they now are, and must remain forever, what they originally were. Hence is inferred the necessity of applying to this corporation, and to other similar corporations, the correcting and improving hand of the legislature. . . .

The opinion of the Court, after mature deliberation, is, that this is a contract, the obligation of which cannot be impaired, without violating the constitution of the United States. This opinion appears to us to be equally supported by reason, and by the former decisions of this Court.

2. We next proceed to the inquiry, whether its obligation has been impaired by those acts of the legislature of New-Hampshire, to which the special verdict refers.

From the review of this charter, which has been taken, it appears, that the whole power of governing the college, of appointing and removing tutors, of fixing their salaries, of directing the course of study to be pursued by the students, and of filling up vacancies created in their own body, was vested in the trustees. On the part of the crown it was expressly stipulated, that this corporation, thus constituted, should continue forever; and that the number of trustees should forever consist of twelve, and no more. By this contract the crown was bound, and could have made no violent alteration in its essential terms, without impairing its obligation.

By the revolution, the duties, as well as the powers, of government devolved on the people of New-Hampshire. It is admitted, that among the latter was comprehended the transcendent power of parliament, as well as that of the executive department. It is too clear to require the support of argument, that all contracts, and rights, respecting property, remained unchanged by the revolution. The obligations then, which were created by the charter to Dartmouth College, were the same in the new, that they had been in the old government. The power of the government was also the same. A repeal of this charter at any time prior to the adoption of the present constitution of the United States, would have been an extraordinary and unprecedented act of power, but one which could have been contested only by the restrictions upon the legislature, to be found in the constitution of the State. But the constitution of the United States has imposed this additional limitation, that the legislature of a State shall pass no act "impairing the obligation of contracts."

It has been already stated, that the act "to amend the charter, and enlarge and improve the corporation of Dartmouth College," increases the number of trustees to twenty-one, gives the appointment of the additional members to the executive of the State, and creates a board of overseers, to consist of twenty-five persons, of whom twenty-one are also appointed by the executive of New-Hampshire who have power to inspect and control the most important acts of the trustees.

On the effect of this law, two opinions cannot be entertained. Between acting directly, and acting through the agency of trustees and overseers, no essential difference is perceived. The whole power of governing the college is transferred from trustees appointed according to the will of the founder, expressed in the charter, to the executive of New-Hampshire. The management and application of the funds of this eleemosynary institution, which are placed by the donors in the hands of trustees named in the charter, and empowered to perpetuate themselves, are placed by this act under the control of the government of the State. The will of the State is substituted for the will of the donors, in every essential operation of the college. This is not an immaterial change. The founders of the college contracted, not merely for the perpetual application of the funds which they gave, to the objects for which those funds were given; they contracted also, to secure that application by the constitution of the corporation. They contracted for a system, which should, as far as human foresight can provide, retain forever the government of the literary institution they had formed, in the hands of persons approved by themselves. This system is totally changed. The charter of 1769 exists no longer. It is reorganized; and reorganized in such a manner, as to convert a literary institution, moulded according to the will of its founders, and placed under the control of private literary men, into a machine entirely subservient to the will of government. This may be for the advantage of this college in particular, and may be for the advantage of literature in general; but it is not according to the will of the donors, and is subversive of that contract, on the faith of which their property was given. . . .

It results from this opinion, that the acts of the legislature of New-Hampshire, which are stated in the special verdict found in this cause, are repugnant to the constitution of the United States; and that the judgment on this special verdict ought to have been for the plaintiffs. The judgment of the State Court must, therefore, be reversed.

6

U. S. SUPREME COURT

Charles River Bridge vs. Warren Bridge (1837)

[11 Pet. 420, 9 L. Ed. 773]

(Mr. Chief Justice Taney delivered the opinion of the Court.)

The plaintiffs in error insist, mainly, upon two grounds: 1st. That by virtue of the grant of 1650, Harvard College was entitled, in perpetuity, to the right of keeping a ferry between Charlestown and Boston; that this right was exclusive; and that the legislature had not the power to establish another ferry on the same line of travel, because it would infringe the rights of the college; and that these rights, upon the erection of the bridge in the place of the ferry, under the charter of 1785, were transferred to, and became vested in "the proprietors of the Charles River Bridge;" and that under, and by virtue of this transfer of the ferry right, the rights of the bridge company were as exclusive in that line of travel, as the rights of the ferry. 2d. That independently of the ferry right, the acts of the legislature of Massachusetts of 1785, and 1792, by their true construction, necessarily implied that the legislature would not authorize another bridge, and especially a free one, by the side of this, and placed in the same line of travel, whereby the franchise granted to the "Proprietors of the Charles River Bridge" should be rendered of no value; and the plaintiffs in error contend, that the grant of the ferry to the college, and of the charter to the proprietors of the bridge, are both contracts on the part of the state; and that the law authorizing the erection of the Warren Bridge in 1828, impairs the obligation of one or both of these contracts. . . .

This brings us to the act of the legislature of Massachusetts, of 1785, by which the plaintiffs were incorporated by the name of "The Proprietors of the Charles River Bridge;" and it is here, and in the law of 1792, prolonging their charter, that we must look for the extent and nature of the franchise conferred upon the plaintiffs.

Much has been said in the argument of the principles of construction by which this law is to be expounded, and what undertakings, on the part of the state, may be implied. The Court think there can be no serious difficulty on that head. It is the grant of certain franchises by the public to a private corporation, and in a matter where the public interest is concerned. The rule of construction in such cases is well settled, both in England, and by the decision of our tribunals. In 2 Barn. & Adol. 793, in the case of the Proprietors of the Stourbridge Canal against Wheeley and others, the Court say, "the canal having been made under an act of parliament, the rights of the plaintiffs are derived entirely from that act. This, like many other cases, is a bargain between a company of adventurers and the public, the terms of which are expressed in the statute; and the rule of construction in all such cases, is now fully established to be this; that any ambiguity in the terms of the contract, must operate against the adventurers, and in favor of the public, and the plaintiffs can claim nothing that is not clearly given them by the act." . . .

Borrowing, as we have done, our system of jurisprudence from the English law; and having adopted, in every other case, civil and criminal, its rules for the construction of statutes; is there anything in our local situation, or in the nature of our political institutions, which should lead us to depart from the principle where corporations are concerned? Are we to apply to acts of incorporation, a rule of construction differing from that of the English law, and, by implication, make the terms of a charter in one of the states, more unfavorable to the public, than upon an act of parliament, framed in the same words, would be sanctioned in an English court? Can any good reason be assigned for excepting this particular class of cases from the operation of the general principle; and for introducing a new and adverse rule of construction in favor of corporations, while we adopt and adhere to the rules of construction known to the English common law, in every other case, without exception? We think not; and it would present a singular spectacle, if, while the courts in England are restraining, within the strictest limits, the spirit of monopoly, and exclusive privileges in nature of monopolies, and confining corporations to the privileges plainly given to them in their charter; the courts of this country should be found enlarging these privileges by implication; and construing a statute more unfavorably to the public, and to the rights of the community, than would be done in a like case in an English court of justice. . . .

Adopting the rule of construction above stated as the settled one, we proceed to apply it to the charter of 1785, to the proprietors of the Charles River Bridge. This act of incorporation is in the usual form, and the privileges such as are commonly given to corporations of that kind. It confers on them the ordinary faculties of a corporation, for the purpose of building the bridge; and establishes certain rates of toll, which the company are authorized to take: this is the whole grant. There is no exclusive privilege given to them over the waters of

Charles River, above or below their bridge. No right to erect
another bridge themselves, nor to prevent other persons from
erecting one. No engagement from the state, that another shall
not be erected; and no undertaking not to sanction competition, nor to make improvements that may diminish the amount
of its income. Upon all these subjects the charter is silent; and
nothing is said in it about a line of travel, so much insisted on
in the argument, in which they are to have exclusive privileges. No words are used, from which an intention to grant
any of these rights can be inferred. If the plaintiff is entitled
to them, it must be implied, simply, from the nature of the
grant; and cannot be inferred from the words by which the
grant is made.

The relative position of the Warren Bridge has already been
described. It does not interrupt the passage over the Charles
River Bridge, nor make the way to it or from it less convenient.
None of the faculties or franchises granted to that corporation, have been revoked by the legislature; and its right to take
the tolls granted by the charter remains unaltered. In short,
all the franchises and rights of property enumerated in the
charter, and there mentioned to have been granted to it, remain unimpaired. But its income is destroyed by the Warren
Bridge; which, being free, draws off the passengers and property which would have gone over it, and renders their franchise of no value. This is the gist of the complaint. For it is
not pretended, that the erection of the Warren Bridge would
have done them any injury, or in any degree affected their
right of property; if it had not diminished the amount of their
tolls. In order then to entitle themselves to relief, it is necessary to show, that the legislature contracted not to do the act
of which they complain; and that they impaired, or in other
words, violated that contract by the erection of the Warren
Bridge.

The inquiry then is, does the charter contain such a contract
on the part of the state? Is there any such stipulation to be
found in that instrument? It must be admitted on all hands,
that there is none—no words that even relate to another bridge,
or to the diminution of their tolls, or to the line of travel. If

a contract on that subject can be gathered from the charter, it must be by implication; and cannot be found in the words used. Can such an agreement be implied? The rule of construction before stated is an answer to the question. In charters of this description, no rights are taken from the public, or given to the corporation, beyond those which the words of the charter, by their natural and proper construction, purport to convey. There are no words which import such a contract as the plaintiffs in error contend for, and none can be implied; and the same answer must be given to them that was given by this Court to Providence Bank. The whole community are interested in this inquiry, and they have a right to require that the power of promoting their comfort and convenience, and of advancing the public prosperity, by providing safe, convenient, and cheap ways for the transportation of produce, and the purposes of travel, shall not be construed to have been surrendered or diminished by the state; unless it shall appear by plain words, that it was intended to be done. . . .

Indeed, the practice and usage of almost every state in the Union, old enough to have commenced the work of internal improvement, is opposed to the doctrine contended for on the part of the plaintiffs in error. Turnpike roads have been made in succession, on the same line of travel; the later ones interfering materially with the profits of the first. These corporations have, in some instances, been utterly ruined by the introduction of newer and better modes of transportation, and traveling. In some cases, rail roads have rendered the turnpike roads on the same line of travel so entirely useless, that the franchise of the turnpike corporation is not worth preserving. Yet in none of these cases have the corporations supposed that their privileges were invaded, or any contract violated on the part of the state. Amid the multitude of cases which have occurred, and have been daily occurring for the last forty or fifty years, this is the first instance in which such an implied contract has been contended for, and this Court called upon to infer it from an ordinary act of incorporation, containing nothing more than the usual stipulations and provisions to be found in every such law. The absence of any such controversy,

when there must have been so many occasions to give rise to
it, proves that neither states, nor individuals, nor corporations,
ever imagined that such a contract could be implied from such
charters. It shows that the men who voted for these laws, never
imagined that they were forming such a contract; and if we
maintain that they have made it, we must create it by a legal
fiction, in opposition to the truth of the fact, and the obvious
intention of the party. We cannot deal thus with the rights
reserved to the states; and by legal intendments and mere
technical reasoning, take away from them any portion of that
power over their own internal police and improvement, which
is so necessary to their well being and prosperity.

And what would be the fruits of this doctrine of implied
contracts on the part of the states, and of property in a line
of travel by a corporation, if it should now be sanctioned by
this Court? To what results would it lead us? If it is to be
found in the charter to this bridge, the same process of reasoning must discover it, in the various acts which have been
passed, within the last forty years, for turnpike companies. And
what is to be the extent of the privileges of exclusion on the
different sides of the road? The counsel who have so ably argued this case, have not attempted to define it by any certain
boundaries. How far must the new improvement be distant
from the old one? How near may you approach, without in-
vading its rights in the privileged line? If this Court should
establish the principles now contended for, what is to become
of the numerous rail roads established on the same line of travel
with turnpike companies; and which have rendered the franchises of the turnpike corporations of no value? Let it once
be understood that such charters carry with them these implied contracts, and give this unknown and undefined property in a line of traveling; and you will soon find the old turnpike corporations awakening from their sleep, and calling upon
this Court to put down the improvements which have taken
their place. The millions of property which have been invested
in rail roads and canals, upon lines of travel which had been
before occupied by turnpike corporations, will be put in jeop-
ardy. We shall be thrown back to the improvements of the

last century, and obliged to stand still, until the claims of the old turnpike corporations shall be satisfied; and they shall consent to permit these states to avail themselves of the lights of modern sciences, and to partake of the benefit of those improvements which are now adding to the wealth and prosperity, and the convenience and comfort, of every other part of the civilized world. Nor is this all. This Court will find itself compelled to fix, by some arbitrary rule, the width of this new kind of property in a line of travel; for if such a right of property exists, we have no lights to guide us in marking out its extent, unless, indeed, we resort to the old feudal grants, and to the exclusive rights of ferries, by prescription, between towns; and are prepared to decide that when a turnpike road from one town to another, had been made, no rail road or canal, between these two points, could afterwards be established. This Court are not prepared to sanction principles which must lead to such results. . . .

The judgment of the supreme judicial court of the commonwealth of Massachusetts, dismissing the plaintiffs' bill, must, therefore, be affirmed, with costs.

D. Central Banking

Every modern and free economy follows the useful but curious practice of permitting private banks to create credit; the state, in effect, cedes to private companies part of its own power to increase or decrease the amount of money available in the country. If this power of the private banks is to be coordinated, some sort of central banking system, subject to public control, must exist. This is now so much taken for granted that it is easy to forget how difficult it was to establish central banking in the United States and how recently the difficulties were overcome.

The objections to a central bank were often presented as an issue of states' rights. Private banks, like corporations of any other sort, were chartered and controlled by the states; a central bank that in any way supervised the state banks could therefore be assailed as a means by which the central government sought to exercise unconstitutional power. This argument could be produced at will by all those who objected to the central bank for whatever reason—its conservative monetary policies, its political influence, its plutocratic appearance or foreign connections, or, more generally, its character as a private institution free of responsibility to the electorate yet enjoying great public powers. All these complaints were leveled against the second Bank of the United States and were summed up in the cry that the Bank was an unlawful attempt to enhance the power of the central government.

The second Bank of the United States, like the first (founded in 1791 and allowed to expire in 1811), was established mainly to serve as the federal government's fiscal agent. But because it held and transferred the government's monies, maintained branches throughout the country, and had much greater assets than other banks, its powers could also be used to regulate the commercial banks, especially by setting the terms on which it accepted their banknotes. Under Nicholas Biddle, its president after 1823, the Bank exercised these powers with imagination and, sometimes, excessive frankness. These activities did not endear it to the banking community or to would-be borrowers. Besides, the Bank also made enemies among Jackson's supporters when they saw their enemies ranged among its chief advocates.

In 1832, four years before its charter was due to expire, the Bank's supporters opened a campaign to renew the charter, and a bill for this purpose was passed by Congress. Jackson promptly vetoed it. The veto message (7) illustrates the prejudices that Democrats held, or were presumed by an astute leader to hold, against the rich, Easterners, bankers, England, and centralized government. Webster's answer (8), among his more famous orations, is an incisive criticism of Jackson's arguments. It does not, however, answer the argument that Jackson hardly suggests, the political danger to a democracy of a privately owned and privately managed institution endowed by law with quasi-sovereign power.

In the end the Bank's charter was not renewed, and the regulation of banks during the next thirty years was managed by the states. A more central system of regulation was established by the National Bank Act of 1863, whose immediate purpose was to help finance the Civil War. Federal incorporation and control of banks survived the War; and since then, but especially after the passage of the Federal Reserve Act in 1913, banks have been subject to detailed supervision by agencies of the federal government. The Federal Reserve System still exhibits, by the considerable measure of its independence from the Treasury and the Executive, and of local autonomy of the Federal Reserve Banks, vestiges of its history.

7
Andrew Jackson (1767–1845)
Veto Message (10 July 1832)
[Richardson, *Messages of the Presidents*, II, 576]

The bill "to modify and continue" the act entitled "An act to incorporate the subscribers to the Bank of the United States" was presented to me on the 4th July instant. Having considered it with that solemn regard to the principles of the Constitution which the day was calculated to inspire, and come to the conclusion that it ought not to become a law, I herewith return it to the Senate, in which it originated, with my objections.

A bank of the United States is in many respects convenient for the Government and useful to the people. Entertaining this opinion, and deeply impressed with the belief that some of the powers and privileges possessed by the existing bank are unauthorized by the Constitution, subversive of the rights of the States, and dangerous to the liberties of the people, I felt it my duty at an early period of my Administration to call the attention of Congress to the practicability of organizing an institution combining all its advantages and obviating these objections. I sincerely regret that in the act before me I can perceive none of those modifications of the bank charter which are necessary, in my opinion, to make it compatible with justice, with sound policy, or with the Constitution of our country.

The present corporate body, denominated the president, directors, and company of the Bank of the United States, will have existed at the time this act is intended to take effect twenty years. It enjoys an exclusive privilege of banking under the authority of the General Government, a monopoly of its favor and support, and, as a necessary consequence, almost a monopoly of the foreign and domestic exchange. The powers, privileges, and favors bestowed upon it in the original charter, by increasing the value of the stock far above its par value, operated as a gratuity of many millions to the stockholders.

An apology may be found for the failure to guard against this result in the consideration that the effect of the original act of incorporation could not be certainly foreseen at the time of its passage. The act before me proposes another gratuity to the holders of the same stock, and in many cases to the same men, of at least seven millions more. This donation finds no apology in any uncertainty as to the effect of the act. On all hands it is conceded that its passage will increase at least 20 or 30 per cent more the market price of the stock, subject to the payment of the annuity of $200,000 per year secured by the act, thus adding in a moment one-fourth to its par value. It is not our own citizens only who are to receive the bounty of our Government. More than eight millions of the stock of this bank are held by foreigners. By this act the American Republic proposes virtually to make them a present of some millions of dollars. For these gratuities to foreigners and to some of our own opulent citizens the act secures no equivalent whatever. They are the certain gains of the present stockholders under the operation of this act, after making full allowance for the payment of the bonus.

Every monopoly and all exclusive privileges are granted at the expense of the public, which ought to receive a fair equivalent. The many millions which this act proposes to bestow on the stockholders of the existing bank must come directly or indirectly out of the earnings of the American people. It is due to them, therefore, if their Government sell monopolies and exclusive privileges, that they should at least exact for them as much as they are worth in open market. The value of the monopoly in this case may be correctly ascertained. The twenty-eight millions of stock would probably be at an advance of 50 per cent, and command in market at least $42,000,000, subject to the payment of the present bonus. The present value of the monopoly, therefore, is $17,000,000, and this the act proposes to sell for three millions, payable in fifteen annual installments of $200,000 each.

It is not conceivable how the present stockholders can have any claim to the special favor of the Government. The present corporation has enjoyed its monopoly during the period stipulated in the original contract. If we must have such a corporation, why should not the Government sell out the whole stock and thus secure to the people the full market value of the privileges granted? Why should not Congress create and sell twenty-eight millions of stock, incorporating the purchasers with all the powers and privileges secured in this act and putting the premium upon the sales into the Treasury?

But this act does not permit competition in the purchase of this monopoly. It seems to be predicated on the erroneous idea that the present stockholders have a prescriptive right not only to the favor but to the bounty of Government. It appears that more than a fourth part of the stock is held by foreigners and the residue is held by a few hundred of our own citizens, chiefly of the richest class. For their benefit does this act exclude the whole American people from competition in the purchase of this monopoly and dispose of it for many millions less than it is worth. This seems the less excusable because some of our citizens not now stockholders petitioned that the door of competition might be opened, and offered to take a charter on terms much more favorable to the Government and country.

But this proposition, although made by men whose aggregate wealth is believed to be equal to all the private stock in the existing bank, has been set aside, and the bounty of our Government is proposed to be again bestowed on the few who have been fortunate enough to secure the stock and at this moment wield the power of the existing institution. I can not perceive the justice or policy of this course. If our Government must sell monopolies, it would seem to be its duty to take nothing less than their full value, and if gratuities must be made once in fifteen or twenty years let them not be bestowed on the subjects of a foreign government nor upon a designated and favored class of men in our own country. It is but justice and good policy, as far as the nature of the case will admit, to confine our favors to our own fellow-citizens, and let each in his turn enjoy an opportunity to profit by our bounty. In the bearings of the act before me upon these points I find ample reasons why it should not become a law.

It has been urged as an argument in favor of rechartering the present bank that the calling in its loans will produce great embarrassment and distress. The time allowed to close its concerns is ample, and if it has been well managed its pressure will be light, and heavy only in case its management has been bad. If, therefore, it shall produce distress, the fault will be its own, and it would furnish a reason against renewing a power which has been so obviously abused. But will there ever be a time when this reason will be less powerful? To acknowledge its force is to admit that the bank ought to be perpetual, and as a consequence the present stockholders and those inheriting their rights as successors be established a privileged order, clothed both with great political power and enjoying immense pecuniary advantages from their connection with the Government.

The modifications of the existing charter proposed by this act are not such, in my view, as make it consistent with the rights of the States or the liberties of the people. The qualification of the right of the bank to hold real estate, the limitation of its power to establish branches, and the power reserved to Congress to forbid the circulation of small notes are restrictions comparatively of little value or importance. All the objectionable principles of the existing corporation, and most of its odious features, are retained without alleviation.

The fourth section provides "that the notes or bills of the said corporation, although the same be, on the faces thereof, respectively made payable at one place only, shall nevertheless be received by the said corporation at the bank or at any of the offices of discount and deposit thereof if tendered in liquidation or payment of any balance or balances due to said corporation or to such office of discount and deposit from any other incorporated bank." This provision secures to the State banks a legal privilege in the Bank of the United States which is withheld from all private citizens. If a State bank in Philadelphia owe the Bank of the United States and have notes issued by the St. Louis branch, it can pay the debt with those notes, but if a merchant, mechanic, or other private citizen be in like circumstances he can not by law pay his debt with those notes, but must sell them at a discount or send them to St. Louis to be cashed. This boon conceded to the State banks, though not unjust in itself, is most odious because it does not measure out equal justice to the high and the low, the rich and the poor. To the extent of its practical effect it is a bond of union among the banking establishments of the nation, erecting them into an interest separate from that of the people, and its necessary tendency is to unite the Bank of the United States and the State banks in any measure which may be thought conducive to their common interest.

The ninth section of the act recognizes principles of worse tendency than any provision of the present charter.

It enacts that "the cashier of the bank shall annually report to the Secretary of the Treasury the names of all stockholders who are not resident citizens of the United States, and on the application of the treasurer of any State shall make out and transmit to such treasurer a list of stockholders residing in or citizens of such State, with the amount of stock owned by each." Although this provision, taken in connection with a decision of the Supreme Court, surrenders, by its silence, the right of the States to tax the banking institutions created by this corporation under the name of branches throughout the Union, it is evidently intended to be construed as a concession of their right to tax that portion of the stock which may be held by their own citizens and residents. In this light, if the act becomes a law, it will be understood by the States, who will probably proceed to levy a tax equal to that paid upon the stock of banks incorporated by themselves. In some States that tax is now 1 per cent, either on the capital or on the shares, and that may be assumed as the amount which all citizen or resident stockholders would be taxed under the operation of this act. As it is only the stock *held* in the States and not that *employed* within them which would be subject to taxation, and as the names of foreign stockholders are not to be reported to the treasurers of the States, it is obvious that the stock held by them will be exempt from this burden. Their annual profits will therefore be 1 per cent more than the citizen stockholders, and as the annual dividends of the bank may be safely estimated at 7 per cent, the stock will be worth 10 or 15 per cent more to foreigners than to citizens of the United States. To appreciate the effects which this state of things will produce, we must take a brief review of the operations and present condition of the Bank of the United States.

By documents submitted to Congress at the present session it appears that on the 1st of January, 1832, of the twenty-eight millions of private stock in the corporation, $8,405,500 were held by foreigners, mostly of Great Britain. The amount of stock held in the nine Western and Southwestern States is $140,200, and in the four Southern States is $5,623,100, and in the Middle and Eastern States is about $13,522,000. The profits of the bank in 1831, as shown in a statement to Congress, were about $3,455,598; of this there accrued in the nine Western States about $1,640,048; in the four Southern States about $352,507, and in the Middle and Eastern States about $1,463,-041. As little stock is held in the West, it is obvious that the debt of the people in that section to the bank is principally a debt to the Eastern and foreign stockholders; that the interest they pay upon it is carried into the Eastern States and into Europe, and that it is a burden upon their industry and a drain of their currency, which no country can bear without inconvenience and occasional distress. To meet this burden and equalize the exchange operations of the bank, the amount of specie drawn from those States through its branches within the last two years, as shown by its official reports, was about $6,000,000. More than half a million of this amount does not stop in the Eastern States, but passes on to Europe to pay the dividends of the foreign stockholders. In the principle of taxation recognized by this act the Western States find no adequate compensation for this perpetual burden on their industry and drain of their currency. The branch bank at Mobile made last year $95,140, yet under the provisions of this act the State of Alabama can raise no revenue from these profitable operations, because not a share of the stock is held by any of her citizens. Mississippi and Missouri are in the same condition in relation to the branches at Natchez and St. Louis, and such, in a greater or less degree, is the condition of every Western State. The tendency of the plan of taxation which this act proposes will be to place the whole United States in the same relation to foreign countries which the Western States now bear to the Eastern. When by a tax on resident stockholders the stock of this bank is made worth 10 or 15 per cent more to foreigners than to residents, most of it will inevitably leave the country.

Thus will this provision in its practical effect deprive the Eastern as well as the Southern and Western States of the means of raising a revenue from the extension of business and great profits of this institution. It will make the American people debtors to aliens in nearly the whole amount due to this bank, and send across the Atlantic from two to five millions of specie every year to pay the bank dividends.

In another of its bearings this provision is fraught with danger. Of the twenty-five directors of this bank five are chosen by the Government and twenty by the citizen stockholders. From all voice in these elections the foreign stockholders are excluded by the charter. In proportion, therefore, as the stock is transferred to foreign holders the extent of suffrage in the choice of directors is curtailed. Already is almost a third of the stock in foreign hands and not represented in elections. It is constantly passing out of the country, and this act will accelerate its departure. The entire control of the institution would necessarily fall into the hands of a few citizen stockholders, and the ease with which the object would be accomplished would be a temptation to designing men to secure that control in their own hands by monopolizing the remaining stock. There is danger that a president and directors would then be able to elect themselves from year to year, and without responsibility or control manage the whole concerns of the bank during the existence of its charter. It is easy to conceive that great evils to our country and its institutions might flow from such a concentration of power in the hands of a few men irresponsible to the people.

Is there no danger to our liberty and independence in a

bank that in its nature has so little to bind it to our country? The president of the bank has told us that most of the State banks exist by its forbearance. Should its influence become concentered, as it may under the operation of such an act as this, in the hands of a self-elected directory whose interests are identified with those of the foreign stockholders, will there not be cause to tremble for the purity of our elections in peace and for the independence of our country in war? Their power would be great whenever they might choose to exert it; but if this monopoly were regularly renewed every fifteen or twenty years on terms proposed by themselves, they might seldom in peace put forth their strength to influence elections or control the affairs of the nation. But if any private citizen or public functionary should interpose to curtail its powers or prevent a renewal of its privileges, it can not be doubted that he would be made to feel its influence.

Should the stock of the bank principally pass into the hands of the subjects of a foreign country, and we should unfortunately become involved in a war with that country, what would be our condition? Of the course which would be pursued by a bank almost wholly owned by the subjects of a foreign power, and managed by those whose interests, if not affections, would run in the same direction there can be no doubt. All its operations within would be in aid of the hostile fleets and armies without. Controlling our currency, receiving our public moneys, and holding thousands of our citizens in dependence, it would be more formidable and dangerous than the naval and military power of the enemy.

If we must have a bank with private stockholders, every consideration of sound policy and every impulse of American feeling admonishes that it should be *purely American*. Its stockholders should be composed exclusively of our own citizens, who at least ought to be friendly to our Government and willing to support it in times of difficulty and danger. So abundant is domestic capital that competition in subscribing for the stock of local banks has recently led almost to riots. To a bank exclusively of American stockholders, possessing the powers and privileges granted by this act, subscriptions for $200,000,000

could be readily obtained. Instead of sending abroad the stock
of the bank in which the Government must deposit its funds
and on which it must rely to sustain its credit in times of
emergency, it would rather seem to be expedient to prohibit
its sale to aliens under penalty of absolute forfeiture.

It is maintained by the advocates of the bank that its constitutionality in all its features ought to be considered as settled by precedent and by the decision of the Supreme Court.
To this conclusion I can not assent. Mere precedent is a dangerous source of authority, and should not be regarded as deciding questions of constitutional power except where the
acquiescence of the people and the States can be considered
as well settled. So far from this being the case on this subject,
an argument against the bank might be based on precedent.
One Congress, in 1791, decided in favor of a bank; another,
in 1811, decided against it. One Congress, in 1815, decided
against a bank; another, in 1816, decided in its favor. Prior to
the present Congress, therefore, the precedents drawn from
that source were equal. If we resort to the States, the expressions of legislative, judicial, and executive opinions against the
bank have been probably to those in its favor as 4 to 1. There
is nothing in precedent, therefore, which, if its authority were
admitted, ought to weigh in favor of the act before me.

If the opinion of the Supreme Court covered the whole
ground of this act, it ought not to control the coordinate authorities of this Government. The Congress, the Executive, and
the Court must each for itself be guided by its own opinion of
the Constitution. Each public officer who takes an oath to support the Constitution swears that he will support it as he understands it, and not as it is understood by others. It is as much
the duty of the House of Representatives, of the Senate, and
of the President to decide upon the constitutionality of any bill
or resolution which may be presented to them for passage or
approval as it is of the supreme judges when it may be brought
before them for judicial decision. The opinion of the judges has
no more authority over Congress than the opinion of Congress
has over the judges, and on that point the President is independent of both. The authority of the Supreme Court must

not, therefore, be permitted to control the Congress or the Executive when acting in their legislative capacities, but to have only such influence as the force of their reasoning may deserve.

But in the case relied upon the Supreme Court have not decided that all the features of this corporation are compatible with the Constitution. It is true that the court have said that the law incorporating the bank is a constitutional exercise of power by Congress; but taking into view the whole opinion of the court and the reasoning by which they have come to that conclusion, I understand them to have decided that inasmuch as a bank is an appropriate means for carrying into effect the enumerated powers of the General Government, therefore the law incorporating it is in accordance with that provision of the Constitution which declares that Congress shall have power "to make all laws which shall be necessary and proper for carrying those powers into execution." Having satisfied themselves that the word *"necessary"* in the Constitution means *"needful," "requisite," "essential," "conducive to,"* and that "a bank" is a convenient, a useful, and essential instrument in the prosecution of the Government's "fiscal operations," they conclude that to "use one must be within the discretion of Congress" and that "the act to incorporate the Bank of the United States is a law made in pursuance of the Constitution;" "but," say they, *"where the law is not prohibited and is really calculated to effect any of the objects intrusted to the Government, to undertake here to inquire into the degree of its necessity would be to pass the line which circumscribes the judicial department and to tread on legislative ground."*

The principle here affirmed is that the "degree of its necessity," involving all the details of a banking institution, is a question exclusively for legislative consideration. A bank is constitutional, but it is the province of the Legislature to determine whether this or that particular power, privilege, or exemption is "necessary and proper" to enable the bank to discharge its duties to the Government, and from their decision there is no appeal to the courts of justice. Under the decision of the Supreme Court, therefore, it is the exclusive province of Congress and the President to decide whether the particular features of this act are *necessary* and *proper* in order to enable the bank to perform conveniently and efficiently the public duties assigned to it as a fiscal agent, and therefore constititional, or *unnecessary* and *improper,* and therefore unconstitutional.

Without commenting on the general principle affirmed by the Supreme Court, let us examine the details of this act in accordance with the rule of legislative action which they have laid down. It will be found that many of the powers and privileges conferred on it can not be supposed necessary for the purpose for which it is proposed to be created, and are not, therefore, means necessary to attain the end in view, and consequently not justified by the Constitution.

The original act of incorporation, section 21, enacts "that no other bank shall be established by any future law of the United States during the continuance of the corporation hereby created, for which the faith of the United States is hereby pledged: *Provided,* Congress may renew existing charters for banks within the District of Columbia not increasing the capital thereof, and may also establish any other bank or banks in said District with capitals not exceeding in the whole $6,000,000 if they shall deem it expedient." This provision is continued in force by the act before me fifteen years from the 3d of March, 1836.

If Congress possessed the power to establish one bank, they had power to establish more than one if in their opinion two or more banks had been "necessary" to facilitate the execution of the powers delegated to them in the Constitution. If they possessed the power to establish a second bank, it was a power derived from the Constitution to be exercised from time to time, and at any time when the interests of the country or the emergencies of the Government might make it expedient. It was possessed by one Congress as well as another, and by all Congresses alike, and alike at every session. But the Congress of 1816 have taken it away from their successors for twenty years, and the Congress of 1832 proposes to abolish it for fifteen years more. It can not be *"necessary"* or *"proper"* for Congress to barter away or divest themselves of any of the powers vested in them by the Constitution to be exercised for the public good.

It is not *"necessary"* to the efficiency of the bank, nor is it *"proper"* in relation to themselves and their successors. They may *properly* use the discretion vested in them, but they may not limit the discretion of their successors. This restriction on themselves and grant of a monopoly to the bank is therefore unconstitutional.

In another point of view this provision is a palpable attempt to amend the Constitution by an act of legislation. The Constitution declares that "the Congress shall have power to exercise exclusive legislation in all cases whatsoever" over the District of Columbia. Its constitutional power, therefore, to establish banks in the District of Columbia and increase their capital at will is unlimited and uncontrollable by any other power than that which gave authority to the Constitution. Yet this act declares that Congress shall *not* increase the capital of existing banks, nor create other banks with capitals exceeding in the whole $6,000,000. The Constitution declares that Congress *shall* have power to exercise exclusive legislation over this District *"in all cases whatsoever,"* and this act declares they shall not. Which is the supreme law of the land? This provision can not be *"necessary"* or *"proper"* or *constitutional* unless the absurdity be admitted that whenever it be "necessary and proper" in the opinion of Congress they have a right to barter away one portion of the powers vested in them by the Constitution as a means of executing the rest.

On two subjects only does the Constitution recognize in Congress the power to grant exclusive privileges or monopolies. It declares that "Congress shall have power to promote the progress of science and useful arts by securing for limited times to authors and inventors the exclusive right to their respective writings and discoveries." Out of this express delegation of power have grown our laws of patents and copyrights. As the Constitution expressly delegates to Congress the power to grant exclusive privileges in these cases as the means of executing the substantive power "to promote the progress of science and useful arts," it is consistent with the fair rules of construction to conclude that such a power was not intended to be granted as a means of accomplishing any other end. On every other subject which comes within the scope of Congressional power there is an ever-living discretion in the use of proper means, which can not be restricted or abolished without an amendment of the Constitution. Every act of Congress, therefore, which attempts by grants of monopolies or sale of exclusive privileges for a limited time, or a time without limit, to restrict or extinguish its own discretion in the choice of means to execute its delegated powers is equivalent to a legislative amendment of the Constitution, and palpably unconstitutional.

This act authorizes and encourages transfers of its stock to foreigners and grants them an exemption from all State and national taxation. So far from being *"necessary and proper"* that the bank should possess this power to make it a safe and efficient agent of the Government in its fiscal operations, it is calculated to convert the Bank of the United States into a foreign bank, to impoverish our people in time of peace, to disseminate a foreign influence through every section of the Republic, and in war to endanger our independence.

The several States reserved the power at the formation of the Constitution to regulate and control titles and transfers of real property, and most, if not all, of them have laws disqualifying aliens from acquiring or holding lands within their limits. But this act, in disregard of the undoubted right of the States to prescribe such disqualifications, gives to alien stockholders in this bank an interest and title, as members of the corporation, to all the real property it may acquire within any of the States of this Union. This privilege granted to aliens is not *"necessary"* to enable the bank to perform its public duties, nor in any sense *"proper,"* because it is vitally subversive of the rights of the States.

The Government of the United States have no constitutional power to purchase lands within the States except "for the erection of forts, magazines, arsenals, dockyards, and other needful buildings," and even for these objects only "by the consent of the legislature of the State in which the same shall be." By making themselves stockholders in the bank and granting to the corporation the power to purchase lands for other purposes they assume a power not granted in the Constitution and grant to others what they do not themselves possess. It is not *necessary* to the receiving, safe-keeping, or transmission of the funds of the Government that the bank should possess this power, and it is not *proper* that Congress should thus enlarge the powers delegated to them in the Constitution.

The old Bank of the United States possessed a capital of only $11,000,000, which was found fully sufficient to enable it with dispatch and safety to perform all the functions required of it by the Government. The capital of the present bank is $35,000,000—at least twenty-four more than experience has proved to be *necessary* to enable a bank to perform its public functions. The public debt which existed during the period of the old bank and on the establishment of the new has been nearly paid off, and our revenue will soon be reduced. This increase of capital is therefore not for public but for private purposes.

The Government is the only *"proper"* judge where its agents should reside and keep their offices, because it best knows where their presence will be *"necessary."* It can not, therefore, be *"necessary"* or *"proper"* to authorize the bank to locate branches where it pleases to perform the public service, without consulting the Government, and contrary to its will. The principle laid down by the Supreme Court concedes that Congress can not establish a bank for purposes of private speculation and gain, but only as a means of executing the delegated powers of the General Government. By the same principle a branch bank can not constitutionally be established for other than public purposes. The power which this act gives to establish two branches in any State, without the injunction or request of the Government and for other than public purposes, is not *"necessary"* to the due *execution* of the powers delegated to Congress.

The bonus which is exacted from the bank is a confession upon the face of the act that the powers granted by it are greater than are *"necessary"* to its character of a fiscal agent. The Government does not tax its officers and agents for the privilege of serving it. The bonus of a million and a half required by the original charter and that of three millions proposed by this act are not exacted for the privilege of giving "the necessary facilities for transferring the public funds from place to place within the United States or the Territories thereof, and for distributing the same in payment of the public creditors without charging commission or claiming allowance on account of the difference of exchange," as required by the act of incorporation, but for something more beneficial to the stockholders. The original act declares that it (the bonus) is granted "in consideration of the exclusive privileges and benefits conferred by this act upon the said bank," and the act before me declares it to be "in consideration of the exclusive benefits and privileges continued by this act to the said corporation for fifteen years, as aforesaid." It is therefore for "exclusive privileges and benefits" conferred for their own use and emolument, and not for the advantage of the Government, that a bonus is exacted. These surplus powers for which the bank is required to pay can not surely be "*necessary*" to make it the fiscal agent of the Treasury. If they were, the exaction of a bonus for them would not be "*proper*."

It is maintained by some that the bank is a means of executing the constitutional power "to coin money and regulate the value thereof." Congress have established a mint to coin money and passed laws to regulate the value thereof. The money so coined, with its value so regulated, and such foreign coins as Congress may adopt are the only currency known to the Constitution. But if they have other power to regulate the currency, it was conferred to be exercised by themselves, and not to be transferred to a corporation. If the bank be established for that purpose, with a charter unalterable without its consent, Congress have parted with their power for a term of years, during which the Constitution is a dead letter. It is neither necessary nor proper to transfer its legislative power to such a bank, and therefore unconstitutional.

By its silence, considered in connection with the decision of the Supreme Court in the case of McCulloch against the State of Maryland, this act takes from the States the power to tax a portion of the banking business carried on within their limits, in subversion of one of the strongest barriers which secured them against Federal encroachments. Banking, like farming, manufacturing, or any other occupation or profession, is *a business*, the right to follow which is not originally derived from the laws. Every citizen and every company of citizens in all of our States possessed the right until the State legislatures deemed it good policy to prohibit private banking by law. If the prohibitory State laws were now repealed, every citizen would again possess the right. The State banks are a qualified restoration of the right which has been taken away by the laws against banking, guarded by such provisions and limitations as in the opinion of the State legislatures the public interest requires. These corporations, unless there be an exemption in their charter, are, like private bankers and banking companies, subject to State taxation. The manner in which these taxes shall be laid depends wholly on legislative discretion. It may be upon the bank, upon the stock, upon the profits, or in any other mode which the sovereign power shall will.

Upon the formation of the Constitution the States guarded their taxing power with peculiar jealousy. They surrendered it only as it regards imports and exports. In relation to every other object within their jurisdiction, whether persons, property, business, or professions, it was secured in as ample a manner as it was before possessed. All persons, though United States officers, are liable to a poll tax by the States within which they reside. The lands of the United States are liable to the usual land tax, except in the new States, from whom agreements that they will not tax unsold lands are exacted when they are admitted into the Union. Horses, wagons, any beasts or vehicles, tools, or property belonging to private citizens, though employed in the service of the United States, are subject to State taxation. Every private business, whether carried on by an officer of the General Government or not, whether it be mixed with public concerns or not, even if it be carried on by the Government of the United States itself, separately or in partnership, falls within the scope of the taxing power of the State. Nothing comes more fully within it than banks and the business of banking, by whomsoever instituted and carried on. Over this whole subject-matter it is just as absolute, unlimited, and uncontrollable as if the Constitution had never been adopted, because in the formation of that instrument it was reserved without qualification.

The principle is conceded that the States can not rightfully tax the operations of the General Government. They can not tax the money of the Government deposited in the State banks, nor the agency of those banks in remitting it; but will any man maintain that their mere selection to perform this public service for the General Government would exempt the State banks and their ordinary business from State taxation? Had the United States, instead of establishing a bank at Philadelphia, employed a private banker to keep and transmit their funds, would it have deprived Pennsylvania of the right to tax his bank and his usual banking operations? It will not be pretended. Upon what principle, then, are the banking establishments of the Bank of the United States and their usual banking operations to be exempted from taxation? It is not their public agency or the deposits of the Government which the States claim a right to tax, but their banks and their banking powers, instituted and exercised within State jurisdiction for their private emolument—those powers and privileges for which they pay a bonus, and which the States tax in their own banks. The exercise of these powers within a State, no matter by whom or under what authority, whether by private citizens in their original right, by corporate bodies created by the States, by foreigners or the agents of foreign governments located within their limits, forms a legitimate object of State taxation. From this and like sources, from the persons, property, and business that are found residing, located, or carried on under their jurisdiction, must the States, since the surrender of their right to raise a revenue from imports and exports, draw all the money necessary for the support of their governments and the maintenance of their independence. There is no more appropriate subject of taxation than banks, banking, and bank stocks, and none to which the States ought more pertinaciously to cling.

It can not be *necessary* to the character of the bank as a fiscal agent of the Government that its private business should be exempted from that taxation to which all the State banks are liable, nor can I conceive it *"proper"* that the substantive and most essential powers reserved by the States shall be thus attacked and annihilated as a means of executing the powers delegated to the General Government. It may be safely assumed that none of those sages who had an agency in forming or adopting our Constitution ever imagined that any portion of the taxing power of the States not prohibited to them nor delegated to Congress was to be swept away and annihilated as a means of executing certain powers delegated to Congress.

If our power over means is so absolute that the Supreme Court will not call in question the constitutionality of an act of Congress the subject of which "is not prohibited, and is really calculated to effect any of the objects intrusted to the Government," although, as in the case before me, it takes away powers expressly granted to Congress and rights scrupulously reserved to the States, it becomes us to proceed in our legislation with the utmost caution. Though not directly, our own powers and the rights of the States may be indirectly legislated away in the use of means to execute substantive powers. We may not enact that Congress shall not have the power of exclusive legislation over the District of Columbia, but we may pledge the faith of the United States that as a means of executing other powers it shall not be exercised for twenty years or forever. We may not pass an act prohibiting the States to tax the banking business carried on within their limits, but we may, as a means of executing our powers over other objects, place that business in the hands of our agents and then declare it exempt from State taxation in their hands. Thus may our own powers and the rights of the States, which we can not directly curtail or invade, be frittered away and extinguished in the use of means employed by us to execute other powers. That a bank of the United States, competent to all the duties which may be required by the Government, might be so organized as not to infringe on our own delegated powers or the reserved rights of the States I do not entertain a doubt. Had the Executive been called upon to furnish the project of such an institution, the duty would have been cheerfully performed. In the absence of such a call it was obviously proper that he should confine himself to pointing out those prominent features in the act presented which in his opinion make it incompatible with the Constitution and sound policy. A general discussion will now take place, eliciting new light and settling important principles; and a new Congress, elected in the midst of such discussion, and furnishing an equal representation of the people according to the last census, will bear to the Capitol the verdict of public opinion, and, I doubt not, bring this important question to a satisfactory result.

Under such circumstances the bank comes forward and asks a renewal of its charter for a term of fifteen years upon conditions which not only operate as a gratuity to the stockholders of many millions of dollars, but will sanction any abuses and legalize any encroachments.

Suspicions are entertained and charges are made of gross abuse and violation of its charter. An investigation unwillingly conceded and so restricted in time as necessarily to make it incomplete and unsatisfactory discloses enough to excite suspicion and alarm. In the practices of the principal bank partially unveiled, in the absence of important witnesses, and in numerous charges confidently made and as yet wholly uninvestigated there was enough to induce a majority of the committee of investigation—a committee which was selected from the most able and honorable members of the House of Representatives—to recommend a suspension of further action upon the bill and a prosecution of the inquiry. As the charter had yet four years to run, and as a renewal now was not necessary to the successful prosecution of its business, it was to have been expected that the bank itself, conscious of its purity and proud of its character, would have withdrawn its application for the present, and demanded the severest scrutiny into all its transactions. In their declining to do so there seems to be an additional reason why the functionaries of the Government should proceed with less haste and more caution in the renewal of their monopoly.

The bank is professedly established as an agent of the executive branch of the Government, and its constitutionality is maintained on that ground. Neither upon the propriety of present action nor upon the provisions of this act was the Executive consulted. It has had no opportunity to say that it neither needs nor wants an agent clothed with such powers and favored by such exemptions. There is nothing in its legitimate functions which makes it necessary or proper. Whatever interest or influence, whether public or private, has given birth to this act, it can not be found either in the wishes or necessities of the executive department, by which present action is deemed premature, and the powers conferred upon its agent not only unnecessary, but dangerous to the Government and country.

It is to be regretted that the rich and powerful too often bend the acts of government to their selfish purposes. Distinctions in society will always exist under every just government. Equality of talents, of education, or of wealth can not be produced by human institutions. In the full enjoyment of the gifts of Heaven and the fruits of superior industry, economy, and virtue, every man is equally entitled to protection by law; but when the laws undertake to add to these natural and just advantages artificial distinctions, to grant titles, gratuities, and exclusive privileges, to make the rich richer and the potent more powerful, the humble members of society—the farmers, mechanics, and laborers—who have neither the time nor the means of securing like favors to themselves, have a right to complain of the injustice of their Government. There are no necessary evils in government. Its evils exist only in its abuses. If it would confine itself to equal protection, and, as Heaven does its rains, shower its favors alike on the high and the low, the rich and the poor, it would be an unqualified blessing. In the act before me there seems to be a wide and unnecessary departure from these just principles.

Nor is our Government to be maintained or our Union preserved by invasions of the rights and powers of the several States. In thus attempting to make our General Government strong we make it weak. Its true strength consists in leaving individuals and States as much as possible to themselves—in making itself felt, not in its power, but in its beneficence; not in its control, but in its protection; not in binding the States more closely to the center, but leaving each to move unobstructed in its proper orbit.

Experience should teach us wisdom. Most of the difficulties our Government now encounters and most of the dangers which impend over our Union have sprung from an abandonment of the legitimate objects of Government by our national legislation, and the adoption of such principles as are embodied in this act. Many of our rich men have not been content with equal protection and equal benefits, but have besought us to make them richer by act of Congress. By attempting to gratify their desires we have in the results of our legislation arrayed section against section, interest against interest, and man against man, in a fearful commotion which threatens to shake the foundations of our Union. It is time to pause in our career to review our principles, and if possible revive that devoted patriotism and spirit of compromise which distinguished the sages of the Revolution and the fathers of our Union. If we can not at once, in justice to interests vested under improvident legislation, make our Government what it ought to be, we can at least take a stand against all new grants of monopolies and exclusive privileges, against any prostitution of our Government to the advancement of the few at the expense of the many, and in favor of compromise and gradual reform in our code of laws and system of political economy.

I have now done my duty to my country. If sustained by my fellow-citizens, I shall be grateful and happy; if not, I shall find in the motives which impel me ample grounds for contentment and peace. In the difficulties which surround us and the dangers which threaten our institutions there is cause for neither dismay nor alarm. For relief and deliverance let us firmly rely on that kind Providence which I am sure watches with peculiar care over the destinies of our Republic, and on the intelligence and wisdom of our countrymen. Through *His* abundant goodness and *their* patriotic devotion our liberty and Union will be preserved.

8
DANIEL WEBSTER (1782–1852)
Address in the Senate (1832)
[Webster, *Works*, (4th ed., 1853), III, 416]

Mr. President, no one will deny the high importance of the subject now before us. Congress, after full deliberation and discussion, has passed a bill, by decisive majorities, in both houses, for extending the duration of the Bank of the United States. It has not adopted this measure until its attention had been called to the subject, in three successive annual messages of the President. The bill having been thus passed by both houses, and having been duly presented to the President, instead of signing and approving it, he has returned it with objections. These objections go against the whole substance of the law originally creating the bank. They deny, in effect, that the bank is constitutional; they deny that it is expedient; they deny that it is necessary for the public service.

It is not to be doubted, that the Constitution gives the President the power which he has now exercised; but while the power is admitted, the grounds upon which it has been exerted become fit subjects of examination. The Constitution makes it the duty of Congress, in cases like this, to reconsider the measure which they have passed, to weigh the force of the President's objections to that measure, and to take a new vote upon the question.

Before the Senate proceeds to this second vote, I propose to make some remarks upon those objections. And, in the first place, it is to be observed, that they are such as to extinguish all hope that the present bank, or any bank at all resembling it, or resembling any known similar institution, can ever receive his approbation. He states no terms, no qualifications, no conditions, no modifications, which can reconcile him to the essential provisions of the existing charter. He is against the bank, and against any bank constituted in a manner known either to this or any other country. One advantage, therefore, is certainly obtained by presenting him the bill. It has caused the President's sentiments to be made known. There is no longer any mystery, no longer a contest between hope and fear, or between those prophets who predicted a *veto* and those who foretold an approval. The bill is negatived; the President has assumed the responsibility of putting an end to the bank; and the country must prepare itself to meet that change in its concerns which the expiration of the charter will produce. Mr. President, I will not conceal my opinion that the affairs of the country are approaching an important and dangerous crisis. At the very moment of almost unparalleled general prosperity, there appears an unaccountable disposition to destroy the most useful and most approved institutions of the government. Indeed, it seems to be in the midst of all this national happiness that some are found openly to question the advantages of the Constitution itself; and many more ready to embarrass the exercise of its just power, weaken its authority, and undermine its foundations. How far these notions may be carried, it is impossible yet to say. We have before us the practical result of one of them. The bank has fallen, or is to fall.

It is now certain, that, without a change in our public counsels, this bank will not be continued, nor will any other be established, which, according to the general sense and language of mankind, can be entitled to the name. Within three years and nine months from the present moment, the charter of the bank expires; within that period, therefore, it must wind up its concerns. It must call in its debts, withdraw its bills from circulation, and cease from all its ordinary operations. All this is to be done in three years and nine months; because, although there is a provision in the charter rendering it lawful to use the corporate name for two years after the expiration of the charter, yet this is allowed only for the purpose of suits and for the sale of the estate belonging to the bank, and for no other purpose whatever. The whole active business of the bank, its custody of public deposits, its transfer of public moneys, its dealing in exchange, all its loans and discounts, and all its issues of bills for circulation, must cease and determine on or before the third day of March, 1836; and within the same period its debts must be collected, as no new contract can be made with it, as a corporation, for the renewal of loans, or discount of notes or bills, after that time.

The President is of opinion, that this time is long enough to close the concerns of the institution without inconvenience. His language is, "The time allowed the bank to close its concerns is ample, and if it has been well managed, its pressure will be light, and heavy only in case its management has been bad. If, therefore, it shall produce distress, the fault will be its own." Sir, this is all no more than general statement, without fact or argument to support it. We know what the management of the bank has been, and we know the present state of its affairs. We can judge, therefore, whether it be probable that its capital can be all called in, and the circulation of its bills withdrawn, in three years and nine months, by any discretion or prudence in management, without producing distress. The bank has discounted liberally, in compliance with the wants of the community. The amount due to it on loans and discounts, in certain large divisions of the country, is great; so great, that I do not perceive how any man can believe that it can be paid, within the time now limited, without distress. Let us look at known facts. Thirty millions of the capital of the bank are now out, on loans and discounts, in the States on the Mississippi and its waters; ten millions of which are loaned on the discount of bills of exchange, foreign and domestic, and twenty millions on promissory notes. Now, Sir, how is it possible that this vast amount can be collected in so short a period without suffering, by any management whatever? We are to remember, that, when the collection of this debt begins, at that same time, the existing medium of payment, that is, the circulation of the bills of the bank, will begin also to be restrained and withdrawn; and thus the means of payment must be limited just when the necessity of making payment becomes pressing. The whole debt is to be paid, and within the same time the whole circulation withdrawn.

The local banks, where there are such, will be able to afford little assistance; because they themselves will feel a full share of the pressure. They will not be in a condition to extend their discounts, but, in all probability, obliged to curtail them. Whence, then, are the means to come for paying this debt? and in what medium is payment to be made? If all this may be done with but slight pressure on the community, what course of conduct is to accomplish it? How is it to be done? What other thirty millions are to supply the place of these thirty millions now to be called in? What other circulation or medium of payment is to be adopted in the place of the bills of the bank? The message, following a singular train of argument, which had been used in this house, has a loud lamentation upon the suffering of the Western States on account of their being obliged to pay even interest on this debt. This payment of interest is itself represented as exhausting their means and ruinous to their prosperity. But if the interest cannot be paid without pressure, can both interest and principal be paid in four years without pressure? The truth is, the interest has been paid, is paid, and may continue to be paid, without any pressure at all; because the money borrowed is profitably employed by those who borrow it, and the rate of interest which they pay is at least 2 per cent lower than the actual value of money in that part of the country. But to pay the whole principal in less than four years, losing, at the same time, the existing and accustomed means and facilities of payment created by the bank itself, and to do this without extreme embarrassment, without absolute distress, is, in my judgment, impossible. I hesitate not to say, that, as this *veto* travels to the West, it will depreciate the value of every man's property from the Atlantic States to the capital of Missouri. Its effects will be felt in the price of lands, the great and leading article of Western property, in the price of crops, in the products of labor, in the repression of enterprise, and in embarrassment to every kind of business and occupation. I state this opinion strongly, because I have no doubt of its truth, and am willing its correctness should be judged by the event. Without personal acquaintance with the Western States, I know enough of their condition to be satisfied that what I have predicted must happen. The people of the West are rich, but their riches consist in their immense quantities of excellent land, in the products of these lands, and in their spirit of enterprise. The actual value of money, or rate of interest, with them is high, because their pecuniary capital bears little proportion to their landed interest. At an average rate, money is not worth less than 8 per cent per annum throughout the whole Western country, notwithstanding that it has now a loan or an advance from the bank of thirty millions, at 6 per cent. To call in this loan, at the rate of eight millions a year, in addition to the interest on the whole, and to take away, at the same time, that circulation which constitutes so great a portion of the medium of payment throughout that whole region, is an operation, which, however wisely conducted, cannot but inflict a blow on the community of tremendous force and frightful consequences. The thing cannot be done without distress, bankruptcy, and ruin, to many. If the President had seen any practical manner in which this change might be effected without producing these consequences, he would have rendered infinite service to the community by pointing it out. But he has pointed out nothing, he has suggested nothing; he contents himself with saying, without giving any reason, that, if the pressure be heavy, the fault will be the bank's. I hope this is not merely an attempt to forestall opinion, and to throw on the bank the responsibility of those evils which threaten the country, for the sake of removing it from himself.

The responsibility justly lies with him, and there it ought to remain. A great majority of the people are satisfied with the bank as it is, and desirous that it should be continued. They wished no change. The strength of this public sentiment has carried the bill through Congress, against all the influence of the administration, and all the power of organized party. But the President has undertaken, on his own responsibility, to arrest the measure, by refusing his assent to the bill. He is answerable for the consequences, therefore, which necessarily follow the change which the expiration of the bank charter may produce; and if these consequences shall prove disastrous, they can fairly be ascribed to his policy only, and the policy of his administration.

Although, Sir, I have spoken of the effects of this *veto* in the Western country, it has not been because I considered that part of the United States exclusively affected by it. Some of the Atlantic States may feel its consequences, perhaps, as sensibly as those of the West, though not for the same reasons. The concern manifested by Pennsylvania for the renewal of the charter shows her sense of the importance of the bank to her own interest, and that of the nation. That great and enterprising State has entered into an extensive system of internal improvements, which necessarily makes heavy demands on her credit and her resources; and by the sound and acceptable currency which the bank affords, by the stability which it gives to private credit, and by occasional advances, made in anticipation of her revenues, and in aid of her great objects, she has found herself benefited, doubtless, in no inconsiderable degree. Her legislature has instructed her Senators here to advocate the renewal of the charter, at this session. They have obeyed her voice, and yet they have the misfortune to find that, in the judgment of the President, *the measure is unconstitutional, unnecessary, dangerous to liberty, and is, moreover, ill-timed.*

But, Mr. President, it is not the local interest of the West, nor the particular interest of Pennsylvania, or any other State, which has influenced Congress in passing this bill. It has been governed by a wise foresight, and by a desire to avoid embarrassment in the pecuniary concerns of the country, to secure the safe collection and convenient transmission of public moneys, to maintain the circulation of the country, sound and safe as it now happily is, against the possible effects of a wild spirit of speculation. Finding the bank highly useful, Congress has thought fit to provide for its continuance. . . .

Before proceeding to the constitutional question, there are some other topics, treated in the message, which ought to be noticed. It commences by an inflamed statement of what it calls the "favor" bestowed upon the original bank by the government, or, indeed, as it is phrased, the "monopoly of its favor and support"; and through the whole message all possible changes are rung on the "gratuity," the "exclusive privileges," and "monopoly," of the bank charter. Now, Sir, the truth is, that the powers conferred on the bank are such, and no others, as are usually conferred on similar institutions. They constitute no monopoly, although some of them are of necessity, and with propriety, exclusively privileges. "The original act," says the message, "operated as a gratuity of many millions to the stockholders." What fair foundation is there for this remark? The stockholders received their charter, not gratuitously, but for a valuable consideration in money, prescribed by Congress, and actually paid. At some times the stock has been above *par*, at other times below *par*, according to prudence in management, or according to commercial occurrences. But if, by a judicious administration of its affairs, it had kept its stock always above *par*, what pretence would there be, nevertheless, for saying that such augmentation of its value was a "gratuity" from government? The message proceeds to declare, that the present act proposes another donation, another gratuity, to the same men, of at least seven millions more. It seems to me that this is an extraordinary statement, and an extraordinary style of argument, for such a subject and on such an occasion. In the first place, the facts are all assumed; they are taken for true without evidence. There are no proofs that any benefit to that amount will accrue to the stockholders, nor any experience to justify the expectation of it. It rests on random estimates, or mere conjecture. But suppose the continuance of the charter should prove beneficial to the stockholders; do they not pay for it? They give twice as much for a charter of fifteen years, as was given before for one of twenty. And if the proposed *bonus*, or premium, be not, in the President's judgment, large enough, would he, nevertheless, on such a mere matter of opinion as that, negative the whole bill? May not Congress be trusted to decide even on such a subject as the amount of the money premium to be received by government for a charter of this kind?

But, Sir, there is a larger and a much more just view of this subject. The bill was not passed for the purpose of benefiting the present stockholders. Their benefit, if any, is incidental

and collateral. Nor was it passed on any idea that they had a
right to a renewed charter, although the message argues
against such right, as if it had been somewhere set up and
asserted. No such right has been asserted by any body. Congress passed the bill, not as a bounty or a favor to the present
stockholders, nor to comply with any demand of right on their
part; but to promote great public interests, for great public
objects. Every bank must have some stockholders, unless it be
such a bank as the President has recommended, and in regard
to which he seems not likely to find much concurrence of
other men's opinions; and if the stockholders, whoever they
may be, conduct the affairs of the bank prudently, the expectation is always, of course, that they will make it profitable
to themselves, as well as useful to the public. If a bank charter
is not to be granted, because, to some extent, it may be profitable to the stockholders, no charter can be granted. The objection lies against all banks. . . .

Allow me, now, Sir, to take notice of an argument founded
on the practical operation of the bank. That argument is this.
Little of the stock of the bank is held in the West, the capital
being chiefly owned by citizens of the Southern and Eastern
States, and by foreigners. But the Western and Southwestern
States owe the bank a heavy debt, so heavy that the interest
amounts to a million six hundred thousand a year. This interest is carried to the Eastern States, or to Europe, annually, and
its payment is a burden on the people of the West, and a drain
of their currency, which no country can bear without inconvenience and distress. The true character and the whole value
of this argument are manifest by the mere statement of it. The
people of the West are, from their situation, necessarily large
borrowers. They need money, capital, and they borrow it,
because they can derive a benefit from its use, much beyond
the interest which they pay. They borrow at 6 per cent of
the bank, although the value of money with them is at least as
high as 8. Nevertheless, although they borrow at this low
rate of interest, and although they use all they borrow thus
profitably, yet they cannot pay the interest without "inconvenience and distress"; and then, Sir, follows the logical con-

clusion, that, although they cannot pay even the interest without inconvenience and distress, yet less than four years is ample time for the bank to call in the whole, both principal and interest, without causing more than a light pressure. This is the argument.

Then follows another, which may be thus stated. It is competent to the States to tax the property of their citizens vested in the stock of this bank; but the power is denied of taxing the stock of foreigners; therefore the stock will be worth 10 or 15 per cent more to foreigners than to residents, and will of course inevitably leave the country, and make the American people debtors to aliens in nearly the whole amount due the bank, and send across the Atlantic from two to five millions of specie every year, to pay the bank dividends.

Mr. President, arguments like these might be more readily disposed of, were it not that the high and official source from which they proceed imposes the necessity of treating them with respect. In the first place, it may safely be denied that the stock of the bank is any more valuable to foreigners than to our own citizens, or an object of greater desire to them, except in so far as capital may be more abundant in the foreign country, and therefore its owners more in want of opportunity of investment. The foreign stockholder enjoys no exemption from taxation. He is, of course, taxed by his own government for his incomes, derived from this as well as other property; and this is a full answer to the whole statement. But it may be added, in the second place, that it is not the practice of civilized states to tax the property of foreigners under such circumstances. Do we tax, or did we ever tax, the foreign holders of our public debt? Does Pennsylvania, New York, or Ohio tax the foreign holders of stock in the loans contracted by either of these States? Certainly not. Sir, I must confess I had little expected to see, on such an occasion as the present, a labored and repeated attempt to produce an impression on the public opinion unfavorable to the bank, from the circumstance that foreigners are among its stockholders. I have no hesitation in saying, that I deem such a train of remark as the message contains on this point, coming from the President of the United

States, to be injurious to the credit and character of the country abroad; because it manifests a jealousy, a lurking disposition not to respect the property, of foreigners invited hither by our own laws. And, Sir, what is its tendency but to excite this jealousy, and create groundless prejudices?

From the commencement of the government, it has been thought desirable to invite, rather than to repel, the introduction of foreign capital. Our stocks have all been open to foreign subscriptions; and the State banks, in like manner, are free to foreign ownership. Whatever State has created a debt has been willing that foreigners should become purchasers, and desirous of it. How long is it, Sir, since Congress itself passed a law vesting new powers in the President of the United States over the cities in this District, for the very purpose of increasing their credit abroad, the better to enable them to borrow money to pay their subscriptions to the Chesapeake and Ohio Canal? It is easy to say that there is danger to liberty, danger to independence, in a bank open to foreign stockholders, because it is easy to say any thing. But neither reason nor experience proves any such danger. The foreign stockholder cannot be a director. He has no voice even in the choice of directors. His money is placed entirely in the management of the directors appointed by the President and Senate and by the American stockholders. So far as there is dependence or influence either way, it is to the disadvantage of the foreign stockholder. He has parted with the control over his own property, instead of exercising control over the property or over the actions of others. And, Sir, let it now be added, in further answer to this class of objections, that experience has abundantly confuted them all. This government has existed forty-three years, and has maintained, in full being and operation, a bank, such as is now proposed to be renewed, for thirty-six years out of the forty-three. We have never for a moment had a bank not subject to every one of these objections. Always, foreigners might be stockholders; always, foreign stock has been exempt from State taxation, as much as at present; always, the same power and privileges; always, all that which is now called a "monopoly," a "gratuity," a "present," have been possessed by the bank. And yet there has been found no danger to liberty, no introduction of foreign influence, and no accumulation of irresponsible power in a few hands. I cannot but hope, therefore, that the people of the United States will not now yield up their judgment to those notions which would reverse all our best experience, and persuade us to discontinue a useful institution from the influence of vague and unfounded declamation against its danger to the public liberties. Our liberties, indeed, must stand upon very frail foundations, if the government cannot, without endangering them, avail itself of those common facilities, in the collection of its revenues and the management of its finances, which all other governments, in commercial countries, find useful and necessary.

In order to justify its alarm for the security of our independence, the message supposes a case. It supposes that the bank should pass principally into the hands of the subjects of a foreign country, and that we should be involved in war with that country, and then it exclaims, "What would be our condition?" Why, Sir, it is plain that all the advantages would be on our side. The Bank would still be our institution, subject to our own laws, and all its directors elected by ourselves; and our means would be enhanced, not by the confiscation and plunder, but by the proper use, of the foreign capital in our hands. And, Sir, it is singular enough, that this very state of war, from which this argument against a bank is drawn, is the very thing which, more than all others, convinced the country and the government of the necessity of a national bank. So much was the want of such an institution felt in the late war, that the subject engaged the attention of Congress, constantly, from the declaration of that war down to the time when the existing bank was actually established; so that in this respect, as well as in others, the argument of the message is directly opposed to the whole experience of the government, and to the general and long-settled convictions of the country.

I now proceed, Sir, to a few remarks upon the President's constitutional objections to the bank; and I cannot forbear to say, in regard to them, that he appears to me to have assumed very extraordinary grounds of reasoning. He denies that the constitutionality of the bank is a settled question. If it be not, will it ever become so, or what disputed question ever can be settled? I have already observed, that for thirty-six years out of the forty-three during which the government has been in being, a bank has existed, such as is now proposed to be continued. . . .

According to that mode of construing the Constitution which was adopted by Congress in 1791, and approved by Washington, and which has been sanctioned by the judgment of the Supreme Court, and affirmed by the practice of nearly forty years, the question upon the constitutionality of the bank involves two inquiries. First, whether a bank, in its general character, and with regard to the general objects with which banks are usually connected, be, in itself, a fit means, a suitable instrument, to carry into effect the powers granted to the government. If it be so, then the second, and the only other question is, whether the powers given in a particular charter are appropriate for a bank. If they are powers which are appropriate for a bank, powers which Congress may fairly consider to be useful to the bank or the country, then Congress may confer these powers; because the discretion to be exercised in framing the constitution of the bank belongs to Congress. One man may think the granted powers not indispensable to the particular bank; another may suppose them injudicious, or injurious; a third may imagine that other powers, if granted in their stead, would be more beneficial; but all these are matters of expediency, about which men may differ; and the power of deciding upon them belongs to Congress.

I again repeat, Sir, that if, for reasons of this kind, the President sees fit to negative a bill, on the ground of its being inexpedient or impolitic, he has a right to do so. But remember, Sir, that we are now on the constitutional question; remember, that the argument of the President is, that, because powers were given to the bank by the charter of 1816 which he thinks unnecessary, that charter is unconstitutional. Now, Sir, it will hardly be denied, or rather it was not denied or doubted before this message came to us, that, if there was to be a bank, the powers and duties of that bank must be pre-scribed in the law creating it. Nobody but Congress, it has been thought, could grant these powers and privileges, or pre-scribe their limitations. It is true, indeed, that the message pretty plainly intimates, that the President should have been *first* consulted, and that he should have had the framing of the bill; but we are not yet accustomed to that order of things in enacting laws, nor do I know a parallel to this claim, thus now brought forward, except that, in some peculiar cases in England, highly affecting the royal prerogative, the assent of the monarch is necessary, before either the House of Peers, or his Majesty's faithful Commons, are permitted to act upon the subject, or to entertain its consideration. But supposing, Sir, that our accustomed forms and our republican principles are still to be followed, and that a law creating a bank is, like all other laws, to originate with Congress, and that the President has nothing to do with it till it is presented for his approval, then it is clear that the powers and duties of a proposed bank, and all the terms and conditions annexed to it, must, in the first place, be settled by Congress.

This power, if constitutional at all, is only constitutional in the hands of Congress. Anywhere else, its exercise would be plain usurpation. If, then, the authority to decide what powers ought to be granted to a bank belong to Congress, and Con-gress shall have exercised that power, it would seem little bet-ter than absurd to say, that its act, nevertheless, would be unconstitutional and invalid, if, in the opinion of a third party, it had misjudged, on a question of expediency, in the arrange-ment of details. According to such a mode of reasoning, a mis-take in the exercise of jurisdiction takes away the jurisdiction. If Congress decide right, its decision may stand; if it decide wrong, its decision is nugatory; and whether its decision be right or wrong another is to judge, although the original power of making the decision must be allowed to be exclusively in Congress. This is the end to which the argument of the mes-sage will conduct its followers.

Sir, in considering the authority of Congress to invest the bank with the particular powers granted to it, the inquiry is not, and cannot be, how appropriate these powers are, but whether they be at all appropriate; whether they come within the range of a just and honest discretion; whether Congress may fairly esteem them to be necessary. The question is not, Are they the fittest means, the best means? or whether the bank might not be established without them; but the question is, Are they such as Congress, *bona fide*, may have regarded as appropriate to the end? If any other rule were to be adopted, nothing could ever be settled. A law would be constitutional to-day and unconstitutional to-morrow. Its constitutionality would altogether depend upon individual opinion on a matter of mere expediency. Indeed, such a case as that is now actually before us. Mr. Madison deemed the powers given to the bank, in its present charter, proper and necessary. He held the bank, therefore, to be constitutional. But the present President, not acknowledging that the power of deciding on these points rests with Congress, nor with Congress and the then President, but setting up his own opinion as the standard, declares the law now in being unconstitutional, because the powers granted by it are, in his estimation, not necessary and proper. I pray to be informed, Sir, whether, upon similar grounds of reasoning, the President's own scheme for a bank, if Congress should do so unlikely a thing as to adopt it, would not become unconstitutional also, if it should so happen that his successor should hold his bank in as light esteem as he holds those established under the auspices of Washington and Madison?

If the reasoning of the message be well founded, it is clear that the charter of the existing bank is not a law. The bank has no legal existence; it is not responsible to government; it has no authority to act; it is incapable of being an agent; the President may treat it as a nullity to-morrow, withdraw from it all the public deposits, and set afloat all the existing national arrangements of revenue and finance. It is enough to state these monstrous consequences, to show that the doctrine, principles, and pretensions of the message are entirely inconsistent with a government of laws. If that which Congress has enacted, and the Supreme Court has sanctioned, be not the law of the land, then the reign of law has ceased, and the reign of individual opinion has already begun.

The President, in his commentary on the details of the existing bank charter, undertakes to prove that one provision, and another provision, is not necessary and proper; because, as he thinks, the same objects proposed to be accomplished by them might have been better attained in another mode; and therefore such provisions are not necessary, and so not warranted by the Constitution. Does not this show, that, according to his own mode of reasoning, his *own* scheme would not be constitutional, since another scheme which probably most people would think a better one, might be substituted for it? Perhaps, in any bank charter, there may be no provisions which may be justly regarded as absolutely indispensable; since it is probable that for any of them some others might be substituted. No bank, therefore, ever could be established; because there never has been, and never could be, any charter, of which every provision should appear to be indispensable, or necessary and proper, in the judgment of every individual. To admit, therefore, that there may be a constitutional bank, and yet to contend for such a mode of judging of its provisions and details as the message adopts, involves an absurdity. Any charter which may be framed may be taken up, and each power conferred by it successively denied, on the ground, that, in regard to each, either no such power is "necessary or proper" in a bank, or, which is the same thing in effect, some other power might be substituted for it, and supply its place. That can never be necessary, in the sense in which the message understands that term, which may be dispensed with; and it cannot be said that any power may not be dispensed with, if there be some other which might be substituted for it, and which would accomplish the same end. Therefore, no bank could ever be constitutional, because none could be established which should not contain some provisions which might have been omitted, and their place supplied by others.

Mr. President, I have understood the true and well-established doctrine to be, that, after it has been decided that it is competent for Congress to establish a bank, then it follows, that

it may create such a bank as it judges, in its discretion, to be
best, and invest it with all such power as it may deem fit and
suitable; with this limitation, always, that all is to be done in
the *bona fide* execution of the power to create a bank. If the
granted powers are appropriate to the professed end, so that
the granting of them cannot be regarded as usurpation of authority by Congress, or an evasion of constitutional restrictions,
under color of establishing a bank, then the charter is constitutional, whether these powers be thought indispensable by
others or not, or whether even Congress itself deemed them
absolutely indispensable, or only thought them fit and suitable, or whether they are more or less appropriate to their
end. It is enough that they are appropriate; it is enough that
they are suited to produce the effects designed; and no comparison is to be instituted, in order to try their constitutionality,
between them and others which may be suggested. A case
analogous to the present is found in the constitutional power
of Congress over the mail. The Constitution says no more than
that "Congress shall have power to establish post-offices and
post-roads"; and, in the general clause, "all powers necessary
and proper" to give effect to this. In the execution of this
power, Congress has protected the mail, by providing that rob-
bery of it shall be punished with death. Is this infliction of
capital punishment constitutional? Certainly it is not, unless it
be both "proper and necessary." The President may not think
it necessary or proper; the law, then, according to the system
of reasoning enforced by the message, is of no binding force,
and the President may disobey it, and refuse to see it executed.

The truth is, Mr. President, that if the general object, the
subject-matter, properly belong to Congress, all its incidents
belong to Congress also. If Congress is to establish post-offices
and post-roads, it may, for that end, adopt one set of regulations or another; and either would be constitutional. So the
details of one bank are as constitutional as those of another, if
they are confined fairly and honestly to the purpose of organizing the institution, and rendering it useful. One *bank* is
as constitutional as another *bank*. If Congress possesses the
power to make a bank, it possesses the power to make it effi-

cient, and competent to produce the good expected from it. It may clothe it with all such power and privileges, not otherwise inconsistent with the Constitution, as may be necessary, in its own judgment, to make it what government deems it should be. It may confer on it such immunities as may induce individuals to become stockholders, and to furnish the capital; and since the extent of these immunities and privileges is matter of discretion, and matter of opinion, Congress only can decide it, because Congress alone can frame or grant the charter. A charter, thus granted to individuals, becomes a contract with them, upon their compliance with its terms. The bank becomes an agent, bound to perform certain duties, and entitled to certain stipulated rights and privileges, in compensation for the proper discharge of these duties; and all these stipulations, so long as they are appropriate to the object professed, and not repugnant to any other constitutional injunction, are entirely within the competency of Congress. And yet, Sir, the message of the President toils through all the commonplace topics of monopoly, the right of taxation, the suffering of the poor, and the arrogance of the rich, with as much painful effort, as if one, or another, or all of them, had something to do with the constitutional question.

What is called the "monopoly" is made the subject of repeated rehearsal, in terms of special complaint. By this "monopoly," I suppose, is understood the restriction contained in the charter, that Congress shall not, during the twenty years, create another bank. Now, Sir, let me ask, Who would think of creating a bank, inviting stockholders into it, with large investments, imposing upon it heavy duties, as connected with the government, receiving some millions of dollars as a *bonus* or premium, and yet retaining the power of granting, the next day, another charter, which would destroy the whole value of the first? If this be an unconstitutional restraint on Congress, the Constitution must be strangely at variance with the dictates both of good sense and sound morals. Did not the first Bank of the United States contain a similar restriction? And have not the States granted bank charters with a condition, that, if the charter should be accepted, they would not grant others?

States have certainly done so; and, in some instances, where no *bonus* or premium was paid at all; but from the mere desire to give effect to the charter, by inducing individuals to accept it and organize the institution. The President declares that this restriction is not necessary to the efficiency of the bank; but that is the very thing which Congress and his predecessor in office were called on to decide, and which they did decide, when the one passed and the other approved the act. And he has now no more authority to pronounce his judgment on that act than any other individual in society. It is not his province to decide on the constitutionality of statutes which Congress has passed, and his predecessors approved. . . .

I beg leave to repeat, Mr. President, that what I have now been considering are the President's objections, not to the policy or expediency, but to the constitutionality of the bank; and not to the constitutionality of any new or proposed bank, but of the bank as it now is, and as it has long existed. If the President had declined to approve this bill because he thought the original charter unwisely granted, and the bank, in point of policy and expediency, objectionable or mischievous, and in that view only had suggested the reasons now urged by him, his argument, however inconclusive, would have been intelligible, and not, in its whole frame and scope, inconsistent with all well-established first principles. His rejection of the bill, in that case, would have been, no doubt, an extraordinary exercise of power; but it would have been, nevertheless, the exercise of a power belonging to his office, and trusted by the Constitution to his discretion. But when he puts forth an array of arguments such as the message employs, not against the expediency of the bank, but against its constitutional existence, he confounds all distinctions, mixes questions of policy and questions of right together, and turns all constitutional restraints into mere matters of opinion. As far as its power extends, either in its direct effects or as a precedent, the message not only unsettles every thing which has been settled under the Constitution, but would show, also, that the Constitution itself is utterly incapable of any fixed construction or definite interpretation, and that there is no possibility of establishing, by its authority, any practical limitations on the powers of the respective branches of the government.

When the message denies, as it does, the authority of the Supreme Court to decide on constitutional questions, it effects, so far as the opinion of the President and his authority can effect it, a complete change in our government. It does two things; first, it converts constitutional limitations of power into mere matters of opinion, and then it strikes the judicial department, as an efficient department, out of our system. But the message by no means stops even at this point. Having denied to Congress the authority of judging what powers may be constitutionally conferred on a bank, and having erected the judgment of the President himself into a standard by which to try the constitutional character of such powers, and having denounced the authority of the Supreme Court to decide finally on constitutional questions, the message proceeds to claim for the President, not the power of approval, but the primary power, the power of originating laws. The President informs Congress, that *he* would have sent them such a charter, if it had been properly asked for, as they ought to confer. He very plainly intimates, that, in his opinion, the establishment of all laws, of this nature at least, belongs to the functions of the executive government; and that Congress ought to have waited for the manifestation of the executive will, before it presumed to touch the subject. Such, Mr. President, stripped of their disguises, are the real pretenses set up in behalf of the executive power in this most extraordinary paper.

Mr. President, we have arrived at a new epoch. We are entering on experiments, with the government and the Constitution of the country, hitherto untried, and of fearful and appalling aspect. This message calls us to the contemplation of a future which little resembles the past. Its principles are at war with all that public opinion has sustained, and all which the experience of the government has sanctioned. It denies first principles; it contradicts truths, heretofore received as indisputable. It denies to the judiciary the interpretation of law, and claims to divide with Congress the power of originating statutes. It extends the grasp of executive pretension over every power of the government. But this is not all. It presents the chief magistrate of the Union in the attitude of arguing away the powers of that government over which he has been chosen to preside; and adopting for this purpose modes of reasoning which, even under the influence of all proper feeling towards high official station, it is difficult to regard as respectable. It appeals to every prejudice which may betray men into a mistaken view of their own interests, and to every passion which may lead them to disobey the impulses of their understanding. It urges all the specious topics of State rights and national encroachment against that which a great majority of the States have affirmed to be rightful, and in which all of them have acquiesced. It sows, in an unsparing manner, the seeds of jealousy and ill-will against that government of which its author is the official head. It raises a cry, that liberty is in danger, at the very moment when it puts forth claims to powers heretofore unknown and unheard of. It affects alarm for the public freedom, when nothing endangers that freedom so much as its own unparalleled pretenses. This, even, is not all. It manifestly seeks to inflame the poor against the rich; it wantonly attacks whole classes of the people, for the purpose of turning against them prejudices and the resentments of other classes. It is a state paper which finds no topic too exciting for its use, no passion too inflammable for its address and its solicitation.

Such is this message. It remains now for the people of the United States to choose between the principles here avowed and their government. These cannot subsist together. The one or the other must be rejected. If the sentiments of the message shall receive general approbation, the Constitution will have perished even earlier than the moment which its enemies originally allowed for the termination of its existence. It will not have survived to its fiftieth year.

PART II

1862-1912

E. Regulation of Railroads

The citizens of the United States, who had done much between 1830 and 1870 to insure themselves an adequate supply of railroads, who had often wildly invested their own funds in railroads and who had pressed their governments to offer the carriers subsidies and encouragement of all sorts, found after 1870 that the railroads were a mixed blessing. Many supposedly pernicious practices were visible, but most of them had a common core: railroads charged rates that many shippers, and particularly the smaller ones, considered exorbitant. A movement developed for statutory regulation of freight charges, and this movement, when augmented by the momentary power of the Granger organization during the early 1870s, led to passage of many such statutes, especially by the midwestern states.

In the case of *Munn vs. Illinois* (9), the Supreme Court examined the two chief constitutional questions brought on by such regulations. Did they interfere unduly with the property rights of railroad owners; and did they interfere with interstate commerce? Chief Justice Waite, in delivering the Court's opinion, held that the regulation was appropriate because the grain elevators in question were property "clothed with the public interest" and as such might be regulated by the state, and because grain elevators resembled certain other businesses that had customarily been subject to regulation. But his opinion does not explain how one can tell when a business is "clothed with the public interest." Neither is the resemblance on which he depended easily visible.

The dissenting opinion fastens on these weaknesses, as well as others. The mention, in Waite's opinion, of the fact that the Chicago grain elevators were organized in a "virtual monopoly" is a hint of what may have swayed the majority of the Court—a feeling that monopolies are inimical to the public welfare and ought therefore naturally to be subject to regulation. Unfortunately, as there was no statute nor even any strong set of common-law precedents prohibiting monopolies, the Court was obliged to rely on a rather indirect mode of argument.

In subsequent decisions, especially the *Wabash* decision of 1886, the Supreme Court held—as it had not in the *Munn* case—that state regulation of interstate traffic was an unconstitutional interference with interstate commerce. This decision was the final step in preparing the ground for a federal regulatory system, embodied in the Interstate Commerce Act of 1887. The Interstate Commerce Commission, created by the act, reviewed in its first report (10) the history of previous regulation and the abuses that it was created to abolish.

These abuses, such as short-haul long-haul discrimination or price discrimination in various other forms, resulted from the fact that railroads competed with each other or with alternative forms of transport in some markets but not in all: wherever a railroad enjoyed a monopoly position—as in towns served by one railroad only—rates were higher than elsewhere. Such discrepancies were not popular with the shippers who faced high rates, and the ICC was assigned the problem of trying to eliminate the discrepancies.

As, however, the commission could not alter the fundamental fact that railroads were partially a competitive and partially a monopolistic industry, the results of its efforts in this field have often been illusory, inefficient, or futile. The prevalence and power of the conviction that railroads, being public carriers, ought to be publicly regulated does not seem however to have been much attenuated by the unsatisfactory experience of regulation. On the contrary, whenever it has become clear that regulation was producing no results or bad results, the argument has been advanced that there should be more or better regulation—and under this motto the Interstate Commerce Act has been "strengthened" again and again.

9

Munn vs. Illinois (1876)

[94 U.S. 113]

Mr. Chief Justice Waite delivered the opinion of the Court. The question to be determined in this case is whether the general assembly of Illinois can, under the limitations upon the legislative power of the States imposed by the Constitution of the United States, fix by law the maximum of charges for the storage of grain in warehouses at Chicago and other places in the State having not less than one hundred thousand inhabitants, "in which grain is stored in bulk, and in which the grain of different owners is mixed together, or in which grain is stored in such a manner that the identity of different lots or parcels cannot be accurately preserved."

It is claimed that such a law is repugnant—

1. To that part of sect. 8, art. 1, of the Constitution of the United States which confers upon Congress the power "to regulate commerce with foreign nations and among the several States;"

2. To that part of sect. 9 of the same article which provides that "no preference shall be given by any regulation of commerce or revenue to the ports of one State over those of another;" and

3. To that part of amendment 14 which ordains that no State shall "deprive any person of life, liberty, or property, without due process of law, nor deny to any person within its jurisdiction the equal protection of the laws."

We will consider the last of these objections first. . . .

The Constitution contains no definition of the word "deprive," as used in the Fourteenth Amendment. To determine its signification, therefore, it is necessary to ascertain the effect which usage has given it, when employed in the same or a like connection.

While this provision of the amendment is new in the Constitution of the United States, as a limitation upon the powers of the States, it is old as a principle of civilized government. It is found in Magna Charta, and, in substance if not in form, in nearly or quite all the constitutions that have been from time to time adopted by the several States of the Union. By the Fifth Amendment, it was introduced into the Constitution of the United States as a limitation upon the powers of the national government, and by the Fourteenth, as a guaranty against any encroachment upon an acknowledged right of citizenship by the legislatures of the States. . . .

When one becomes a member of society, he necessarily parts with some rights or privileges which, as an individual not affected by his relations to others, he might retain. "A body politic," as aptly defined in the preamble of the Constitution of Massachusetts, "is a social compact by which the whole people covenants with each citizen, and each citizen with the whole people, that all shall be governed by certain laws for the common good." This does not confer power upon the whole people to control rights which are purely and exclusively private . . . but it does authorize the establishment of laws requiring each citizen to so conduct himself, and so use his own property, as not unnecessarily to injure another. This is the very essence of government, and has found expression in the maxim *sic utere tuo ut alienum non lædas.** From this source come the police powers, which, as was said by Mr. Chief Justice Taney in the *License Cases*, 5 How. 583, "are nothing more or less than the powers of government inherent in every sovereignty, . . . that is to say, . . . the power to govern men and things." Under these powers the government regulates the conduct of its citizens one towards another, and the manner in which each shall use his own property, when such regulation becomes necessary for the public good. In their exercise it has been customary in England from time imme-

* [Act so as to injure no other.]

morial, and in this country from its first colonization, to regulate ferries, common carriers, hackmen, bakers, millers, wharfingers, innkeepers, &c., and in so doing to fix a maximum of charge to be made for services rendered, accommodations furnished, and articles sold. To this day, statutes are to be found in many of the States upon some or all these subjects; and we think it has never yet been successfully contended that such legislation came within any of the constitutional prohibitions against interference with private property. With the Fifth Amendment in force, Congress, in 1820, conferred power upon the city of Washington "to regulate . . . the rates of wharfage at private wharves, . . . the sweeping of chimneys, and to fix the rates of fees therefor, . . . and the weight and quality of bread," 3 Stat. 587, sect. 7; and, in 1848, "to make all necessary regulations respecting hackney carriages and the rates of fare of the same, and the rates of hauling by cartmen, wagoners, carmen, and draymen, and the rates of commission of auctioneers," 9 id. 224, sect. 2.

From this it is apparent that, down to the time of the adoption of the Fourteenth Amendment, it was not supposed that statutes regulating the use, or even the price of the use, of private property necessarily deprived an owner of his property without due process of law. Under some circumstances they may, but not under all. The amendment does not change the law in this particular: it simply prevents the States from doing that which will operate as such a deprivation.

This brings us to inquire as to the principles upon which this power of regulation rests, in order that we may determine what is within and what without its operative effect. Looking, then, to the common law, from whence came the right which the Constitution protects, we find that when private property is "affected with a public interest, it ceases to be *juris privati* only." This was said by Lord Chief Justice Hale more than two hundred years ago, in his treatise *De Portibus Maris* . . . and has been accepted without objection as an essential element in the law of property ever since. Property does become clothed with a public interest when used in a manner to make it of public consequence, and affect the community at large.

When, therefore, one devotes his property to a use in which
the public has an interest, he, in effect, grants to the public
an interest in that use, and must submit to be controlled by
the public for the common good, to the extent of the interest
he has thus created. He may withdraw his grant by discontinuing the use; but, so long as he maintains the use, he must
submit to the control. . . .

From the same source comes the power to regulate the
charges of common carriers, which was done in England as
long ago as the third year of the reign of William and Mary,
and continued until within a comparatively recent period. And
in the first statute we find the following suggestive preamble,
to wit:—

"And whereas divers wagoners and other carriers, by combination amongst themselves, have raised the prices of carriage of goods in many places to excessive rates, to the great
injury of the trade: Be it, therefore, enacted, . . ."

Common carriers exercise a sort of public office, and have
duties to perform in which the public is interested. . . . Their
business is, therefore, "affected with a public interest," within
the meaning of the doctrine which Lord Hale has so forcibly
stated.

But we need not go further. Enough has already been said
to show that, when private property is devoted to a public
use, it is subject to public regulation. It remains only to ascertain whether the warehouses of these plaintiffs in error, and
the business which is carried on there, come within the operation of this principle.

For this purpose we accept as true the statements of fact
contained in the elaborate brief of one of the counsel of the
plaintiffs in error. . . .

In this connection it must also be borne in mind that, although in 1874 there were in Chicago fourteen warehouses
adapted to this particular business, and owned by about thirty
persons, nine business firms controlled them, and that the
prices charged and received for storage were such "as have
been from year to year agreed upon and established by the
different elevators or warehouses in the city of Chicago, and

which rates have been annually published in one or more newspapers printed in said city, in the month of January in each year, as the established rates for the year then next ensuing such publication." Thus it is apparent that all the elevating facilities through which these vast productions "of seven or eight great States of the West" must pass on the way "to four or five of the States on the sea-shore" may be a "virtual" monopoly.

Under such circumstances it is difficult to see why, if the common carrier, or the miller, or the ferryman, or the innkeeper, or the wharfinger, or the baker, or the cartman, or the hackney-coachman, pursues a public employment and exercises "a sort of public office," these plaintiffs in error do not. They stand, to use again the language of their counsel, in the very "gateway of commerce," and take toll from all who pass. Their business most certainly "tends to a common charge, and is become a thing of public interest and use." . . . Certainly, if any business can be clothed "with a public interest and cease to be *juris privati* only," this has been. It may not be made so by the operation of the Constitution of Illinois or this statute, but it is by the facts. . . .

. . . For our purposes we must assume that, if a state of facts could exist that would justify such legislation, it actually did exist when the statute now under consideration was passed. For us the question is one of power, not of expediency. If no state of circumstances could justify such a statute, then we may declare this one void, because in excess of the legislative power of the State. But if it could, we must presume it did. Of the propriety of legislative interference within the scope of legislative power, the legislature is the exclusive judge.

Neither is it a matter of any moment that no precedent can be found for a statute precisely like this. It is conceded that the business is one of recent origin, that its growth has been rapid, and that it is already of great importance. And it must also be conceded that it is a business in which the whole public has a direct and positive interest. It presents, therefore, a case for the application of a long-known and well-established principle in social science, and this statute simply extends the law so as to meet this new development of commercial progress. There is no attempt to compel these owners to grant the public an interest in their property, but to declare their obligations, if they use it in this particular manner.

It matters not in this case that these plaintiffs in error had built their warehouses and established their business before the regulations complained of were adopted. What they did was from the beginning subject to the power of the body politic to require them to conform to such regulations as might be established by the proper authorities for the common good. They entered upon their business and provided themselves with the means to carry it on subject to this condition. If they did not wish to submit themselves to such interference, they should not have clothed the public with an interest in their concerns. The same principle applies to them that does to the proprietor of a hackney-carriage, and as to him it has never been supposed that he was exempt from regulating statutes or ordinances because he had purchased his horses and carriage and established his business before the statute or the ordinance was adopted.

It is insisted, however, that the owner of property is entitled to a reasonable compensation for its use, even though it be clothed with a public interest, and that what is reasonable is a judicial and not a legislative question.

As has already been shown, the practice has been otherwise. In countries where the common law prevails, it has been customary from time immemorial for the legislature to declare what shall be a reasonable compensation under such circumstances, or, perhaps more properly speaking, to fix a maximum beyond which any charge made would be unreasonable. Undoubtedly, in mere private contracts, relating to matters in which the public has no interest, what is reasonable must be ascertained judicially. But this is because the legislature has no control over such a contract. So, too, in matters which do affect the public interest, and as to which legislative control may be exercised, . . . the courts must determine what is reasonable. The controlling fact is the power to regulate at all.

If that exists, the right to establish the maximum of charge, as one of the means of regulation, is implied. . . .

We know that this is a power which may be abused; but that is no argument against its existence. For protection against abuses by legislatures the people must resort to the polls, not to the courts. . . .

We come now to consider the effect upon this statute of the power of Congress to regulate commerce.

. . . The warehouses of these plaintiffs in error are situated and their business carried on exclusively within the limits of the State of Illinois. They are used as instruments by those engaged in State as well as those engaged in inter-state commerce. . . . Incidentally they may become connected with inter-state commerce, but not necessarily so. Their regulation is a thing of domestic concern and, certainly, until Congress acts in reference to their inter-state relations, the State may exercise all the powers of government over them, even though in so doing it may indirectly operate upon commerce outside its immediate jurisdiction. . . .

Judgment affirmed.

Mr. Justice Field and Mr. Justice Strong dissented.

Mr. Justice Field. I am compelled to dissent from the decision of the court in this case, and from the reasons upon which that decision is founded. The principle upon which the opinion of the majority proceeds is, in my judgment, subversive of the rights of private property, heretofore believed to be protected by constitutional guaranties against legislative interference, and is in conflict with the authorities cited in its support.

The defendants had constructed their warehouse and elevator in 1862 with their own means, upon ground leased by them for that purpose, and from that time until the filing of the information against them had transacted the business of receiving and storing grain for hire. The rates of storage charged by them were annually established by arrangement with the owners of different elevators in Chicago, and were published in the month of January. In 1870 the State of Illinois adopted a new constitution, and by it "all elevators or storehouses where grain or other property is stored for a compensation, whether the property stored be kept separate or not, are declared to be public warehouses."

In April, 1871, the legislature of the State passed an act to regulate these warehouses, thus declared to be public, and the warehousing and inspection of grain, and to give effect to this article of the Constitution. By that act public warehouses, as defined in the Constitution, were divided into three classes, the first of which embraced all warehouses, elevators, or granaries located in cities having not less than one hundred thousand inhabitants, in which grain was stored in bulk, and the grain of different owners was mixed together, or stored in such manner that the identity of different lots or parcels could not be accurately preserved. To this class the elevator of the defendants belonged. The act prescribed the maximum of charges which the proprietor, lessee, or manager of the warehouse was allowed to make for storage and handling of grain, including the cost of receiving and delivering it, for the first thirty days or any part thereof, and for each succeeding fifteen days or any part thereof; and it required him to procure from the Circuit Court of the county a license to transact business as a public warehouseman, and to give a bond to the people of the State in the penal sum of $10,000 for the faithful performance of his duty as such warehouseman of the first class, and for his full and unreserved compliance with all laws of the State in relation thereto. The license was made revocable by the Circuit Court upon a summary proceeding for any violation of such laws. And a penalty was imposed upon every person transacting business as a public warehouseman of the first class, without first procuring a license, or continuing in such business after his license had been revoked, of not less than $100 or more than $500 for each day on which the business was thus carried on. The court was also authorized to refuse for one year to renew the license, or to grant a new one to any person whose license had been revoked. The maximum of charges prescribed by the act for the receipt and storage of grain was different from that which the defendants had previously charged, and which had been agreed to by the owners of the grain. More extended periods of storage were required of them than they formerly gave for the same charges. What they formerly charged for the first twenty days of storage, the act allowed them to charge only for the first thirty days of storage; and what they formerly charged for each succeeding ten days after the first twenty, the act allowed them to charge only for each succeeding fifteen days after the first thirty. The defendants, deeming that they had a right to use their own property in such manner as they desired, not inconsistent with the equal right of others to a like use, and denying the power of the legislature to fix prices for the use of their property, and their services in connection with it, refused to comply with the act by taking out the license and giving the bond required, but continued to carry on the business and to charge for receiving and storing grain such prices as they had been accustomed to charge, and as had been agreed upon between them and the owners of the grain. For thus transacting their business without procuring a license, as required by the act, they were prosecuted and fined, and the judgment against them was affirmed by the Supreme Court of the State.

The question presented, therefore, is one of the greatest importance,—whether it is within the competency of a State to fix the compensation which an individual may receive for the use of his own property in his private business, and for his services in connection with it.

The declaration of the Constitution of 1870, that private buildings used for private purposes shall be deemed public institutions, does not make them so. The receipt and storage of grain in a building erected by private means for that purpose does not constitute the building a public warehouse. There is no magic in the language, though used by a constitutional convention, which can change a private business into a public one, or alter the character of the building in which the business is transacted. A tailor's or a shoemaker's shop would still retain its private character, even though the assembled wisdom of the State should declare, by organic act or legislative ordinance, that such a place was a public workshop, and that the workmen were public tailors or public shoemakers. One might as well attempt to change the nature of colors, by giving them a new designation. The defendants were no more public warehousemen, as justly observed by counsel, than the merchant who sells his merchandise to the public is a public merchant, or the blacksmith who shoes horses for the public is a public blacksmith; and it was a strange notion that by calling them so they would be brought under legislative control.

The Supreme Court of the State—divided, it is true, by three to two of its members—has held that this legislation was a legitimate exercise of State authority over private business; and the Supreme Court of the United States, two only of its members dissenting, has decided that there is nothing in the Constitution of the United States, or its recent amendments, which impugns its validity. It is, therefore, with diffidence I presume to question the soundness of the decision.

The validity of the legislation was, among other grounds, assailed in the State court as being in conflict with that provision of the State Constitution which declares that no person shall be deprived of life, liberty, or property without due process of law, and with that provision of the Fourteenth Amendment of the Federal Constitution which imposes a similar restriction upon the action of the State. The State court held, in substance, that the constitutional provision was not violated so long as the owner was not deprived of the title and possession of his property; and that it did not deny to the legislature the power to make all needful rules and regulations respecting the use and enjoyment of the property, referring, in support of the position, to instances of its action in prescribing the interest on money, in establishing and regulating public ferries and public mills, and fixing the compensation in the shape of tolls, and in delegating power to municipal bodies to regulate the charges of hackmen and draymen, and the weight and price of bread. In this court the legislation was also assailed on the same ground, our jurisdiction arising upon the clause of the Fourteenth Amendment, ordaining that no State shall deprive any person of life, liberty, or property without due process of law. But it would seem from its opinion that the court holds that property loses something of its private character when employed in such a way as to be generally useful. The doctrine declared is that property "becomes clothed with a public interest when used in a manner to make it of public consequence, and affect the community at large;" and from such clothing the right of the legislature is deduced to control the use of the property, and to determine the compensation which the owner may receive for it. When Sir Matthew Hale, and the sages of the law in his day, spoke of property as affected by a public interest, and ceasing from that cause to be *juris privati* solely, that is, ceasing to be held merely in private right, they referred to property dedicated by the owner to public uses, or to property the use of which was granted by the government, or in connection with which special privileges were conferred. Unless the property was thus dedicated, or some right bestowed by the government was held with the property, either by specific grant or by prescription of so long a time as to imply a grant originally, the property was not affected by any public interest so as to be taken out of the category of property held in private right. But it is not in any such sense that the terms "clothing property with a public interest" are used in this case. From the nature of the business under consideration—the storage of grain—which, in any sense in which the words can be used, is a private business, in which the public are interested only as they are interested in the storage of other products of the soil, or in articles of manufacture, it is clear that the court intended to declare that, whenever one devotes his property to a business which is useful to the public,—"affects the community at large,"—the legislature can regulate the compensation which the owner may receive for its use, and for his own services in connection with it. "When, therefore," says the court, "one devotes his property to a use in which the public has an interest, he, in effect, grants to the public an interest in that use, and must submit to be controlled by the public for the common good, to the extent of the interest he has thus created. He may withdraw his grant by discontinuing the use; but, so long as he maintains

the use, he must submit to the control." The building used by
the defendants was for the storage of grain: in such storage,
says the court, the public has an interest; therefore the defendants, by devoting the building to that storage, have granted
the public an interest in that use, and must submit to have
their compensation regulated by the legislature.

If this be sound law, if there be no protection, either in the
principles upon which our republican government is founded,
or in the prohibitions of the Constitution against such invasion
of private rights, all property and all business in the State are
held at the mercy of a majority of its legislature. The public
has no greater interest in the use of buildings for the storage
of grain than it has in the use of buildings for the residences
of families, nor, indeed, any thing like so great an interest;
and, according to the doctrine announced, the legislature may
fix the rent of all tenements used for residences, without reference to the cost of their erection. If the owner does not like
the rates prescribed, he may cease renting his houses. He has
granted to the public, says the court, an interest in the use of
the buildings, and "he may withdraw his grant by discontinuing the use; but, so long as he maintains the use, he must submit to the control." The public is interested in the manufacture of cotton, woollen, and silken fabrics, in the construction
of machinery, in the printing and publication of books and
periodicals, and in the making of utensils of every variety, useful and ornamental; indeed, there is hardly an enterprise or
business engaging the attention and labor of any considerable
portion of the community, in which the public has not an interest in the sense in which that term is used by the court in
its opinion; and the doctrine which allows the legislature to
interfere with and regulate the charges which the owners of
property thus employed shall make for its use, that is, the rates
at which all these different kinds of business shall be carried
on, has never before been asserted, so far as I am aware, by
any judicial tribunal in the United States.

The doctrine of the State court, that no one is deprived of
his property, within the meaning of the constitutional inhibition, so long as he retains its title and possession, and the doc-

trine of this court, that, whenever one's property is used in such a manner as to affect the community at large, it becomes by that fact clothed with a public interest, and ceases to be *juris privati* only, appear to me to destroy, for all useful purposes, the efficacy of the constitutional guaranty. All that is beneficial in property arises from its use, and the fruits of that use; and whatever deprives a person of them deprives him of all that is desirable or valuable in the title and possession. If the constitutional guaranty extends no further than to prevent a deprivation of title and possession, and allows a deprivation of use, and the fruits of that use, it does not merit the encomiums it has received. Unless I have misread the history of the provision now incorporated into all our State constitutions, and by the Fifth and Fourteenth Amendments into our Federal Constitution, and have misunderstood the interpretation it has received, it is not thus limited in its scope, and thus impotent for good. It has a much more extended operation than either court, State, or Federal has given to it. The provision, it is to be observed, places property under the same protection as life and liberty. Except by due process of law, no State can deprive any person of either. The provision has been supposed to secure to every individual the essential conditions for the pursuit of happiness; and for that reason has not been heretofore, and should never be, construed in any narrow or restricted sense.

No State "shall deprive any person of life, liberty, or property without due process of law," says the Fourteenth Amendment to the Constitution. By the term "life," as here used, something more is meant than mere animal existence. The inhibition against its deprivation extends to all those limbs and faculties by which life is enjoyed. The provision equally prohibits the mutilation of the body by the amputation of an arm or leg, or the putting out of an eye, or the destruction of any other organ of the body through which the soul communicates with the outer world. The deprivation not only of life, but of whatever God has given to every one with life, for its growth and enjoyment, is prohibited by the provision in question, if its efficacy be not frittered away by judicial decision.

By the term "liberty," as used in the provision, something more is meant than mere freedom from physical restraint or the bounds of a prison. It means freedom to go where one may choose, and to act in such manner, not inconsistent with the equal rights of others, as his judgment may dictate for the promotion of his happiness; that is, to pursue such callings and avocations as may be most suitable to develop his capacities, and give to them their highest enjoyment.

The same liberal construction which is required for the protection of life and liberty, in all particulars in which life and liberty are of any value, should be applied to the protection of private property. If the legislature of a State, under pretence of providing for the public good, or for any other reason, can determine, against the consent of the owner, the uses to which private property shall be devoted, or the prices which the owner shall receive for its uses, it can deprive him of the property as completely as by a special act for its confiscation or destruction. If, for instance, the owner is prohibited from using his building for the purposes for which it was designed, it is of little consequence that he is permitted to retain the title and possession; or, if he is compelled to take as compensation for its use less than the expenses to which he is subjected by its ownership, he is, for all practical purposes, deprived of the property, as effectually as if the legislature had ordered his forcible dispossession. If it be admitted that the legislature has any control over the compensation, the extent of that compensation becomes a mere matter of legislative discretion. The amount fixed will operate as a partial destruction of the value of the property, if it fall below the amount which the owner would obtain by contract, and, practically, as a complete destruction, if it be less than the cost of retaining its possession. There is, indeed, no protection of any value under the constitutional provision, which does not extend to the use and income of the property, as well as to its title and possession.

This court has heretofore held in many instances that a constitutional provision intended for the protection of rights of private property should be liberally construed. It has so held in the numerous cases where it has been called upon to give effect to the provision prohibiting the States from legislation impairing the obligation of contracts; the provision being construed to secure from direct attack not only the contract itself, but all the essential incidents which give it value and enable its owner to enforce it. . . .

The power of the State over the property of the citizen under the constitutional guaranty is well defined. The State may take his property for public uses, upon just compensation being made therefor. It may take a portion of his property by way of taxation for the support of the government. It may control the use and possession of his property, so far as may be necessary for the protection of the rights of others, and to secure to them the equal use and enjoyment of their property. The doctrine that each one must so use his own as not to injure his neighbor—*sic utere tuo ut alienum non lædas*—is the rule by which every member of society must possess and enjoy his property; and all legislation essential to secure this common and equal enjoyment is a legitimate exercise of State authority. Except in cases where property may be destroyed to arrest a conflagration or the ravages of pestilence, or be taken under the pressure of an immediate and overwhelming necessity to prevent a public calamity, the power of the State over the property of the citizen does not extend beyond such limits.

It is true that the legislation which secures to all protection in their rights, and the equal use and enjoyment of their property, embraces an almost infinite variety of subjects. Whatever affects the peace, good order, morals, and health of the community, comes within its scope; and every one must use and enjoy his property subject to the restrictions which such legislation imposes. What is termed the police power of the State, which, from the language often used respecting it, one would suppose to be an undefined and irresponsible element in government, can only interfere with the conduct of individuals in their intercourse with each other, and in the use of their property, so far as may be required to secure these objects. The compensation which the owners of property, not having any special rights or privileges from the government in connection with it, may demand for its use, or for their own services in union with it, forms no element of consideration in prescribing regulations for that purpose. If one construct a building in a city, the State, or the municipality exercising a delegated power from the State, may require its walls to be of sufficient thickness for the uses intended; it may forbid the employment of inflammable materials in its construction, so as not to endanger the safety of his neighbors; if designed as a theatre, church, or public hall, it may prescribe ample means of egress, so as to afford facility for escape in case of accident; it may forbid the storage in it of powder, nitro-glycerine, or other explosive material; it may require its occupants daily to remove decayed vegetable and animal matter, which would otherwise accumulate and engender disease; it may exclude from it all occupations and business calculated to disturb the neighborhood or infect the air. Indeed, there is no end of regulations with respect to the use of property which may not be legitimately prescribed, having for their object the peace, good order, safety, and health of the community, thus securing to all the equal enjoyment of their property; but in establishing these regulations it is evident that compensation to the owner for the use of his property, or for his services in union with it, is not a matter of any importance: whether it be one sum or another does not affect the regulation, either in respect to its utility or mode of enforcement. One may go, in like manner, through the whole round of regulations authorized by legislation, State or municipal, under what is termed the police power, and in no instance will he find that the compensation of the owner for the use of his property has any influence in establishing them. It is only where some right or privilege is conferred by the government or municipality upon the owner, which he can use in connection with his property, or by means of which the use of his property is rendered more valuable to him, or he thereby enjoys an advantage over others, that the compensation to be received by him becomes a legitimate matter of regulation. Submission to the regulation of compensation in such cases is an implied condition of the grant, and the State, in exercising its power of prescribing the compensation, only determines the conditions upon which its concession shall be enjoyed. When the privilege ends, the power of regulation ceases. . . .

The citations show what I have already stated to be the case, that the regulations which the State, in the exercise of its police power, authorizes with respect to the use of property are entirely independent of any question of compensation for such use, or for the services of the owner in connection with it.

There is nothing in the character of the business of the defendants as warehousemen which called for the interference complained of in this case. Their buildings are not nuisances; their occupation of receiving and storing grain infringes upon no rights of others, disturbs no neighborhood, infects not the air, and in no respect prevents others from using and enjoying their property as to them may seem best. The legislation in question is nothing less than a bold assertion of absolute power by the State to control at its discretion the property and business of the citizen, and fix the compensation he shall receive. The will of the legislature is made the condition upon which the owner shall receive the fruits of his property and the just reward of his labor, industry, and enterprise. "That government," says Story, "can scarcely be deemed to be free where the rights of property are left solely dependent upon the will of a legislative body without any restraint. The fundamental maxims of a free government seem to require that the rights of personal liberty and private property should be held sacred." *Wilkeson* v. *Leland,* 2 Pet. 657. The decision of the court in this case gives unrestrained license to legislative will.

The several instances mentioned by counsel in the argument, and by the court in its opinion, in which legislation has fixed the compensation which parties may receive for the use of their property and services, do not militate against the views I have expressed of the power of the State over the property of the citizen. They were mostly cases of public ferries, bridges, and turnpikes, of wharfingers, hackmen, and draymen, and of interest on money. In all these cases, except that of interest on money, which I shall presently notice, there was some special privilege granted by the State or municipality; and no one, I suppose, has ever contended that the State had not a right to prescribe the conditions upon which such privilege should be enjoyed. The State in such cases exercises no greater right than an individual may exercise over the use of his own property when leased or loaned to others. The conditions upon which the privilege shall be enjoyed being stated or implied in the legislation authorizing its grant, no right is, of course, impaired by their enforcement. The recipient of the privilege, in effect, stipulates to comply with the conditions. It matters not how limited the privilege conferred, its acceptance implies an assent to the regulation of its use and the compensation for it. The privilege which the hackman and drayman have to the use of stands on the public streets, not allowed to the ordinary coachman or laborer with teams, constitutes a sufficient warrant for the regulation of their fares. In the case of the warehousemen of Chicago, no right or privilege is conferred by the government upon them; and hence no assent of theirs can be alleged to justify any interference with their charges for the use of their property.

The quotations from the writings of Sir Matthew Hale, so far from supporting the positions of the court, do not recognize the interference of the government, even to the extent which I have admitted to be legitimate. They state merely that the franchise of a public ferry belongs to the king, and cannot be used by the subject except by license from him, or prescription time out of mind; and that when the subject has a public wharf by license from the king, or from having dedicated his private wharf to the public, as in the case of a street opened by him through his own land, he must allow the use of the wharf for reasonable and moderate charges. Thus, in the first quotation which is taken from his treatise *De Jure Maris*, Hale says that the king has "a right of franchise or privilege, that no man may set up a common ferry for all passengers without a prescription time out of mind or a charter from the king. He may make a ferry for his own use or the use of his family, but not for the common use of all the king's subjects passing that way; because it doth in consequent tend to a common charge, and is become a thing of public interest and use, and every man for his passage pays a toll, which is a common charge, and every ferry ought to be under a public regulation, viz., that it give attendance at due times, keep a boat in due order, and take but reasonable toll; for if he fail in these he is finable." Of course, one who obtains a license from the king to establish a public ferry, at which "every man for his passage pays a toll," must take it on condition that he charge only reasonable toll, and, indeed, subject to such regulations as the king may prescribe.

In the second quotation, which is taken from his treatise *De Portibus Maris*, Hale says:—

"A man, for his own private advantage, may, in a port or town, set up a wharf or crane, and may take what rates he and his customers can agree for cranage, wharfage, housellage, pesage; for he doth no more than is lawful for any man to do, viz., makes the most of his own. If the king or subject have a public wharf, unto which all persons that come to that port must come and unlade or lade their goods as for the purpose, because they are the wharves only licensed by the king, or because there is no other wharf in that port, as it may fall out where a port is newly erected, in that case there cannot be taken arbitrary and excessive duties for cranage, wharfage, pesage, &c.: neither can they be enhanced to an immoderate rate, but the duties must be reasonable and moderate, though settled by the king's license or charter. For now the wharf and crane and other conveniences are affected with a public interest, and they cease to be *juris privati* only; as if a man set out a street in new building on his own land, it is now no longer bare private interest, but is affected by the public interest."

The purport of which is, that if one have a public wharf, by license from the government or his own dedication, he must exact only reasonable compensation for its use. By its dedication to public use, a wharf is as much brought under the common-law rule of subjection to reasonable charges as it would be if originally established or licensed by the crown. All property dedicated to public use by an individual owner, as in the case of land for a park or street, falls at once, by force of the dedication, under the law governing property appropriated by the government for similar purposes.

I do not doubt the justice of the encomiums passed upon Sir Matthew Hale as a learned jurist of his day; but I am unable to perceive the pertinency of his observations upon public ferries and public wharves, found in his treatises on "The Rights of the Sea" and on "The Ports of the Sea," to the questions presented by the warehousing law of Illinois, undertaking to regulate the compensation received by the owners of private property, when that property is used for private purposes.

The principal authority cited in support of the ruling of the court is that of *Alnutt* v. *Inglis*, decided by the King's Bench, and reported in 12 East. But that case, so far from sustaining the ruling, establishes, in my judgment, the doctrine that every one has a right to charge for his property, or for its use, whatever he pleases, unless he enjoys in connection with it some right or privilege from the government not accorded to others; and even then it only decides what is above stated in the quotations from Sir Matthew Hale, that he must submit, so long as he retains the right or privilege, to reasonable rates. In that case, the London Dock Company, under certain acts of Parliament, possessed the exclusive right of receiving imported goods into their warehouses before the duties were paid; and the question was whether the company was bound to receive them for a reasonable reward, or whether it could arbitrarily fix its compensation. In deciding the case, the Chief Justice, Lord Ellenborough, said:—

"There is no doubt that the general principle is favored, both in law and justice, that every man may fix what price he pleases upon his own property, or the use of it; but if, for a particular purpose, the public have a right to resort to his premises and make use of them, and he have a monopoly in them for that purpose, if he will take the benefit of that monopoly, he must, as an equivalent, perform the duty attached to it on reasonable terms."

And, coming to the conclusion that the company's warehouses were invested with "the monopoly of a public privilege," he held that by law the company must confine itself to take reasonable rates; and added, that if the crown should thereafter think it advisable to extend the privilege more generally to other persons and places, so that the public would not be restrained from exercising a choice of warehouses for the purpose, the company might be enfranchised from the restriction which attached to a monopoly; but, so long as its warehouses were the only places which could be resorted to for that purpose, the company was bound to let the trade have the use of them for a reasonable hire and reward. The other judges of the court placed their concurrence in the decision upon the ground that the company possessed a legal monopoly of the business, having the only warehouses where goods imported could be lawfully received without previous payment of the duties. From this case it appears that it is only where some privilege in the bestowal of the government is enjoyed in connection with the property, that it is affected with a public interest in any proper sense of the terms. It is the public privilege conferred with the use of the property which creates the public interest in it.

In the case decided by the Supreme Court of Alabama, where a power granted to the city of Mobile to license bakers, and to regulate the weight and price of bread, was sustained so far as regulating the weight of the bread was concerned, no question was made as to the right to regulate the price. 3 Ala. 137. There is no doubt of the competency of the State to prescribe the weight of a loaf of bread, as it may declare what weight shall constitute a pound or a ton. But I deny the power of any legislature under our government to fix the price which one shall receive for his property of any kind. If the power can be exercised as to one article, it may as to all articles, and the prices of every thing, from a calico gown to a city mansion, may be the subject of legislative direction.

Other instances of a similar character may, no doubt, be cited of attempted legislative interference with the rights of property. The act of Congress of 1820, mentioned by the court, is one of them. There Congress undertook to confer upon the city of Washington power to regulate the rates of wharfage at private wharves, and the fees for sweeping chimneys. Until some authoritative adjudication is had upon these and similar provisions, I must adhere, notwithstanding the legislation, to my opinion, that those who own property have the right to fix the compensation at which they will allow its use, and that those who control services have a right to fix the compensation at which they will be rendered. The chimney-sweeps may, I think, safely claim all the compensation which they can obtain by bargain for their work. In the absence of any contract for property or services, the law allows only a reasonable price or compensation; but what is a reasonable price in any case will depend upon a variety of considerations, and is not a matter for legislative determination.

The practice of regulating by legislation the interest receivable for the use of money, when considered with reference to its origin, is only the assertion of a right of the government to control the extent to which a privilege granted by it may be exercised and enjoyed. By the ancient common law it was unlawful to take any money for the use of money: all who did so were called usurers, a term of great reproach, and were exposed to the censure of the church; and if, after the death of a person, it was discovered that he had been a usurer whilst living, his chattels were forfeited to the king, and his lands escheated to the lord of the fee. No action could be maintained on any promise to pay for the use of money, because of the unlawfulness of the contract. Whilst the common law thus condemned all usury, Parliament interfered, and made it lawful to take a limited amount of interest. It was not upon the theory that the legislature could arbitrarily fix the compensation which one could receive for the use of property, which, by the general law, was the subject of hire for compensation, that Parliament acted, but in order to confer a privilege which the common law denied. The reasons which led to this legislation originally have long since ceased to exist; and if the legislation is still persisted in, it is because a long acquiescence in the exercise of a power, especially when it was rightfully assumed in the first instance, is generally received as sufficient evidence of its continued lawfulness. 10 Bac. Abr. 264.*

There were also recognized in England, by the ancient common law, certain privileges as belonging to the lord of the manor, which grew out of the state of the country, the condition of the people, and the relation existing between him and his tenants under the feudal system. Among these was the right of the lord to compel a!l the tenants within his manor to grind their corn at his mill. No one, therefore, could set up a mill except by his license, or by the license of the crown, unless he claimed the right by prescription, which presupposed a grant from the lord or crown, and, of course, with such license went the right to regulate the tolls to be received. Woolrych on the Law of Waters, c. 6, of Mills. Hence originated the doctrine which at one time obtained generally in this country, that there could be no mill to grind corn for the public, without a grant or license from the public authorities. It is still, I believe, asserted in some States. This doctrine being recognized, all the rest followed. The right to control the toll accompanied the right to control the establishment of the mill.

It requires no comment to point out the radical differences between the cases of public mills and interest on money, and that of the warehouses in Chicago. No prerogative or privilege of the crown to establish warehouses was ever asserted at the common law. The business of a warehouseman was, at common law, a private business, and is so in its nature. It has no special privileges connected with it, nor did the law ever extend to it any greater protection than it extended to all other private business. No reason can be assigned to justify legislation interfering with the legitimate profits of that business, that would not equally justify an intermeddling with the business

---

* The statute of 13 Eliz. c. 8, which allows ten per cent interest, recites "that all usury, being forbidden by the law of God, is sin, and detestable;" and the statute of 21 James the First, reducing the rate to eight per cent, provided that nothing in the law should be "construed to allow the practice of usury in point of religion or conscience,"—a clause introduced, it is said, to satisfy the bishops, who would not vote for the bill without it.

of every man in the community, so soon, at least, as his business became generally useful.

I am of opinion that the judgment of the Supreme Court of Illinois should be reversed.

10

INTERSTATE COMMERCE COMMISSION
First Annual Report (1887)

THE ACT TO REGULATE COMMERCE

. . . The leading features of the act are the following:

All charges made for services by carriers subject to the act must be reasonable and just. Every unjust and unreasonable charge is prohibited and declared to be unlawful.

The direct or indirect charging, demanding, collecting, or receiving, for any service rendered, a greater or less compensation from any one or more persons than from any other for a like and contemporaneous service, is declared to be unjust discrimination and is prohibited.

The giving of any undue or unreasonable preference, as between persons or localities, or kinds of traffic, or the subjecting any one of them to undue or unreasonable prejudice or disadvantage, is declared to be unlawful.

Reasonable, proper, and equal facilities for the interchange of traffic between lines, and for the receiving, forwarding, and delivering of passengers and property between connecting lines is required, and discrimination in rates and charges as between connecting lines is forbidden.

It is made unlawful to charge or receive any greater compensation in the aggregate for the transportation of passengers or the like kind of property under substantially similar circumstances and conditions for a shorter than for a longer distance over the same line in the same direction, the shorter being included within the longer distance.

Contracts, agreements, or combinations for the pooling of freights of different and competing railroads, or for dividing between them the aggregate or net earnings of such railroads or any portion thereof, are declared to be unlawful.

All carriers subject to the law are required to print their tariffs for the transportation of persons and property, and to keep them for public inspection at every depot or station on their roads. An advance in rates is not to be made until after ten days' public notice, but a reduction in rates may be made to take effect at once, the notice of the same being immediately and publicly given. The rates publicly notified are to be the maximum as well as the minimum charges which can be collected or received for the services respectively for which they purport to be established.

Copies of all tariffs are required to be filed with this Commission, which is also to be promptly notified of all changes that shall be made in the same. The joint tariffs of connecting roads are also required to be filed, and also copies of all contracts, agreements, or arrangements between carriers in relation to traffic affected by the act.

It is made unlawful for any carrier to enter into any combination, contract, or agreement, expressed or implied, to prevent, by change of time schedules, carriage in different cars, or by other means or devices, the carriage of freights from being continuous from the place of shipment to the place of destination. . . .

II.—THE LONG AND SHORT HAUL CLAUSE OF THE ACT

Another question presenting itself immediately on the organization of the Commission was that respecting the proper construction of the fourth section of the act, which, after providing

That it shall be unlawful for any common carrier subject to the provisions of this act to charge or receive any greater compensation in the aggregate for the transportation of passengers or of like kind of property, under substantially similar circumstances and conditions, for a shorter than for a longer distance over the same line, in the same direction, the shorter being included within the longer distance,

proceeds to say—

That, upon application to the Commission appointed under the provisions of this act, such common carrier may, in special cases, after investigation by the Commission, be authorized to charge less for longer than for shorter distances for the transportation of passengers or property, and the Commission may from time to time prescribe the extent to which such designated common carrier may be relieved from the operation of this section of this act.

The provision against charging more for the shorter than for the longer haul under the like circumstances and conditions over the same line and in the same direction, the shorter being included within the longer distance, is one of obvious justice and propriety. Indeed, unless one is familiar with the conditions of railroad traffic in sections of the country where the enactment of this provision is found to have its principal importance, he might not readily understand how it could be claimed that circumstances and conditions could be such as to justify the making of any exceptions to the general rule.

It is a part of the history of the act that one house of Congress was disposed to make the rule of the fourth section imperative and absolute, and it is likely that in some sections of the country many railroad managers would very willingly have conformed to it, because for the most part they could have done so without loss, and with very little disturbance to general business. But in some other parts of the country the immediate enforcement of an iron-clad rule would have worked changes so radical that many localities in their general interests, many great industries, as well as many railroads, would have found it impossible to conform without suffering very serious injury. In some cases probably the injury would have been overbalanced by a greater good; in others it would have been irremediable. To enforce it strictly would have been, in some of its consequences in particular cases, almost like establishing, as to vested interests, a new rule of property.

A study of the conditions under which railroad traffic in certain sections of the country has sprung up is necessary to an understanding of the difficulties which surround the subject. The territory bounded by the Ohio and the Potomac on the north and by the Mississippi on the west presented to the Commission an opportunity, and also an occasion, for such a study. The railroad business of that section has grown to be what it is in sharp competition with water carriers, who not only have had the ocean at their service, but by means of navigable streams were able to penetrate the interior in all directions. The carriers by water were first in the field, and were having a very thriving business while railroads were coming into existence; but when the roads were built the competition between them and the water-craft soon became sharp and close, and at the chief competing points the question speedily came to be, not what the service in transportation was worth, or even what it would cost to the party performing it, but at what charge for its service the one carrier or the other might obtain the business. In this competition the boat owners had great advantages: the capital invested in their business was much smaller; they were not restricted closely to one line, but could change from one to another as the exigencies of business might require; the cost of operation was less. But the railroads had an advantage in greater speed, which at some times, and in respect to some freight, was controlling.

In this competition of boat and railroad the rates of transportation which were directly controlled by it soon reached a point to which the railroads could not possibly have reduced all their tariffs and still maintain a profitable existence. They did not attempt such a reduction, but on the contrary, while reducing their rates at the points of water competition to any figures that should be necessary to enable them to obtain the freights, they kept them up at all other points to such figures as they deemed the service to be worth, or as they could obtain. It often happened, therefore, that the rates for transporting property over the whole length of a road to a terminus on a water highway would not exceed those for the transportation for half the distance only, to a way station not similarly favored with competition. The seeming injustice was excused on the plea of necessity. The rates to the terminus, it was said, were fixed by the competition and could not be advanced without abandoning the business to the boats. The greater rates to the local points were no more than was reasonable, and they were not by reason of the low rates to the competitive point made greater than they otherwise would have been. On the contrary, if the rates on the railroad were established on a mileage basis throughout, with no regard to special competitive forces at particular points, the effect in diminishing the volume of business would be so serious that local rates at non-competitive points would necessarily be advanced beyond what they are made when the competitive business can be taken also, even though the competitive business be taken at rates which leave little margin above the actual cost of movement. Such is the common argument advanced in support of the short-haul rates.

But the lower rates on the longer hauls have not been due altogether to water competition; railroad competition has been allowed to have a similar effect in reducing them. But as the railroad tariffs are commonly agreed upon between the parties making them, the necessity which controlled the water competition was not so apparent here, and to some extent the lower rates have been conceded to important towns in order to equalize advantages as between them and the other towns which were their rivals, and to which low rates had been given under a pressure of necessity. But they were given also in many cases as a means of building up a long-haul traffic that could not possibly bear the local rates, and which consequently would not exist at all if rates were established on a mileage basis, or on any basis which, as between the long and short haul traffic, undertook to preserve anything like relative equality.

It would be foreign to the purposes of this report to discuss at this time the question whether in this system of rate-making the evils or the advantages were most numerous and important. Some of the evils are obvious; not the least of which is the impossibility of making it apparent to those who have not considered the subject in all its bearings, that the greater charge for the shorter haul can in any case be just. The first impression necessarily is that it must be extortionate; and until that is removed it stands as an impeachment of the fairness and relative equity of railroad rates. But, on the other hand, it must be conceded that this method of making rates represents the best judgment of experts who have spent many years in solving the problems of railroad transportation; and its sudden termination without allowing opportunity for business to adapt itself to the change would, to some extent, check the prosperity of many important places, render unprofitable many thriving enterprises, and probably put an end to some long-haul traffic now usefully carried on between distant parts of the country. It is also quite clear that the more powerful corporations of the country, controlling the largest traffic and operating on the chief lines of trade through the most thickly settled districts, can conform to the statutory rule with much more ease and much less apparent danger of loss of income than can the weaker lines, whose business is comparatively light and perhaps admits of no dividends, and the pressure of whose fixed charges imposes a constant struggle to avoid bankruptcy.

If Congress intended this immediate change of system, it was not for the Commission to inquire whether the evils of making it at once would or would not exceed the benefits. The law must stand as the conclusive evidence of its own wisdom, and the authorities charged with enforcing it were not to question but to obey it. With the Commission, therefore, the first question was one of interpretation; and when it was clearly perceived what Congress intended, the line of duty was plain. The intent should be given effect, not only because it was enacted, but because in the enactment it was determined by the proper authority that the public good required it. . . .

XI.—REASONABLE CHARGES

Of the duties devolved upon the Commission by the act to regulate commerce, none is more perplexing and difficult than that of passing upon complaints made of rates as being unreasonable. The question of the reasonableness of rates involves so many considerations and is affected by so many circumstances and conditions which may at first blush seem foreign, that it is quite impossible to deal with it on purely mathematical principles, or on any principles whatever, without a consciousness that no conclusion which may be reached can by demonstration be shown to be absolutely correct. Some of the difficulties in the way have been indicated in what has been said on classification; and it has been shown that to take each class of freight by itself and measure the reasonableness of charges by reference to the cost of transporting that particular class, though it might seem abstractly just, would neither be practicable for the carriers nor consistent with the public interest.

The public interest is best served when the rates are so apportioned as to encourage the largest practicable exchange of products between different sections of our country and with foreign countries; and this can only be done by making value an important consideration, and by placing upon the higher classes of freight some share of the burden that on a relatively equal apportionment, if service alone were considered, would fall upon those of less value. With this method of arranging tariffs little fault is found, and perhaps none at all by persons who consider the subject from the stand-point of public interest. Indeed, in the complaints thus far made to the Commission little fault has been found with the principles on which tariffs for transportation of freight are professedly arranged, while applications of those principles in particular cases have been complained of frequently and very earnestly.

Among the reasons most frequently operating to cause complaints of rates may be mentioned:

The want of steadiness in rates.

The disproportion between the charges for long and those for short distances.

The great disparity between the charges made for transportation by roads differently circumstanced as to advantages.

The extremely low rates which are compelled by competition in some cases, and which may make rates which are not unreasonable seem, on comparison, extremely high.

Some others will be mentioned further on.

The want of steadiness in rates is commonly the fault of railroad managers, and may come from want of care in arranging their schedules, or from want of business foresight. But more often perhaps it grows out of disagreements between competing companies which when they become serious may result in wars of rates between them. Wars of rates, when mutual injury is the chief purpose in view, as is sometimes the case, are not only mischievous in their immediate effects upon the parties to them, and upon the business community whose calculations and plans must for a time be disturbed, but they have a permanently injurious influence upon the railroad service because of their effect upon the public mind. When railroad companies determine for themselves what their rates shall be, it is not unnatural for the public to infer that the lowest rates charged at any time are not below what can be afforded at all times, and that when these are advanced, the company is reaching out for extortionate profits.

Now, there are few important lines in the country that have not at some time in their history been carrying freight at prices that if long continued would cause bankruptcy. But to a large proportion of the public the fact that the rates were accepted was proof that they were reasonable; and when advanced rates are complained of, the complainants, to demonstrate their unreasonableness, go back to the war prices, and cite them as conclusive proof of what the companies then charging them can afford to accept. Many popular complaints have their origin in the ideas regarding rates which these wars have engendered or fed, and the evils of the controversies do not end when the controversies are over, but may continue to disturb the relations of railroad companies with their patrons for many years afterwards.

It may be truly said, also, that while railroad competition is to be protected, wars in railroad rates unrestrained by competitive principles are disturbers in every direction; if the community reaps a temporary advantage, it is one whose benefits are unequally distributed, and these are likely to be more than counterbalanced by the incidental unsettling of prices and interference with safe business calculations. The public authorities at the same time find that the task of regulation has been made more troublesome and difficult through the effect of war rates upon the public mind. These are consequences which result so inevitably from this species of warfare, that it would naturally be expected they would be kept constantly in mind by railroad managers. It is inevitable that the probability that any prescribed rates will be accepted by the public as just shall to some extent be affected by the fact that at some previous time they have been lower; perhaps considerably lower.

The disproportion between the rate charged and the distance the property is carried is also important in its effect upon the minds of those who have not the time or perhaps the opportunity to study the subject and understand the reasons. There are grounds on which short-haul traffic may be charged more in proportion to the distance of transportation than long-haul traffic, some of which any one would readily understand and appreciate. Thus, it is seen that a considerable proportion of the carrier's service is the same whether the transportation is for the short or for the long distance; there must be the same loading and unloading, the same number of papers and entries on books, and so on. It is also seen that short-haul traffic is more often taken up and laid down in small quantities, and that for this reason the proportionate train service is much greater.

But when all these considerations are taken into account it will still appear that the long-haul traffic is given an advantage in rates which must be accounted for on grounds which are not so readily apparent. When the reasons are seen it may perhaps appear that there is in fact no wrong either to the shippers who are apparently discriminated against, or to the general public.

It is not uncommon that in railroad freight service the rates for the transportation of a particular kind of property, instead of being regularly progressive, shall be found arranged on a system of grouping, whereby the charges to all points within a defined territory shall be the same, though the distances will vary. Thus, at the present time the rates which are made from New York to Chicago are also made from New York to all points within a territory about Chicago, which includes some important towns in western Indiana and western Michigan. A question might be made by such towns whether grouping them with Chicago and making them pay the same rates is just; but the grouping system in general departs so little from the distance proportions that it is seldom the ground of complaint.

There are cases, however, in which the distance proportions are purposely disregarded, and the doing so is justified by the managers on the negative ground that no one is wronged by it, and on the affirmative ground that the public is benefited. Cases of the sort may perhaps be found about all our large cities in which the railroads, as to some particular agricultural production needed for daily consumption in the city, have gradually extended the area from which they would receive and transport it at the lowest rates, until they may be found carrying the article at the same price for 100 miles as for 20. The low rate for the long distance has extended the area of production and benefited the city; and it is possible to conceive of cases in which the opposite course, of taking distance into the account in all rate making, would have kept production so far restricted in territory that producers near the city could never have been given as low rates as they receive now, when they are charged the same as their more distant competitors. Where such a case appears, the failure to measure the charges from regard to distance could not dogmatically be pronounced unjust, if it appeared that the railroad on the one side, and the public on the other, was benefited by the course actually adopted. But to increase the rates to the nearer producers, or even to keep them at a point which, though fair in the first place, has in the course of events become unreasonably high, in order to be able to put those at a distance on an equal footing in the market with such nearer producers, would be manifestly unjust. Not even on grounds of general public advantage do we understand that this would be justified; for public benefits, when they are to be had at the cost of individual citizens, can not rightfully, nor we suppose lawfully, be assessed on one class of the people exclusively.

The great disparity in the charges of different roads for the transportation of the same kind of property is a prolific cause of complaint, sometimes justly founded and sometimes not. It is apparent sometimes, in the complaints which are made to the Commission, that the parties complaining hold the opinion, or at least have an impression, that the cost of transporting a particular species of property is substantially the same on all roads, and that consequently the charges made by one road may prove with tolerable certainty that the higher charges made by another road are unjust. If the circumstances and conditions under which the traffic is carried by the two roads are substantially the same, the comparison would be legitimate and the argument from it of very great force. But when any such comparison is made, there are some circumstances having an important bearing upon rates which can not be left out of view. Among these may be specified:

The length of haul.—A thousand tons of wheat can be loaded, transported a thousand miles, and delivered much more cheaply in proportion to distance than the same quantity can be loaded, transported one hundred miles, and delivered.

The quantity hauled.—A train load of coal can be transported more cheaply in proportion to quantity than a single car load, and a car load more cheaply than a hundred pounds. So if the business is large, though it be the transportation of many kinds of property, it can be done relatively more cheaply than if it were small.

Return freights.—If lumber or other property in quantity is to be delivered at points where there will be return loads for the same cars, the delivery can be made much more cheaply than at points where return freights could not be expected. *Cost of moving trains.*—This is very much less on some roads than on others by reason of lighter grades, cheaper fuel, less liability to obstruction from storms, and other causes which may disturb the track or delay trains.

These are among the causes which have an important bearing on relative rates. Beyond these the relative cost of roads must be allowed force also, if the owners are to be permitted to charge such rates as will make their investments remunerative. A complaint that rates are unreasonable may therefore require for its proper adjudication a careful inquiry not only into the circumstances and conditions of the road which makes them and of the traffic upon it, but also into those of other roads whose lower rates are supposed by comparison to show the injustice of the rates complained of.

But there are reasons which make it necessary, in adjudicating a case of alleged excessive rates, to consider rates on other lines or at other points, even when the complaining party makes no argument or draws no conclusion from them. Questions of rates on one line or at one point can not be considered by themselves exclusively; a change in them may affect the rates in a considerable part of the country. Rates from the interior to New York necessarily have close relation to rates from the same points to Philadelphia, Boston, and Baltimore; rates from the sea-board to Toledo must have a similar relation to those from the sea-board to Detroit and other towns whose business men compete with those of Toledo in a common territory. Just rates are always relative; the act itself provides for its being so when it forbids unjust discrimination as between localities. This prohibition may sometimes give to competition an effect upon rates beyond what it would have if the competitive forces alone were considered.

The Commission has had occasion, where a railroad company operated lines which run parallel to each other, to hold that if the company yielded to competitive forces so far as to give the towns on one line very low rates, the effect of such low rates upon the business of rival towns on the other line could not be ignored when their rates came under consideration. The natural influence of just competitive forces ought to be allowed as it would be as between two lines owned by different companies; and if the rates on one line were made very low because of competition, keeping the others high because the absence of competition enabled it to be done might amount, within the meaning of the law, to unjust discrimination. Consolidation of rival lines, or the bringing them under the same management, cannot justify ignoring on one line the effect of competitive forces on the other; those forces always, when not unnaturally restrained, have an influence which reaches beyond the points whose business is controlled by it, and by secondary effect modifies prices to more distant points. This is well understood in the transportation business; the modifying effect of rates by lake and canal is perceived in the charges on all lines from the Mississippi to the sea-board; the rates to and from Duluth affect all charges in the Northwest to and from Chicago. Any arrangement by consolidation or otherwise that should undertake to eliminate this influence would, if made on a large scale, be futile, because it would antagonize laws of trade and communication which would be too powerful for it, and on a small scale, affecting particular towns or small districts, it might be illegal from its manifest inequality or injustice.

Competition.—A study of the act to regulate commerce has satisfied the members of the Commission that it was intended in its passage to preserve for the people the benefits of competition as between the several transportation lines of the country. If that shall be done the towns which have great natural advantages, or advantages acquired by large expenditures of money in establishing new thoroughfares of commerce, will have cheaper rates than can ordinarily be obtained by towns less favorably situated. New York with its noble harbor, its central location, the Hudson River, and the Erie Canal for interior water-ways, can not be deprived of the benefits which spring from these great natural and acquired advantages without altogether eliminating competition as a force in transportation charges, and by an exercise of sovereign legislative power establishing arbitrary rates over the whole country.

It might possibly be within the competency of legislative power to prescribe for the several interstate railroads equal mileage rates for the whole country; but this, if enforced, would put an end to competition as a factor in making rates, and to a very large extent deprive the great business centers of the country of their several natural advantages, and also of the benefit of expenditures made by them in creating for themselves new channels of trade. It would, in fact, work a revolution in the business of the country, which, though it might be greatly beneficial in some directions, would be fearfully destructive in others. Congress has not by the existing legislation undertaken to inaugurate such a revolution; nothing in the act to regulate commerce looks in that direction, unless it be the prohibition to charge more for a shorter than for a longer haul on the same line in the same direction, the shorter being included in the longer distance. But that prohibition is not absolute, and if it were, a strict enforcement would necessarily be at the expense of the competitive centers which have heretofore had the exceptionally low rates. The rates have made them centers for a valuable wholesale trade which they cannot expect to retain permanently in its entirety if they are deprived even in part of the advantages which they have hitherto had from the competition of rival carriers. The benefit which non-competitive points receive must be largely at the expense of the competitive. This is one of the inevitable consequences of perfecting the reform in the direction of basing rates upon distance more than has been the case hitherto. It is an incidental disadvantage to some which is supposed to be more than made up by the more equal apportionment of transportation benefits.

The competition by water is the most important factor in forcing rates to a low level at the points where the lines of land and water transportation intersect. Where there are good channels of water transportation, the cost of moving traffic upon it is so very greatly below the cost of rail transportation that the railroads would scarcely be able to compete at all if rapidity of transit were not in most cases a matter of such importance that it enables the railroads to demand and obtain higher rates than are made by boat. But even when compensated for the extra speed, the rates which the roads can obtain in competition with the natural water-ways must be extremely low and in some cases leave little if any margin for profit. The experience of the country has demonstrated that the artificial waterways can not be successful competitors with the railroads on equal terms. If the effort is to make the business upon them pay the cost of their maintenance and a fair return upon the capital invested in them, its futility must soon appear. The railroads long since deprived the great canals of Ohio, Indiana, and Illinois of nearly all their importance, and the Erie Canal is only maintained as a great channel of trade by the liberality of the State of New York in making its use free; the State thus taking upon itself a large share of the cost of transportation which would be assessed upon the property carried if the canal were owned and held for the profit of operation as the railroads are.

In their competitive struggles with each other towns can not ignore the effect which the existence of natural waterways must have upon railroad tariffs; the railroad companies can not ignore it, nor can the Commission ignore it if competition is still to exist and be allowed its force according to natural laws. Neither can the great free Erie Canal be ignored; it influences the rates to New York more than any other one cause, and indirectly, through its influence upon the rates to New York, it influences those to all other sea-board cities, and indeed to all that section of the country.

Other considerations bearing upon the reasonableness of rates might be mentioned, but enough has been said to show the difficulty of the task which the law has cast upon the Commission, and the impossibility that that task shall be so performed as to give satisfaction to all complaints. The question of rates, as has already been shown, is often quite as much a question between rival interests and localities as between the railroads and any one or more of such localities or interests; but while each strives to secure such rates as will most benefit itself, the Commission must look beyond the parties complaining and complained of, and make its decisions on a survey of the whole field, that either directly or indirectly, will be affected by them.

The act to regulate commerce has now been in operation nearly eight months. One immediate effect was to cause inconvenience in many quarters, and even yet the business of some parts of the country is not fully adjusted to it. Some carriers also are not as yet in their operations conforming in all respects to its spirit and purpose. Nevertheless the Commission feels justified in saying that the operation of the act has in general been beneficial. In some particulars, as we understand has also been the case with similar statutes in some of the States, it has operated directly to increase railroad earnings, especially in the cutting off of free passes on interstate passenger traffic, and in putting an end to rebates, drawbacks, and special rates upon freight business. The results of the law in these respects are also eminently satisfactory to the general public, certainly to all who had not been wont to profit by special or personal advantages. In connection with the abolition of the pass system, there has been some reduction in passenger fares, especially in the charge made for mileage tickets in the Northwest, the section of the country where they are perhaps most employed.

Freight traffic for the year has been exceptionally large in volume and is believed to have been in no small degree stimulated by a growing confidence that the days of rebates and special rates were ended, and that open rates on an equal basis were now offered to all comers. The reflex action of this development of confidence among business men has been highly favorable to the roads.

In some localities the passage of the act was made the occasion on the part of dissatisfied and short-sighted railroad managers for new exactions, through a direct raising of rates, by change in classification and otherwise. The manifestation of the spirit which induced such action is not but seldom observed, and the wrongs resulting from it have in general been corrected. The effect of the operation of the fourth section has been specially described above, and the Commission repeats in this place its opinion that, however serious may have been the results in some cases, the general effect has been beneficial. The changes in classification made since the act took effect have been in the direction of greater uniformity, and have also in general, it is believed, been concessions to business interests.

The tendency of rates has been downward, and they have seldom been permanently advanced except when excessive competition had reduced them to points at which they could not well be maintained. No destructive rate wars have occurred, but increased stability in rates has tended in the direction of stability in general business. There is still, however, great mischief resulting from frequent changes in freight rates on the part of some companies; changes that in some cases it is difficult to suggest excuse for.

The general results of the law have been in important ways favorable to both the roads and the public; while the comparatively few complaints that have been heard of its results are either made with imperfect knowledge of the facts, or spring from the remembrance of practices which the law was deliberately framed to put an end to. . . .

F. Antitrust Policy

The inconvenient absence from the federal statute books of any law against monopolies became more noticeable than ever during the 1880s, when a great wave of industrial mergers began and a number of industries, following the example of the Standard Oil Company, organized themselves as "Trusts." Some of these encompassing organizations deliberately set out to reap the profits available to successful monopolists. Others merely wished to grow to a scale that would enable them to take advantage of steam power and electricity, of the wider markets available as a result of cheaper transportation and a growing population, or of large-scale industrial financing newly available through the New York Stock Exchange. Nevertheless, the public reaction to these new large firms was sharp enough to produce anti-monopoly laws in a number of states, and finally to evoke the Sherman Antitrust Law of 1890.

During the years immediately after 1890, the government began to prosecute trusts, not as vigorously as some would have liked and with mixed success. By 1900 the law had become a fairly forceful instrument, although this became clear to the public only after the government's victory in the *Northern Securities* case—popularly construed as President Theodore Roosevelt's defeat of J. P. Morgan. The case concerned a railroad combination organized by Morgan. Justice Harlan, sole dissenter in the *E. C. Knight* case, appeared as spokesman for the majority of the court; Justice Holmes was one of the four dissenters.

Despite victories such as the *Northern Securities* decision, there was still much feeling that the Sherman Act was very imperfect. It was regarded by some as too weak because, although it might eventually destroy a monopolistic growth, it could not be used to stop an incipient monopoly from growing up or a prospective one from using methods of competition that gave it unfair advantage. On the other hand, it was considered too powerful because it might be used against good trusts as well as bad ones and because it was said to keep businessmen in a perpetual state of nervous uncertainty.

At times both objections might be found on the lips of the same people, and the solution they proposed was to regulate rather than prohibit monopolistic organizations. Hearings held in 1912 before the Senate Committee on Interstate Commerce (12) took testimony from many witnesses, among them George Perkins, a partner of J. P. Morgan, and Louis Brandeis, a lawyer subsequently appointed to the Supreme Court. The spirit of the changes they and others proposed in their testimony was embodied in provisions of the Clayton Antitrust and Federal Trade Commission acts of 1914.

11

U. S. SUPREME COURT

Northern Securities Company vs. U. S. (14 March 1904)
[193 U.S. 197]

Opinion of the Court, delivered by Justice Harlan

This suit was brought by the United States against the Northern Securities Company, a corporation of New Jersey; the Great Northern Railway Company, a corporation of Minnesota; the Northern Pacific Railway Company, a corporation of Wisconsin; James J. Hill, a citizen of Minnesota; and William P. Clough, D. Willis James, John S. Kennedy, J. Pierpont Morgan, Robert Bacon, George F. Baker and Daniel S. Lamont, citizens of New York.

Its general object was to enforce, as against the defendants, the provisions of the statute of July 2, 1890, commonly known as the Anti-Trust Act, and entitled "An act to protect trade and commerce against unlawful restraints and monopolies." 26 Stat. 209. By the decree below the United States was given substantially the relief asked by it in the bill.

As the act is not very long, and as the determination of the particular questions arising in this case may require a consideration of the scope and meaning of most of its provisions, it is here given in full:

"SEC. 1. Every contract, combination in the form of trust or otherwise, or conspiracy, in restraint of trade or commerce among the several States, or with foreign nations, is hereby declared to be illegal. Every person who shall make any such contract or engage in any such combination or conspiracy, shall be deemed guilty of a misdemeanor, and, on conviction thereof, shall be punished by fine not exceeding five thousand dollars, or by imprisonment not exceeding one year, or by both said punishments, in the discretion of the court.

"SEC. 2. Every person who shall monopolize, or attempt to monopolize, or combine or conspire with any other person or persons, to monopolize any part of the trade or commerce among the several States, or with foreign nations, shall be deemed guilty of a misdemeanor, and, on conviction thereof, shall be punished by fine not exceeding five thousand dollars, or by imprisonment not exceeding one year, or by both said punishments, in the discretion of the court.

"SEC. 3. Every contract, combination in form of trust or otherwise, or conspiracy, in restraint of trade or commerce in any Territory of the United States or of the District of Columbia, or in restraint of trade or commerce between any such Territory and another, or between any such Territory or Territories and any State or States or the District of Columbia, or with foreign nations, is hereby declared illegal. Every person who shall make any such contract or engage in any such combination or conspiracy, shall be deemed guilty of a misdemeanor, and, on conviction thereof, shall be punished by fine not exceeding five thousand dollars, or by imprisonment not exceeding one year, or by both said punishments, in the discretion of the court.

"SEC. 4. The several Circuit Courts of the United States are hereby invested with jurisdiction to prevent and restrain violations of this act; and it shall be the duty of the several district attorneys of the United States, in their respective districts, under the direction of the Attorney-General, to institute proceedings in equity to prevent and restrain such violations. Such proceedings may be by way of petition setting forth the case and praying that such violation shall be enjoined or otherwise prohibited. When the parties complained of shall have been duly notified of such petition the court shall proceed, as soon as may be, to the hearing and determination of the case; and, pending such petition and before final decree, the court may at any time make such temporary restraining order or prohibition as shall be deemed just in the premises.

"SEC. 5. Whenever it shall appear to the court before which any proceeding under section four of this act may be pending, that the ends of justice require that other parties should be brought before the court, the court may cause them to be summoned, whether they reside in the district in which the court is held or not; and subpoenas to that end may be served in any district by the marshal thereof.

"SEC. 6. Any property owned under any contract or by any combination, or pursuant to any conspiracy (and being the subject thereof) mentioned in section one of this act, and being in the course of transportation from one State to another, or to a foreign country, shall be forfeited to the United States, and may be seized and condemned by like proceedings as those provided by law for the forfeiture, seizure, and condemnation of property imported into the United States contrary to law.

"SEC. 7. Any person who shall be injured in his business or property by any other person or corporation by reason of anything forbidden or declared to be unlawful by this act, may sue therefor in any Circuit Court of the United States in the district in which the defendant resides or is found, without respect to the amount in controversy, and shall recover three-fold the damages by him sustained, and the costs of suit, including a reasonable attorney's fee.

"SEC. 8. That the word 'person,' or 'persons,' wherever used in this act shall be deemed to include corporations and associations existing under or authorized by the laws of either the United States, the laws of any of the Territories, the laws of any State, or the laws of any foreign country."

Is the case as presented by the pleadings and the evidence one of a combination or a conspiracy in restraint of trade or commerce among the States, or with foreign states? Is it one in which the defendants are properly chargeable with monopolizing or attempting to monopolize any part of such trade or commerce? Let us see what are the facts disclosed by the record.

The Great Northern Railway Company and the Northern Pacific Railway Company owned, controlled and operated separate lines of railway—the former road extending from Superior, and from Duluth and St. Paul, to Everett, Seattle, and Portland, with a branch line to Helena; the latter, extending from Ashland, and from Duluth and St. Paul, to Helena, Spokane, Seattle, Tacoma and Portland. The two lines, main and branches, about 9,000 miles in length, were and are parallel and competing lines across the continent through the northern tier of States between the Great Lakes and the Pacific, and the two companies were engaged in active competition for freight and passenger traffic, each road connecting at its respective terminals with lines of railway, or with lake and river steamers, or with seagoing vessels.

Prior to 1893 the Northern Pacific system was owned or controlled and operated by the Northern Pacific Railroad Company, a corporation organized under certain acts and resolutions of Congress. That company becoming insolvent, its road and property passed into the hands of receivers appointed by courts of the United States. In advance of foreclosure and sale a majority of its bondholders made an arrangement with the Great Northern Railway Company for a virtual consolidation of the two systems, and for giving the practical control of the Northern Pacific to the Great Northern. That was the arrangement declared in *Pearsall* v. *Great Northern Railway Company*, 161 U.S. 646, to be illegal under the statutes of Minnesota which forbade any railroad corporation or the purchasers or managers of any corporation, to consolidate the stock, property or franchises of such corporation, or to lease or purchase the works or franchises of, or in any way control, other railroad corporations owning or having under their control parallel or competing lines. Gen. Laws, Minn. 1874, c. 29; ch. 1881.

Early in 1901 the Great Northern and Northern Pacific Railway companies, having in view the ultimate placing of their two systems under a common control, united in the purchase of the capital stock of the Chicago, Burlington and Quincy Railway Company, giving in payment, upon an agreed basis of exchange, the joint bonds of the Great Northern and Northern Pacific Railway companies, payable in twenty years from date, with interest at 4 per cent per annum. In this manner the two purchasing companies became the owners of $107,000,000 of the $112,000,000 total capital stock of the Chicago, Burlington and Quincy Railway Company, whose lines aggregated about 8,000 miles, and extended from St. Paul to Chicago and from St. Paul and Chicago to Quincy, Burlington, Des Moines, St. Louis, Kansas City, St. Joseph, Omaha, Lincoln, Denver, Cheyenne and Billings, where it connected with the Northern Pacific railroad. By this purchase of stock the Great Northern and Northern Pacific acquired full control of the Chicago, Burlington and Quincy main line and branches.

Prior to November 13, 1901, defendant Hill and associate stockholders of the Great Northern Railway Company, and defendant Morgan and associate stockholders of the Northern Pacific Railway Company, entered into a combination to form, under the laws of New Jersey, a *holding* corporation, to be called the Northern Securities Company, with a capital stock of $400,000,000, and to which company, in exchange for its own capital stock upon a certain basis and at a certain rate, was to be turned over the capital stock, or a controlling interest in the capital stock, of each of the constituent railway companies, with power in the holding corporation to vote such stock and in all respects to act as the owner thereof, and to do whatever it might deem necessary in aid of such railway companies to enhance the value of their stocks. In this manner the interests of individual stockholders in the property and franchises of the two independent and competing railway companies were to be converted into an interest in the property and franchises of the holding corporation. Thus, as stated in Article VI of the bill, "by making the stockholders of each system jointly interested in both systems, and by practically pooling the earnings of both for the benefit of the former stockholders of each, and by vesting the selection of the directors and officers of each system in a common body, to wit, the holding corporation, with not only the power but the duty to pursue a policy which would promote the interests, not of one system at the expense of the other, but of both at the expense of the public, all inducement for competition between the two systems was to be removed, a virtual consolidation effected, and a monopoly of the interstate and foreign commerce formerly carried on by the two systems as independent competitors established."

In pursuance of this combination and to effect its objects, the defendant, the Northern Securities Company, was organized November 13, 1901, under the laws of New Jersey.

Its certificate of incorporation stated that the objects for which the company was formed were: "1. To acquire by purchase, subscription or otherwise, and to hold as investment, any bonds or other securities or evidences of indebtedness, or any shares of capital stock created or issued by any other corporation or corporations, association or associations, of the State of New Jersey, or of any other State, Territory or country. 2. To purchase, hold, sell, assign, transfer, mortgage, pledge or otherwise dispose of any bonds or other securities or evidences of indebtedness created or issued by any other corporation or corporations, association or associations, of the State of New Jersey, or of any other State, Territory or country, and while owner thereof to exercise all the rights, powers and privileges of ownership. 3. To purchase, hold, sell, assign, transfer, mortgage, pledge or otherwise dispose of shares of the capital stock of any other corporation or corporations, association or associations, of the State of New Jersey, or of any other State, Territory or country, and while owner of such stock to exercise all the rights, powers and privileges of ownership, including the right to vote thereon. 4. To aid in any manner any corporation or association of which any bonds or other securities or evidences of indebtedness or stock are held by the corporation, and to do any acts or things designed to protect, preserve, improve or enhance the value of any such bonds or other securities or evidences of indebtedness or stock. 5. To acquire, own and hold such real and personal property as may be necessary or convenient for the transaction of its business."

It was declared in the certificate that the business or purpose of the corporation was from time to time to do any one or more of such acts and things, and that the corporation should have power to conduct its business in other States and in foreign countries, and to have one or more offices, and hold, purchase, mortgage and convey real and personal property, out of New Jersey.

The total authorized capital stock of the corporation was fixed at $400,000,000, divided into 4,000,000 shares of the par value of $100 each. The amount of the capital stock with which the corporation should commence business was fixed at $30,000. The duration of the corporation was to be perpetual.

This charter having been obtained, Hill and his associate stockholders of the Great Northern Railway Company, and Morgan and associate stockholders of the Northern Pacific Railway Company, assigned to the Securities Company a controlling amount of the capital stock of the respective constituent companies upon an agreed basis of exchange of the capital stock of the Securities Company for each share of the capital stock of the other companies.

In further pursuance of the combination, the Securities Company acquired additional stock of the defendant railway companies, issuing in lieu thereof its own stock upon the above basis, and, at the time of the bringing of this suit, held, as owner and proprietor, substantially all the capital stock of the Northern Pacific Railway Company, and, it is alleged, a controlling interest in the stock of the Great Northern Railway Company, "and is voting the same and is collecting the dividends thereon, and in all respects is acting as the owner thereof, in the organization, management and operation of said railway companies and in the receipt and control of their earnings."

No consideration whatever, the bill alleges, has existed or will exist, for the transfer of the stock of the defendant railway companies to the Northern Securities Company, other than the issue of the stock of the latter company for the purpose, after the manner, and upon the basis stated.

The Securities Company, the bill also alleges, was not organized in good faith to purchase and pay for the stocks of the Great Northern and Northern Pacific Railway companies, but solely "to incorporate the pooling of the stocks of said companies," and carry into effect the above combinations; that it is a mere depositary, custodian, holder or trustee of the stocks of the Great Northern and Northern Pacific Railway companies; that its shares of stock are but beneficial certificates against said railroad stocks to designate the interest of the holders in the pool; that it does not have and never had any capital to warrant such an operation; that its subscribed capital was but $30,000, and its authorized capital stock of $400,000,000 was just sufficient, when all issued, to represent and cover the exchange value of substantially the entire stock of the Great Northern and Northern Pacific Railway companies, upon the basis and at the rate agreed upon, which was about $122,-000,000 in excess of the combined capital stock of the two railway companies taken at par; and that, unless prevented, the Securities Company would acquire as owner and proprietor substantially all the capital stock of the Great Northern and Northern Pacific Railway companies, issuing in lieu thereof its own capital stock to the full extent of its authorized issue, of which, upon the agreed basis of exchange, the former stockholders of the Great Northern Railway Company have received or would receive and hold about fifty-five per cent, the balance going to the former stockholders of the Northern Pacific Railway Company.

The Government charges that if the combination was held

not to be in violation of the act of Congress, then all efforts of the National Government to preserve to the people the benefits of free competition among carriers engaged in interstate commerce will be wholly unavailing, and all transcontinental lines, indeed the entire railway systems of the country, may be absorbed, merged and consolidated, thus placing the public at the absolute mercy of the holding corporation.

The several defendants denied all the allegations of the bill imputing to them a purpose to evade the provisions of the act of Congress, or to form a combination or conspiracy having for its object either to restrain or to monopolize commerce or trade among the States or with foreign nations. They denied that any combination or conspiracy was formed in violation of the act.

In our judgment, the evidence fully sustains the material allegations of the bill, and shows a violation of the act of Congress, in so far as it declares illegal every combination or conspiracy in restraint of commerce among the several States and with foreign nations, and forbids attempts to monopolize such commerce or any part of it.

Summarizing the principal facts, it is indisputable upon this record that under the leadership of the defendants Hill and Morgan the stockholders of the Great Northern and Northern Pacific Railway corporations, having competing and substantially parallel lines from the Great Lakes and the Mississippi River to the Pacific Ocean at Puget Sound combined and conceived the scheme of organizing a corporation under the laws of New Jersey, which should *hold* the shares of the stock of the constituent companies, such shareholders, in lieu of their shares in those companies, to receive, upon an agreed basis of value, shares in the holding corporation; that pursuant to such combination the Northern Securities Company was organized as the holding corporation through which the scheme should be executed; and under that scheme such holding corporation has become the holder—more properly speaking, the custodian—of more than nine-tenths of the stock of the Northern Pacific, and more than three-fourths of the stock of the Great Northern, the stockholders of the companies who delivered their stock receiving upon the agreed basis shares of stock in the holding corporation. The stockholders of these two competing companies disappeared, as such, for the moment, but immediately reappeared as stockholders of the holding company which was thereafter to guard the interests of both sets of stockholders as a unit, and to manage, or cause to be managed, both lines of railroad as if held *in one ownership*. Necessarily by this combination or arrangement the holding company in the fullest sense dominates the situation in the interest of those who were stockholders of the constituent companies; as much so, for every practical purpose, as if it had been itself a railroad corporation which had built, owned, and operated both lines for the exclusive benefit of its stockholders. Necessarily, also, the constituent companies ceased, under such a combination, to be in active competition for trade and commerce along their respective lines, and have become, practically, one powerful consolidated corporation, by the name of a holding corporation the principal, if not the sole, object for the formation of which was to carry out the purpose of the original combination under which competition between the constituent companies would cease. Those who were stockholders of the Great Northern and Northern Pacific and became stockholders in the holding company are now interested in preventing all competition between the two lines, and as owners of stock or of certificates of stock in the holding company, they will see to it that no competition is tolerated. They will take care that no persons are chosen directors of the holding company who will permit competition between the constituent companies. The result of the combination is that all the earnings of the constituent companies make a common fund in the hands of the Northern Securities Company to be distributed, not upon the basis of the earnings of the respective constituent companies, each acting exclusively in its own interest, but upon the basis of the certificates of stock issued by the holding company. No scheme or device could more certainly come within the words of the act—"combination in the form of a trust or otherwise . . . in restraint of commerce among the several States or with foreign nations,"—or could more effectively and certainly suppress free competition between the constituent companies. This combination is, within the meaning of the act, a "trust;" but if not, it is a *combination in restraint of interstate and international commerce;* and that is enough to bring it under the condemnation of the act. The mere existence of such a combination and the power acquired by the holding company as its trustee, constitute a menace to, and a restraint upon, that freedom of commerce which Congress intended to recognize and protect, and which the public is entitled to have protected. If such combination be not destroyed, all the advantages that would naturally come to the public under the operation of the general laws of competition, as between the Great Northern and Northern Pacific Railway companies, will be lost, and the entire commerce of the immense territory in the northern part of the United States between the Great Lakes and the Pacific at Puget Sound will be at the mercy of a single holding corporation, organized in a State distant from the people of that territory.

The Circuit Court was undoubtedly right when it said—all the Judges of that court concurring—that the combination referred to "led inevitably to the following results: First, it placed the control of the two roads in the hands of a single person, to wit, the Securities Company, by virtue of its ownership of a large majority of the stock of both companies; second, it destroyed every motive for competition between two roads engaged in interstate traffic, which were natural competitors for business, by pooling the earnings of the two roads for the common benefit of the stockholders of both companies." 120 Fed. Rep. 721, 724.

Such being the case made by the record, what are the principles that must control the decision of the present case? Do former adjudications determine the controlling questions raised by the pleadings and proofs?

The contention of the Government is that, if regard be had to former adjudications, the present case must be determined in its favor. That view is contested and the defendants insist that a decision in their favor will not be inconsistent with anything heretofore decided and would be in harmony with the act of Congress.

Is the act to be construed as forbidding every combination or conspiracy in restraint of trade or commerce among the States or with foreign nations? Or, does it embrace only such restraints as are unreasonable in their nature? Is the motive with which a forbidden combination or conspiracy was formed at all material when it appears that the necessary tendency of the particular combination or conspiracy in question is to restrict or suppress free competition between competing railroads engaged in commerce among the States? Does the act of Congress prescribe, as a *rule* for *interstate* or *international* commerce, that the operation of the natural laws of competition between those engaged in *such* commerce shall not be restricted or interfered with by any contract, combination or conspiracy? How far may Congress go in regulating the affairs or conduct of state corporations engaged as carriers in commerce among the States or of state corporations which, although not directly engaged themselves in *such* commerce, yet have control of the business of interstate carriers? If state corporations, or their stockholders, are found to be parties to a combination, in the form of a trust or otherwise, which restrains interstate or international commerce, may they not be compelled to respect any rule for such commerce that may be lawfully prescribed by Congress?

These questions were earnestly discussed at the bar by able counsel, and have received the full consideration which their importance demands. . . .

We will not incumber this opinion by extended extracts from the former opinions of this court. It is sufficient to say that from the decisions in the above cases certain propositions are plainly deducible and embrace the present case. Those propositions are:

That although the act of Congress known as the Anti-Trust Act has no reference to the mere manufacture or production of articles or commodities within the limits of the several States, it does embrace and declare to be illegal every contract, combination or conspiracy, in whatever form, of whatever nature, and whoever may be parties to it, which directly or necessarily operates *in restraint* of trade or commerce *among the several States or with foreign nations;*

That the act is not limited to restraints of interstate and international trade or commerce that are unreasonable in their nature, but embraces *all* direct *restraints* imposed by any combination, conspiracy or monopoly upon such trade or commerce;

That railroad carriers engaged in interstate or international trade or commerce are embraced by the act;

That combinations even among *private* manufacturers or dealers whereby *interstate or international commerce* is restrained are equally embraced by the act;

That Congress has the power to establish *rules* by which *interstate and international* commerce shall be governed, and, by the Anti-Trust Act, has prescribed the rule of free competition among those engaged in such commerce;

That *every* combination or conspiracy which would extinguish competition between otherwise competing railoads engaged in *interstate trade or commerce,* and which would *in that way* restrain *such* trade or commerce, is made illegal by the act;

That the natural effect of competition is to increase commerce, and an agreement whose direct effect is to prevent this play of competition restrains instead of promotes trade and commerce;

That to vitiate a combination, such as the act of Congress condemns, it need not be shown that the combination, in fact, results or will result in a total suppression of trade or in a complete monopoly, but it is only essential to show that by its necessary operation it tends to restrain interstate or international trade or commerce or tends to create a monopoly in such trade or commerce and to deprive the public of the advantages that flow from free competition;

That the constitutional guarantee of liberty of contract does not prevent Congress from prescribing the rule of free competition for those engaged in *interstate and international* commerce; and,

That under its power to regulate commerce among the several States and with foreign nations, Congress had authority to enact the statute in question.

No one, we assume, will deny that these propositions were distinctly announced in the former decisions of this court. They cannot be ignored or their effect avoided by the intimation that the court indulged in *obiter dicta*. What was said in those cases was within the limits of the issues made by the parties. In our opinion, the recognition of the principles announced in former cases must, under the conceded facts, lead to an affirmance of the decree below, unless the special objections, or some of them, which have been made to the application of the act of Congress to the present case are of a substantial character. We will now consider those objections.

Underlying the argument in behalf of the defendants is the idea that as the Northern Securities Company is a state corporation, and as its acquisition of the stock of the Great Northern and Northern Pacific Railway companies is not inconsistent with the powers conferred by its charter, the enforcement of the act of Congress, as against those corporations, will be an unauthorized interference by the national government with the internal commerce of the States creating those corporations. This suggestion does not at all impress us. There is no reason to suppose that Congress had any purpose to interfere with the internal affairs of the States, nor, in our opinion, is there any ground whatever for the contention that the Anti-Trust Act regulates their domestic commerce. By its very terms the act regulates only commerce among the States and with foreign states. Viewed in that light, the act, if within the powers of Congress, must be respected; for, by the explicit words of the Constitution, that instrument and the laws enacted by Congress in pursuance of its provisions, are the supreme law of the land, "anything in the constitution or laws of any State to the contrary notwithstanding"—supreme over the States, over the courts, and even over the people of the United States, the source of all power under our governmental system in respect of the objects for which the National Government was ordained. An act of Congress constitutionally passed under its power to regulate commerce among the States and with foreign nations is binding upon all; as much so as if it were embodied, in terms, in the Constitution itself. Every judicial officer, whether of a national or a state court, is under the obligation of an oath so to regard a lawful enactment of Congress. Not even a State, still less one of its artificial creatures, can stand in the way of its enforcement. If it were otherwise, the Government and its laws might be prostrated at the feet of local authority. *Cohens* v. *Virginia,* 6 Wheat. 264, 385, 414. These views have been often expressed by this court.

It is said that whatever may be the power of a State over such subjects Congress cannot forbid single individuals from disposing of their stock in a state corporation, even if such corporation be engaged in interstate and international commerce; that the holding or purchase by a state corporation, or the purchase by individuals, of the stock of another corporation, for whatever purpose, are matters in respect of which Congress has no authority under the Constitution; that, so far as the power of Congress is concerned, citizens or state corporations may dispose of their property and invest their money in any way they choose; and that in regard to all such matters, citizens and state corporations are subject, if to any authority, only to the lawful authority of the State in which such citizens reside, or under whose laws such corporations are organized. It is unnecessary in this case to consider such abstract, general questions. The court need not now concern itself with them. They are not here to be examined and determined, and may well be left for consideration in some case necessarily involving their determination.

In this connection, it is suggested that the contention of the Government is that the acquisition and *ownership* of stock in a state railroad corporation is itself interstate commerce, if that corporation be engaged in interstate commerce. This suggestion is made in different ways, sometimes in express words, at other times by implication. For instance, it is said that the question here is whether the power of Congress over interstate commerce extends to the regulation of the ownership of the stock in state railroad companies, by reason of their being engaged in such commerce. Again, it is said that the only issue in this case is whether the Northern Securities Company can acquire and hold stock in other state corporations. Still further, it is asked, generally, whether the organization or ownership of railroads is not under the control of the States under whose laws they came into existence? Such statements as to the issues in this case are, we think, wholly unwarranted and are very wide of the mark; it is the setting up of mere men of straw to be easily stricken down. We do not understand that the Government makes any such contentions or takes any such positions as those statements imply. It does not contend that Congress may control the mere acquisition or the mere ownership of stock in a state corporation engaged in interstate commerce. Nor does it contend that Congress can control the organization of state corporations authorized by their charters to engage in interstate and international commerce. But it does contend that Congress may protect the freedom of interstate commerce by any means that are appropriate and that are lawful and not prohibited by the Constitution. It does contend that no state corporation can stand in the way of the enforcement of the national will, legally expressed. What the Government particularly complains of, indeed, all that it complains of here, is the existence of a combination among the stockholders of competing railroad companies which in violation of the act of Congress restrains interstate and international commerce through the agency of a common corporate trustee designated to act for both companies in repressing free competition between them. Independently of any question of the mere ownership of stock or of the organization of a state corporation, can it in reason be said that such a combination is not embraced by the very terms of the Anti-Trust Act? May not Congress declare that *combination* to be illegal? If Congress legislates for the protection of the public, may it not proceed on the ground that wrongs when effected by a powerful combination are more dangerous and require more stringent supervision than when they are to be effected by a single person? *Callan v. Wilson*, 127 U.S. 540, 556. How far may the courts go in order to give effect to the act of Congress, and remedy the evils it was designed by that act to suppress? These are confessedly questions of great moment, and they will now be considered.

By the express words of the Constitution, Congress has power to "regulate commerce with foreign nations and among the several States, and with the Indian tribes." In view of the numerous decisions of this court there ought not, at this day, to be any doubt as to the general scope of such power. In some circumstances regulation may properly take the form and have the effect of prohibition. *In re Rahrer*, 140 U.S. 545; *The Lottery Case*, 188 U.S. 321, 355, and authorities there cited. Again and again this court has reaffirmed the doctrine announced in the great judgment rendered by Chief Justice Marshall for the court in *Gibbons* v. *Ogden*, 9 Wheat. 1, 196, 197, that the power of Congress to regulate commerce among the States and with foreign nations is the power "to prescribe the *rule* by which commerce *is to be governed;*" that such power "is complete in itself, may be exercised to its utmost extent, and acknowledges no limitations other than are prescribed in the Constitution;" that "if, as has always been understood, the sovereignty of Congress, though limited to specified objects, is plenary as to those objects, the power over commerce with foreign nations and among the several States, is vested in Congress *as absolutely as it would be in a single government having in its constitution the same restrictions on the exercise of the power as are found in the Constitution of the United States;*" that a sound construction of the Constitution allows to Congress a large discretion, "with respect to the means by which the powers it confers are to be carried into execution, which enable that body to perform the high duties assigned to it, in the manner most beneficial to the people;" and that if the end to be accomplished is within the scope of the Constitution, "all means which are appropriate, which are plainly adapted to that end and which are not prohibited, are constitutional." *Brown* v. *Maryland*, 12 Wheat. 419; *Sinnot* v. *Davenport*, 22 How. 227, 238; *Henderson* v. *The Mayor*, 92 U.S. 259; *Railroad Company* v. *Husen*, 95 U.S. 465, 472; *County of Mobile* v. *Kimball*, 102 U.S. 691; *M., K. & Texas Ry. Co.* v. *Haber*, 169 U.S. 613, 626; *The Lottery Case*, 188

U.S. 321, 348. In *Cohens* v. *Virginia*, 6 Wheat. 264, 413, this court said that the United States were for many important purposes "a single nation," and that "in all commercial regulations we are one and the same people;" and it has since frequently declared that commerce among the several States was a *unit*, and subject to national control. Previously, in *McCulloch* v. *Maryland*, 4 Wheat. 316, 405, the court has said that the Government ordained and established by the Constitution was, within the limits of the powers granted to it, "the Government of all; its powers are delegated by all; it represents all, and acts for all," and was "supreme within its sphere of action." As late as the case of *In re Debs*, 158 U.S. 564, 582, this court, every member of it concurring, said: "The entire strength of the Nation may be used to enforce in any part of the land the full and free exercise of all National powers and the security of all rights entrusted by the Constitution to its care. The strong arm of the National Government may be put forth to brush away all obstructions to the freedom of interstate commerce or the transportation of the mails. If the emergency arises, the army of the Nation, and all its militia, are at the service of the Nation to compel obedience to its laws."

The means employed in respect of the combinations forbidden by the Anti-Trust Act, and which Congress deemed germane to the end to be accomplished, was to prescribe as *a rule* for *interstate and international* commerce, (not for domestic commerce,) that it should not be vexed by combinations, conspiracies or monopolies which restrain commerce by destroying or restricting competition. We say that Congress has prescribed such a rule, because in all the prior cases in this court the Anti-Trust Act has been construed as forbidding any combination which by its necessary operation destroys or restricts free competition among those engaged in interstate commerce; in other words, that to destroy or restrict free competition in interstate commerce was to restrain such commerce. Now, can this court say that such a rule is prohibited by the Constitution or is not one that Congress could appropriately prescribe when exerting its power under the commerce clause of the Constitution? Whether the free operation of the normal laws of competition is a wise and wholesome rule for trade and commerce is an economic question which this court need not consider or determine. Undoubtedly, there are those who think that the general business interests and prosperity of the country will be best promoted if the rule of competition is not applied. But there are others who believe that such a rule is more necessary in these days of enormous wealth than it ever was in any former period of our history. Be all this as it may, Congress has, in effect, recognized the rule of free competition by declaring illegal every combination or conspiracy in restraint of interstate and international commerce. As in the judgment of Congress the public convenience and the general welfare will be best subserved when the natural laws of competition are left undisturbed by those engaged in interstate commerce, and as Congress has embodied that rule in a statute, that must be, for all, the end of the matter, if this is to remain a government of laws, and not of men.

It is said that railroad corporations created under the laws of a State can only be consolidated with the authority of the State. Why that suggestion is made in this case we cannot understand, for there is no pretense that the combination here in question was under the authority of the States under whose laws these railroad corporations were created. But even if the State allowed consolidation it would not follow that the stockholders of two or more state railroad corporations, having *competing lines and engaged in interstate commerce,* could lawfully combine and form a distinct corporation to hold the stock of the constituent corporations, and, by destroying competition between them, in violation of the act of Congress, restrain commerce among the States and with foreign nations.

The rule of competition, prescribed by Congress, was not at all new in trade and commerce. And we cannot be in any doubt as to the reason that moved Congress to the incorporation of that rule into a statute. That reason was thus stated in *United States* v. *Joint Traffic Association:* "Has not Congress with regard to interstate commerce and in the course of regulating it, in the case of railroad corporations, the power to say that no contract or combination shall be legal which shall restrain trade and commerce by shutting out the operation of the general law of competition? We think it has. . . . It is the combination of these large and powerful corporations, covering vast sections of territory and influencing trade throughout the whole extent thereof, and acting *as one body* in all the matters over which the combination extends, that constitutes the alleged evil, and in regard to which, *so far as the combination operates upon and restrains interstate commerce*, Congress has power to legislate and to prohibit." (pp. 569, 571.) That such a rule was applied to interstate commerce should not have surprised any one. Indeed, when Congress declared contracts, combinations and conspiracies in restraint of trade or commerce to be illegal, it did nothing more than apply to interstate commerce a rule that had been long applied by the several States when dealing with combinations that were in restraint of their domestic commerce. The decisions in state courts upon this general subject are not only numerous and instructive but they show the circumstances under which the Anti-Trust Act was passed. It may well be assumed that Congress, when enacting that statute, shared the general apprehension that a few powerful corporations or combinations sought to obtain, and, unless restrained, would obtain such absolute control of the entire trade and commerce of the country as would be detrimental to the general welfare. . . .

The question of the relations of the General Government with the States is again presented by the specific contention of each defendant that Congress did not intend "to limit the power of the several States to create corporations, define their purposes, fix the amount of their capital, and determine who may buy, own and sell their stock." All that is true, generally speaking, but the contention falls far short of meeting the controlling questions in this case. To meet this contention we must repeat some things already said in this opinion. But if what we have said be sound, repetition will do no harm. So far as the Constitution of the United States is concerned, a State may, indeed, create a corporation, define its powers, prescribe the amount of its stock and the mode in which it may be transferred. It may even authorize one of its corporations to engage

in commerce of every kind; domestic, interstate and international. The regulation or control of purely domestic commerce of a State is, of course, with the State, and Congress has
no direct power over it so long as what is done by the State
does not interfere with the operations of the General Government, or any legal enactment of Congress. A State, if it chooses
so to do, may even submit to the existence of combinations
within its limits that restrain its internal trade. But neither a
state corporation nor its stockholders can, by reason of the
non-action of the State or by means of any combination among
such stockholders, interfere with the complete enforcement of
any rule lawfully devised by Congress for the conduct of commerce among the States or with foreign nations; for, as we have
seen, interstate and international commerce is by the Constitution under the control of Congress, and it belongs to the
legislative department of the Government to prescribe rules
for the conduct of that commerce. If it were otherwise, the
declaration in the Constitution of its supremacy, and of the
supremacy as well of the laws made in pursuance of its provisions, was a waste of words. Whilst every instrumentality of
domestic commerce is subject to state control, every instrumentality of interstate commerce may be reached and controlled
by national authority, *so far as to compel it to respect the
rules for such commerce lawfully established by Congress*. No
corporate person can excuse a departure from or violation of
that rule under the plea that that which it has done or omitted
to do is permitted or not forbidden by the State under whose
authority it came into existence. We repeat that no State can
endow any of its corporations, or any combination of its
citizens, with authority to restrain interstate or international
commerce, or to disobey the national will as manifested in
legal enactments of Congress. So long as Congress keeps within
the limits of its authority as defined by the Constitution, in-
fringing no rights recognized or secured by that instrument,
its regulations of interstate and international commerce,
whether founded in wisdom or not, must be submitted to by
all. Harm and only harm can come from the failure of the
courts to recognize this fundamental principle of constitutional

construction. To depart from it because of the circumstances of special cases, or because the rule, in its operation, may possibly affect the interests of business, is to endanger the safety and integrity of our institutions and make the Constitution mean not what it says but what interested parties wish it to mean at a particular time and under particular circumstances. The supremacy of the law is the foundation rock upon which our institutions rest. The law, this court said in *United States* v. *Lee*, 106 U.S. 196, 220, is the only supreme power in our system of government. And no higher duty rests upon this court than to enforce, by its decrees, the will of the legislative department of the Government, as expressed in a statute, unless such statute be plainly and unmistakably in violation of the Constitution. If the statute is beyond the constitutional power of Congress, the court would fail in the performance of a solemn duty if it did not so declare. But if nothing more can be said than that Congress has erred—and the court must not be understood as saying that it has or has not erred—the remedy for the error and the attendant mischief is the selection of new Senators and Representatives, who, by legislation, will make such changes in existing statutes, or adopt such new statutes, as may be demanded by their constituents and be consistent with law.

Many suggestions were made in argument based upon the thought that the Anti-Trust Act would in the end prove to be mischievous in its consequences. Disaster to business and widespread financial ruin, it has been intimated, will follow the execution of its provisions. Such predictions were made in all the cases heretofore arising under that act. But they have not been verified. It is the history of monopolies in this country and in England that predictions of ruin are habitually made by them when it is attempted, by legislation, to restrain their operations and to protect the public against their exactions. In this, as in former cases, they seek shelter behind the reserved rights of the States and even behind the constitutional guarantee of liberty of contract. But this court has heretofore adjudged that the act of Congress did not touch the rights of the States, and that liberty of contract did not involve a right to

deprive the public of the advantages of free competition in
trade and commerce. Liberty of contract does not imply liberty
in a corporation or individuals to defy the national will, when
legally expressed. Nor does the enforcement of a legal enactment of Congress infringe, in any proper sense, the general
inherent right of every one to acquire and hold property. That
right, like all other rights, must be exercised in subordination
to the law.

But even if the court shared the gloomy forebodings in
which the defendants indulge, it could not refuse to respect
the action of the legislative branch of the Government if what
it has done is within the limits of its constitutional power. The
suggestions of disaster to business have, we apprehend, their
origin in the zeal of parties who are opposed to the policy
underlying the act of Congress or are interested in the result
of this particular case; at any rate, the suggestions imply that
the court may and ought to refuse the enforcement of the
provisions of the act if, in its judgment, Congress was not wise
in prescribing as a rule by which the conduct of interstate and
international commerce is to be governed, that every combination, whatever its form, in restraint of such commerce and
the monopolizing or attempting to monopolize such commerce
shall be illegal. These, plainly, are questions as to the policy of
legislation which belong to another department, and this court
has no function to supervise such legislation from the stand-
point of wisdom or policy. We need only say that Congress
has authority to declare, and by the language of its act, as
interpreted in prior cases, has, in effect declared, that the freedom of interstate and international commerce shall not be
obstructed or disturbed by any combination, conspiracy or
monopoly that will restrain such commerce, by preventing the
free operation of competition among interstate carriers engaged in the transportation of passengers and freight. This
court cannot disregard that declaration unless Congress, in
passing the statute in question, be held to have transgressed
the limits prescribed for its action by the Constitution. But, as
already indicated, it cannot be so held consistently with the
provisions of that instrument.

The combination here in question may have been for the pecuniary benefit of those who formed or caused it to be formed. But the interests of private persons and corporations cannot be made paramount to the interests of the general public. Under the Articles of Confederation commerce among the original States was subject to vexatious and local regulations that took no account of the general welfare. But it was for the protection of the general interests, as involved in interstate and international commerce, that Congress, representing the whole country, was given by the Constitution full power to regulate commerce among the States and with foreign nations. . . .

Mr. Justice Holmes, with whom concurred the Chief Justice, Mr. Justice White, and Mr. Justice Peckham, dissenting.

I am unable to agree with the judgment of the majority of the court, and although I think it useless and undesirable, as a rule, to express dissent, I feel bound to do so in this case and to give my reasons for it.

Great cases like hard cases make bad law. For great cases are called great, not by reason of their real importance in shaping the law of the future, but because of some accident of immediate overwhelming interest which appeals to the feelings and distorts the judgment. These immediate interests exercise a kind of hydraulic pressure which makes what previously was clear seem doubtful, and before which even well settled principles of law will bend. What we have to do in this case is to find the meaning of some not very difficult words. We must try, I have tried, to do it with the same freedom of natural and spontaneous interpretation that one would be sure of if the same question arose upon an indictment for a similar act which excited no public attention, and was of importance only to a prisoner before the court. Furthermore, while at times judges need for their work the training of economists or statesmen, and must act in view of their foresight of consequences, yet when their task is to interpret and apply the words of a statute, their function is merely academic to begin with—to read English intelligently—and a consideration of consequences comes into play, if at all, only when the meaning of the words used is open to reasonable doubt.

The question to be decided is whether, under the act of July 2, 1890, c. 647, 26 Stat. 209, it is unlawful, at any stage of the process, if several men unite to form a corporation for the purpose of buying more than half the stock of each of two competing interstate railroad companies, if they form the corporation, and the corporation buys the stock. I will suppose further that every step is taken, from the beginning, with the single intent of ending competition between the companies. I make this addition not because it may not be and is not disputed but because, as I shall try to show, it is totally unimportant under any part of the statute with which we have to deal.

The statute of which we have to find the meaning is a criminal statute. The two sections on which the Government relies both make certain acts crimes. That is their immediate purpose and that is what they say. It is vain to insist that this is not a criminal proceeding. The words cannot be read one way in a suit which is to end in fine and imprisonment and another way in one which seeks an injunction. The construction which is adopted in this case must be adopted in one of the other sort. I am no friend of artificial interpretations because a statute is of one kind rather than another, but all agree that before a statute is to be taken to punish that which always has been lawful it must express its intent in clear words. So I say we must read the words before us as if the question were whether two small exporting grocers should go to jail.

Again the statute is of a very sweeping and general character. It hits "every" contract or combination of the prohibited sort, great or small, and "every" person who shall monopolize or attempt to monopolize, in the sense of the act, "any part" of the trade or commerce among the several States. There is a natural inclination to assume that it was directed against certain great combinations and to read it in that light. It does not say so. On the contrary, it says "every," and "any part." Still less was it directed specially against railroads. There even was a reasonable doubt whether it included railroads until the point was decided by this court.

Finally, the statute must be construed in such a way as not merely to save its constitutionality but, so far as is consistent with a fair interpretation, not to raise grave doubts on that score. I assume, for the purposes of discussion, although it would be a great and serious step to take, that in some case that seemed to it to need heroic measures, Congress might regulate not only commerce, but instruments of commerce or contracts the bearing of which upon commerce would be only indirect. But it is clear that the mere fact of an indirect effect upon commerce not shown to be certain and very great, would not justify such a law. The point decided in *United States* v. *E. C. Knight Co.*, 156 U.S. 1, 17, was that "the fact that trade or commerce might be indirectly affected was not enough to entitle complainants to a decree." Commerce depends upon population, but Congress could not, on that ground, undertake to regulate marriage and divorce. If the act before us is to be carried out according to what seems to me the logic of the argument for the Government, which I do not believe that it will be, I can see no part of the conduct of life with which on similar principles Congress might not interfere.

This act is construed by the Government to affect the purchasers of shares in two railroad companies because of the effect it may have, or, if you like, is certain to have, upon the competition of these roads. If such a remote result of the exercise of an ordinary incident of property and personal freedom is enough to make that exercise unlawful, there is hardly any transaction concerning commerce between the States that may not be made a crime by the finding of a jury or a court. The personal ascendency of one man may be such that it would give to his advice the effect of a command, if he owned but a single share in each road. The tendency of his presence in the stockholders' meetings might be certain to prevent competition, and thus his advice, if not his mere existence, become a crime.

I state these general considerations as matters which I should have to take into account before I could agree to affirm

the decree appealed from, but I do not need them for my
own opinion, because when I read the act I cannot feel sufficient doubt as to the meaning of the words to need to fortify
my conclusion by any generalities. Their meaning seems to me
plain on their face.

The first section makes "Every contract, combination in the
form of trust or otherwise, or conspiracy in restraint of trade
or commerce among the several States, or with foreign nations" a misdemeanor, punishable by fine, imprisonment or
both. Much trouble is made by substituting other phrases assumed to be equivalent, which then are reasoned from as if
they were in the act. The court below argued as if maintaining
competition were the expressed object of the act. The act says
nothing about competition. I stick to the exact words used.
The words hit two classes of cases, and only two—Contracts in
restraint of trade and combinations or conspiracies in restraint
of trade, and we have to consider what these respectively are.
Contracts in restraint of trade are dealt with and defined by
the common law. They are contracts with a stranger to the
contractor's business, (although in some cases carrying on a
similar one,) which wholly or partially restrict the freedom of
the contractor in carrying on that business as otherwise he
would. The objection of the common law to them was primarily on the contractor's own account. The notion of monopoly
did not come in unless the contract covered the whole of England. *Mitchel* v. *Reynolds*, 1 P. Wms. 181. Of course this objection did not apply to partnerships or other forms, if there
were any, of substituting a community of interest where there
had been competition. There was no objection to such combinations merely as in restraint of trade, or otherwise unless
they amounted to a monopoly. Contracts in restraint of trade,
I repeat, were contracts with strangers to the contractor's business, and the trade restrained was the contractor's own.

Combinations or conspiracies in restraint of trade, on the
other hand, were combinations to keep strangers to the agreement out of the business. The objection to them was not an
objection to their effect upon the parties making the contract,
the members of the combination or firm, but an objection to

their intended effect upon strangers to the firm and their supposed consequent effect upon the public at large. In other words, they were regarded as contrary to public policy because they monopolized or attempted to monopolize some portion of the trade or commerce of the realm. See *United States v. E. C. Knight Co.*, 156 U.S. 1. All that is added to the first section by §2 is that like penalties are imposed upon every single person who, without combination, monopolizes or attempts to monopolize commerce among the States; and that the liability is extended to attempting to monopolize any part of such trade or commerce. It is more important as an aid to the construction of §1 than it is on its own account. It shows that whatever is criminal when done by way of combination is equally criminal if done by a single man. That I am right in my interpretation of the words of §1 is shown by the words "in the form of trust or otherwise." The prohibition was suggested by the trusts, the objection to which, as every one knows, was not the union of former competitors, but the sinister power exercised or supposed to be exercised by the combination in keeping rivals out of the business and ruining those who already were in. It was the ferocious extreme of competition with others, not the cessation of competition among the partners, that was the evil feared. Further proof is to be found in §7, giving an action to any person injured in his business or property by the forbidden conduct. This cannot refer to the parties to the agreement and plainly means that outsiders who are injured in their attempt to compete with a trust or other similar combination may recover for it. *Montague & Co. v. Lowry*, 193 U.S. 38. How effective the section may be or how far it goes, is not material to my point. My general summary of the two classes of cases which the act affects is confirmed by the title, which is "An Act to protect Trade and Commerce against unlawful Restraints and Monopolies."

What I now ask is under which of the foregoing classes this case is supposed to come, and that question must be answered as definitely and precisely as if we were dealing with the indictments which logically ought to follow this decision. The provision of the statute against contracts in restraint of trade has been held to apply to contracts between railroads, otherwise remaining independent, by which they restricted their respective freedom as to rates. This restriction by contract with a stranger to the contractor's business is the ground of the decision in *United States* v. *Joint Traffic Association*, 171 U.S. 505, following and affirming *United States* v. *Trans-Missouri Freight Association*, 166 U.S. 290. I accept those decisions absolutely, not only as binding upon me, but as decisions which I have no desire to criticise or abridge. But the provision has not been decided, and, it seems to me, could not be decided without perversion of plain language, to apply to an arrangement by which competition is ended through community of interest—an arrangement which leaves the parties without external restriction. That provision, taken alone, does not require that all existing competitions shall be maintained. It does not look primarily, if at all, to competition. It simply requires that a party's freedom in trade between the States shall not be cut down by contract with a stranger. So far as that phrase goes, it is lawful to abolish competition by any form of union. It would seem to me impossible to say that the words "every contract in restraint of trade is a crime punishable with imprisonment," would send the members of a partnership between, or a consolidation of, two trading corporations to prison—still more impossible to say that it forbade one man or corporation to purchase as much stock as he liked in both. Yet those words would have that effect if this clause of §1 applies to the defendants here. For it cannot be too carefully remembered that that clause applies to "every" contract of the forbidden kind—a consideration which was the turning point of the Trans-Missouri Freight Association's case.

If the statute applies to this case it must be because the parties, or some of them, have formed, or because the Northern Securities Company is, a combination in restraint of trade among the States, or, what comes to the same thing in my opinion, because the defendants, or some or one of them, are monopolizing or attempting to monopolize some part of the commerce between the States. But the mere reading of those words shows that they are used in a limited and accurate sense.

According to popular speech, every concern monopolizes whatever business it does, and if that business is trade between two States it monopolizes a part of the trade among the States. Of course the statute does not forbid that. It does not mean that all business must cease. A single railroad down a narrow valley or through a mountain gorge monopolizes all the railroad transportation through that valley or gorge. Indeed every railroad monopolizes, in a popular sense, the trade of some area. Yet I suppose no one would say that the statute forbids a combination of men into a corporation to build and run such a railroad between the States.

I assume that the Minnesota charter of the Great Northern and the Wisconsin charter of the Northern Pacific both are valid. Suppose that, before either road was built, Minnesota, as part of a system of transportation between the States, had created a railroad company authorized singly to build all the lines in the States now actually built, owned or controlled by either of the two existing companies. I take it that that charter would have been just as good as the present one, even if the statutes which we are considering had been in force. In whatever sense it would have created a monopoly the present charter does. It would have been a large one, but the act of Congress makes no discrimination according to size. Size has nothing to do with the matter. A monopoly of "any part" of commerce among the States is unlawful. The supposed company would have owned lines that might have been competing—probably the present one does. But the act of Congress will not be construed to mean the universal disintegration of society into single men, each at war with all the rest, or even the prevention of all further combinations for a common end.

There is a natural feeling that somehow or other the statute meant to strike at combinations great enough to cause just anxiety on the part of those who love their country more than money, while it viewed such little ones as I have supposed with just indifference. This notion, it may be said, somehow breathes from the pores of the act, although it seems to be contradicted in every way by the words in detail. And it has occurred to me that it might be that when a combination reached a certain size it might have attributed to it more of the character of a monopoly merely by virtue of its size than would be attributed to a smaller one. I am quite clear that it is only in connection with monopolies that size could play any part. But my answer has been indicated already. In the first place size in the case of railroads is an inevitable incident and if it were an objection under the act, the Great Northern and the Northern Pacific already were too great and encountered the law. In the next place in the case of railroads it is evident that the size of the combination is reached for other ends than those which would make them monopolies. The combinations are not formed for the purpose of excluding others from the field. Finally, even a small railroad will have the same tendency to exclude others from its narrow area that great ones have to exclude others from a greater one, and the statute attacks the small monopolies as well as the great. The very words of the act make such a distinction impossible in this case and it has not been attempted in express terms.

If the charter which I have imagined above would have been good notwithstanding the monopoly, in a popular sense, which it created, one next is led to ask whether and why a combination or consolidation of existing roads, although in actual competition, into one company of exactly the same powers and extent, would be any more obnoxious to the law. Although it was decided in *Louisville & Nashville Railroad Co.* v. *Kentucky,* 161 U.S. 677, 701, that since the statute, as before, the States have the power to regulate the matter, it was said, in the argument, that such a consolidation would be unlawful, and it seems to me that the Attorney General was compelled to say so in order to maintain his case. But I think that logic would not let him stop there, or short of denying the power of a State at the present time to authorize one company to construct and own two parallel lines that might compete. The monopoly would be the same as if the roads were consolidated after they had begun to compete—and it is on the footing of monopoly that I now am supposing the objection made. But to meet the objection to the prevention of competition at the same time, I will suppose that three parties apply to a State

for charters; one for each of two new and possibly competing lines respectively, and one for both of these lines, and
that the charter is granted to the last. I think that charter
would be good, and I think the whole argument to the contrary rests on a popular instead of an accurate and legal conception of what the word "monopolize" in the statute means.
I repeat, that in my opinion there is no attempt to monopolize,
and what, as I have said, in my judgment amounts to the same
thing, that there is no combination in restraint of trade, until
something is done with the intent to exclude strangers to the
combination from competing with it in some part of the business which it carries on.

Unless I am entirely wrong in my understanding of what a
"combination in restraint of trade" means, then the same
monopoly may be attempted and effected by an individual,
and is made equally illegal in that case by §2. But I do not
expect to hear it maintained that Mr. Morgan could be sent
to prison for buying as many shares as he liked of the Great
Northern and the Northern Pacific, even if he bought them
both at the same time and got more than half the stock of each
road.

There is much that was mentioned in argument which I
pass by. But in view of the great importance attached by both
sides to the supposed attempt to suppress competition, I must
say a word more about that. I said at the outset that I should
assume, and I do assume, that one purpose of the purchase was
to suppress competition between the two roads. I appreciate
the force of the argument that there are independent stockholders in each; that it cannot be presumed that the respective
boards of directors will propose any illegal act; that if they
should they could be restrained, and that all that has been
done as yet is too remote from the illegal result to be classed
even as an attempt. Not every act done in furtherance of an
unlawful end is an attempt or contrary to the law. There must
be a certain nearness to the result. It is a question of proximity
and degree. *Commonwealth* v. *Peaslee,* 177 Massachusetts,
267, 272. So, as I have said, is the amenability of acts in
furtherance of interference with commerce among the States

to legislation by Congress. So, according to the intimation of this court, is the question of liability under the present statute. *Hopkins* v. *United States*, 171 U.S. 578; *Anderson* v. *United States*, 171 U.S. 604. But I assume further, for the purposes of discussion, that what has been done is near enough to the result to fall under the law, if the law prohibits that result, although that assumption very nearly if not quite contradicts the decision in *United States* v. *E. C. Knight Co.*, 156 U.S. 1. But I say that the law does not prohibit the result. If it does it must be because there is some further meaning than I have yet discovered in the words "combinations in restraint of trade." I think that I have exhausted the meaning of those words in what I already have said. But they certainly do not require all existing competitions to be kept on foot, and, on the principle of the Trans-Missouri Freight Association's case, invalidate the continuance of old contracts by which former competitors united in the past.

A partnership is not a contract or combination in restraint of trade between the partners unless the well known words are to be given a new meaning invented for the purposes of this act. It is true that the suppression of competition was referred to in *United States* v. *Trans-Missouri Freight Association*, 166 U.S. 290, but, as I have said, that was in connection with a contract with a stranger to the defendant's business— a true contract in restraint of trade. To suppress competition in that way is one thing, to suppress it by fusion is another. The law, I repeat, says nothing about competition, and only prevents its suppression by contracts or combinations in restraint of trade, and such contracts or combinations derive their character as restraining trade from other features than the suppression of competition alone. To see whether I am wrong, the illustrations put in the argument are of use. If I am, then a partnership between two stage drivers who had been competitors in driving across a state line, or two merchants once engaged in rival commerce among the States, whether made after or before the act, if now continued, is a crime. For, again I repeat, if the restraint on the freedom of the members of a combination caused by their entering into partnership is a restraint of trade, every such combination, as well the small as the great, is within the act.

In view of my interpretation of the statute I do not go further into the question of the power of Congress. That has been dealt with by my brother White and I concur in the main with his views. I am happy to know that only a minority of my brethren adopt an interpretation of the law which in my opinion would make eternal the *bellum omnium contra omnes* and disintegrate society so far as it could into individual atoms. If that were its intent I should regard calling such a law a regulation of commerce as a mere pretense. It would be an attempt to reconstruct society. I am not concerned with the wisdom of such an attempt, but I believe that Congress was not entrusted by the Constitution with the power to make it and I am deeply persuaded that it has not tried.

I am authorized to say that the Chief Justice, Mr. Justice White and Mr. Justice Peckham concur in this dissent.

12

SENATE COMMITTEE ON INTERSTATE COMMERCE

Hearings (1912)

[62 Cong., Hearing . . . pursuant to S. Res. 98, pp. 1173 ff.]

TESTIMONY OF LOUIS D. BRANDEIS

Senator Cummins: What regulations that will restrict competition within reasonable limits do you suggest?

Mr. Brandeis: I think this might be a very brief statement of some of the practices which ought to be deemed in and of themselves unreasonable, and therefore illegal, if connected with the restraint of trade: Selling in one locality at discriminating prices in order to force out local competition; selling one grade or variety at discriminating prices to force out competition; discriminating against producers who will not agree not to deal with a rival; imposing terms in leases that the lessees shall not buy or lease anything from anyone else; spying on competitors; bribing methods; buying trade secrets; establishing bogus competition.

I think practices of that nature, which are all what might be called methods of destruction, and are not properly called competition at all, ought to be made impossible.

Senator Cummins: We have acquired the term "in restraint of trade," which we have been told many times, both here and from the decisions of the Supreme Court, is based upon the common law. Of course you recognize that some of those things were not known in the common law as restraint of trade. Now, your idea is that we ought to, say, enlarge upon the common law so as to make these things which experience has shown are opposed to the public welfare restraint of trade, and thereby bring them within the prohibition of the antitrust law.

Mr. Brandeis: Yes; if it is necessary to do that. That is, I have no hesitation in saying that those practices are not proper practices for business; and it is clear to me that if they are exercised in connection with any restraint of trade they ought to be conclusively accepted as evidence of illegality or unreasonableness, as the court expresses it.

Senator Cummins: There are some of us who hesitate—and I am one—to accept the idea that there can be any reasonable restraint of trade. I can easily imagine a restraint upon competition that is not a restraint upon trade; but if the given thing is in restraint of trade, which means of course that freedom of commerce which is necessary for the public good, then it ought to be illegal, and I take it that your general notion is that, viewed from the standpoint of our experience in modern times, we ought to make the words "restraint of trade" mean what the people of this country believe they ought to mean in order to accomplish their own welfare.

Mr. Brandeis: That is my belief, decidedly.

Senator Cummins: I think that is all.

Senator Newlands: Mr. Brandeis, what limit would you place upon the size of corporations?

Mr. Brandeis: I should not think that we are in a position to-day to fix a limit, stated in millions of dollars, but I think we are in a position, after the experience of the last 20 years, to state two things: In the first place, that a corporation may well be too large to be the most efficient instrument of production and of distribution, and, in the second place, whether it has exceeded the point of greatest economic efficiency or not, it may be too large to be tolerated among the people who desire to be free. I think, therefore, that the recognition of those propositions should underlie any administration of the law. As I stated before, I believe that it was a very serious mistake on the part of our legislators to remove the limit of the assets and of capitalization of corporations; that they did not fully consider what they were doing. I believe it is historically true that that limit was removed without serious consideration by the legislators of the country of the probable effect of their action.

Senator Newlands: Do you think it would be in the power of the United States Government, by act of Congress, to limit the size of State corporations engaged in interstate commerce, either in point of size, capitalization, or area of their operations?

Mr. Brandeis: I do not suppose it would be constitutional in one sense to limit their size, but I suppose Congress would possess the constitutional power to confine the privilege of interstate commerce to corporations of a particular character.

Senator Newlands: You have no question about that power?

Mr. Brandeis: I should think not.

Senator Newlands: It would be necessary to fix some standard, would it not?

Mr. Brandeis: I think so; yes, sir.

Senator Newlands: Upon which or by which the administrative bureau or commission charged with the duty could determine whether the corporation was of a size that threatened to become a monopoly or that threatened, as you say, social efficiency. Now, what standard would you fix; how would you phrase it?

Mr. Brandeis: I do not think that I am able at this time to state the exact provision which I should make. I feel very clear on the proposition, but I do not feel equally clear as to what machinery should be invoked or the specific provision by which that proposition could be enforced.

Senator Newlands: You do not think that standard should be fixed in dollars; you have already stated that.

Mr. Brandeis: I am very clear that the maximum limit could not be properly fixed in dollars, because what would be just enough for one business would be far too much for many others.

Senator Newlands: Then, if it is not fixed in dollars, would it not be necessary to fix it in respect to the area of the operations, the proportion of the business, or of the industry which the corporation would be likely to absorb?

Mr. Brandeis: There is embodied some such suggestion in the La Follette bill. It seems to me that probably this goes rather to the volume of business than to capitalization, but the more I have thought of the subject in connection with the tobacco disintegration, in which case I acted as counsel and investigated trade facts, it seems to me that there is a distinct peril in the community in having one organization control a very large percentage of the market. The La Follette bill provides that where there is found to be a combination in restraint of trade, if the combination controls 40 per cent or more of the market, that creates a presumption of unreasonableness. I am inclined to think that an inquiry into our experience of the last 20 years would justify making of that presumption irrefutable, and that no corporation ought to control so large a percentage if we desire to maintain competition at all. I found, for instance, in the tobacco company this situation—and it was one of the many objections to the plan of so-called disintegration—that the American Tobacco Co. in various departments were controlling about 40 per cent or over of the American business. We found there that in this way the American Tobacco Co. alone, and each one of the other two large companies, would control a proportion of the total business of the country in certain departments of the trade which was from one to seven times the aggregate of the business of all the independents. Now, I believe that fair competition is not possible under those conditions, because the mere power of endurance of the large company would be sufficient to give it mastery of the field.

Senator Newlands: And yet, if you were establishing to-day a standard to which corporations hereafter organized, we will say, for the purpose of engaging in both interstate and State commerce, should conform, you would not permit any such corporation to control 40 per cent of the business, would you?

Mr. Brandeis: I do not think I should. I mean the more I have thought of it the less inclined I have been to allow that.

Senator Newlands: Would you be willing to allow one-tenth in a country as large as this?

Mr. Brandeis: I am inclined to think it could control one-tenth with perfect safety.

Senator Newlands: You would not go below that?

Mr. Brandeis: I would not prohibit it, and I should be perfectly prepared to allow any appreciable larger percentage to be controlled by one company.

Senator Newlands: You say you would be?

Mr. Brandeis: I would be prepared to allow considerably more than one-tenth. The doubt I had was whether 40 was not too much, and I was going down from 40.

Senator Newlands: Now, if you were to establish such a standard, would you apply it only to corporations hereafter organized or endeavor to apply it to corporations already organized?

Mr. Brandeis: I should, in the first place, naturally apply it to those corporations already organized which had been organized in violation of the Sherman antitrust law. I think that is the real question which confronts the country, and it is one on which there ought not to be hesitation, because, as I indicated to-day in another connection, it seems to me that it goes to the very foundations of society. The things which have been done in defiance of law should not be ratified. The danger of so doing is infinitely greater to society than any danger from the fall of securities or questions of credit, or anything of that kind. As I view it, we are in a position that is serious because of the distrust of our laws, and of our courts, and such an act as the validation of things illegal will be one of the most

serious steps that could be taken. We have been confronted
with that situation in Massachusetts. We validated on one occasion violations of the law by a great corporation which are
comparable to the violation of the Sherman law, and I think
the demoralizing effect upon the community has been great,
the unrest in the community increased, and also the doubt
whether the law is being applied equally to the rich and to the
poor. I look with the greatest apprehension upon any action
on the part of Congress that would seem to condone violations
of the law, particularly those committed by the rich.

Senator Newlands: You would apply, then, this standard as
to the percentage of the business, or the proportion of the
business, or the area of the operations, whatever it may be, of
corporations, not only to corporations that are hereafter to be
organized, but also to those now organized that have been
condemned under the Sherman Act, and I presume you would
extend it to those that may be organized hereafter.

Mr. Brandeis: Yes; that should be those that have been
guilty of violations of the law.

Senator Newlands: Now, as applied to those great aggregations of capital that now exist, whose securities are now upon
the market, and are in use as securities for bank loans, etc.,
what importance do you attach to a movement that would
practically retire those securities and result in the issue of
securities of a different character, perhaps very much less in
amount—I am speaking now of the effect not so much upon the
owners of securities but upon the general prosperity of the
country itself?

Mr. Brandeis: I believe it would have very slight effect
upon the general prosperity of the country—I mean slight evil
effects—and that it will have very great effect, ultimately beneficial effect, upon the prosperity of the country if the people
should understand that the law will be enforced equally
against the rich and the poor, or against the capitalist or the
laborer.

Senator Newlands: You would regard it as a wise thing to
have a gradual process of adjustment, would you not, rather
than an immediate one?

Mr. Brandeis: I think certainly it is very desirable to have the community accustom itself to the idea of change before a change is made, but I think Mr. Perkins's statement yesterday in answer to a somewhat similar question put to him by you, that a large amount of money is borrowed on such collateral for commercial purposes, would be found to be entirely unfounded.

I do not believe people who are engaging in commercial business are to any large extent investing in Standard Oil and Tobacco and similar securities and then borrowing money on them for the benefit of their business. I happen to know, from investigations which have been made in connection with another trust—the Sugar Trust—that its securities are held in the main by a very different class of persons than business men. The women of New England seem to own the great bulk of the securities of the American Sugar Refining Co., and I think it will be found so with regard to a very large number of our other securities. Of course there are those who are speculating in securities.

Senator Newlands: Your idea then is that they are held either for investment or speculation as a rule?

Mr. Brandeis: To a very large extent—not exclusively.

Senator Newlands: But the case you speak of in Massachusetts, where the stocks are held largely by women—who never do wrong, of course, and who must be innocent purchasers—what do you say regarding the effect upon them of a radical readjustment in these securities that would inflict a loss upon them?

Mr. Brandeis: I think that is the effect which would be very unfortunate, but to my mind there is no such thing as an innocent purchaser of stocks—I mean innocent in the sense in which we are considering the purchasers of stock in the organization. It is entirely contrary, not only to our laws but what ought to be our whole attitude toward investments, that the person who has a chance of profit where, by going into an enterprise, or the chance of getting a larger return than he could get on a perfectly safe mortgage or bond, that he should have the chance of gain without any responsibility. The idea of such persons being innocent in the sense of not letting them take the consequences of their acts is, to my mind, highly immoral, and is bound to work out, if pursued, in very evil results to the community. When a person buys stock in the American Tobacco Co. and buys stock in the Standard Oil Co., and buys stock in any of those organizations of doubtful validity and of doubtful practices, they are not innocent; they are guilty constructively by law, and they should be deemed so by the community and held up to a responsibility; precisely to the same responsibility that the English owners of Irish estates should have been held up, although it was their bailiffs who were guilty of nearly every oppression that attended the absentee landlordism of Ireland.

Senator Newlands: How do you account for it that the stock of the Sugar Trust drifted into the hands of the women of New England?

Mr. Brandeis: I think the women of New England, like other investors, desire a large return and a larger return than they could get upon the absolute safe investments. They were driven to that larger return by peculiarly unwise tax laws in Massachusetts and other New England States. So far as they did not invest in tax-exempt property, they found the rate of taxation so high—for instance, in the city of Boston it would be one and nearly seven-tenths per cent on the market value of the security—that they had to go into something more or less speculative in order to get satisfactory returns unless they were content with a very low return which would come from the tax-exempt security like municipal bonds or Massachusetts guaranteed stock, something of that sort. With the idea of getting a larger return, which was reasonably safe, they extended the realm of their investments to industrials.

Senator Newlands: But men are just as desirous of large returns as women, are they not?

Mr. Brandeis: But the men are usually in a different position. Women's property is apt to be held either in trust estates or in some way akin to trust estates. When the men are investing they, of course, invest largely in their own businesses and invest very largely also in more speculative business—business in which the prospective return is often larger than on preferred stocks. Then there is another reason for this situation. Through the incidence of death a very large part of our wealth in Massachusetts is really held for the benefit of women. It is inherited wealth which is passing along that way and is maintained in trust estates.

Senator Newlands: You referred to the unfair methods of killing competition, and you gave a statement of a number of things which should be forbidden. How would you make those unfair methods impossible? Would you punish the corporation, or the individual, or the officials?

Mr. Brandeis: I should punish both; I mean I think the law as it stands, giving an opportunity of fine and giving an opportunity of improvement, is proper; but I should give—what I should expect would be even more effective as a deterrent—the rights to the injured individual to enforce through the Government action, in a practically automatic way, his claim for treble damages, as set forth in the La Follette bill. That would prove a very serious burden upon law-violating corporations.

Senator Newlands: You spoke of community of interests being a factor in the prevention of competition. Take the shoe factories in New England. There are a number of them, I presume, are there not?

Mr. Brandeis: Yes, sir.

Senator Newlands: A very large number?

Mr. Brandeis: In Massachusetts there are over 400.

Senator Newlands: Would it be practicable there, do you think, to prevent individuals from owning stock in half a dozen shoe factories, or otherwise?

Mr. Brandeis: I think it would be perfectly practicable. I think as a matter of fact it is very uncommon to-day.

Senator Newlands: Do you say it is very uncommon?

Mr. Brandeis: It is very uncommon to-day. I think in the shoe industry—I mean in the mere manufacture, say, of shoes —there is at present the most perfect instance of competition and evidences of the value of competition probably of any industry in the country.

Senator Newlands: Do you mean to say that a person seeking investments in the stock of a shoe factory would always confine his investment to any particular factory?

Mr. Brandeis: I do not mean to say they would always do so; but I should feel perfectly sure that there was no appreciable number of persons who invest in more than one company except in those instances which I happen to know about of particular men who are now practically partners in three or four or five businesses.

Senator Newlands: What I wanted to get at is, would you forbid an investor in the stock of one corporation from holding stock in another corporation doing the same business?

Mr. Brandeis: I do not believe that the situation requires such legislation. Take it in the shoe business. There are 1,918 shoe manufacturers in the United States, or there were at the time of the last census. The largest shoe manufacturer in the United States does only a very large percentage of the total business. You have a situation in that business where there is not the slightest danger at the present time of the suppression of competition. But when you are dealing, for instance, with the Tobacco case, where you are trying to break up a combination, or where the control of the business has gone into such few hands that it is easy for three or four or five or seven or nine people to come together and control an industry, then you have a situation where common ownership is absolutely destructive of competition.

Senator Newlands: Would you meet that situation by a general law that absolutely prevents such common ownership in any case, or would you meet it simply in the case of the individual corporation that is condemned under the Sherman Act?

Mr. Brandeis: I would do the latter; that is, the La Follette bill, in its more recent amendments, specifically meets that situation and provides that in the case of an adjudication of illegality that it would be in the power—as indeed I think it is now—of the court. The bill makes clear a point—as to which the judges in New York seem to have had doubt—makes clear the proposition that a court may, in breaking up a combination, put such a limitation upon ownership in the segments.

Senator Newlands: And you would have a limitation as to community of directorship?

Mr. Brandeis: Absolutely. That is, there ought to be the fullest power in the court to put limitations upon all segments of the trust so as to make competition actual and not paper competition thereafter.

Senator Newlands: You stated that labor unions were not permitted in the steel industry?

Mr. Brandeis: Yes, sir.

Senator Newlands: Are there no labor organizations of any kind among the workingmen?

Mr. Brandeis: There are a few independent shops, where the amalgamated association is effective, and perhaps I may add there has been the most striking instances of progress toward humanity, and, to a certain extent, toward efficiency in some of those.

For instance, on this very question that I was speaking of this morning, of the horrible 12-hour day, there are no trade unions. In the shop of one of the small independents where the trade-unions prevailed the union insisted upon an 8-hour day. A good many of the workmen in that shop did not want to have an 8-hour day because they thought their wages would be reduced. The management thought that they could not compete with other businesses on the basis of an 8-hour day, but the union insisted that they must have an 8-hour day and the management consented to try it. They tried it, and the 8-hour day was very successful. After it had been in operation a little while there was nobody who would speak of changing it. That, of course, was an independent organization and not only independent but was one of the smaller industries. I think it employed only about 1,200 people.

Senator Newlands: Do you think this movement for regulation of the unions of capital will, or ought to, be followed by regulation of the unions of labor?

Mr. Brandeis: I do not believe that the conditions in America are such that we are in any appreciable danger from the trade-unions, except that danger of their unwisdom which is inherent in man. I think the time has passed, owing to these larger aggregations, when we have any reason to regard the combination of men in trade-unions as a real menace. I think, on the other hand, that we should have a reasonable publicity as to the organization, etc., of trade-unions.

Now, I want to state, while I believe in the instruments of trade-unions, there is very much that I definitely oppose in their actions as unions as well as of individual members. I am definitely opposed to the closed shop; but I do not consider that the trade-union is to-day a menace, and I think, with all its faults, with all the abuses of the individual man, or of the individual union, we owe to it more than to any other agency for the preservation of what there is that is good in the condition of the American laborer—the reduction of hours, the increase of wages, and very great improvement in the conditions under which men work.

Senator Newlands: Do you regard the closed shop in labor as a tendency toward monopoly, just as you do a combination of plants?

Mr. Brandeis: Yes.

Senator Newlands: You regard it as a tendency toward monopoly?

Mr. Brandeis: I think there is no man or body of men whose intelligence or whose character will stand absolute power, and I should no more think of giving absolute power to unions than I should of giving to capital monopoly power.

Senator Newlands: We are seeking legislation that is doing away practically with the closed shop to capital, are we not?

Mr. Brandeis: Yes.

Senator Newlands: Does not consistency require us to extend that to labor?

Mr. Brandeis: I do not believe it does. I think that the labor situation is such that we do not need any limitation upon their power. That comes now from the difficulty of keeping in line those thousands of men in any organization. I think the difficulty is such that we do not require special prohibitions to curb the unions' power.

I believe that experience will teach the labor unions that

they can never succeed in a large way as long as they insist upon the closed shop.

Senator Newlands: Do you think that labor troubles have had anything to do with the capitalistic unions? Do you think that the creation of the labor unions led in some degree to the formation of capitalistic unions as the only way of meeting them upon equal terms, or that the organization of the capitalistic unions led to the formation of the labor unions?

Mr. Brandeis: No; I do not think the formation of the capitalistic union led to the labor union. I think the labor union historically would be found to have been the necessary development of the factory conditions. I think, on the other hand, that the existence of labor unions has nothing to do appreciably with the formation of trusts. Of course it had a great deal to do with the formation of employers' associations.

Senator Newlands: Take the case of the steel industry; assume that we determine that no capitalistic union in steel can absorb more than one-twentieth of the entire industry, and now, on the other hand, a union of the laborers employed by all the steel industries to be one body capable of working as one. Would the capitalistic unions have a fair show under those conditions?

Mr. Brandeis: The mind can conceive of that, but experience will teach us that it would not be possible because the whole tendency in the steel industry—indeed, in a large part of all industries—is to the limitation in numbers of skilled workmen and to the rapid increase of the unskilled labor.

Now, the formation of a union under all circumstances is extremely difficult with unskilled labor. It becomes a matter almost of impossibility, when you are dealing as you do in the steel industry—and you must in so many of the large trades, with not only foreign labor but with the temporary foreign labor—the labor in which the inflow and outgo each year or every few years is such as to make labor practically as fluid as capital.

Now, under these conditions the formation and the control of the union within the control of a large part of the working people is a very difficult proposition. It is extremely difficult to hold the organization together. While I believe that the closed-shop idea is radically wrong and is illegal, in the sense that no court could enforce it (and to a certain extent the courts—our Massachusetts court—has interfered by injunctions with the closed shop) yet I should not think that the necessities of the situation were such as to require the same protection against the union which we now require against trusts. I mean we are dealing here with a condition and not a theory.

Senator Newlands: In other words, you do not think that the labor union constitutes the same menace to society that the capitalistic union does?

Mr. Brandeis: I do not.

Senator Newlands: But if it does you would be prepared to act on that?

Mr. Brandeis: Absolutely, I think. Society must protect itself.

G. Monetary Policy

One of the fundamental conflicts of interest in any community is that between debtors and creditors, and the natural field on which the contenders fight it out is monetary policy. An easy-money or inflationary policy favors the debtor, for it eases the task of repayment. A stable or deflationary policy, on the other hand, assures the creditor that the real value of what he receives on repayment equals or exceeds the real value of the amount he loaned. Conflict of this sort has never had a sharper effect on American politics than during the period between the Civil War and the First World War, when it focused on the silver question.

The great silver dispute had for its background a series of episodes related to the Civil War. The Comstock Lode in Nevada, a rich deposit of silver, was discovered in 1859, but its exploitation was interrupted by the war and the great increase in silver production that it permitted therefore took place only after 1870. Moreover, the Coinage Act of 1873 eliminated the silver dollar from the coinage, an omission that the free silver movement labeled the "Crime of '73." And most important, the violent inflation that took place during the Civil War was followed by a long and steady fall in prices, which persisted from 1865 to 1895. Those personally affected by the deflation, as well as many who believed that the cure for all economic problems is plenty of money, joined in urging that the government buy and coin silver as quickly as it could. Others who for personal reasons found deflation beneficial, or who were mystically attached to a gold currency, or who recognized the real difficulty of maintaining a bimetallic currency, opposed the monetization of silver. The parties divided, although only roughly, so that the Republicans favored gold and the Democrats—but especially the third parties—silver.

Still, both parties were prepared to make concessions. The Republicans, under the leadership of Senator Sherman, made one when they passed the Sherman Silver Purchase Act in 1890; the Democratic administration of Grover Cleveland made another when, during the panic of 1893, it forced the repeal of that Act. At the next Democratic convention, however, the party's leadership was captured by the Free-Silver contingent, who repudiated their President and nominated William Jennings Bryan, largely, it is said, because of the impact of his "Cross of Gold" speech (13). Bryan's successive defeats, however, and the rapid and steady rise of prices after 1895, ended that campaign for unlimited coinage of silver.

Some of the energy of the silver movement transferred itself to the antitrust and other populist drives of the early 1900s, and especially to the persistent complaint that money was hard to get because it was in the control of a Money Trust. J. P. Morgan served as the bête noire for those people who held that private power over monetary policy was unduly concentrated. In 1913 a congressional committee under the chairmanship of A. P. Pujo reported on its investigation of the money market (14). The report was one of the elements that led to the new system of banking regulation created by the Federal Reserve Act of 1913.

13

WILLIAM JENNINGS BRYAN (1860–1925)
Cross of Gold Speech (8 July 1896)
[Bryan, *Speeches* (1909), I, 238]

I would be presumptuous, indeed, to present myself against the distinguished gentlemen to whom you have listened if this were a mere measuring of abilities; but this is not a contest between persons. The humblest citizen in all the land, when clad in the armor of a righteous cause, is stronger than all the hosts of error. I come to speak to you in defense of a cause as holy as the cause of liberty—the cause of humanity.

When this debate is concluded, a motion will be made to lay upon the table the resolution offered in commendation of the administration, and also the resolution offered in condemnation of the administration. We object to bringing this question down to the level of persons. The individual is but an atom; he is born, he acts, he dies; but principles are eternal; and this has been a contest over a principle.

Never before in the history of this country has there been witnessed such a contest as that through which we have just passed. Never before in the history of American politics has a great issue been fought out as this issue has been, by the voters of a great party. On the fourth of March, 1895, a few Democrats, most of them members of Congress, issued an address to the Democrats of the nation, asserting that the money question was the paramount issue of the hour; declaring that a majority of the Democratic party had the right to control the action of the party on this paramount issue; and concluding with the request that the believers in the free coinage of silver in the Democratic party should organize, take charge of, and control the policy of the Democratic party. Three months later, at Memphis, an organization was perfected, and the silver Democrats went forth openly and courageously proclaiming their belief, and declaring that, if successful, they would crystallize into a platform the declaration which they had made. Then began the conflict. With a zeal approaching the zeal which inspired the crusaders who followed Peter the Hermit, our silver Democrats went forth from victory unto victory until they are now assembled, not to discuss, not to debate, but to enter up the judgment already rendered by the plain people of this country. In this contest brother has been arrayed against brother, father against son. The warmest ties of love, acquaintance and association have been disregarded; old leaders have been cast aside when they have refused to give expression to

the sentiments of those whom they would lead, and new leaders have sprung up to give direction to this cause of truth.
Thus has the contest been waged, and we have assembled
here under as binding and solemn instructions as were ever
imposed upon representatives of the people.

We do not come as individuals. As individuals we might
have been glad to compliment the gentleman from New York,
but we know that the people for whom we speak would never
be willing to put him in a position where he could thwart the
will of the Democratic party. I say it was not a question of
persons; it was a question of principle, and it is not with glad-
ness, my friends, that we find ourselves brought into conflict
with those who are now arrayed on the other side.

The gentleman who preceded me spoke of the State of Massachusetts; let me assure him that not one present in all this
convention entertains the least hostility to the people of the
State of Massachusetts, but we stand here representing people
who are the equals, before the law, of the greatest citizens in
the State of Massachusetts. When you come before us and tell
us that we are about to disturb your business interests, we
reply that you have disturbed our business interests by your
course.

We say to you that you have made the definition of a business man too limited in its application. The man who is employed for wages is as much a business man as his employer,
the attorney in a country town is as much a business man as
the corporation counsel in a great metropolis; the merchant
at the cross-roads store is as much a business man as the merchant of New York; the farmer who goes forth in the morning
and toils all day—who begins in the spring and toils all summer—and who by the application of brain and muscle to the
natural resources of the country creates wealth, is as much a
business man as the man who goes upon the board of trade
and bets upon the price of grain; the miners who go down a
thousand feet into the earth, or climb two thousand feet upon
the cliffs, and bring forth from their hiding places the precious
metals to be poured into the channels of trade are as much
business men as the few financial magnates who, in a back

room, corner the money of the world. We come to speak for this broader class of business men.

Ah, my friends, we say not one word against those who live upon the Atlantic coast, but the hardy pioneers who have braved all the dangers of the wilderness, who have made the desert to blossom as the rose—the pioneers away out there, who rear their children near to Nature's heart, where they can mingle their voices with the voices of the birds—out there where they have erected schoolhouses for the education of their young, churches where they praise their Creator, and cemeteries where rest the ashes of their dead—these people, we say, are as deserving of the consideration of our party as any people in this country. It is for these that we speak. We do not come as aggressors. Our war is not a war of conquest; we are fighting in the defense of our homes, our families, and posterity. We have petitioned, and our petitions have been scorned; we have entreated, and our entreaties have been disregarded; we have begged, and they have mocked when our calamity came. We beg no longer; we entreat no more, we petition no more. We defy them.

The gentleman from Wisconsin has said that he fears a Robespierre. My friends, in this land of the free you need not fear that a tyrant will spring up from among the people. What we need is an Andrew Jackson to stand, as Jackson stood, against the encroachments of organized wealth.

They tell us that this platform was made to catch votes. We reply to them that changing conditions make new issues; that the principles upon which Democracy rests are as everlasting as the hills, but that they must be applied to new conditions as they arise. Conditions have arisen, and we are here to meet these conditions. They tell us that the income tax ought not to be brought in here; that it is a new idea. They criticize us for our criticism of the Supreme Court of the United States. My friends, we have not criticized; we have simply called attention to what you already know. If you want criticisms, read the dissenting opinions of the court. There you will find criticisms. They say that we passed an unconstitutional law; we deny it. The income tax law was not unconstitutional when it was passed; it was not unconstitutional when it went before the Supreme Court for the first time; it did not become unconstitutional until one of the judges changed his mind, and we cannot be expected to know when a judge will change his mind. The income tax is just. It simply intends to put the burdens of government justly upon the backs of the people. I am in favor of an income tax. When I find a man who is not willing to bear his share of the burdens of the government which protects him, I find a man who is unworthy to enjoy the blessings of a government like ours.

They say that we are opposing national bank currency; it is true. If you will read what Thomas Benton said, you will find he said that, in searching history, he could find but one parallel to Andrew Jackson; that was Cicero, who destroyed the conspiracy of Cataline and saved Rome. Benton said that Cicero only did for Rome what Jackson did for us when he destroyed the bank conspiracy and saved America. We say in our platform that we believe that the right to coin and issue money is a function of government. We believe it. We believe that it is a part of sovereignty, and can no more with safety be delegated to private individuals than we could afford to delegate to private individuals the power to make penal statutes or levy taxes. Mr. Jefferson, who was once regarded as good Democratic authority, seems to have differed in opinion from the gentleman who has addressed us on the part of the minority. Those who are opposed to this proposition tell us that the issue of paper money is a function of the bank, and that the government ought to go out of the banking business. I stand with Jefferson rather than with them, and tell them, as he did, that the issue of money is a function of government, and that the banks ought to go out of the governing business.

They complain about the plank which declares against life tenure in office. They have tried to strain it to mean that which it does not mean. What we oppose by that plank is the life tenure which is being built up in Washington, and which excludes from participation in official benefits the humbler members of society.

Let me call your attention to two or three important things.

The gentleman from New York says that he will propose an amendment to the platform providing that the proposed change in our monetary system shall not affect contracts already made. Let me remind you that there is no intention of affecting those contracts which according to present laws are made payable in gold; but if he means to say that we cannot change our monetary system without protecting those who have loaned money before the change was made, I desire to ask him where, in law or in morals, he can find justification for not protecting the debtors when the act of 1873 was passed, if he now insists that we must protect the creditors.

He says he will also propose an amendment which will provide for the suspension of free coinage if we fail to maintain the parity within a year. We reply that when we advocate a policy which we believe will be successful, we are not compelled to raise a doubt as to our own sincerity by suggesting what we shall do if we fail. I ask him, if he would apply his logic to us, why he does not apply it to himself. He says he wants this country to try to secure an international agreement. Why does he not tell us what he is going to do if he fails to secure an international agreement? There is more reason for him to do that than there is for us to provide against the failure to maintain the parity. Our opponents have tried for twenty years to secure an international agreement, and those are waiting for it most patiently who do not want it at all.

And now, my friends, let me come to the paramount issue. If they ask us why it is that we say more on the money question than we say upon the tariff question, I reply that, if protection has slain its thousands, the gold standard has slain its tens of thousands. If they ask us why we do not embody in our platform all the things that we believe in, we reply that when we have restored the money of the Constitution all other necessary reforms will be possible; but that until this is done there is no other reform that can be accomplished.

Why is it that within three months such a change has come over the country? Three months ago, when it was confidently asserted that those who believe in the gold standard would frame our platform and nominate our candidates, even the advocates of the gold standard did not think that we could elect a President. And they had good reason for their doubt, because there is scarcely a State here to-day asking for the gold standard which is not in the absolute control of the Republican party. But note the change. Mr. McKinley was nominated at St. Louis upon a platform which declared for the maintenance of the gold standard until it can be changed into bimetalism by international agreement. Mr. McKinley was the most popular man among the Republicans, and three months ago everybody in the Republican party prophesied his election. How is it to-day? Why, the man who was once pleased to think that he looked like Napoleon—that man shudders to-day when he remembers that he was nominated on the anniversary of the battle of Waterloo. Not only that, but as he listens he can hear with ever-increasing distinctness the sound of the waves as they beat upon the lonely shores of St. Helena.

Why this change? Ah, my friends, is not the reason for the change evident to any one who will look at the matter? No private character, however pure, no personal popularity, however great, can protect from the avenging wrath of an indignant people a man who will declare that he is in favor of fastening the gold standard upon this country, or who is willing to surrender the right of self-government and place the legislative control of our affairs in the hands of foreign potentates and powers.

We go forth confident that we shall win. Why? Because upon the paramount issue of this campaign there is not a spot of ground upon which the enemy will dare to challenge battle. If they tell us that the gold standard is a good thing, we shall point to their platform and tell them that their platform pledges the party to get rid of the gold standard and substitute bimetalism. If the gold standard is a good thing, why try to get rid of it? I call your attention to the fact that some of the very people who are in this convention to-day and who tell us that we ought to declare in favor of international bimetalism—thereby declaring that the gold standard is wrong and that the principle of bimetalism is better—these very people four months ago were open and avowed advocates of the

gold standard, and were then telling us that we could not legislate two metals together, even with the aid of all the world.
If the gold standard is a good thing, we ought to declare in
favor of its retention and not in favor of abandoning it; and
if the gold standard is a bad thing why should we wait until
other nations are willing to help us to let go? Here is the line
of battle, and we care not upon which issue they force the
fight; we are prepared to meet them on either issue or on both.
If they tell us that the gold standard is the standard of civilization, we reply to them that this, the most enlightened of all
the nations of the earth, has never declared for a gold standard
and that both the great parties this year are declaring against
it. If the gold standard is the standard of civilization, why, my
friends, should we not have it? If they come to meet us on
that issue we can present the history of our nation. More than
that; we can tell them that they will search the pages of history in vain to find a single instance where the common people of any land have ever declared themselves in favor of the
gold standard. They can find where the holders of fixed investments have declared for a gold standard, but not where
the masses have.

Mr. Carlisle said in 1878 that this was a struggle between
"the idle holders of idle capital" and "the struggling masses,
who produce the wealth and pay the taxes of the country";
and, my friends, the question we are to decide is: Upon which
side will the Democratic party fight; upon the side of "the idle
holders of idle capital" or upon the side of "the struggling
masses"? That is the question which the party must answer
first, and then it must be answered by each individual hereafter. The sympathies of the Democratic party, as shown by
the platform, are on the side of the struggling masses who have
ever been the foundation of the Democratic party. There are
two ideas of government. There are those who believe that, if
you will only legislate to make the well-to-do prosperous, their
prosperity will leak through on those below. The Democratic
idea, however, has been that if you legislate to make the masses
prosperous, their prosperity will find its way up through every
class which rests upon them.

You come to us and tell us that the great cities are in favor of the gold standard; we reply that the great cities rest upon our broad and fertile prairies. Burn down your cities and leave our farms, and your cities will spring up again as if by magic; but destroy our farms and the grass will grow in the streets of every city in the country.

My friends, we declare that this nation is able to legislate for its own people on every question, without waiting for the aid or consent of any other nation on earth; and upon that issue we expect to carry every State in the Union. I shall not slander the inhabitants of the fair State of Massachusetts nor the inhabitants of the State of New York by saying that, when they are confronted with the proposition, they will declare that this nation is not able to attend to its own business. It is the issue of 1776 over again. Our ancestors, when but three millions in number, had the courage to declare their political independence of every other nation; shall we, their descendants, when we have grown to seventy millions, declare that we are less independent than our forefathers? No, my friends, that will never be the verdict of our people. Therefore, we care not upon what lines the battle is fought. If they say bimetalism is good, but that we cannot have it until other nations help us, we reply that, instead of having a gold standard because England has, we will restore bimetalism, and then let England have bimetalism because the United States has it. If they dare to come out in the open field and defend the gold standard as a good thing, we will fight them to the uttermost. Having behind us the producing masses of this nation and the world, supported by the commercial interests, the laboring interests, and the toilers everywhere, we will answer their demand for a gold standard by saying to them: You shall not press down upon the brow of labor this crown of thorns, you shall not crucify mankind upon a cross of gold.

14

PUJO COMMITTEE

Conclusions

[Comm. on Banking and Currency, Investigation of Financial and Monetary Conditions (1913), 62 Cong. 3 Sess.; H. Rep. 1593, III, 129–33, 136–38, 159–61]

SECTION 1.—EVOLUTION OF THE CONTROLLING GROUPS

Your committee is satisfied from the proofs submitted, even in the absence of data from the banks, that there is an established and well-defined identity and community of interest between a few leaders of finance, created and held together through stock ownership, interlocking directorates, partnership and joint account transactions, and other forms of domination over banks, trust companies, railroads, and public-service and industrial corporations, which has resulted in great and rapidly growing concentration of the control of money and credit in the hands of these few men.

The bulk of the oral and documentary evidence taken before your committee was directed toward ascertaining whether, in current phrase, there is a "money trust."

If by such a trust is meant a combination or arrangement created and existing pursuant to a definite agreement between designated persons with the avowed and accomplished object of concentrating unto themselves the control of money and credit, we are unable to say that the existence of a money trust has been established in that broad bald sense of the term, although the committee regrets to find that even adopting that extreme definition surprisingly many of the elements of such a combination exist.

One of the witnesses presented a statement or argument following his examination, from which it appears that he read the charts, statistics, and other testimony produced before the committee, showing among other things the total resources of various financial, railway, and industrial corporations, as intended to imply that all such resources were in the form of actual cash. It was assumed that it would be understood that the resources of railroads include their rails, station equipment, materials, and other assets as well as their cash in hand, and that the resources of industrial corporations include their plants, accounts, and other assets, and those of financial institutions their loans, discounts, and other property and investments. There is no ground for the deduction that the term "resources" as used in the exhibits was not used in the universal acceptation of the word.

It would of course be absurd to suggest that control of the bulk of the widely distributed wealth of a great nation can be corralled by any set of men. If that is what is meant by gentlemen who deny the existence of a money trust, your committee agrees with them. Such a thing would of course be impossible, and its suggestion is ridiculous. It is not, however, necessary that a group of men shall directly control the small savings in the banks nor the scattered resources of the country in order to monopolize the great financial transactions or to be able to dictate the credits that shall be extended or withheld from the more important and conspicuous business enterprises. This is substantially what has been accomplished and fairly represents the existing condition.

Under our system of issuing and distributing corporate securities the investing public does not buy directly from the corporation. The securities travel from the issuing house through middlemen to the investor. It is only the great banks or bankers with access to the mainsprings of the concentrated resources made up of other people's money in the banks, trust companies, and life insurance companies, and with control of the machinery for creating markets and distributing securities, who have had the power to underwrite or guarantee the sale of large-scale security issues. The men who through their control over the funds of our railroad and industrial companies are able to direct where such funds shall be kept, and thus to create these great reservoirs of the people's money are the ones who are in position to tap those reservoirs for the ventures in which they are interested and to prevent their being tapped for purposes of which they do *not* approve. The latter is quite as important a factor as the former. It is a controlling consideration in its effect on competition in the railroad and industrial world.

When we consider, also, in this connection that into these reservoirs of money and credit there flow a large part of the reserves of the banks of the country, that they are also the agents and correspondents of the out-of-town banks in the loaning of their surplus funds in the only public money market of the country, and that a small group of men and their partners and associates have now further strengthened their hold upon the resources of these institutions by acquiring large stock holdings therein, by representation on their boards and through valuable patronage, we begin to realize something of the extent to which this practical and effective domination and control over many of our greatest financial, railroad, and industrial corporations has developed, largely within the past five years, and that it is fraught with peril to the welfare of the country.

If, therefore, by a "money trust" is meant—

An established and well-defined identity and community of interest between a few leaders of finance which has been created and is held together through stock holdings, interlocking directorates, and other forms of domination over banks, trust companies, railroads, public-service and industrial corporations, and which has resulted in a vast and growing concentration of control of money and credit in the hands of a comparatively few men—

your committee, as before stated, has no hesitation in asserting as the result of its investigation up to this time that the condition thus described exists in this country to-day.

Some of the endless ramifications of this power have been traced and presented and it is upon these that we have based our findings. Many others can be fully discovered and analyzed only after a close scrutiny of the internal affairs of the great

national banks that will disclose the ways in which their resources are used, to whom their funds are loaned, what securities they have been buying and selling and how their vast
profits have been earned. Whilst your committee has been denied access to this data, sufficient has been learned to reveal
the relations of these banks and of the State banks and trust
companies and the use that has been made of them in upbuilding a power over our financial system and in consequence
over our railroads and greater industries that permits real competition on a large scale in the various fields of enterprise only
by sufferance, if at all.

The parties to this combination or understanding or community of interest, by whatever name it may be called, may
be conveniently classified, for the purpose of differentiation,
into four separate groups.

First. The first, which for convenience of statement we will
call the inner group, consists of J. P. Morgan & Co., the recognized leaders, and George F. Baker and James Stillman in their
individual capacities and in their joint administration and control of the First National Bank, the National City Bank, the
National Bank of Commerce, the Chase National Bank, the
Guaranty Trust Co., and the Bankers Trust Co., with total
known resources, in these corporations alone, in excess of
$1,300,000,000, and of a number of smaller but important
financial institutions. This takes no account of the personal fortunes of these gentlemen.

Second. Closely allied with this inner or primary group, and
indeed related to them practically as partners in many of their
larger financial enterprises, are the powerful international banking houses of Lee, Higginson & Co. and Kidder, Peabody & Co.,
with three affiliated banks in Boston—the National Shawmut
Bank, the First National Bank, and the Old Colony Trust Co.
—having at least more than half of the total resources of all
the Boston banks; also with interests and representation in
other important New England financial institutions.

Third. In New York City the international banking house
of Messrs. Kuhn, Loeb & Co., with its large foreign clientele
and connections, whilst only qualifiedly allied with the inner

group, and only in isolated transactions, yet through its close relations with the National City Bank and the National Bank of Commerce and other financial institutions with which it has recently allied itself has many interests in common, conducting large joint-account transactions with them, especially in recent years, and having what virtually amounts to an understanding not to compete, which is defended as a principle of "banking ethics." Together they have with a few exceptions pre-empted the banking business of the important railways of the country.

Fourth. In Chicago this inner group associates with and makes issues of securities in joint account or through underwriting participations primarily with the First National Bank and the Illinois Trust & Savings Bank, and has more or less friendly business relations with the Continental & Commercial National Bank, which participates at times in the underwriting of security issues by the inner group. These are the three largest financial institutions in Chicago, with combined resources (including the two affiliated and controlled State institutions of the two national banks) of $561,000,000.

Radiating from these principal groups and closely affiliated with them are smaller but important banking houses, such as Kissel Kinnicut & Co., White, Weld & Co., and Harvey Fisk & Sons, who receive large and lucrative patronage from the dominating groups and are used by the latter as jobbers or distributors of securities the issuing of which they control, but which for reasons of their own they prefer not to have issued or distributed under their own names. Messrs. Lee, Higginson & Co., besides being partners with the inner group, are also frequently utilized in this service because of their facilities as distributors of securities.

Beyond these inner groups and subgroups are banks and bankers throughout the country who cooperate with them in underwriting or guaranteeing the sale of securities offered to the public and who also act as distributors of such securities. It was impossible to learn the identity of these corporations, owing to the unwillingness of the members of the inner group to disclose the names of their underwriters, but sufficient appears to justify the statement that there are at least hundreds of them and that they extend into many of the cities throughout this and foreign countries.

The patronage thus proceeding from the inner group and its subgroups is of great value to these banks and bankers, who are thus tied by self-interest to the great issuing houses and may be regarded as a part of this vast financial organization. Such patronage yields no inconsiderable part of the income of these banks and bankers and without much risk on account of the facilities of the principal groups for placing issues of securities through their domination of great banks and trust companies and their other domestic affiliations and their foreign connections. The underwriting commissions on issues made by this inner group are usually easily earned and do not ordinarily involve the underwriters in the purchase of the underwritten securities. Their interest in the transaction is generally adjusted, unless they choose to purchase part of the securities, by the payment to them of a commission. There are however occasions on which this is not the case. The underwriters are then required to take the securities. Bankers and brokers are so anxious to be permitted to participate in these transactions under the lead of the inner group that as a rule they join when invited to do so, regardless of their approval of the particular business, lest by refusing they should thereafter cease to be invited.

It can hardly be expected that the banks, trust companies, and other institutions that are thus seeking participations from this inner group would be likely to engage in business of a character that would be displeasing to the latter or that would interfere with their plans or prestige. And so the protection that can be offered by the members of this inner group constitutes the safest refuge of our great industrial combinations and railroad systems against future competition. The powerful grip of these gentlemen is upon the throttle that controls the wheels of credit, and upon their signal those wheels will turn or stop.

In the case of the pending New York subway financing of $170,000,000 of bonds by Messrs. Morgan & Co. and their associates, Mr. Davison estimated that there were from 100 to 125 such underwriters who were apparently glad to agree that Messrs. Morgan & Co., the First National Bank, and the National City Bank should receive 3 per cent—equal to $5,100,-000—for forming this syndicate, thus relieving themselves from all liability, whilst the underwriters assumed the risk of what the bonds would realize and of being required to take their share of the unsold portion.

This transaction furnishes a fair illustration of the basis on which this inner group is able to capitalize its financial power. Included among the underwriters are the banks and trust companies that are controlled by Messrs. Morgan, Baker, and Stillman under voting trusts, through stock ownerships, and in the other ways described. Thus, they utilize this control for their own profit and that of the stockholders of the institutions. But the advantage to the depositors whose money and credit may be used in financing such enterprises is not apparent.

It may be that this recently concentrated money power so far has not been abused otherwise than in the possible exaction of excessive profits through absence of competition. Whilst no evidence of abuse has come to the attention of the committee from impartial sources, neither has there been adequate proof or opportunity for proof on the subject. Here again the data has not been available.

Sufficient has, however, been developed to demonstrate that neither potentially competing banking institutions or competing railroad or industrial corporations should be subject to a common source of private control.

Your committee is convinced that however well founded may be the assurances of good intentions by those now holding the places of power which have been thus created, the situation is fraught with too great peril to our institutions to be tolerated. . . .

SECTION 3.—CONCENTRATION OF CONTROL OF MONEY
AND CREDIT ADMITTED

That a rapid concentration of the sources of credit in the forms we have described has taken place in this country in very recent years was admitted by witnesses of the highest qualifications.

Mr. Morgan, however, was not one of these. He said (R., 1051, 1052):

Q. There is no way one man can get a monopoly of money?

A. Or control of it.

Q. He can make a try at it?

A. No, sir; he can not. He may have all the money in Christendom, but he can not do it.

Q. Let us go on. If you owned all the banks of New York, with all their resources, would you not come pretty near having a control of credit?

A. No, sir; not at all.

   *   *   *   *   *   *   *

* * * What I mean to say is this—allow me: The question of control, in this country, at least, is personal; that is, in money.

Q. How about credit?

A. In credit also.

Q. Personal to whom—to the man who controls?

A. No, no; he never has it; he can not buy it.

Q. No; but he gets—

A. All the money in Christendom and all the banks in Christendom can not control it.

Q. That is what you wanted to say, is it not?

A. Yes, sir.

And again (R., 1082, 1083, 1084, 1085):

Q. If you had the control of all that represents the assets in the banks of New York, you would have the control of money—of all that money?

A. No; you would not.

   *   *   *   *   *   *   *

But money can not be controlled.

Q. Is not the credit based upon the money?

A. No, sir.

Q. It has no relation?

A. No, sir.

Q. None whatever?

A. No, sir; none whatever.

* * * * * * *

Q. Commercial credits are based upon the possession of money or property?

A. What?

Q. Commercial credits?

A. Money or property or character.

Q. Is not commercial credit based primarily upon money or property?

A. No, sir; the first thing is character.

Q. Before money or property?

A. Before money or anything else. Money can not buy it.

Q. So that a man with character, without anything at all behind it can get all the credit he wants, and a man with the property can not get it?

A. That is very often the case.

Q. But that is the rule of business?

A. That is the rule of business, sir.

* * * * * * *

Q. Do you mean to say that when people lend, as when loans are made on stock-exchange collateral, to the extent of hundreds of millions of dollars, they look to anything except the collateral?

A. Yes; they do.

Q. They do?

A. Yes. Right on that point, what I did, what I used to do—and I think it is pretty generally done now—is this: If I see there is a loan to Mr. Smith, I say, "You call that loan right away." I would not have that loan in the box. I would not have that loan.

Q. That is not the way money is loaned on the stock exchange?

A. That is the way I loan it.

Q. No matter what collateral a man has on the stock exchange—

A. If he is not satisfactory to me, I call the loan at once, personally.

Q. I am not talking about you, personally.

A. I call that loan personally. I am not talking of anybody else's way of doing business, but I tell you what I think is the basis of business.

None of the other witnesses who were interrogated on this subject were able to agree with Mr. Morgan as to the factors that enter into the current business of loaning money on collateral. Thus Mr. Baker said (R., 1503):

Q. As a matter of fact, Mr. Baker, in the current loans made on stock-exchange collateral, does not the bank look to the security and not to the borrower?

A. Generally.

It is thus seen that Mr. Morgan's view that group control of credit is impossible, rests upon the theory that credit is not based on money or resources, but wholly on character, and this even as regards loans on the stock exchange. This is an obvious economic fallacy, as the every-day transactions of business demonstrates.

Following out this theory, Mr. Morgan further stated that he was not conscious that he had the slightest power (R., 1061):

Q. Your power in any direction is entirely unconscious to you, is it not?

A. It is, sir; if that is the case.

Q. You do not think you have any power in any department of industry in this country, do you?

A. I do not.

Q. Not the slightest?
A. Not the slightest.

This again illustrates that Mr. Morgan's conception of what constitutes power and control in the financial world is so peculiar as to invalidate all his conclusions based upon it.

It seems to your committee that among other things his testimony as to the circumstances under which he obtained control of the Equitable Life Assurance Co. from Mr. Ryan demonstrates his possession of power in the fullest sense, and also that he knows how to exercise it. He said (R., 1069, 1070):

Q. * * * Did Mr. Ryan offer this stock to you?
A. I asked him to sell it to me.
Q. You asked him to sell it to you?
A. Yes.
Q. Did you tell him why you wanted it?
A. No; I told him I thought it was a good thing for me to have.
Q. Did he tell you that he wanted to sell it?
A. No; but he sold it.
Q. He did not want to sell it; but when you said you wanted it, he sold it?
A. He did not say that he did not want to sell it.
Q. What did he say when you told him you would like to have it and thought you ought to have it?
A. He hesitated about it, and finally sold it.

It will be noted that the only reason that Mr. Morgan gave for Mr. Ryan's surrender of the stock was that he told Mr. Ryan that he "thought it was a good thing" for him (Mr. Morgan) to have. (R., 1069.)

It may be that behind the reluctance of Mr. Morgan to furnish a business or other reason for this transaction lies a hidden motive, based on a high disinterested sense of public duty. If so, we have been unable to discover it. The incident is cited here primarily to show that however he may feel about it himself, the dominating power of Mr. Morgan is so universally recognized in the financial world that even the leaders humbly bow to it.

Again, Mr. Morgan's conceptions of the duty of a bank director with regard to the knowledge a director is entitled to secure and is required to possess as to loans made by his bank demonstrates that his views on these questions are peculiar to himself and represent neither the generally understood point nor do they correctly state the legal obligation resting on a director (R., 1090, 1091):

Q. You do not think a director has a right to look at the loans in his bank?

A. In the aggregate stocks, but not as to whose they are.

Q. You do not think the director of a corporation has a right to find out to whom the bank lends its money?

A. Yes; to whom they loan, but not to examine it for that purpose.

Q. They have a right to see to whom they loan their money and on what collateral, have they not?

A. Yes; in blank.

Q. They would not be allowed to know the name?

A. No, sir.

On the proposition that there is not and can not be concentration of control of money or credit, it will be observed that Mr. Morgan is directly at variance with his associate, Mr. Baker, who deprecated further concentration in this regard, saying it has gone far enough, because in the hands of the wrong men "it would be very bad"; that the safety of the situation lies in the personnel of the control. (R., 1567, 1568.) He evidently does not agree that the situation would correct itself.

That such concentration is an existing condition and not a myth seems indeed to be agreed on all sides. Mr. Reynolds considers it a menace (R., 1654, 1655), whilst Mr. Schiff has been an interested observer of its rapid growth during the past few years, but is not worried, because his firm is now so rich and powerful that it no longer requires credit (R., 1686, 1688). We note, however, that he has been something more than a mere observer. His firm has acquired also within the past few years interests and representation in the National Bank of Commerce, Equitable Trust Co., United States Mortgage & Trust Co., and Fourth National Bank. (Exhibit 200, R., 1696, 1765.)

Mr. Perkins said he had also observed the growth of concentration. (R., 1635.) . . .

We are not unmindful of the important and valuable part that the gentlemen who dominate this inner group and their allies have played in the development of our prosperity. There should be no disposition to hamper their activities if a situation can be brought about where their capital, prestige, and connections can be independently employed in free and open competition. Without the aid of their invaluable enterprise and initiative and their credit and financial power the money requirements of our vast ventures could not have been financed in the past, and much less so in the future.

It is also recognized that cooperation between them is frequently valuable, and often essential to the public interest as well as their own, in order to permit of the furnishing or guaranteeing of the requirements of our vast enterprises of the present day and of the still larger ones that are probably in store for us.

But these considerations do not involve their taking control of the resources of our financial institutions or of the savings of the people in our life insurance companies nor that they shall be able to levy tribute upon every large enterprise; nor that commercial credits or stock exchange markets and values shall wait upon their beck and call. Other countries finance enterprises quite as important as our own without employing these methods.

Far more dangerous than all that has happened to us in the past in the way of elimination of competition in industry is the control of credit through the domination of these groups over our banks and industries. It means that there can be no hope of revived competition and no new ventures on a scale commensurate with the needs of modern commerce or that could live against existing combinations, without the consent of those

who dominate these sources of credit. A banking house that
has organized a great industrial or railway combination or that
has offered its securities to the public, is represented on the
board of directors and acts as its fiscal agent, thereby assumes
a certain guardianship over that corporation. In the ratio in
which that corporation succeeds or fails the prestige of the
banking house and its capacity for absorbing and distributing
future issues of securities is affected. If competition is threatened it is manifestly the duty of the bankers from their point
of view of the protection of the stockholders, as distinguished
from the standpoint of the public, to prevent it if possible. If
they control the sources of credit they can furnish such protection. It is this element in the situation that unless checked
is likely to do more to prevent the restoration of competition
than all other conditions combined. This power standing between the trusts and the economic forces of competition is the
factor most to be dreaded and guarded against by the advocates of revived competition.

Mr. Morgan was unable to name an instance in the past 10
years in which there had been any railroad building in competition with any of the existing systems. He attributed it to
the restrictions of the Interstate Commerce Commission. The
fact is, however, as we all know, that railroad construction is
constantly being prosecuted—necessarily so with our rapidly
growing population—but that instead of being done independently as formerly it is now done by the great systems.

It is impossible that there should be competition with all
the facilities for raising money or selling large issues of bonds
in the hands of these few bankers and their partners and allies,
who together dominate the financial policies of most of the existing systems. There never will be, until this combination or
community of interest can be dissolved by either closing to
them the vaults of the banks, life insurance companies, and
other trustees of other people's money or by opening them to
meritorious competing enterprises.

Mr. Baker, when upon the witness stand, was unable to
name a single issue of as much as $10,000,000 of any security,
either in the railroad or industrial world, that had been made

within 10 years without the participation or cooperation of one of the members of this small group. He subsequently wrote naming only the case of a single issue of $13,500,000. It was proved as to this instance by the notice issued to stockholders that Morgan & Co. were in fact largely interested and received a part of the profits from the issue. Yet it appears that within *six* years the *joint* account transactions of that group in *public issues alone* (not including any issues made by them alone or privately), amounted to over *three billion dollars*, of which a $10,000,000 issue would have been less than one-third of 1 per cent.

Issues of securities of local or small enterprises requiring moderate sums of money are frequently financed without the cooperation of these gentlemen; but from what we have learned of existing conditions in finance and of the vast ramifications of this group throughout the country and in foreign countries we are satisfied that their influence is sufficiently potent to prevent the financing of any enterprise in any part of the country requiring $10,000,000 or over, of which for reasons satisfactory to themselves they do not approve. Therein lies the peril of this money power to our progress, far greater than the combined danger of all existing combinations. The latter may at last fall of their own weight, especially if deprived of the protection and support against competition referred to, or they may be disintegrated as unlawful.

The men who established our great industries have added to the prosperity of the country during the period of the upbuilding of these industries; but they none the less violated the law when they reversed the processes under which the country had grown and prospered by combining to throttle the competition upon which they had thrived. Whilst they were struggling against one another for supremacy they were a valuable asset to the country; since they have pursued the opposite policy they have become a menace.

The gentlemen constituting this inner circle have, however, violated no law in what they have done, so far as we are able to gather; but that is rather because of the loose, intangible character of this recently developed community of interest and because the law has not yet properly safeguarded the community against this form of control.

The acts of this inner group, as here described, have nevertheless been more destructive of competition than anything accomplished by the trusts, for they strike at the very vitals of potential competition in every industry that is under their protection, a condition which, if permitted to continue, will render impossible all attempts to restore normal competitive conditions in the industrial world.

It accordingly behooves us to see to it that the bankers who require and are bidding for the money held by our banks, trust companies, and life insurance companies to use in their ventures are not permitted to control and utilize these funds as though they were their own.

If the arteries of credit now clogged well-nigh to choking by the obstructions created through the control of these groups are opened so that they may be permitted freely to play their important part in the financial system, competition in large enterprises will become possible and business can be conducted on its merits instead of being subject to the tribute and the good will of this handful of self-constituted trustees of the national prosperity.

H. Conservation

To the early settlers of the United States, each new region they entered offered raw materials in abundance, or land which, once cleared, was unusually rich. Americans reacted to this abundance as reasonable men anywhere might. They cut down as many trees as repaid the cost of cutting, for when they had used up the forests nearby they could—and did—move on to the next forest. They grew as much cotton as they could on the Eastern seaboard lands, and when those were exhausted moved on into the Mississippi delta. When they hunted, they shot what they could, unless, presumably, the skin and meat of still another beast were not worth as much as the powder and ball that might kill it. Perhaps they took more than they needed, but since they did not all become wealthy it is not clear that they all behaved as wastrels.

In time, of course, this enthusiastic use of what was given reduced the supplies, and after the Civil War men began to be conscious that certain simple natural goods were no longer so abundant. Trees, especially, were not. A fear that soon no single tree would be left in the country—just as hardly a single bison was—began to spread among the prudent and farsighted. It did not occur to them that when trees become scarce, more can be grown; that when land becomes exhausted, it can be revived with fertilizer; and that when wild animals are no more, tame ones can be raised as cattle are. Or, if this did occur to them, they thought that private businesses would be unwilling to incur the costs of so restoring the stock of natural resources.

They argued, therefore, that government should launch a program of conservation.

One of the earliest American proponents of conservation was Franklin B. Hough, whose essay in 1873 on public preservation of forests put him at the forefront of the movement that led to the National Forest scheme. But the notion spread much more widely, and by 1908 even James J. Hill was to be found urging a conference of Governors to promote the good work (15). His audience may have been amused by the irony that Hill, who as founder of the Great Northern Railroad might qualify as a Robber Baron, now appeared to bewail the poverty of the victims.

The notion that conservation is desirable was readily accepted as an axiom of American economic policy, and remains so today. The conviction has not had much effect on public policy, except in fostering the development of national parks and forest reserves, and in giving the curious title of "reclamation" to irrigation schemes. Under the name of "conservation" much useful work has been done in teaching farmers that techniques such as contour plowing are in the long run very productive, and in teaching lumbermen more sophisticated methods of harvesting timber.

But in its purer sense—which implies that government should slow down private exploitation of raw materials—conservation has not gone very far. This may be because the somber predictions that conservationists made at the turn of the century have not come true. Supplies of iron and coal, petroleum and other important mineral products have not, as they predicted, been exhausted. On the contrary, either the "proven reserves" have steadily increased, or, more important, substitutes have been found for many presumably essential raw materials and economic methods of recovery for others. It now seems possible that the supply of raw materials will outlast the supply of humans.

15
James J. Hill (1838–1916)
The Natural Wealth of the Land and Its Conservation
(14 May 1908)
[W. J. McGee (ed.), Proceedings of A Conference of
Governors (1909) 63]

In some respects the occasion that calls together this as-
semblage is unprecedented. The dignity and public influence
of those present mark its importance. It is in effect a directors'
meeting of the great political and economic corporation known
as the United States of America. The stockholders are the 87,-
000,000 People of this country; the directors are the State and
Federal officers, whose position brings them in touch with the
operation of the whole country. We should not fail to recognize
the high note that has been struck and the immensity of the
interests involved upon the lives of millions yet to be.

The two-fold significance of this meeting is found in the
comparative novelty of its subject matter and of the method by
which it has been approached. The subject is the conservation
of our national wealth, and a careful study of our national
economic resources.

Two years ago, in an address delivered before the meeting
of the Minnesota State Agricultural Society in St. Paul, I reviewed the practical consequences and the statistical proof of
that national wastefulness which competent scientific authority
has already set down as distinguishing the American people.
From data of the highest certainty, no one of which has ever
since been called in question, I then forecast some of the conditions certain to arise within the next half-century, when the
population of this country will have grown to more than 200,-
000,000. The facts were pointed out not in the spirit of the
alarmist, but in order that attention might be directed to the

way by which the nation may escape future disaster. So rapidly do events move in our time, so swiftly do ideas spread and grasp the public mind, that some policy directed to the ends then set forth has already become a national care. It is this policy—the conservation of national resources, the best means of putting an end to the waste of the sources of wealth —which largely forms the subject-matter of this Conference. For the first time there is a formal national protest, under seal of the highest authority, against economic waste.

The method by which this end is to be reached is scarcely less interesting or significant. This body has no legal status, and its conclusions will not be of binding effect upon Nation, the State, or the citizen. Yet they will carry a weight greater than legislatures can impart, a force that even courts could not strengthen, because they will not be subject to repeal. They will represent a truly national opinion expressed with fidelity to our national constitutional form. The People of the United States are represented here through the several States. May we not hope that from this gathering there may be born not only a wiser system of using the still remaining resources of this country, but a cooperation between Nation and State that shall be as helpful in our political as these deliberations ought to be in our economic future?

"Of all the sinful wasters of man's inheritance on earth," said the late Professor Shaler, "and all are in this regard sinners, the very worst are the people of America." This is not a popular phrase, but a scientific judgment. It is borne out by facts. In the movement of modern times, which has made the world commercially a small place and has produced a solidarity of the race such as never before existed, we have come to the point where we must to a certain extent regard the natural resources of this planet as a common asset, compare them with demands now made and likely to be made upon them, and study their judicious use. Commerce, wherever untrammeled, is wiping out boundaries and substituting the world-relation of demand and supply for smaller systems of local economy. The changes of a single generation have brought the Nations of the Earth closer together than were the States of this Union at the close of the Civil War. If we fail to consider what we possess of wealth available for the uses of mankind, and to what extent we are wasting a national patrimony that can never be restored, we might be likened to the directors of a company who never examine a balance sheet.

The sum of resources is simple and fixed. From the sea, the mine, the forest and the soil must be gathered everything that can sustain the life of man. Upon the wealth that these supply must be conditioned forever, as far as we can see, not only his progress but his continued existence on earth. How stands the inventory of property for our own people? The resources of the sea furnish less than 5% of the food supply, and that is all. The forests of this country, the product of centuries of growth, are fast disappearing. The best estimates reckon our standing merchantable timber at less than 2,000,000,000,000 feet. Our annual cut is about 40,000,000,000 feet. The lumber cut rose from 18,000,000,000 feet in 1880 to 34,000,000,000 feet in 1905; that is, it nearly doubled in 25 years. We are now using annually 500 feet board measure of timber per capita, as against an average of 60 feet for all Europe. The New England supply is gone. The Northwest furnishes small growths that would have been rejected by the lumberman 30 years ago. The South has reached its maximum production and begins to decline. On the Pacific Coast only is there now any considerable body of merchantable standing timber. We are consuming yearly three or four times as much timber as forest growth restores. Our supply of some varieties will be practically exhausted in 10 or 12 years; in the case of others, without reforesting, the present century will see the end. When will we take up in a practical and intelligent way the restoration of our forests?

Turning now to one of the only two remaining sources of wealth, the mine, we find it different from the others in an important essential. It is incapable of restoration or recuperation. The mineral wealth stored in the earth can be used only once. When iron and coal are taken from the mine, they cannot be restored; and upon iron and coal our industrial civilization is built. When fuel and iron become scarce and high-priced, civilization, so far as we can now foresee, will suffer as man would suffer by the gradual withdrawal of the air he breathes.

The exhaustion of our coal supply is not in the indefinite future. The startling feature of our coal production is not so much the magnitude of the annual output as its rate of growth. For the decade ending in 1905 the total product was 2,832,-402,746 tons, which is almost exactly one-half the total product previously mined in this country. For the year 1906 the output was 414,000,000 tons, an increase of 46% on the average annual yield of the 10 years preceding. In 1907 our production reached 470,000,000 tons. Fifty years ago the annual per capita production was a little more than one-quarter of a ton; it is now about five tons. It is but eight years since we took the place of Great Britain as the leading coal producing nation of the world, and already our product exceeds hers by over 43%, and is 37% of the known production of the world. Estimates of coal deposits still remaining must necessarily be somewhat vague, but they are approximately near the mark.

The iron industry tells a similar story. The total of iron ore mined in the United States doubles about once in seven years. It was less than 12,000,000 tons in 1893, over 24,000,000 tons in 1899, 47,740,000 tons in 1906 and over 52,000,000 tons in 1907. The rising place of iron in the world's life is the most impressive phenomenon of the last century. In 1850 the pig iron production of the United States amounted to 563,757 tons, or about 50 pounds per capita. Our production now is over 600 pounds per capita. We do not work a mine, build a house, weave a fabric, prepare a meal or cultivate an acre of ground under modern methods without the aid of iron. We turn out over 25,000,000 tons of pig iron every year, and the production for the first half of 1907 was at the rate of 27,000,000 tons. This is two and one-half times the product of Great Britain. It is nearly half the product of the whole world. And the supply of this most precious of all the metals is so far from inexhaustible that it seems as if iron and coal might be united in their disappearance from common life.

The large deposits of iron ore in this country are now located. For cheap iron we depend on the Lake Superior district, because of its high grade, the ease of extracting the ore from the mines, and its nearness to cheap transportation. At the rate of over 50,000,000 tons per year, our present consumption, it would require over 2,000,000,000 tons to supply the demand for the next 40 years, supposing it to remain stationary. This would approach the end of all the higher grade ore in large deposits now in sight in this country. The product of other workings would be of inferior quality and higher cost, and remote from market. But production is certain to increase even more rapidly than in the past. A few years ago a Swedish geologist prepared for his government a report which stated that the entire supply of the iron ore in the United States would be exhausted within the present century. The United States Geological Survey declared this an over-estimate; but here is the conclusion of its own report, after a careful examination of the question in the light of the best authorities. I quote the official published document:

Assuming the demand for iron ore during the present century may range from 50,000,000 to 100,000,000 tons per year, the Lake Superior district would last for from 25 to 50 years, if it supplied the entire United States. But counting on the known supply elsewhere in the United States, the ore will last for a much longer period, though, of course, it must necessarily show a gradual but steady increase in value and in cost of mining, along with an equally steady decrease in grade.

The most favorable view of the situation forces the conclusion that iron and coal will not be available for common use on anything like present terms before the end of this century; and our industrial, social and political life must be readjusted to meet the strains imposed by new conditions. Yet we forbid to our consumers access to the stores of other countries, while we boast of our increased exports, of that material for want of which one day the nation must be reduced to the last extremity.

We now turn to the only remaining resource of man upon

this earth, which is the soil itself. How are we caring for that, and what possibilities does it hold out to the People of future support? We are only beginning to feel the pressure upon the land. The whole interior of this continent, aggregating more than 1,500,000,000 acres, has been occupied by settlers within the last 50 years. What is there left for the next 50 years? Excluding arid and irrigable areas, the latter limited by nature, and barely enough of which could be made habitable in each year to furnish a farm for each immigrant family, the case stands as follows: In 1906 the total unappropriated public lands in the United States consisted of 792,000,000 acres. Of this area the divisions of Alaska, Arizona, California, Colorado, Idaho, Montana, Nevada, New Mexico and Wyoming contained 195,700,000 acres of surveyed and 509,000,000 acres of unsurveyed land. Little of Alaska is fitted for general agriculture, while practically all of the rest is semiarid land, available only for grazing or irrigation. We have, subtracting these totals, 50,000,000 acres of surveyed and 36,500,000 acres of unsurveyed land as our actual remaining stock. And 21,000,000 acres were disposed of in 1907. How long will the remainder last? No longer can we say that "Uncle Sam has land enough to give us all a farm."

Equally threatening is the change in quality. There are two ways in which the productive power of the earth is lessened; first by erosion and the sweeping away of the fertile surface into streams and thence to the sea, and second by exhaustion through wrong methods of cultivation. The former process has gone far. Thousands of acres in the East and South have been made unfit for tillage. North Carolina was, a century ago, one of the greatest agricultural states of the country and one of the wealthiest. Today as you ride through the South you see everywhere land gullied by torrential rains; red and yellow clay banks exposed where once were fertile fields; and agriculture reduced because its main support has been washed away. Millions of acres, in places to the extent of one-tenth of the entire arable area, have been so injured that no industry and no care can restore them.

Far more ruinous, because universal and continuing in its

effects, is the process of soil exhaustion. It is creeping over the
land from East to West. The abandoned farms that are now
the playthings of the city's rich or the game preserves of patrons of sport, bear witness to the melancholy change. New
Hampshire, Vermont, Northern New York, show long lists of
them. In Western Massachusetts, which once supported a
flourishing agriculture, farm properties are now for sale for
half the cost of the improvements. Professor Carver, of Harvard, has declared after a personal examination of the country
that "Agriculture as an independent industry, able in itself to
support a community, does not exist in the hilly parts of New
England."

The same process of deterioration is affecting the farm lands
of Western New York, Ohio and Indiana. Where prices of
farms should rise by increase of population, in many places
they are falling. Between 1880 and 1900 the land values of
Ohio shrank $60,000,000. Official investigation of two counties
in Central New York disclosed a condition of agricultural de-
cay. In one, land was for sale for about the cost of improvements, and 150 vacant houses were counted in a limited area;
in the other, the population in 1905 was nearly 4,000 less than
it was in 1855.

Practically identical soil conditions exist in Maryland and
Virginia, where lands sell at from $10 to $30 an acre. In a
hearing before an Industrial Commission, the chief of the Bureau of Soils of the Department of Agriculture said: "One of
the most important causes of deterioration, and I think I should
put this first of all, is the method and system of agriculture
that prevails throughout these states. Unquestionably the soil
has been abused." The richest region of the West is no more
exempt than New England or the South. The soil of the West
is being reduced in agricultural potency by exactly the same
processes which have driven the farmer of the East, with all
his advantage of nearness to markets, practically from the field.

Within the last 40 years a great part of the richest land in
the country has been brought under cultivation. We should,
therefore, in the same time, have raised proportionately the
yield of our principal crops per acre; because the yield of old

lands, if properly treated, tends to increase rather than to diminish. The year 1906 was one of large crops and can scarcely be taken as a standard. We produced, for example, more corn that year than had ever been grown in the United States in a single year before. But the average yield per acre was less than it was in 1872. We are barely keeping the acre-product stationary. The average wheat crop of the country now ranges from 12½ bushels in ordinary years to 15 bushels per acre in the best seasons. And so it is on down the line.

But the fact of soil waste becomes startlingly evident when we examine the record of some states where single cropping and other agricultural abuses have been prevalent. Take the case of wheat, the mainstay of single-crop abuse. Many of us can remember when New York was the great wheat-producing state of the Union. The average yield of wheat per acre in New York for the last 10 years was about 18 bushels. For the first five years of that 10-year period it was 18.4 bushels, and for the last five years 17.4 bushels. Farther west, Kansas takes high rank as a wheat producer. Its average yield per acre for the last 10 years was 14.16 bushels. For the first five of those years it was 15.14 and for the last five years 13.18. Up in the Northwest, Minnesota wheat has made a name all over the world. Her average yield per acre for the same 10 years was 12.96 bushels. For the first five years it was 13.12, and for the last five 12.8. We perceive here the working of a uniform law, independent of location, of soil, or of climate. It is the law of diminishing return due to soil destruction. Apply this to the country at large, and it reduces agriculture to the condition of a bank whose depositors are steadily drawing out more money than they put in.

What is true in this instance is true of our agriculture as a whole. In no other important country in the world, with the exception of Russia, is the industry that must be the foundation of every state at so low an ebb as in our own. According to the last census the average annual product per acre of the farms of the whole United States was worth $11.38. It is little more than a respectable rental in communities where the soil is properly cared for and made to give a reasonable return for cultivation. There were but two states in the Union whose total value of farm products was over $30 per acre of improved land. The great state of Illinois gave but $12.48, and Minnesota showed only $8.74. No discrimination attaches to these figures, where all are so much at fault. Nature has given to us the most valuable possession ever committed to man. It can never be duplicated, because there is none like it upon the face of the earth. And we are racking and impoverishing it exactly as we are felling the forests and rifling the mines. Our soil, once the envy of every other country, the attraction which draws millions of immigrants across the seas, gave an average yield for the whole United States during the 10 years beginning with 1896 of 13.5 bushels of wheat per acre. Austria and Hungary each produced over 17 bushels per acre, France 19.8, Germany 27.6, and the United Kingdom 32.2 bushels per acre. For the same decade our average yield of oats was less than 30 bushels, while Germany produced 46 and Great Britain 42. For barley the figures are 25 against 33 and 34.6; for rye 15.4 against 24 for Germany and 26 for Ireland. In the United Kingdom, Belgium, the Netherlands, and Denmark a yield of more than 30 bushels of wheat per acre has been the average for the past five years.

When the most fertile land in the world produces so much less than that of poorer quality elsewhere, and this low yield shows a tendency toward steady decline, the situation becomes clear. We are robbing the soil, in an effort to get the largest cash returns from each acre of ground in the shortest possible time and with the least possible labor. This soil is not mere dead matter, subject to any sort of treatment with impunity. Chemically, it contains elements which must be present in certain proportions for the support of vegetation. Physically, it is made up of matter which supplies the principal plant food. This food, with its chemical constituents in proper admixture, is furnished by the decomposition of organic matter and the disintegration of mineral matter that proceed together. Whatever disturbs either factor of the process, whatever takes out of the soil an excessive amount of one or more of the chemical elements upon which plant growth depends, ends in sterility.

Any agricultural methods that move in this direction mean soil impoverishment; present returns at the cost of future loss; the exhaustion of the land—exactly as the animal system is enfeebled by lack of proper nourishment.

Our agricultural lands have been abused in two principal ways: first, by single cropping, and second, by neglecting fertilization. It is fortunate for us that nature is slow to anger, and that we may arrest the consequence of this ruinous policy before it is too late. In all parts of the United States, with only isolated exceptions, the system of tillage has been to select the crop which would bring in most money at the current market rate, to plant that year after year, and to move on to virgin fields as soon as the old farm rebelled by lowering the quality and quantity of its return. It is still the practice; although diversification of industry and the rotation of crops have been urged for nearly a century and are today taught in every agricultural college in this country. The demonstration of the evils of single cropping is mathematical in its completeness. At the experiment station of the Agricultural College of the University of Minnesota they have maintained 44 experimental plots of ground, adjoining one another, and as nearly identical in soil, cultivation, and care as scientific handling can make them. On these have been tried and compared different methods of crop rotation and fertilization, together with systems of single cropping. The results of ten years' experiment are now available. On a tract of good ground sown continuously for 10 years to wheat, the average yield per acre for the first five years was 20.22 bushels and for the next five 16.92 bushels. Where corn was grown continuously on one plot while on the plot beside it corn was planted but once in five years in a system of rotation, the average yield of the latter for the two years it was under corn was 48.2 bushels per acre. The plot where corn only was grown gave 20.8 bushels per acre for the first five and 11.1 bushels for the last five-year period, an average of 16 bushels. The difference in average of these two plots was 32.2 bushels, or twice the total yield of the ground exhausted by the single-crop system. The corn grown at the end of the 10 years was hardly hip high, the ears small and the grains light. But the cost of cultivation remained the same. And the same is true of every other grain or growth when raised continuously on land unfertilized. We frequently hear it said that the reduction in yield is due to the wearing out of the soil as if it was a garment to be destroyed by the wearing. The fact is that soils either increase or maintain their productivity indefinitely under proper cultivation. If the earth, the great mother of human and animal life, is to "wear out," what is to become of the race?

The two remedies are as well ascertained as is the evil. Rotation of crops and the use of fertilizers act as tonics upon the soil. We might expand our resources and add billions of dollars to our national wealth by conserving soil resources, instead of exhausting them as we have the forests and the contents of our mines. For there is good authority for the assertion that the farmer could take from the same area of ground in four years' grain crops as much as seven years now give him; leaving the products of the other three years when the land rested from grain as a clear profit due to better methods.

He can do far more than that by joining livestock raising with grain raising. Nature has provided the cattle to go with the land. There is as much money in livestock as there is in grain. Looked at in any way there is money in livestock: money for dairy products, money for beef, money for the annual increase, and most money of all for the next year's crop when every particle of manure is saved and applied to the land.

We need not consider at present really intensive farming, such as is done by market gardeners with high profit, or such culture as in France, in Holland, in Belgium, and in the island of Jersey produces financial returns per acre that seem almost beyond belief. The average in money per acre of the island of Jersey for each acre of cultivated land is over $250. What our people have to do is to cover less ground, cultivate smaller farms so as to make the most of them instead of getting a scant and uncertain yield from several hundred acres, and raise productivity by intelligent treatment to twice or three times its present level.

There is more money in this system. The net profit from an

acre of wheat on run-down soils is very small; consequently decreasing the acreage of wheat under certain conditions will not materially decrease profits. Here are some reliable estimates. The price of wheat is given from the United States Department of Agriculture Yearbook, average for ten years:

Yield in bushels	Price	Market value per acre	Cost of production, including rent	Net profit or loss, per acre
20	$0.638	$12.76	$7.89	+ $4.87
16	.638	10.21	7.89	+ 2.32
12	.638	7.66	7.89	− .23
10	.638	6.38	7.89	− 1.51
8	.638	5.10	7.89	− 2.79

From the above table it will be seen that as large a net profit is realized from one crop of 20 bushels per acre as from two crops of 16 bushels; and that a 12-bushel crop or less yields a net loss—that is, provided the land is charged with a rental of $2.50 an acre. It is a safe conclusion that 75 acres of land, growing a crop of clover every fourth year will yield a larger net profit than will 100 acres sown to grain continually. A small field of eight acres of clover in the Red River Valley last year yielded 42 bushels (worth over $60) per acre, the value coming from the sale of seed.

I have dwelt upon the conservation of farm resources because of the commanding importance of this industry and because of its relation to our future. Nearly 36% of our people are engaged directly in agriculture. But all the rest depend on it. In the last analysis, commerce, manufactures, our home market, every form of activity, run back to the bounty of the earth by which every worker, skilled and unskilled, must be fed, and by which his wages are ultimately paid. The farm products of the United States in 1906 were valued at $6,794,-000,000 and in 1907 at $7,412,000,000. All of our vast domestic commerce, equal in value to the foreign trade of all the nations combined, is supported and paid for by the land. Of our farm areas only one-half is improved. It does not produce one-half of what it could be made to yield; not by some complex system of intensive culture, but merely by ordinary care and industry intelligently applied. It is the capital upon which alone we can draw through all the future, but the amount of the draft that will be honored depends on the care and intelligence given to its cultivation. Were any statesman to show us how to add $7,000,000,000 annually to our foreign trade, it would be the sensation of the hour. The way to do this in agriculture is open. Our share in the increase would not be the percentage of profit allowed by successful trading, but the entire capital sum. On the other side stands the fact that the unappropriated area suitable to farm purposes is almost gone, and that we have been for the last century reducing the producing power of the country. Nowhere in the range of national purposes is the reward for conservation of a national resource so ample. Nowhere is the penalty of neglect so threatening.

By the fixed rate of increase in the past, we must count upon a population of over 200,000,000 in the United States in the year 1950. The annual increase from natural growth is about one and one-half per cent each year. Adding for immigration only 750,000 a year, which is less than three-quarters of the figures reached in recent years, we shall have about 130,000,000 people in 1925, and at least 200,000,000 by the middle of the century. Where are they to go, how are they to be employed, how fed, how enabled to earn a living wage? The pressure of all the nations upon the waste places of the earth grows more intense as the last of them are occupied. We are approaching the point where all our wheat product will be needed for our own uses, and we shall cease to be an exporter of grain. There is still some room in Canada, but it will soon be filled. The relief will be but temporary. Our own people, whose mineral resources will by that time have greatly diminished, must find themselves thrown back upon the soil for a living. If continued abuse of the land should mark the next fifty years as it has the last, what must be our outlook?

Even the unintelligent are now coming to understand that we cannot look to our foreign trade for relief from future embarrassment. Our total exports, about one-fourth in value of the products of our farms, consist to the extent of more than 70% of articles grown on the soil or directly sustained by it, such as livestock, or made from soil products, such as flour. Of all the materials used in manufacture in this country, 42% are furnished by the soil. We shall have less and less of this agricultural wealth to part with as population increases. And as to enlarging greatly our sale of manufactured products in the world's markets, it is mostly a dream. We cannot finally compete there, except in a few selected lines, without a material lowering of the wage scale at home and a change in the national standard of living which our people are not ready to accept without a struggle. When capital cannot find a profit, there will be no money for the payrolls of an unprofitable business. Doubtless as we grow we shall buy more and sell more, but our main dependence half a century ahead must be on ourselves. The Nation can no more escape the operation of that law than can the man. It is time to set our house in order.

Not only the economic but the political future is involved. No people ever felt the want of work or the pinch of poverty for a long time without reaching out violent hands against their political institutions, believing that they might find in a change some relief from their distress. Although there have been moments of such restlessness in our country, the trial has never been so severe or so prolonged as to put us to the test. It is interesting that one of the ablest men in England during the last century, a historian of high merit, a statesman who saw active service, and a profound student of men and things, put on record his prophecy of such a future ordeal. Writing to an American correspondent 50 years ago, Lord Macaulay used these words:

As long as you have a boundless extent of fertile and unoccupied land your laboring population will be found more at ease than the laboring population of the Old World; but the time will come when wages will be as low and will fluctuate as much with you as they do with us. Then your institutions will be brought to the test. Distress everywhere makes the laborer mutinous and discontented and inclines him to listen with eagerness to agitators who tell him that it is a monstrous iniquity that one man should have a million and another cannot get a full meal. . . . The day will come when the multitudes of people, none of whom has had more than half a breakfast or expects to have more than half a dinner, will choose a legislature. Is it possible to doubt what sort of legislature will be chosen? . . . There will be, I fear, spoliation. The spoliation will increase the distress; the distress will produce fresh spoliation . . . Either civilization or liberty will perish. Either some Caesar or Napoleon will seize the reins of government with a strong hand, or your Republic will be as fearfully plundered and laid waste by barbarians in the twentieth century as the Roman Empire in the fifth.

We need not accept this gloomy picture too literally, but we have been already sufficiently warned to prevent us from dismissing the subject as unworthy of attention. Every nation finds its hour of peril when there is no longer free access to the land, or when the land will no longer support the people. Disturbances within are more to be feared than attacks from without. Our Government is built upon the assumption of a fairly contented, happy, and prosperous people, ruling their passions, with power to change their institutions when such change is generally desired. It would not be strange if they should in their desire for change attempt to pull down the pillars of their national temple. Far may this day be from us! But since the unnecessary destruction of our land will bring new conditions of danger, its conservation, its improvement to the highest point of productivity promised by scientific intelligence and practical experiment, appears to be a first command of any political economy worthy of the name.

I have endeavored to outline some of the principal issues at stake in the better conservation of our national resources, and especially that one about which all the others revolve and by whose fortunes we shall eventually stand or fall—the land itself. They are for us quite literally the issues of national existence. The era of unlimited expansion on every side, of having but to reach out and seize any desired good, ready provided for us by the hand that laid the foundations of the earth, is drawing to a close. The first task, it seems to me, must be to force home the facts of the situation into the public consciousness; to make men realize their duty toward coming generations exactly as the father feels it a duty to see that his children do not suffer want. In a democracy this is a first essential. In other forms of government one or two great men may have power to correct mistakes, and to put in motion wise policies that centuries do not unsettle. A part of the price of self-government is the acceptance of that high office and imperative duty as a whole by the people themselves. They must know, they must weigh, they must act. Only as they form and give effect to wise decisions can the nation go forward. And we should not be here today were it not that the principle of a conservation of national resources as the foremost and controlling policy of the United States henceforth is coming to be seen by many, and must be heartily accepted by all, as the first condition not only of continued material prosperity, but also of the perpetuation of free institutions and a government by the People. The work now being done by the Department of Agriculture and the agricultural colleges of the various states, furnishes a broad and intelligent foundation upon which to build up a new era of national progress and prosperity. It calls for a wise, generous and continuing policy on the part of both Federal and State governments.

If this patriotic gospel is to make headway, it must be by just such organized missionary work as is here begun. It cannot go on and conquer if imposed from without. It must come to represent the fixed idea of the People's mind, their determination and their hope. It can not be incorporated in our practical life by the dictum of any individual or any officer of Nation or State in his official capacity. It needs the cooperation of all the influences, the help of every voice, the commendation of Nation and State that has been the strength and inspiration of every worthy work on American soil for 120 years. We return, for our gathering in council and for our plan of action for the future, to the model given us by the Fathers. State and Nation are represented here, without jealousy or any ambition of superiority on either side, to apply to the consideration of our future such cooperation as that out of which this Nation was born and by which it has won to worthy manhood. Reviving the spirit of the days that created our Constitution, the days that carried us through civil conflict, the spirit by which all our enduring work in the world has been wrought, taking thought as Washington and Lincoln took thought, only for the highest good of all the People, we may, as a result of the deliberations held and the conclusions reached here today, give new meaning to our future, new lustre to the ideal of a Republic of living federated states, may shape anew the fortunes of this country, and enlarge the borders of hope for all mankind.

I. Income Taxation

Although the income tax has a fairly long history in the United States, surprisingly little has ever been said either to justify or condemn it. It was introduced for the first time by the North as a measure to finance the Civil War. Applied to only a small part of the population and only mildly progressive, it was imposed in 1861 and persisted until 1872. Although some debate took place when the law was first passed, little enough was said then about the two basic questions this form of taxation raises. Supposing that it has been decided to tax income, what reason is there for choosing to tax it progressively? (A proportional tax—of 20 per cent, for instance—on all incomes would equally well satisfy the criterion that those who earn more should pay more and would provide as much revenue as a progressive tax whose basic rate was only slightly lower.) Secondly, how could the tax be reconciled with the Constitutional provision requiring "direct taxation" to be levied on the states in proportion to their population, since, if "direct tax" meant anything, it meant a tax on individuals?

These two questions, on the whole neatly avoided during the Civil War experiment, were forced into open debate during the second attempt to establish an income tax. This took place when Congress, in 1894, enacted the tax as an amendment to the Wilson-Gorman Tariff Act, presumably in an effort to make the high tariffs more palatable to small consumers.

The statute had hardly come into effect when one Pollock, a stockholder in the Farmers' Loan Company, sought a court order to prevent the company from paying the tax. The action was posed in this slightly fictitious form because American courts refuse to consider abstract questions and will decide the constitutionality of a law only in the context of a concrete and specific case.

When the case reached the Supreme Court, W. D. Guthrie was one of the group of distinguished lawyers who, appearing for Pollock, argued against the law. Attorney-General Olney appeared as a "friend of the court," since the United States was not a party to the action. (Parts of their arguments are given in 16 and 17.) The Court invalidated part of the law but divided 4 to 4 on the central issue of whether the income tax was direct and therefore unconstitutional.

A rehearing was held several weeks later, and this time Justice Jackson rose from his sickbed to fill the bench. The Court now held by a majority of 5 to 4 that the tax was unconstitutional (18). Since Jackson was known to have dissented, it followed that one of the other justices had during the six weeks changed his earlier view. The belief that in holding an income tax unconstitutional the Court was reversing a long line of its own decisions was perhaps less important in stimulating hostility toward the Court than the conclusion that the legality of an important and popular statute might turn on the apparently unstable views of a single justice.

The constitutional difficulty was solved by the ratification in 1913 of the Sixteenth Amendment. But neither then nor since has much been said to justify the notion of progressive taxation —which by now has acquired the appearance of being justifiable because it is habitual.

16

W. D. Guthrie

Opening Argument for Pollock (1895)
[in *Pollock vs. Farmers' Loan and
Trust Co.* (157 U.S. 429)]

The provisions as to an income tax contained in the act of
August 28, 1894, are unconstitutional, in that they violate the
requirement of the Constitution as to apportionment in respect
of direct taxes, or as to uniformity in respect of duties, imposts, and excises.

Congress has no constitutional power to impose taxes, duties,
or excises which shall vary according to ownership of the
subject-matter of the tax, and which shall be at one rate upon
the income of individuals, and at an entirely different rate upon
the income of corporations and of those who derive their income from corporate profits. It has no power to foster and aid
favored classes of corporations and associations by arbitrarily
exempting them from taxation. It is the fundamental rule of
all taxation that there shall be equality of burden among those
of the same class; and that, under well-settled principles, if a
tax be levied upon any citizens at a higher rate than is imposed
upon others of the same class, having like property, it is depriving the former of their property without due process of
law and taking the same for public use without just compensation. It is also submitted that Congress cannot tax income derived from state, county, and municipal bonds. . . .

The provisions of the act of 1894 impose a tax of two per
cent upon the gains, profits, and income derived from any kind
of property, including rent and the growth and produce of
land and profits made upon the sale of land if purchased within
two years. Every element that could make real or personal
property a source of value or income to an owner is taxed.

An excise or duty is also imposed upon income derived from any profession, trade, employment, or avocation. The tax upon persons generally is not upon their entire income, but upon the excess over and above $4000. All persons having incomes of $4000 or under are exempted. The whole burden of the tax falls upon less than two per cent of the population of the country.

The rate of taxation upon corporations and associations is in excess of the rate imposed upon individuals and associations. Persons having incomes of $4000 or under pay nothing; corporations having like incomes pay two per cent. Persons having incomes of over $4000 pay on the excess. Corporations having like incomes, derived from like property and like values, pay two per cent upon the entire amount. Partnerships are expressly exempted from the operation of the act. An individual owning lands, the rents of which net him $8000, pays $80, or two per cent upon the excess over $4000. A corporation or association having like property pays a tax of two per cent upon the whole $8000, or $160, double the tax upon the individual. Five individuals as partners own property or carry on business netting them, after paying all taxes and expenses, $20,000, which they divide equally. The partnership is entirely exempted from taxation, and each member is exempted. If those same five individuals organized a private trading corporation or association under the laws of one of the States, and held the property in that form, they would have to pay an income tax of $400, simply and solely because they had united their interest in a corporate or associate form instead of a partnership. In a word, the rate varies according to the form or nature of ownership. Citizens whose income is $4000 and under, derived from profits and dividends of corporations, are deprived of the benefit of the exemption, because their shares or interests in the profits of corporations are subjected to a tax of two per cent, while the same income derived from similar business and similar property by those who carry on business individually or as partners would be wholly exempted. If the exemption of the $4000 was to cover the expenses of a household, certainly all persons having all their means invested in corporate shares equally have their household expenses. Why not exempt them?

The act of 1894 is new in the provisions discriminating against those whose income is derived from dividends of corporations and in the exemptions from taxation of favored private corporations and associations. Under the old income tax laws, the business of certain selected classes of corporations, such as banks, saving institutions, insurance companies and railroads was taxed. The language of the present act is "all corporations, companies, or associations, doing business for profit in the United States, no matter how created and organized, but not including partnerships." The tax upon classes of corporations under the old law was sustained, not because it was a tax upon the property of the corporations selected, but upon the distinct ground that it was an excise upon their business. Such was the reason assigned by Mr. Justice Swayne in the case of *Pacific Insurance Co.* v. *Soule,* 7 Wall. 433, and such the ground reiterated by Mr. Justice Miller in delivering the opinion of the court in *Railroad Co.* v. *Collector,* 100 U.S. 595. The bank tax was held to be a tax, not upon property or income, but upon the act of issuing notes; not on the obligation itself, but on its use in a particular way. The judgment in *Veazie Bank* v. *Fenno,* 8 Wall. 533, followed by *National Bank* v. *United States,* 101 U.S. 1, clearly shows this to be the true ground.

The act of 1894 not only exempts charitable, religious, and educational institutions, but it specially excepts from the operation of the tax certain private business concerns, such as building and loan associations, savings banks and mutual insurance companies—not merely mutual life companies, but all mutual insurance companies or associations, whether life, fire, marine, inland, or accident. The exemption is granted without regard to the amount of property or income. If the business of an insurance company is conducted on the stock plan for the benefit of its shareholders, every dollar of profit is taxed; if it is carried on for the benefit of its members or policy-holders, who are but another form of shareholders, it is wholly exempted. The census reports show the immense accumulations of estates in the hands of these exempted corporations or institutions. In the State of New York, the act exempts hundreds of millions of property.

The census reports show that when the statistics were compiled in 1890 there were 1926 insurance companies transacting insurance business relating to property, of which 1689 were doing business on the mutual plan. The assets of all these companies are not reported, but taking those ascertained, we find $278,000,000 of assets owned by stock insurance companies and $1,200,000,000 of assets owned by mutual companies: the former are subjected to the income tax; the latter are absolutely freed from any such burden simply because the method or manner of conducting the very same business happens to be the mutual plan. The amount of tax saved to these favored mutual companies is at least $1,200,000 per annum.

It is not contended that any doubt exists as to the power of Congress to tax the property or income of private corporations organized under state laws in the same manner and at the same rate that it taxes the property and income of individuals; but it is insisted that the property cr income of corporations or of citizens deriving their income therefrom cannot be singled out to be assessed and taxed at a higher rate than the property or income of other individuals or partnerships. If exemptions are to be granted, then such exemptions must be equally allowed to those who have their means invested in corporations and who derive their income from the corporate profits. The question is not whether Congress can select particular classes of property or income for taxation,—whether it can tax one article at one rate and another article at a different rate,—but whether it can prescribe rules of taxation upon like property or like income which shall vary as it is held or collected by individuals and partnerships on the one hand or by corporations and their stockholders on the other. The power of Congress to impose an excise upon certain peculiar or distinct businesses or occupations is not challenged; the question is regarding its right to impose an excise tax upon a particular business or occupation which shall vary as it is carried on by individuals or by corporations.

Congress has no power, at the expense of others owning
property of the same character, to foster and aid private trading
corporations, such as building and loan associations, savings
banks and mutual life, fire, marine, inland, and accident insurance companies or associations, which serve no national
purpose or public interest whatsoever and which exist solely
for the pecuniary profit of their members. There seems to be a
notion that the courts have held that the right to exempt is
one of legislative discretion, and that there is no check upon
it and no limit to its exercise. With us, under the American
system, no power of government is untrammelled or unrestrained. The exercise of the discretion to exempt must be regulated by some public interest; it cannot be arbitrary or capricious; there must be some principle of public policy to support
the presumption that the public and not private interests will
be subserved by the exemptions which are allowed. Private
enterprises for the pecuniary profit of their members can never
be aided under the guise of the exercise of the discretion to
exempt. . . .

We now come to the question whether these gross inequalities and discriminations are unconstitutional. Section 8 of Article I of the Constitution is as follows: "The Congress shall
have power to lay and collect taxes, duties, imposts, and excises; to pay the debts and provide for the common defence
and general welfare of the United States; but all duties, imposts, and excises shall be uniform throughout the United
States." The contention of the government and of the appel-
lees, in support of the act, seems to be that the uniformity
required is simply geographical in character, and does not
prohibit inequality among persons in regard to the same property or subject of the tax, provided the inequality be uniform
throughout the United States. This contention is without merit,
and is certainly not sustained by authority. The true meaning
of that clause in the Constitution is that duties, imposts, and
excises shall bear equally upon the subject of taxation and be
uniform throughout the United States. . . .

A tax which imposes one rate upon individuals and a higher
rate upon corporations, which exempts individuals generally to

the extent of $4000, but practically denies any such exemption to those deriving their income from corporate investments, and which arbitrarily exempts immense accumulations of property in the hands of favored private corporations and associations, is not uniform in any sense or in any part of the United States.

The court cannot strike out the exemptions and itself remodel the act so as to make it uniform. The act of 1894 must fall because of its utter lack of uniformity. It is not within the judicial province to make a new law. It would be decreeing as law what Congress deliberately refused to enact. If these immense accumulations of property had not been exempted, if corporations had not been discriminated against, the law might never have been passed: at all events, the rate of taxation would probably have been reduced to one per cent. The court will not strike out these exceptions and exemptions so as to give the act an operation which Congress confessedly never meant. If you annul the exemptions, what warrant of law would exist for collecting a tax from these mutual concerns? As Mr. Justice Matthews said in the case of *Spraigue* v. *Thompson*, 118 U.S. 90, 95, delivering the opinion of the whole court, this would confer "upon the statute a positive operation beyond the legislative intent, and beyond what any one can say it would have enacted in view of the illegality of the exceptions."

But, irrespective of the constitutional limitation, the grant to Congress of the power to tax necessarily implied the limitation that all taxes should be equal, impartial, and uniform as to all similarly situated.

The requirement of approximate equality inheres in the very nature of the power to tax, and it exists whether declared or not in the written Constitution. It may be difficult, if not impracticable, to obtain absolute equality as between all classes of property. We recognize that; but there must be absolute equality as between persons or owners of the same kind of property. The taxing power may select land and omit personal property, or select any particular kind of personal property and omit land, and the courts cannot interfere; but on whatever subject the tax is imposed, it must apply equally and uniformly to all owning similar property; it cannot vary according to ownership; it cannot tax one and arbitrarily exempt another; it cannot be at one rate for the individual, and at another rate for the corporation.

The provisions of the Fifth Amendment, prescribing due process of law and just compensation if private property be taken for public use, restrain the Federal government from enforcing unequal and partial tax laws.

When the Constitution was adopted, the people expressed their apprehension that powers not intended to be conferred might be claimed and exercised by the Federal government, and that there might be an abuse of taxation. Hamilton had argued in the Federalist that adequate precautions had been inserted, and that the door had been closed to partiality and oppression; but the people insisted on further specific restrictions upon Congress, and to that end ten amendments were proposed at the first session of the First Congress in March, 1789.

The Fifth Amendment, thus adopted to restrict the powers of Congress, provides that no person shall be deprived of life, liberty, or property, without due process of law, nor shall private property be taken for public use without just compensation. We contend that an act of Congress which imposes the burden of a tax upon the property or income of certain citizens, while others owning like property or having like income are exempted, or which imposes a rate of taxation upon like subjects which varies according to their ownership, deprives those discriminated against of their property without due process of law and arbitrarily takes such property for public use without just compensation. To impose a tax on A and B, and exempt C and D similarly situated, is not taxation, but exaction and confiscation. Our conception of the rights of our clients under the shield and protection of due process of law finds its definition in the language of the Chief Justice in *Caldwell* v. *Texas*, 137 U.S. 692, 697: " 'Due process of law' is so secured by laws operating on all alike and not subjecting the individual to the arbitrary exercise of the powers of government, unrestrained by the established principles of private right and distributive justice."

And further, there can be no doubt that in enacting the income tax law of 1894, it was the deliberate intention of Congress to tax the income derived from state, county, and municipal securities. The precise question as to the power of Congress to tax income derived from state, county, and municipal bonds has never been decided, but it has often been held that the instrumentalities of the state governments cannot be, directly or indirectly, taxed, and of course, a municipal corporation is but a branch of the government of the State. The authorities fully sustain the proposition that Congress cannot tax the borrowing powers of the States or their municipalities; for clearly if the right to tax existed, it would place the borrowing powers of the States completely at the mercy of a majority in Congress. . . .

The discrimination in the present case cannot be sustained upon the theory that the taxing power may classify the various kinds of property or the various kinds of business for purposes of taxation. It is not classification to impose a tax at one rate on the income or business of corporations and at a different rate upon the same income or the same business if carried on by individuals or partnerships. Classification to be lawful must distinguish between different kinds of property, not different ownership, or between different business pursuits, not between particular or selected individuals or corporations of the same class. If the difference in the rate of taxation is not based upon the nature of the property, nor upon the use made of the property, irrespective of its ownership, then it is based on ownership and involves a discrimination against particular owners, which is unlawful. In the present case, corporations have not been classified as a class, but the same tax is imposed upon companies or associations as distinguished from corporations, no matter how created and organized. Besides, under this act, a large class of these corporations, companies, and associations are withdrawn from the operation of the act, and it cannot be said, therefore, that Congress has classified corporations as a class, even if it had the power to do so.

We are not instructed to present any argument which shall abridge the taxing power of Congress or embarrass the government in any emergency that may now exist or hereafter arise. Let Congress remodel the act, apportioning direct taxes and equalizing indirect taxes, within the limitations of the Constitution, and none more willingly than our clients will contribute their share of the burden to maintain, defend, and preserve the national government, even if it shall take all their property. We ask you to impose no limitation upon the right of Congress to tax up to the full measure of the requirements of the Nation. Recognizing that authority to tax in its nature must be without limitations except equality of burden, and that it involves the power to destroy, we are here to plead that the destruction must result from some necessity or peril of the Union, and that however the occasion may arise, the destruction must be equal and uniform and not of selected individuals or classes: we are here to plead that Congress cannot sacrifice one—the lowliest or the richest—for the benefit of others.

17
Richard Olney (1835-1917)
Oral Argument of the Attorney General (1895)
[in *Pollock vs. Farmers' Loan and Trust Co.*,
(157 U.S. 429)]

. . . This brings me to the only remaining point—to *the* constitutional objection which, notwithstanding all that has been so earnestly and forcibly said on the direct tax part of this controversy, is, I am satisfied, the plaintiffs' main reliance. The point is that the income tax imposed by the statute under consideration is not uniform. But what does the Constitution mean by "uniform" as applied to a tax? But for the strong pressure upon the plaintiffs' counsel to find objections to this statute there would be no controversy as to the meaning. It is clearly

shown by the debates in the constitutional convention and by
the repeated and unequivocal utterances of the framers of the
Constitution themselves. It is set forth by the writers on constitutional law, who are unanimous in their interpretation. It
is judicially expounded by this court in the well-known judgments in the so-called *Head Money cases.* The uniformity of
tax prescribed by the Constitution is a territorial uniformity.
A Federal tax, which is not a poll tax nor a tax on land, must
be the same in all parts of the country. It cannot be one thing
in Maine and another thing in Florida. The law providing for
such a tax must be like a bankruptcy law or a naturalization
law. It must have the same operation everywhere, wholly irrespective of state lines.

It is manifestly impossible for the plaintiffs to assent to this
settled construction of the word "uniform," and they do not
assent to it. They are compelled to insist that a tax, to be "uniform" within the meaning of the Constitution, must be uniform,
not only geographically but as between taxpayers. In other
words, they make it prescribe the nature and quality of a tax
as well as its local application. I submit that their contention
is hopeless and may fairly be regarded as already decided
against them. Let it be, however, for present purposes that the
adjective "uniform" describes and regulates the properties of a
tax. I then beg leave to submit that the plaintiffs gain nothing
by the concession, and that, so far as the validity of this income-tax law or any other tax law is concerned, the word
"uniform" might as well be out of the Constitution as in it. The
word is surplusage. It simply designates and describes an essential element of every tax—an element which is inherent in
every valid tax and the absence of which would be sufficient
to annul any attempted exercise of the taxing power.

For the basis and the truth of this position it is only necessary to refer for a moment to the nature of the taxing power.
The power to tax is wholly legislative, and in its essence is the
power to raise money *from* the public *for* the public. That the
object of a tax must be public is undeniable. To force money
from the pockets of the people at large to enrich a private
individual is so clear an abuse of the taxing power that every

court would so declare on general principles without the aid of any express constitutional prohibition. Conversely, to take the property of a single individual for public uses is not to exercise the power to tax but the power of eminent domain, and can be done only on the condition of rendering the individual full indemnity. These inherent limitations of the taxing power necessarily enter into and control every scheme of taxation and determine the mode and extent of its operation upon private persons and estates. Theoretically, a tax for the benefit of the public should fall equally upon all persons composing the public; should, as text writers and judges often express it, be ratable and proportional, and be so adjusted that every member of the community shall contribute his just and equal share toward the common defence and the general welfare. Moreover, under theoretical and ideal conditions such as can be conceived of, these general maxims would be actually and exactly applicable. If, for example, every individual in a community were like every other in respect of property, of the ability to bear taxation, and of the benefit to accrue from taxation, the question how he should be taxed could receive but one answer. Nothing would have to be done but to apply the rule of three, and any other rule would be inadmissible for obvious reasons. To make one man pay a higher rate of tax than another when all the conditions in both cases are exactly alike would, to the extent of the excess be a taking of private property for public uses without making that special compensation which alone can justify such a taking.

Taxation, however, is an uncommonly practical affair. The power to tax is for practical use and is necessarily to be adapted to the practical conditions of human life. These are never the same for any two persons, and for any community, however small, are infinitely diversified. Regard being paid to them, nothing is more evident, nothing has been oftener declared by courts and jurists, than that absolute equality of taxation is impossible—is, as characterized in an opinion of this court, only "a baseless dream." No system has been or can be devised that will produce any such result. Suppose, for instance, manhood taxation were resorted to, as a sort of offset to manhood suffrage, and that the public exchequer were sought to be filled by a tax levied on adult males at so much per head—the inequity and impolicy of such a tax would be universally recognized and universally denounced. But if such would be the fate of a capitation tax employed as the sole source of public revenue, hardly less objection lies to an ad valorem property tax which should make every owner, without exception or discrimination of any sort, pay in exact proportion to the value of his estate. Logically and theoretically, no criticism could be made on such a tax. But practically it loses sight of a most important element, to wit, the ability to bear taxation, and ignores the fact that exacting $5 from a man whose annual income is $500 puts upon him an infinitely greater burden than the exaction of $500 from one whose annual income is $50,000. There is at first blush plausibility in the suggestion that the rule should be that every person should contribute to a tax ratably to the benefits derived from it. But nothing could be more objectionable or would be more certainly objected to than an attempt to collect the public revenue on any such plan. The principal beneficiaries of almost all taxes, of the taxes for highways and schools and sewers, and almost all other objects of state and municipal expenditure, are the poorer classes of the community. To impose taxes solely upon the principle of the ensuing advantages realized would in effect largely exempt the more fortunate and wealthy classes and place the greater part of the burden upon those least able to bear it.

These considerations serve to show the nature of the taxing power; that it offers little, if any, opportunity for the exploitation of theories or for experiment with abstract generalizations; that it calls for the highest practical wisdom to be applied to the actual and infinitely varied affairs of a particular community and people; and that in its exercise, in the selection of the subjects of taxation, in taxing some persons and estates and in exempting others, the legislature is vested with the largest and widest discretion. It by no means follows that the power to tax is without any limits. They are, so to speak, self-imposed, that is, as already observed, they result from the very nature of the power itself. No country, for example, no State of this

Union, ever adopted a plan of taxation that did not except some portions of the community from a burden that was imposed upon others. The power to do so is unquestioned and is universally exercised. Nevertheless, the power to exempt has bounds. It cannot be used without regard to the end in view, nor to gratify a mere whim or caprice. A law, for instance, providing for a tax to be paid by the light-complexioned members of the community and exempting the dark, would be unhesitatingly pronounced void as being not a use but an abuse of the taxing power. It would be an abuse because the discrimination made by it could not be traced to any line of public policy. So, having classified the community for the purpose of a tax, the legislature cannot then proceed by arbitrary selection to take individuals out of the class to which they belong. That is the rule of uniformity—that is what "uniform" means as applied to a tax—and that is its whole meaning as used in the Federal Constitution, even when it is conceded that it prescribes the nature of a tax, not merely as between localities, but as between taxpayers. The rule of uniformity places no restrictions upon any division of the community into classes for taxable purposes which the legislature may deem wise. It merely declares that, the classes being formed, the members of each shall be on the same footing, and shall be taxed alike or be exempted alike without arbitrary discriminations in individual cases. Uniformity between members of a class created for taxable purposes is required upon the same grounds which prevent a purely senseless and capricious division into classes. The classification must be such that it can be referred to some view of public policy. Being made and justified only on that principle, any exemption of particular members of a class is void because necessarily in conflict with the principle and preventing its operation.

For these reasons I maintain that the term "uniform" in the Constitution, even if it describes the properties of a tax, puts no limitations upon the taxing power of Congress that are not inherent in the very nature of the power. It is a power to enforce money from the public for public uses. Could it be exercised so as to produce equality of taxation, it could be exercised in no other manner. That not being feasible in the nature of things, it is for Congress and Congress alone to decide how the taxing power shall be applied so as best to approximate that result. In making that application, Congress is of course bound to keep in view the fundamental purpose of the power and to aim at its accomplishment. Hence, in taxing this class or exempting that, Congress must proceed upon considerations of public policy, and cannot adopt a classification which has no relation to the end to be attained and is founded only in whim or caprice. Hence, and on the same ground, classes for the purpose of taxation being constituted, the rule of taxation or exemption must be uniform between members of the class. But, these limitations upon its taxing power being granted, the right of Congress to determine who shall be taxed and what shall be taxed and all the ways and means of assessment and collection, is practically uncontrolled. It is quite beside the issue to argue in this or any other case that Congress has mistaken what public policy requires. On that point Congress is the sole and final authority, and its decision once made controls every other department of the government.

These familiar principles, so well established that any citation of authorities and decisions is, I think, quite unnecessary, effectually dispose, I submit, of the plaintiffs' contention in the present cases. What do they complain of? It is not that Congress has determined to tax and has taxed income generally. It is that Congress has made exemptions in favor of certain classes, and the plaintiffs' contention, if pushed to its logical conclusion, means that Congress cannot tax income at all without taxing ratably the income of every man, woman, and child in the country. The preposterously harsh and impolitic operation of any such tax as that it is not necessary to descant upon. Congress has rightfully repudiated any such plan. While taxing incomes generally, it had full power to make such exemptions as its views of public policy required, and the only real question now and here is, has it abused or exceeded that power of exemption? The tests already stated are applicable, and being applied render but one answer to the question possible. The statute makes no exemption in favor of a class that is not based on some obvious line of public policy, and, the class being established, one uniform rule is applicable to its members. Take, for example, the principal classification of all —the grand division by which the entire population of the country is separated into people with incomes of $4000 and under who are non-taxable, and people with incomes of over $4000 who are taxable. It is manifest that in this distinction Congress was proceeding upon definite views of public policy and was aiming at accomplishing a great public object. It was seeking to adjust the load of taxation to the shoulders of the community in the manner that would make it most easily borne and most lightly felt. Having so much revenue to raise, it might have got it by a proportional tax upon the entire income of all the people of the country. But it bore in mind the fact that a small sum taken from a small income is an infinitely greater deprivation than a large sum taken from a large income; that in the one case the very means of decent support might be impaired, while in the other the power to command all the luxuries of life would hardly be affected. Acting upon these considerations or considerations such as these, Congress undertook to exempt moderate incomes from the tax altogether. It had to draw the line somewhere, and it drew it at $4000. The same objections in point of principle would have existed if it had drawn the line at $400, or at any other figure. But no objection in truth lies at all, because it is entirely evident that, as well in exempting incomes of $4000 and under as in taxing incomes of over $4000, Congress has been governed by what it deemed sound public policy. Take another illustration —an example of a class formed by way of exception to a larger class. The statutory general rule is that every taxpayer is entitled to a fixed deduction of $4000 before taxable income is reached. In the case, however, of a family consisting of husband and wife, or parent and a minor child or children, there is but one $4000 deduction from the aggregate income of all the members of the family. Here is a differentiation of a special class whose members may be taxed higher than others having incomes of the same amount. But the discrimination is not arbitrary nor senseless, but is founded on obvious views of equity and policy. It assumes—what is undoubtedly true—that as a rule there is but one income and one breadwinner to one family, but, recognizing the fact that the rule has many exceptions, it makes the existence of several incomes to a family the just and proper basis of a somewhat higher rate of tax. It is an attempt, in short, to tax with some regard to the capacity of the taxpayer to bear it. Take another illustration—that of a class which the plaintiffs' counsel dwell upon at great length and with exceeding unction—the class, namely, of business corporations. Their net incomes are taxed at the standard rate of two per cent undiminished by the standard deduction of $4000. The result is that a man in business as a member of a corporation is taxable at a little higher rate than a man in the same business by himself or as a copartner. Here, it is claimed, is a distinction without a difference, is the establishment of a special class without special reasons of equity and policy to justify it. But I venture to submit that that is not so, and that the higher statutory rate of tax for corporate incomes is founded upon and vindicated by essential differences in the conditions under which corporations and individuals respectively carry on business. The advantages acquired by doing business as a corporation, rather than as individuals or partners, are plain and are notorious. The interest of a corporator is in distinct and tangible shape, is marketable at any moment, and is unaffected by the insolvency or decease of other corporators. It is an interest attended with a definite and limited liability for debts. It is an interest through which the corporator ratably participates in all the benefits arising from the transaction of business on a large scale. These and other like commercial advantages of incorporation are wholly dependent upon legislative grant, which is the only fountain of corporate franchises. But so pronounced and so general has been the appreciation of these advantages that there is hardly a State of the Union which does not facilitate the formation of business corporations by a general corporation law, and that the great and evergrowing multitude and variety of such corporations is one of the striking phenomena of modern times. It is common knowledge, indeed, that corporations are so successful an agency for

the conduct of business and the accumulation of wealth that a
large section of the community views them with intense dis-
favor as malicious and cunningly devised inventions for making
rich people richer and poor people poorer. When, then, this
income-tax law takes a special class of business corporations
and taxes their incomes at a higher rate than that applied to
the incomes of persons not incorporated, it simply recognizes
existing social facts and conditions which it would be the
height of folly to ignore. It but classifies and discriminates
upon the plainest basis of equity and public policy, upon a
superiority of business conditions both enabling those enjoying
them to pay a special and higher rate of tax and making it
just and equitable that they should pay it. Other like exemptions of the statute, covering religious, educational, charitable
and semicharitable companies, and embracing institutions
where wage-earners lodge their scanty earnings and by which
persons of small means are enabled to cooperate in various ways
for mutual security and benefits, these exemptions rest firmly
upon the same legal footing of a wise and humane public
policy. It would be tedious and cannot be necessary to consider each in detail. Suffice it to say that the statute lays down
a rule for the taxation of incomes generally, and then adds
qualifications, exceptions, and exemptions, as to no one of
which can it be fairly said that it does not represent an honest
attempt of Congress to make the operation of the tax just and
equitable, and that it does not reflect the honest views of Congress respecting the requirements of true public policy. That
being so, it avails nothing for the plaintiffs to point out instances in which the law taxes property twice over or produces
other inequalities and incongruities in the way of taxation.
Nothing else could be expected and nothing different, it is safe
to predict, would result from any other law, even if the plaintiffs had the drawing of it. It avails nothing, also, for the
learned counsel to convince themselves, and perhaps the court
also, that Congress's views of public policy are quite mistaken.
When they have done that, what have they accomplished?
They have gone through an intellectual exercise which from
the character of counsel is bound to be both interesting and

brilliant. But they have accomplished nothing else because, be Congress's views of public policy ever so mistaken, this court cannot avoid ruling that it is absolutely bound by them.

My endeavor has been to eliminate and discuss such of the legal issues presented as are not already too conclusively settled to admit of discussion, and to do so succinctly, without unnecessary elaboration of details, and without being betrayed into those bypaths of metaphysical and economical and historical inquiry which, however fascinating in themselves, have so little connection with the real business of the case. It would be a mistake—I am aware that the court is in no danger of falling into it—but it would certainly be a mistake to infer that this great array of counsel, this elaborate argumentation, and these many and voluminous treatises miscalled by the name of briefs, indicate anything specially intricate or unique either in the facts before the court or in the rules of law which are applicable to them. An income tax is pre-eminently a tax upon the rich, and all the circumstances just adverted to prove the immense pecuniary stake which is now played for. It is so large that counsel fees and costs and printers' bills are mere bagatelles. It is so large and so stimulates the efforts of counsel that no legal or constitutional principle that stands in the way, however venerable or however long and universally acquiesced in, is suffered to pass unchallenged. It is a matter of congratulation, indeed, that the existence of the Constitution itself is not impeached, and that we are not threatened with a logical demonstration that we are still living, for all taxable purposes at least, under the regime of the old Articles of Confederation. Seriously speaking, however, I venture to suggest that all this laborious and erudite and formidable demonstration must necessarily be without result on one distinct ground. In its essence and in its last analysis, it is nothing but a call upon the judicial department of the government to supplant the political in the exercise of the taxing power; to substitute its discretion for that of Congress in respect of the subjects of taxation, the plan of taxation, and all the distinctions and discriminations by which taxation is sought to be equitably adjusted to the resources and capacities of the different classes of society. Such an effort, however weightily supported, cannot, I am bound to believe, be successful. It is inevitably predestined to failure unless this court shall, for the first time in its history, overlook and overstep the bounds which separate the judicial from the legislative power—bounds, the scrupulous observance of which it has so often declared to be absolutely essential to the integrity of our constitutional system of government.

18

Pollock vs. Farmers' Loan and Trust Co. (1895)
[158 U.S. 601]

Chief Justice Fuller, delivering the opinion of the court upon rehearing:

Whenever this court is required to pass upon the validity of an act of Congress as tested by the fundamental law enacted by the people, the duty imposed demands in its discharge the utmost deliberation and care, and invokes the deepest sense of responsibility. And this is especially so when the question involves the exercise of a great governmental power, and brings into consideration, as vitally affected by the decision, that complex system of government, so sagaciously framed to secure and perpetuate "an indestructible Union, composed of indestructible States."

We have, therefore, with an anxious desire to omit nothing which might in any degree tend to elucidate the questions submitted, and aided by further able arguments embodying the fruits of elaborate research, carefully re-examined these cases, with the result that, while our former conclusions remain unchanged, their scope must be enlarged by the acceptance of their logical consequences.

The very nature of the Constitution, as observed by Chief Justice Marshall, in one of his greatest judgments, "requires that only its great outlines should be marked, its important objects designated, and the minor ingredients which compose those objects be deduced from the nature of the objects themselves." "In considering this question, then, we must never forget that it is *a Constitution* that we are expounding." *McCulloch* v. *Maryland*, 4 Wheat. 316, 407.

As heretofore stated, the Constitution divided Federal taxation into two great classes, the class of direct taxes, and the class of duties, imposts, and excises; and prescribed two rules which qualified the grant of power as to each class.

The power to lay direct taxes apportioned among the several States in proportion to their representation in the popular branch of Congress, a representation based on population as ascertained by the census, was plenary and absolute; but to lay direct taxes without apportionment was forbidden. The power to lay duties, imposts, and excises was subject to the qualification that the imposition must be uniform throughout the United States.

Our previous decision was confined to the consideration of the validity of the tax on the income from real estate, and on the income from municipal bonds. The question thus limited was whether such taxation was direct or not, in the meaning of the Constitution; and the court went no farther, as to the tax on the income from real estate, than to hold that it fell within the same class as the source whence the income was derived, that is, that a tax upon the realty and a tax upon the receipts therefrom were alike direct; while as to the income from municipal bonds, that could not be taxed because of want of power to tax the source, and no reference was made to the nature of the tax as being direct or indirect.

We are now permitted to broaden the field of inquiry, and to determine to which of the two great classes a tax upon a person's entire income, whether derived from rents, or products, or otherwise, of real estate, or from bonds, stocks, or other forms of personal property, belongs; and we are unable to conclude that the enforced subtraction from the yield of all the owner's real or personal property, in the manner prescribed, is so different from a tax upon the property itself, that it is not a direct, but an indirect tax, in the meaning of the Constitution.

The words of the Constitution are to be taken in their obvious sense, and to have a reasonable construction. In *Gibbons* v. *Ogden,* Mr. Chief Justice Marshall, with his usual felicity, said: "As men, whose intentions require no concealment, generally employ the words which most directly and aptly express the ideas they intend to convey, the enlightened patriots who framed our Constitution, and the people who adopted it must be understood to have employed words in their natural sense, and to have intended what they have said." 9 Wheat. 1, 188. And in *Rhode Island* v. *Massachusetts,* where the question was whether a controversy between two States over the boundary between them was within the grant of judicial power, Mr. Justice Baldwin, speaking for the court, observed: "The solution of this question must necessarily depend on the words of the Constitution; the meaning and intention of the convention which framed and proposed it for adoption and ratification to the conventions of the people of and in the several States; together with a reference to such sources of judicial information as are resorted to by all courts in construing statutes, and to which this court has always resorted in construing the Constitution." 12 Pet. 657, 721.

We know of no reason for holding otherwise than that the words "direct taxes," on the one hand, and "duties, imposts and excises," on the other, were used in the Constitution in their natural and obvious sense. Nor, in arriving at what those terms embrace, do we perceive any ground for enlarging them beyond, or narrowing them within, their natural and obvious import at the time the Constitution was framed and ratified.

And, passing from the text, we regard the conclusion reached as inevitable, when the circumstances which surrounded the convention and controlled its action and the views of those who framed and those who adopted the Constitution are considered.

We do not care to retravel ground already traversed; but some observations may be added.

In the light of the struggle in the convention as to whether or not the new Nation should be empowered to levy taxes directly on the individual until after the States had failed to respond to requisitions—a struggle which did not terminate until the amendment to that effect, proposed by Massachusetts and concurred in by South Carolina, New Hampshire, New York, and Rhode Island, had been rejected—it would seem beyond reasonable question that direct taxation, taking the place as it did of requisitions, was purposely restrained to apportionment according to representation, in order that the former system as to ratio might be retained, while the mode of collection was changed.

This is forcibly illustrated by a letter of Mr. Madison of January 29, 1789, recently published, written after the ratification of the Constitution, but before the organization of the government and the submission of the proposed amendment to Congress, which, while opposing the amendment as calculated to impair the power, only to be exercised in "extraordinary emergencies," assigns adequate ground for its rejection as substantially unnecessary, since, he says, "every State which chooses to collect its own quota may always prevent a Federal collection, by keeping a little beforehand in its finances, and making its payment at once into the Federal treasury."

The reasons for the clauses of the Constitution in respect of direct taxation are not far to seek. The States, respectively, possessed plenary powers of taxation. They could tax the property of their citizens in such manner and to such extent as they saw fit; they had unrestricted powers to impose duties or imposts on imports from abroad, and excises on manufactures, consumable commodities, or otherwise. They gave up the great sources of revenue derived from commerce; they retained the concurrent power of levying excises, and duties if covering anything other than excises; but in respect of them the range of taxation was narrowed by the power granted over interstate commerce, and by the danger of being put at disadvantage in dealing with excises on manufactures. They retained the power of direct taxation, and to that they looked as their chief resource; but even in respect of that, they granted the concurrent power, and if the tax were placed by both governments on the same subject, the claim of the United States had preference. Therefore, they did not grant the power of direct taxation without regard to their own condition and resources as States; but they granted the power of apportioned direct taxation, a power just as efficacious to serve the needs of the general government, but securing to the States the opportunity to pay the amount apportioned, and to recoup from their own citizens in the most feasible way, and in harmony with their systems of local self-government. If, in the changes of wealth and population in particular States, apportionment produced inequality, it was an inequality stipulated for, just as the equal representation of the States, however small, in the Senate, was stipulated for. The Constitution ordains affirmatively that each State shall have two members of that body, and negatively that no State shall by amendment be deprived of its equal suffrage in the Senate without its consent. The Constitution ordains affirmatively that representatives and direct taxes shall be apportioned among the several States according to numbers, and negatively that no direct tax shall be laid unless in proportion to the enumeration.

The founders anticipated that the expenditures of the States, their counties, cities, and towns, would chiefly be met by direct taxation on accumulated property, while they expected that those of the Federal government would be for the most part met by indirect taxes. And in order that the power of direct taxation by the general government should not be exercised, except on necessity; and, when the necessity arose, should be so exercised as to leave the States at liberty to discharge their respective obligations, and should not be so exercised, unfairly and discriminatingly, as to particular States or otherwise, by a mere majority vote, possibly of those whose constituents were intentionally not subjected to any part of the burden, the qualified grant was made. Those who made it knew that the power to tax involved the power to destroy, and that, in the language of Chief Justice Marshall, in *McCulloch* v. *Maryland,* "the only security against the abuse of this power is found in the structure of the government itself. In imposing a tax, the legislature acts upon its constituents. This is, in general, a sufficient security against erroneous and oppressive taxation." 4 Wheat. 428. And they retained this security by providing that direct taxation and representation in the lower house of Congress should be adjusted on the same measure.

Moreover, whatever the reasons for the constitutional provisions, there they are, and they appear to us to speak in plain language. . . .

At the time the Constitution was framed and adopted, under the systems of direct taxation of many of the States, taxes were laid on incomes from professions, business, or employments, as well as from "offices and places of profit;" but if it were the fact that there had then been no income tax law, such as this, it would not be of controlling importance. A direct tax cannot be taken out of the constitutional rule because the particular tax did not exist at the time the rule was prescribed. As Chief Justice Marshall said in the *Dartmouth College case:* "It is not enough to say, that this particular case was not in the mind of the convention, when the article was framed, nor of the American people, when it was adopted. It is necessary to go further, and to say that, had this particular case been suggested, the language would have been so varied, as to exclude it, or it would have been made a special exception. The case being within the words of the rule, must be within its operation likewise, unless there be something in the literal construction so obviously absurd, or mischievous, or repugnant to the general spirit of the instrument, as to justify those who expound the Constitution in making it an exception." 4 Wheat. 518, 644.

Being direct, and therefore to be laid by apportionment, is there any real difficulty in doing so? Cannot Congress, if the necessity exist of raising thirty, forty, or any other number of million dollars for the support of the government, in addition to the revenue from duties, imposts, and excises, apportion the quota of each State upon the basis of the census, and thus advise it of the payment which must be made, and proceed to assess that amount on all the real and personal property and the income of all persons in the State, and collect the same if the State does not in the meantime assume and pay its quota and collect the amount according to its own system and in its own way? Cannot Congress do this, as respects either or all these subjects of taxation, and deal with each in such manner as might be deemed expedient, as indeed was done in the act of July 14, 1798, c. 75, 1 Stat. 597? Inconveniences might possibly attend the levy of an income tax, notwithstanding the listing of receipts, when adjusted, furnishes its own valuation; but that it is apportionable is hardly denied, although it is asserted that it would operate so unequally as to be undesirable.

In the disposition of the inquiry whether a general unapportioned tax on the income of real and personal property can be sustained, under the Constitution, it is apparent that the suggestion that the result of compliance with the fundamental law would lead to the abandonment of that method of taxation altogether, because of inequalities alleged to necessarily accompany its pursuit, could not be allowed to influence the conclusion; but the suggestion not unnaturally invites attention to the contention of appellants' counsel, that the want of uniformity and equality in this act is such as to invalidate it. Figures drawn from the census are given, showing that enormous assets of mutual insurance companies; of building associations; of mutual savings banks; large productive property of ecclesiastical organizations; are exempted, and it is claimed that the exemptions reach so many hundred millions that the rate of taxation would perhaps have been reduced one-half, if they had not been made. We are not dealing with the act from that point of view; but, assuming the data to be substantially reliable, if the sum desired to be raised had been apportioned, it may be doubted whether any State, which paid its quota and collected the amount by its own methods, would, or could under its constitution, have allowed a large part of the property alluded to to escape taxation. If so, a better measure of equality would have been attained than would be otherwise possible, since, according to the argument for the government, the rule of equality is not prescribed by the Constitution as to Federal taxation, and the observance of such a rule as inherent in all just taxation is purely a matter of legislative discretion.

Elaborate argument is made as to the efficacy and merits of an income tax in general, as on the one hand, equal and just, and on the other, elastic and certain; not that it is not open to abuse by such deductions and exemptions as might make taxation under it so wanting in uniformity and equality as in substance to amount to deprivation of property without due process of law; not that it is not open to fraud and evasion and is inquisitorial in its methods; but because it is pre-eminently a tax upon the rich, and enables the burden of taxes on consumption and of duties on imports to be sensibly diminished. And it is said that the United States as "the representative of an indivisible nationality, as a political sovereign equal in authority to any other on the face of the globe, adequate to all emergencies, foreign or domestic, and having at its command for offence and defence and for all governmental purposes all the resources of the nation," would be "but a maimed and crippled creation after all," unless it possesses the power to lay a tax on the income of real and personal property throughout the United States without apportionment.

The power to tax real and personal property and the income from both, there being an apportionment, is conceded; that such a tax is a direct tax in the meaning of the Constitution has not been, and, in our judgment, cannot be successfully denied; and yet we are thus invited to hesitate in the enforcement of the mandate of the Constitution, which prohibits Congress from laying a direct tax on the revenue from property of the citizen without regard to state lines, and in such manner that the States cannot intervene by payment in regulation of their own resources, lest a government of delegated powers should be found to be, not less powerful, but less absolute, than the imagination of the advocate had supposed.

We are not here concerned with the question whether an income tax be or be not desirable, nor whether such a tax would enable the government to diminish taxes on consumption and duties on imports, and to enter upon what may be believed to be a reform of its fiscal and commercial system. Questions of that character belong to the controversies of political parties, and cannot be settled by judicial decision. In these cases our province is to determine whether this income tax on the revenue from property does or does not belong to the class of direct taxes. If it does, it is, being unapportioned, in violation of the Constitution, and we must so declare.

Differences have often occurred in this court—differences exist now—but there has never been a time in its history when there has been a difference of opinion as to its duty to announce its deliberate conclusions unaffected by considerations not pertaining to the case in hand.

If it be true that the Constitution should have been so framed that a tax of this kind could be laid, the instrument defines the way for its amendment. In no part of it was greater sagacity displayed. Except that no State, without its consent, can be deprived of its equal suffrage in the Senate, the Constitution may be amended upon the concurrence of two-thirds of both houses, and the ratification of the legislatures or conventions of the several States, or through a Federal convention when applied for by the legislatures of two-thirds of the States, and upon like ratification. The ultimate sovereignty may thus be called into play by a slow and deliberate process, which gives time for mere hypothesis and opinion to exhaust themselves, and for the sober second thought of every part of the country to be asserted. . . .

PART III

1912-1935

J. Immigration Policy

Believing that their land was fully populated and their natural resources near exhaustion, Americans toward the end of the nineteenth century began to look with a more critical eye at the flood of immigrants crowding the country still further. During the period between 1880 and 1914, the number of immigrants each year averaged about 1 per cent of the population, and about one of every seven inhabitants of the United States was foreign-born. Any native who felt crowded or any native workman who was for any reason unemployed might easily resent the great and continuing flow of foreigners. There were, of course, many grounds, other than the purely economic one, that had long since created hostility towards immigration, or at least some immigrant groups. But although antipathy founded on differences of religion, race, language, manners and political habits had previously given rise to local disturbances, no federal control of immigration existed until well after the Civil War. Indeed, as late as 1889 the control of immigration was still in part exercised by the states, as the report of a congressional committee (19) shows.

Recommendations to restrict the entry of immigrants "undesirable" because of physical or moral defects were heard with increasing regularity and fervor after 1880. On the other hand, there was also much opposition to measures that proposed to limit immigration by imposing, for example, a literacy test. The opposition was based on diverse grounds: that the country still needed immigrant labor, that it should continue to offer asylum to the poor and oppressed, and that in any event illiteracy was usually a sign of lack of opportunity rather than of incapacity to learn. On such grounds, literacy tests were vetoed by Presidents Cleveland and Taft and by President Wilson in 1915 (20), although the test was passed over Wilson's veto in 1917.

The debate during the thirty or forty years around the turn of the century was couched in terms of "selection" versus "restriction," and the defense of immigration was strong enough so that even would-be restrictionists felt obliged to represent their intentions as selection, an effort to improve the quality of immigrants rather than to reduce their number. All this, however, had changed by the time the Per Centum Limit Act was passed in 1921 (21). That law established the system of national quotas, which, though modified in detail, is still in effect today.

19

Report of the Select Committee to Inquire into the Importation of Contract Laborers, etc. (January 1889)
[50 Cong. 2 Sess., H. Rep. 3792]

PAUPERS, ETC.

. . . The great majority of immigrants landing in the United States are received at the port of New York; therefore the investigation of the committee was more extended in that city than at any other place. The local affairs of immigration at New York are in charge of the commissioners of immigration of the State of New York, by virtue of a contract entered into with the Secretary of the Treasury on the 27th day of September, 1883. During the fiscal year 1888 the number of immigrants landing at the different sea-ports of the United States was 546,889. Of this number, 418,423 (or about 76 per cent) came via the port of New York, and the greater portion of them arrived between the months of April and September; and during this period the daily arrival of immigrants is exceedingly large, sometimes amounting to as many as 9,000.

When the vessel containing them has been moored to her dock, the immigrants are transferred to barges, which are towed to Castle Garden. There they disembark, and are required to pass in single file through narrow passage-ways, separated from each other by wooden railings. In about the center of each of these passage-ways there is a desk at which sits a registry clerk, who interrogates the immigrant as to his nationality, occupation, destination, etc.—questions calculated to elicit whether or not he is disqualified by law from landing.

Owing to the large number of immigrants received each day during the spring and summer months these questions must be asked rapidly, and the inspection is necessarily done in a very hurried manner, in order that there may be no undue delay in landing them.

The committee visited Castle Garden on several occasions and witnessed the arrival and inspection of immigrants, and it was very obvious to them that it was almost impossible to properly inspect the large number of persons who arrive daily during the immigrant season with the facilities afforded; and the testimony taken puts it beyond question that large numbers of persons not lawfully entitled to land in the United States are annually received at this port. In fact, one of the commissioners of immigration himself testified that the local administration of affairs at Castle Garden, by the method and system now followed, was a perfect farce.

Upon this subject the committee invite attention to the testimony of Dr. Hoyt, for twenty years connected with the board of charities and corrections, who testified that every charitable institution in the State of New York is now not only filled with occupants, but overflowing, and that the State annually expends in taking care of paupers, insane persons, etc., $20,000,-000, and that this condition of affairs is largely due to improper immigration.

The investigation at Pittsburgh, Pa., elicited the fact that over 500 immigrant paupers and insane persons were received at that city within the last six years, the great majority of whom were admitted through the port of New York, and that many of these pauper immigrants bore upon their clothing the branded name of the work-house of which they had recently been inmates in Ireland.

The investigation at Boston disclosed that a few years ago an organized effort was made by the officials of Great Britain and Ireland, through and by means of an association known as the "Tuke Society," to assist poor persons, paupers, etc., to immigrate to this country, by furnishing them with tickets for the necessary transportation, and that the number of such assisted immigrants who were landed in Boston between April 3, 1882, and July 8, 1888, was 4,922, a great many of whom subsequently became inmates of charitable institutions in this country.

And by certain English statutes guardians of the poor are authorized to appropriate funds at their disposal for the purpose of exporting to other lands persons who have become public charges; that the English authorities have made liberal use of these laws is absolutely attested by the number of aliens who are inmates of charitable institutions in this country. In fact, the testimony upon the subject of pauper immigration conclusively shows that there are thousands of alien paupers, insane persons, and idiots annually landed in this country, who become a burden and a charge upon the States where they happen to gain a settlement, many of whom are aided and assisted to emigrate by the officials of the country from whence they came.

IMMIGRATION ALONG THE CANADIAN BORDER

Along the border between Canada and the United States no inspection whatever is made of immigrants; and alien paupers, insane persons, etc., may land at Quebec and at once proceed to this country without any let or hindrance. The number of persons not lawfully entitled to land in the United States who thus arrive in this country by way of the Canadian frontier is rapidly assuming large proportions, and has become a matter of serious contemplation. The testimony shows that in many instances immigrants coming by steamer to Quebec have within forty-eight hours after the arrival there been applicants for shelter in the almshouses of the State of New York. . . .

CONVICTS

It was also shown that many persons belonging to the criminal class have been sent to the United States by officials of the European Governments. In Germany there exists an association whose object is the exportation of their incorrigible convicts, and their vicious and lawless members of society. Quite a number of this class of persons have been assisted by this society to immigrate here, and they have succeeded in effecting a landing. According to the testimony, this practice has also been carried on by officials of Great Britain and of the Swiss Republic, and in this manner this country has been made the refuge for a great many criminals whose character was such that they were deemed to be irreclaimable; and therefore the officials of the Governments from whence they came have purchased tickets for them, opened the prison doors, conducted them on board a steamer, and shipped them to the United States, some of them being sent as cabin passengers, in order thereby to render detection more difficult. And they have persisted in this course even after having been requested by officials of our Government to discontinue it.

The result of the investigation into the enforcement of the law of 1882 demonstrates beyond a doubt that it has been and is being repeatedly violated, and to such an extent, in fact, that it has become a matter of grave concern and demands immediate remedial legislation.

CONTRACT LABORERS

By the act of February 26, 1885, it is made unlawful to prepay the transportation or in anywise assist or encourage the importation of aliens into the United States under a contract to perform labor or service of any kind, except skilled work-

men in a new industry when such workmen can not be otherwise obtained. The Secretary of the Treasury is given the same
power in this act as is conferred by the act of 1882, to contract
with such State commission or board as may be designated by
the governor to examine passengers arriving at ports within
such State, in reference to detecting violations of this law.

   The enforcement of this act is not easily accomplished.
Evasions of the law are much more numerous than convictions, for the reason that it is a difficult matter to prove in
court a violation of it. The committee have discovered some
cases of actual transgression of the act, but still the instances
of failure to obey the letter of the law have been, comparatively
speaking, few, yet the proof disclosed that the spirit of the law
has been violated with impunity. A reference to the testimony
will show that it is constantly evaded to a large extent, and
also the manner in which it is done.

   In the opinion of the committee the non-enforcement of
these acts of 1882 and 1885 is not so much due to a want of
diligence on the part of the officials having their administration
in charge as it is to a lack of proper machinery to carry them
into effect. The committee believe that the enforcement of all
acts designed to regulate immigration should be intrusted to
the Federal Government and not to the States. The regulation
of immigration is a matter affecting the whole Union, and is
pre-eminently a proper subject for Federal control. . . .

VIEWS OF THE MINORITY

   The undersigned, [Richard Guenther] member of the Select
Committee to Inquire into the Importation of Contract Laborers, Convicts, Paupers, etc., agrees with the majority of
the committee in reaching the conclusion that some law should
be enacted which would, more effectually than the present
laws, restrict and if possible stop entirely the influx into the
United States of all such persons who, instead of benefiting
our country, as the large majority of immigrants undoubtedly
do, are a direct source of evil in many ways.

   The undersigned thinks that a large number of people who

now fill our poor-houses, insane asylums, hospitals, and other charitable institutions, . . . should never have been admitted to land in the United States. He is, however, of the opinion that no law should be passed to lessen the immigration of industrious, law-abiding people, who come here in good faith with the intention of making this country their permanent home, who bring their families with them, and who in due course of time become useful and valuable citizens of the Republic, especially when every unprejudiced mind must admit that that class of immigrants for the last fifty years has been one of the main causes of our unexampled progress in every field of industry and enterprise.

The undersigned opposes any measure that would unnecessarily annoy the desirable immigrant, but he is in favor of all such measures as would most likely result in excluding all such foreign elements whose coming is not a benefit to our country, but rather the opposite. . . .

20

WOODROW WILSON (1856–1924)
Veto Message of 1915
[*Cong. Rec.*, LII, 2481–2]

To the House of Representatives:

It is with unaffected regret that I find myself constrained by clear conviction to return this bill (H.R. 6060, "An act to regulate the immigration of aliens to and the residence of aliens in the United States") without my signature. Not only do I feel it to be a very serious matter to exercise the power of veto in any case, because it involves opposing the single judgment of the President to the judgment of the majority of both the Houses of the Congress, a step which no man who realizes his own liability to error can take without great hesitation, but also because this particular bill is in so many important respects admirable, well conceived, and desirable. Its enactment into law would undoubtedly enhance the efficiency and improve the methods of handling the important branch of the public service to which it relates. But candor and a sense of duty with regard to the responsibility so clearly imposed upon me by the Constitution in matters of legislation leave me no choice but to dissent.

In two particulars of vital consequence this bill embodies a radical departure from the traditional and long-established policy of this country, a policy in which our people have conceived the very character of their Government to be expressed, the very mission and spirit of the Nation in respect of its relations to the peoples of the world outside their borders. It seeks to all but close entirely the gates of asylum which have always been open to those who could find nowhere else the right and opportunity of constitutional agitation for what they conceived to be the natural and inalienable rights of men; and it excludes those to whom the opportunities of elementary education have been denied, without regard to their character, their purposes, or their natural capacity.

Restrictions like these, adopted earlier in our history as a Nation, would very materially have altered the course and cooled the humane ardors of our politics. The right of political asylum has brought to this country many a man of noble character and elevated purpose who was marked as an outlaw in his own less fortunate land, and who has yet become an ornament to our citizenship and to our public councils. The children and the compatriots of these illustrious Americans must stand amazed to see the representatives of their Nation now resolved, in the fullness of our national strength and at the maturity of our great institutions, to risk turning such men back from our shores without test of quality or purpose. It is difficult for me to believe that the full effect of this feature of the bill was realized when it was framed and adopted, and it is impossible for me to assent to it in the form in which it is here cast.

The literacy test and the tests and restrictions which accompany it constitute an even more radical change in the policy of the Nation. Hitherto we have generously kept our doors open to all who were not unfitted by reason of disease or incapacity for self-support or such personal records and antecedents as were likely to make them a menace to our peace and order or to the wholesome and essential relationships of life. In this bill it is proposed to turn away from tests of character and of quality and impose tests which exclude and restrict; for the new tests here embodied are not tests of quality or of character or of personal fitness, but tests of opportunity. Those who come seeking opportunity are not to be admitted unless they have already had one of the chief of the opportunities they seek, the opportunity of education. The object of such provisions is restriction, not selection.

If the people of this country have made up their minds to limit the number of immigrants by arbitrary tests and so reverse the policy of all the generations of Americans that have gone before them, it is their right to do so. I am their servant and have no license to stand in their way. But I do not believe that they have. I respectfully submit that no one can quote their mandate to that effect. Has any political party ever avowed a policy of restriction in this fundamental matter, gone to the country on it, and been commissioned to control its legislation? Does this bill rest upon the conscious and universal assent and desire of the American people? I doubt it. It is because I doubt it that I make bold to dissent from it. I am willing to abide by the verdict, but not until it has been rendered. Let the platforms of parties speak out upon this policy and the people pronounce their wish. The matter is too fundamental to be settled otherwise.

I have no pride of opinion in this question. I am not foolish enough to profess to know the wishes and ideals of America better than the body of her chosen representatives know them. I only want instruction direct from those whose fortunes, with ours and all men's, are involved.

21

COMMISSIONER GENERAL OF IMMIGRATION
Annual Report, 1923

THE PER CENTUM LIMIT ACT OF 1921

The fiscal year just ended was the second during which the so-called per centum limit immigration act of May 19, 1921, was in operation, and because of this the statistical records of the Immigration Service are peculiarly interesting and significant. The law is still new, and there is so much evidence that its purpose and provisions are not fully understood that a brief discussion of what it is and of the events which led to its enactment by Congress may be appropriate at this time.

Perhaps it is not very generally realized that the per centum limit law marked the beginning of actual restriction or limitation of immigration to the United States from Europe, Africa, Australasia, and a considerable part of Asia. The Chinese exclusion act of 1882, the passport agreement with Japan which became effective in 1908, and the "barred zone" provision in the general immigration law of 1917 had already stopped or greatly reduced the influx of oriental peoples, but so far as others, and particularly Europeans, were concerned, all applicants who met the various tests prescribed in the general law were admitted. This general law, first enacted in 1882 and several times revised and strengthened, was and still is based on the principle of selection rather than of numerical restriction. It is probably true that the provision barring illiterate aliens from admission, which was added to the general law in 1917, was intended as a restrictive measure rather than a quality test, but in its practical effect it was only another addition to the already numerous class of alleged undesirables who were denied admission, and obviously could not be relied upon actually to limit the volume of immigration.

The immigration act of 1882, which, as already indicated, was the first general law upon the subject, provided for the exclusion from the United States of the following classes only: Convicts, lunatics, idiots, and persons likely to become a public charge. This law underwent more or less important revisions in 1891, 1893, 1903, 1907, and 1917, until the last-mentioned act, which is the present general immigration law, denies admission to many classes of aliens, including the following: Idiots, imbeciles, feeble-minded persons, epileptics, insane persons; persons who have had one or more attacks of insanity at any time previously; persons of constitutional psychopathic inferiority; persons with chronic alcoholism; paupers; professional beggars; vagrants; persons afflicted with tuberculosis in any form or with a loathsome or dangerous contagious disease; persons certified by the examining physician as being mentally or physically defective, such physical defect being of a nature which may affect the ability of the alien to earn a living; persons who have been convicted of or admit having committed a felony or other crime or misdemeanor involving moral turpitude; polygamists, or persons who practice polygamy or believe in or advocate the practice of polygamy; anarchists and similar classes; immoral persons and persons coming for an immoral purpose; contract laborers; persons likely to become a public charge; persons seeking admission within one year of date of previous debarment or deportation; persons whose ticket or passage is paid for with the money of another or who are assisted by others to come, unless it is affirmatively shown that such persons do not belong to one of the foregoing excluded classes; persons whose ticket or passage is paid for by any corporation, association, society, municipality, or foreign government, either directly or indirectly; stowaways; children under 16 years of age unless accompanied by one or both of their parents; persons who are natives of certain geographically defined territory; aliens over 16 years of age who are unable to read some language or dialect; certain accompanying aliens, as described in the last proviso of section 18 of the act; and persons who have arrived in Canada or Mexico by certain steamship lines. Persons who fail to meet certain passport requirements were added to the excluded classes in subsequent legislation.

Obviously it would be difficult to find, or even to invent, many other terms denoting individual undesirability which might be added to the foregoing list, but, as already pointed out, the general law is essentially selective in theory, for even its most rigid application with respect to the excludable classes above enumerated could not be depended upon to prevent the coming of unlimited numbers of aliens who were able to meet the tests imposed.

Even a casual survey of congressional discussions of the immigration problem during the past quarter of a century demonstrates very clearly that while the law makers were deeply concerned with the mental, moral, and physical quality of immigrants, there developed as time went on an even greater concern as to the fundamental racial character of the constantly increasing numbers who came. The record of alien arrivals year by year had shown a gradual falling off in the immigration of northwest European peoples, representing racial stocks which were common to America even in colonial days, and a rapid and remarkably large increase in the movement from southern and eastern European countries and Asiatic Turkey. Immigration from the last-named sources reached an annual average of about 750,000 and in some years nearly a million came, and there seems to have been a general belief in Congress that it would increase rather than diminish. At the same time no one seems to have anticipated a revival of the formerly large influx from the "old sources," as the countries of northwest Europe came to be known.

This remarkable change in the sources and racial character of our immigrants led to an almost continuous agitation of the immigration problem both in and out of Congress, and there was a steadily growing demand for restriction, particularly of the newer movement from the south and east of Europe. During the greater part of this period of agitation the so-called literacy test for aliens was the favorite weapon of the restrictionists, and its widespread popularity appears to have been based quite largely on a belief, or at least a hope, that it would reduce to some extent the stream of "new" immigration, about one-third of which was illiterate, without seriously interfering with the coming of the older type, among whom illiteracy was at a minimum.

Presidents Cleveland and Taft vetoed immigration bills because they contained a literacy test provision, and President Wilson vetoed two bills largely for the same reason. In 1917, however, Congress passed a general immigration bill which included the literacy provision over the President's veto, and, with certain exceptions, aliens who are unable to read are no longer admitted to the United States. At that time, however, the World War had already had the effect of reducing immigration from Europe to a low level, and our own entry into the conflict a few days before the law in question went into effect practically stopped it altogether. Consequently, the value of the literacy provision as a means of restricting European immigration was never fairly tested under normal conditions.

The Congress, however, seemingly realized that even the comprehensive immigration law of 1917, including the literacy test, would afford only a frail barrier against the promised rush from the war-stricken countries of Europe, and in December 1920, the House of Representatives, with little opposition, passed a bill to suspend practically all immigration for the time being. The per centum limit plan was substituted by the Senate, however, and the substitute prevailed in Congress, but it failed to become a law at the time because President Wilson withheld executive approval. Nevertheless, favorable action was not long delayed, for at the special session called at the beginning of the present administration the measure was quickly enacted, and, with President Harding's approval, became a law on May 19, 1921. This law expired by limitation June 30, 1922, but by the act of May 11, 1922, its life was extended to June 30, 1924, and some strengthening amendments were added.

The principal provisions of the per centum limit act, or the "quota law," as it is popularly known, are as follows:

The number of aliens of any nationality who may be admitted to the United States in any fiscal year shall not exceed

3 per cent of the number of persons of such nationality who were resident in the United States according to the census of 1910.

Monthly quotas are limited to 20 per cent of the annual quota.

For the purposes of the act, "nationality" is determined by country of birth.

The law does not apply to the following classes of aliens: Government officials; aliens in transit; aliens visiting the United States as tourists or temporarily for business or pleasure; aliens from countries immigration from which is regulated in accordance with treaties or agreement relating solely to immigration, otherwise China and Japan; aliens from the so-called Asiatic barred zone; aliens who have resided continuously for at least five years in Canada, Newfoundland, Cuba, Mexico, Central or South America, or adjacent islands; aliens under the age of 18 who are children of citizens of the United States.

Certain other classes of aliens who are counted against quotas are admissible after a quota is exhausted. The following are included in this category: Aliens returning from a temporary visit abroad; aliens who are professional actors, artists, lecturers, singers, ministers of any religious denomination, professors for colleges or seminaries, members of any recognized learned profession, or aliens employed as domestic servants.

So far as possible preference is given to the wives and certain near relatives of citizens of the United States, applicants for citizenship, and honorably discharged soldiers, eligible to citizenship, who served in the United States military or naval forces at any time between April 6, 1917, and November 11, 1918.

Transportation companies are liable to a fine of $200 for each alien brought to a United States port in excess of the quota and where such fine is imposed the amount paid for passage must be returned to the rejected alien.

The quota limit law is in addition to and not in substitution for the provisions of the immigration laws.

In the annual report for the preceding fiscal year it was pointed out that the operation of the per centum limit law had necessitated the introduction of a new, although limited, series of immigration statistics which, for the following reasons, are not comparable with existing statistics:

1. In the quota-law figures country of birth rules, whereas country of last permanent residence is regarded as country of origin in our ordinary immigration tables.

2. Both immigrant and nonimmigrant aliens may appear in quota-law statistics, or, by reason of exemptions already referred to, arriving aliens of both classes may not be counted against quotas at all, or, in other cases, after a quota is exhausted.

For example, during the fiscal year just ended 335,480 aliens were charged to the various quotas, while a total of 522,919 immigrant aliens were admitted during the same period, or an excess of 187,439. However, this difference is readily accounted for by the fact that during the fiscal year 117,011 immigrant aliens were admitted from British North America, 63,768 from Mexico, 13,181 from the West Indies, and smaller numbers from other sources, only a minor part of such immigration being subject to the provisions of the quota law. . . .

The chief significance of the foregoing figures lies in the fact that while in the fiscal year 1922 only 46.4 per cent of the combined quotas of northern and western European countries was exhausted, 90 per cent of the total allotment was utilized in the past fiscal year, the increase in numbers being from 91,862 in 1921–22 to 177,943 in 1922–23. Table I shows that the quotas of the United Kingdom, Sweden, Norway, Denmark, Belgium, the Netherlands, and Switzerland were either completely or practically exhausted, the German quota being the only one of this group which reached the end of the fiscal year with any considerable balance.

On the other hand the quotas of the southern and eastern European and Near East group were substantially exhausted in both years, the small increase in 1922–23 being due to the fact that more favorable conditions surrounding the immigration of natives of Russia made possible the coming of increased numbers of that nationality.

As already explained, the law provides that not more than

20 per cent of a quota allotment may be admitted in any month, and it has been judicially determined that adherence to a monthly allotment is as mandatory as in the case of an annual quota. While this provision has resulted in more or less confusion at times and has necessitated the rejection of considerable numbers of otherwise admissible aliens, nevertheless the experience of the past two years has amply justified the wisdom of fixing a monthly limit. Under the present plan, however, it is possible to admit a full year's quota of any nationality, and consequently all nationalities subject to the law, within the first five months of a fiscal year. As a matter of fact several of the nationalities concerned did completely exhaust their quotas for the fiscal year 1923 in November. Fortunately for the Immigration Service applications for admission under some of the larger quotas were better distributed. The Russian quota, for example, was not exhausted until April and that of the United Kingdom until May.

The trend of immigration during the last few months of the fiscal year, however, indicates that most of the quotas, large and small, for the fiscal year 1924 may be exhausted early in November. This naturally suggests the advisability of decreasing the monthly limit somewhat in order to insure a better distribution throughout the year.

The quota limit law has created new and in some instances difficult problems for the Immigration Service, as it has intensified already existing problems, particularly that of preventing illegal entries over the land boundaries and at seaports. On the whole, however, its administration has been attended with fewer difficulties than during the preceding fiscal year, and if the law were amended in some particulars it is doubtful whether any other equally effective method of restricting immigration could be devised that would present fewer administrative difficulties or cause less hardship to aliens or inconvenience to their friends in the United States. . . .

RACES OR PEOPLES

Since 1899 all aliens admitted to the United States have been classified in the bureau's statistics under the head of "Races or peoples" as well as by country of origin. Accordingly there is a continuous record of 25 years which is based on the racial rather than the political or geographical status of admitted aliens and, therefore, not at all affected by shifting political boundaries, newly created countries, or changed place of residence on the part of the aliens themselves. Thus an Englishman is counted as such whether he comes from England, Canada, or China. The value of this classification is clearly apparent when it is considered that during the past fiscal year the aliens admitted from Turkey in Asia included only 158 persons of the Turkish race compared with 658 Armenians, 631 Syrians, 417 Hebrews, 179 Greeks, and 140 of various other races or peoples, and what is true of Turkey is true in some degree of every other country from which immigrants come. . . .

In 1913–14, which, as already stated, was a fairly typical pre-war immigration year, 75.6 per cent of the 1,218,480 immigrant aliens admitted from all sources were of the varied racial stocks indigenous to southern and eastern Europe and Turkey and only 20.8 per cent were of north and west European peoples. All but 3.6 per cent of the total, therefore, were European stock, including a relatively small number, mostly Armenians, Syrians, Hebrews, and so-called Ottoman Greeks, who came from Turkey in Asia. The number of Mexicans recorded as admitted in 1913–14 was relatively insignificant, being only about 1 per cent of the total, and the remainder, including Chinese, Japanese, African (black), Cuban, Spanish American, etc., was only 2.5 per cent of the whole immigration of the year.

Then came the World War, and it was not until the fiscal year 1921 that immigration from Europe was resumed to any considerable extent, and even then some of the principal sources of pre-war years, including Russia, Austria, and Hungary, were still largely shut off from the United States so far as immigration was concerned. In the fiscal year last mentioned a total of 805,228 immigrants were admitted to the United States and of this number 537,144, or 66.7 per cent of the whole, were of races or peoples peculiar to south and east Europe and Asiatic Turkey, Italians (north and south) leading with 222,496, followed by 119,036 Hebrews, 35,047 Slovaks, 27,448 Spanish, 21,146 Poles, and 18,856 Portuguese. In fact, it seemed very clear that wherever possible immigration was rapidly approaching pre-war proportions and there was every indication that as time went on the influx, especially from the south and east of Europe and the Near East, would reach even greater proportions than ever before. As explained elsewhere, it is very evident that this prospect was what led Congress to enact the quota limit law of May 19, 1921.

Any attempt to estimate the effect of the quota law in the matter of checking immigration from Europe during the past two fiscal years would of necessity be largely speculative. It is known, however, that hundreds of thousands have been prevented from coming, and probably this is literally true even of some countries alone. Following the destruction of Smyrna, for example, and the exile of a million, more or less, Armenian and Greek residents of Turkey, it was commonly reported that had it not been for the quota law a considerable proportion of these refugees would have come to the United States. The bureau was advised that in the spring of 1923 there were 150,-000 persons in Greece alone who desired to emigrate to the United States, and it is said that the number in Italy who would come if they could greatly exceeds even this estimate. Undoubtedly many of the reports of this nature which have reached the bureau are exaggerated, perhaps greatly so in some instances, but however that may be it seems very certain that except for the quota limit law immigration from Europe and Asiatic Turkey during the past fiscal year would have been far in excess of any year in our history.

Turning for a moment from speculation as to what might have happened, it is of interest to note to what extent operations under the quota law have fulfilled the evident purpose of Congress in enacting it; this purpose, as already suggested, having been to materially lessen the tide of immigration from the so-called new sources without unduly interfering with the normal movement of northwest European peoples into the United States. The answer seems to appear when comparison is made of the records of the years 1913–14 and 1922–23, as presented in the two tables next foregoing. These tables, and particularly the latter, show not only a numerical decrease of 758,465 in the newer immigrant types in the year just ended but that the proportion of these peoples in the total immigration fell from 75.6 per cent in 1913–14 to 31.1 per cent in 1922–23. On the other hand, while there was only a small increase in numbers among northwest European peoples or racial stocks they formed 52.5 per cent of all our immigration in 1922–23 compared with only 20.8 per cent of the whole in 1913–14, and considering the two European groups alone the proportion of old-type immigrants was practically 63 per cent of the total. In pointing to these facts it will, of course, be understood that the bureau is not commenting on the relative merits of the various alien peoples or groups composing our immigration, but rather that it is merely attempting to show from statistical records to what extent the quota limit law has met the purpose of Congress as that purpose is understood. . . .

K. Agricultural Price Supports

The end of World War I was succeeded by a sharp but fairly short depression. While the rest of the United States began to emerge from it into the happy days of the boom, farmers found that the recovery of farm commodity prices and, to a lesser extent, of their incomes, was faltering. They remembered their golden age, the five years before the War, and the comparison disgruntled them. The prices of industrial products had regained their prewar levels, but the prices of agricultural products had not. This, farmers concluded, was an inequity not to be borne. The term "parity" was invented, and with it the remarkable doctrine that justice required the maintenance of parity, that is, government must keep the relation between prices of goods farmers sell and prices of goods they buy at the same level as it had been between 1909 and 1914.

One way to do this, the farmers—or rather, certain of their spokesmen—maintained, was to remove from the market the "demoralizing surpluses," the name given to as much of the produce as lowered its price below parity levels. A great stumbling block to this policy, however, was doubt as to what should be done with these surpluses after they had been removed from the market. To sell them abroad cheaply would offend foreign farmers, to store them was expensive and perhaps self-defeating, to destroy them was an outrageous waste.

In fact, at first, the whole notion encountered intransigent opposition, the tenor of which is clear in Coolidge's speech on the farm problem during 1925. The principal sentiments of the speech—reverence for the independent farmer as a foundation of American institutions and the conviction that he should be helped but not controlled—might have been uttered by any American statesman between 1789 and 1933.

But the McNary-Haugen bill (22)—passed in 1927 and 1928 and twice vetoed—showed that federal price-fixing as a remedy for depression in farm prices was gathering a good deal of support. Coolidge's veto message (23) rehearsed the deleterious consequences, especially over-production, that have since been observed and objected to as consequences of price supports of this kind.

But with the Great Depression, the pressure for farm subsidies could no longer be contained and indeed was vigorously favored by the Roosevelt administration. The Agricultural Adjustment Act of 1933 (24) was passed as an essential part of the New Deal. It was invalidated by the Supreme Court in 1936, but later laws eliminated the aspects held unconstitutional and restored the foundation on which American agricultural policy has rested since.

22
McNary-Haugen Bill (1927)
[*Cong. Rec.*, LXVIII, 3869]

Section 1. It is hereby declared to be the policy of Congress to promote the orderly marketing of basic agricultural commodities in interstate and foreign commerce and to that end to provide for the control and disposition of surpluses of such commodities, to enable producers of such commodities to stabilize their markets against undue and excessive fluctuations, to preserve advantageous domestic markets for such commodities, to minimize speculation and waste in marketing such commodities, and to encourage the organization of producers of such commodities into cooperative marketing associations.

Sec. 2. (a) A Federal Farm Board is hereby created which

shall consist of the Secretary of Agriculture, who shall be a member ex officio, and 12 members, one from each of the 12 Federal land-bank districts, appointed by the President of the United States, by and with the advice and consent of the Senate, from lists of eligibles submitted by the nominating committee for the district, as hereinafter in this section provided.

(b) There is hereby established a nominating committee in each of the 12 Federal land-bank districts, to consist of seven members. Four of the members of the nominating committee in each district shall be elected by the bona fide farm organizations and cooperative associations in such district at a convention of such organizations and associations, to be held at the office of the Federal land bank in such district, or at such other place, in the city where such Federal land bank is located, to which the convention may adjourn. Two of the members of the nominating committee in each district shall be elected by a majority vote of the heads of the agricultural departments of the several States of each Federal land-bank district, at a meeting to be held in the same city and at the same time of the meeting of the convention of the bona fide farm organizations and cooperative associations in each district. One of the members of the nominating committee in each district shall be appointed by the Secretary of Agriculture. . . .

Sec. 6. (a) For the purposes of this act, cotton, wheat, corn, rice, tobacco, and swine shall be known and are referred to as "basic agricultural commodities," except that the board may, in its discretion, treat as a separate basic agricultural commodity one or more of such classes or types of tobacco as are designated in the classification of the Department of Agriculture.

(b) Whenever the board finds that the conditions of production and marketing of any other agricultural commodity are such that the provisions of this act applicable to a basic agricultural commodity should be made applicable to such other agricultural commodity, the board shall submit its report thereon to Congress.

(c) Whenever the board finds, first, that there is or may

be during the ensuing year either (1) a surplus above the domestic requirements for wheat, corn, rice, tobacco, or swine, or (2) a surplus above the requirements for the orderly marketing of cotton, or of wheat, corn, rice, tobacco, or swine; and, second, that both the advisory council hereinafter created for the commodity and a substantial number of cooperative associations or other organizations representing the producers of the commodity favor the full cooperation of the board in the stabilization of the commodity, then the board shall publicly declare its findings and commence, upon a date to be fixed by the board and published in such declaration, the operations in such commodity authorized by this act: . . .

(d) During the continuance of such operations in any basic agricultural commodity, the board is authorized to enter into agreements, for the purpose of carrying out the policy declared in section 1, with any cooperative association engaged in handling the basic agricultural commodity, or with a corporation created by one or more of such cooperative associations, or with processors of the basic agricultural commodity.

(e) Such agreements may provide for (1) removing or disposing of any surplus of the basic agricultural commodity, (2) withholding such surplus, (3) insuring such commodity against undue and excessive fluctuations in market conditions, and (4) financing the purchase, storage, or sale or other disposition of the commodity. The moneys in the stabilization fund of the basic agricultural commodity shall be available for carrying out such agreements. In the case of any agreement in respect of the removal or disposal of the surplus of a basic agricultural commodity, the agreement shall provide both for the payment from the stabilization fund for the commodity of the amount of losses, costs, and charges, arising out of the purchase, storage, or sale or other disposition of the commodity or out of contracts therefor, and for the payment into the stabilization fund for the commodity of profits (after deducting all costs and charges provided for in the agreement) arising out of such purchase, storage, or sale or other disposition, or contracts therefor. In the case of agreements insuring such commodity against undue and excessive fluctuations in market conditions, the board may insure any cooperative marketing association against decline in the market price for the commodity at the time of sale by the association, from the market price for such commodity at the time of delivery to the association. . . .

Sec. 7. (a) The board is hereby authorized and directed to create for each basic agricultural commodity an advisory council of seven members fairly representative of the producers of such commodity. . . .

Sec. 8. In order that each marketed unit of a basic agricultural commodity may contribute ratably its equitable share to the stabilization fund hereinafter established for such commodity; in order to prevent any unjust discrimination against, any direct burden or undue restraint upon, and any suppression of commerce with foreign nations in basic agricultural commodities in favor of interstate or intrastate commerce in such commodities; and in order to stabilize and regulate the current of foreign and interstate commerce in such commodities—there shall be apportioned and paid as a regulation of such commerce an equalization fee as hereinafter provided.

Sec. 9. Prior to the commencement of operations in respect of any basic agricultural commodity, and thereafter from time to time, the board shall estimate the probable advances, losses, costs, and charges to be paid in respect of the operations in such commodity. Having due regard to such estimates, the board shall from time to time determine and publish the amount for each unit of weight, measure, or value designated by it, to be collected upon such unit of such basic agricultural commodity during the operations in such commodity. Such amount is hereinafter referred to as the "equalization fee." At the time of determining and publishing an equalization fee the board shall specify the period during which it shall remain in effect, and the place and manner of its payment and collection.

Sec. 10. (a) Under such regulations as the board may prescribe there shall be paid, during operations in a basic agricultural commodity and in respect of each unit of such commodity, an equalization fee upon one of the following: The transportation, processing, or sale of such unit. . . .

(b) The board may by regulation require any person engaged in the transportation, processing, or acquisition by sale of a basic agricultural commodity—

(1) To file returns under oath and to report, in respect of his transportation, processing, or acquisition of such commodity, the amount of equalization fees payable thereon and such other facts as may be necessary for their payment or collection.

(2) To collect the equalization fee as directed by the board, and to account therefor.

(3) In the case of cotton, to issue to the producer a serial receipt for the commodity which shall be evidence of the participating interest of the producer in the equalization fund for the commodity. The board may in such case prepare and issue such receipts and prescribe the terms and conditions thereof. The Secretary of the Treasury, upon the request of the board, shall have such receipts prepared at the Bureau of Engraving and Printing.

(c) Every person who, in violation of the regulations prescribed by the board, fails to collect or account for any equalization fee shall be liable for its amount and to a penalty equal to one-half its amount. Such amount and penalty may be recovered together in a civil suit brought by the board in the name of the United States.

Sec. 11. (a) In accordance with regulations prescribed by the board, there shall be established a stabilization fund for each basic agricultural commodity. Such funds shall be administered by and exclusively under the control of the board, and the board shall have the exclusive power of expending the moneys in any such fund. There shall be deposited to the credit of the stabilization fund for a basic agricultural commodity, advances from the revolving fund hereinafter established, premiums paid for insurance under section 12, and the equalization fees and profits in connection with operations by the board in the basic agricultural commodity or its food products. . . .

Sec. 12. (a) The board is authorized, upon such terms and conditions and in accordance with such regulations as it may prescribe, to make loans out of the revolving fund to any cooperative association engaged in the purchase, storage, or sale or other disposition of any agricultural commodity (whether or not a basic agricultural commodity) for the purpose of assisting such cooperative association in controlling the surplus of such commodity in excess of the requirements for orderly marketing.

(b) For the purpose of developing continuity of cooperative services, including unified terminal marketing facilities and equipment, the board is authorized, upon such terms and conditions and in accordance with such regulations as it may prescribe, to make loans out of the revolving fund to any cooperative association engaged in the purchase, storage, sale, or other disposition, or processing of any agricultural commodity, (1) for the purpose of assisting any such association in the acquisition, by purchase, construction, or otherwise, of facilities to be used in the storage, processing, or sale of such agricultural commodity, or (2) for the purpose of furnishing funds to such associations for necessary expenditures in federating, consolidating, or merging cooperative associations, or (3) for the purpose of furnishing to any such association funds to be used by it as capital for any agricultural credit corporation eligible for receiving rediscounts from an intermediate-credit bank. In making any such loan the board may provide for the payment of such charge, to be determined by the board from time to time, upon each unit of the commodity handled by the association, as will within a period of not more than 20 years repay the amount of such loan, together with interest thereon. The aggregate amounts loaned under this subdivision and remaining unpaid shall not exceed at any one time the sum of $25,000,000.

(c) Any loan under subdivision (a) or (b) shall bear interest at the rate of 4 per cent per annum.

(d) The board may at any time enter into a contract with any cooperative marketing association engaged in marketing any basic agricultural commodity, insuring such association for periods of 12 months against decline in the market price for such commodity at the time of sale by the association from the market price for such commodity at the time of delivery to the association. For such insurance the association shall pay such premium, to be determined by the board, upon each unit of the basic agricultural commodity reported by the association for coverage under the insurance contract, as will cover the risks of the insurance. . . .

Sec. 16. (a) There is hereby authorized to be appropriated, out of any money in the Treasury not otherwise appropriated, the sum of $250,000,000, which shall be administered by the board and used as a revolving fund, in accordance with the provisions of this act. . . .

23

CALVIN COOLIDGE (1872–1933)
Veto of the McNary-Haugen Bill (25 Feb. 1927)
[*Cong. Rec.*, LXVIII, 4771]

To the Senate:

The conditions which Senate bill 4808 is designed to remedy have been and still are unsatisfactory in many cases. No one can deny that the prices of many farm products have been out of line with the general price level for several years. No one could fail to want every proper step taken to assure to agriculture a just and secure place in our economic scheme. Reasonable and constructive legislation to that end would be thoroughly justified and would have the hearty support of all who have the interests of the Nation at heart. The difficulty with this particular measure is that it is not framed to aid farmers as a whole, and it is, furthermore, calculated to injure rather than promote the general public welfare.

It is axiomatic that progress is made through building on the good foundations that already exist. For many years—indeed, from before the day of modern agricultural science—balanced and diversified farming has been regarded by thoughtful farmers and scientists as the safeguard of our agriculture. The bill under consideration throws this aside as of no consequence. It says in effect that all the agricultural scientists and all the thinking farmers of the last 50 years are wrong, that what we ought to do is not to encourage diversified agriculture but instead put a premium on one-crop farming.

The measure discriminates definitely against products which make up what has been universally considered a program of safe farming. The bill upholds as ideals of American farming the men who grow cotton, corn, rice, swine, tobacco, or wheat, and nothing else. These are to be given special favors at the expense of the farmer who has toiled for years to build up a constructive farming enterprise to include a variety of crops and livestock that shall, so far as possible, be safe, and keep the soil, the farmer's chief asset, fertile and productive.

The bill singles out a few products, chiefly sectional, and proposes to raise the prices of those regardless of the fact that thousands of other farmers would be directly penalized. If this is a true farm-relief measure, why does it leave out the producers of beef cattle, sheep, dairy products, poultry products, potatoes, hay, fruit, vegetables, oats, barley, rye, flax, and the other important agricultural lines? So far as the farmers as a whole are concerned, this measure is not for them. It is for certain groups of farmers in certain sections of the country. Can it be thought that such legislation could have the sanction of the rank and file of the Nation's farmers?

This measure provides specifically for the payment by the Federal board of all losses, costs, and charges of packers, millers, cotton spinners, or other processors who are operating under contract with the board. It contemplates that the packers may be commissioned by the Government to buy hogs enough to create a near scarcity in this country, slaughter the hogs, sell the pork products abroad at a loss, and have their losses, costs, and charges made good out of the pockets of farm taxpayers. The millers would be similarly commissioned to operate in wheat or corn and have their losses, costs, and charges paid by farm taxpayers. . . .

It seems almost incredible that the producers of hogs, corn, wheat, rice, tobacco, and cotton should be offered a scheme of legislative relief in which the only persons who are guaranteed a profit are the exporters, packers, millers, cotton spinners, and other processors.

Clearly this legislation involves governmental fixing of prices. It gives the proposed Federal board almost unlimited authority to fix prices on the designated commodities. This is price fixing, furthermore, on some of the Nation's basic foods and materials. Nothing is more certain than that such price fixing would upset the normal exchange relationships existing in the open market and that it would finally have to be extended to cover a multitude of other goods and services. Government price fixing, once started, has alike no justice and no end. It is an economic folly from which this country has every right to be spared.

This legislation proposes, in effect, that Congress shall delegate to a Federal farm board, nominated by farmers, the power to fix and collect a tax, called an equalization fee, on certain products produced by those farmers. That certainly contemplates a remarkable delegation of the taxing power. The purpose of that tax, it may be repeated, is to pay the losses incurred in the disposition of the surplus products in order to raise the price on that portion of the products consumed by our own people.

This so-called equalization fee is not a tax for purposes of revenue in the accepted sense. It is a tax for the special benefit of particular groups. As a direct tax on certain of the vital necessaries of life it represents the most vicious form of taxation. Its real effect is an employment of the coercive powers of Government to the end that certain special groups of farmers and processors may profit temporarily at the expense of other farmers and of the community at large.

The chief objection to the bill is that it would not benefit the farmer. Whatever may be the temporary influence of arbitrary interference, no one can deny that in the long run prices will be governed by the law of supply and demand. To expect to increase prices and then to maintain them on a higher level by means of a plan which must of necessity increase production while decreasing consumption is to fly in the face of an economic law as well established as any law of nature. Experience shows that high prices in any given year mean greater acreage the next year. This does not necessarily mean a larger crop the following year, because adverse weather conditions may produce a smaller crop on a larger acreage, but in the long run a constantly increasing acreage must of necessity mean a larger average crop. . . .

A board of 12 men are granted almost unlimited control of the agricultural industry and can not only fix the price which the producers of five commodities shall receive for their goods, but can also fix the price which the consumers of the country shall pay for these commodities. The board is expected to obtain higher prices for the American farmer by removing the surplus from the home market and dumping it abroad at a below-cost price. To do this, the board is given the authority by implication to fix the domestic price level, either by means of contracts which it may make with processors or cooperatives, or by providing for the purchase of the commodities in such quantities as will bring the prices up to the point which the board may fix.

Except as it may be restrained by fear of foreign importations, the farm board, composed of representatives of producers, is given the power to fix the prices of these necessities of life at any point it sees fit. The law fixes no standards, imposes no restrictions, and requires no regulation of any kind. There could be no appeal from the arbitrary decision of these men, who would be under constant pressure from their constituents to push prices as high as possible. To expect moderation under these circumstances is to disregard experience and credit human nature with qualities it does not possess. It is not so long since the Government was spending vast sums and through the Department of Justice exerting every effort to break up combinations that were raising the cost of living to a point conceived to be excessive. This bill, if it accomplishes its purpose, will raise the price of the specified agricultural commodities to the highest possible point, and in doing so the board will operate without any restraint imposed by the antitrust laws. The granting of any such arbitrary power to a Government board is to run counter to our traditions, the philosophy of our Government, the spirit of our institutions, and all principles of equity.

The administrative difficulties involved are sufficient to wreck the plan. No matter how simple an economic conception may be, its application on a large scale in the modern world is attended by infinite complexities and difficulties. The principle underlying this bill, whether fallacious or not, is simple and easy to state; but no one has outlined in definite and detailed terms how the principle is to be carried out in practice. How can the board be expected to carry out after the enactment of the law what can not even be described prior to its passage? In the meanwhile, existing channels and methods of distribution and marketing must be seriously dislocated.

This is even more apparent when we take into consideration the problem of administering the collection of the equalization fee. The bureau states that the fee will have to be collected either from the processors or the transportation companies, and dismisses as impracticable collections at the point of sale. In the case of transportation companies it points out the enormous difficulties of collecting the fee in view of the possibility of shipping commodities by unregistered vehicles. In so far as processors are concerned, it estimates the number at 6,632, without considering the number of factories engaged in the business of canning corn or manufacturing food products other than millers. Some conception of the magnitude of the task may be had when we consider that if the wheat, the corn, and the cotton crops had been under operation in the year 1925, collection would have been required from an aggregate of 16,-034,466,679 units. The bureau states that it will be impossible to collect the equalization fee in full.

The bill will not succeed in providing a practical method of controlling the agricultural surplus, which lies at the heart of the whole problem. In the matter of controlling output, the farmer is at a disadvantage as compared with the manufacturer. The latter is better able to gauge his market, and in the face of falling prices can reduce production. The farmer, on the other hand, must operate over a longer period of time in producing his crops and is subject to weather conditions and disturbances in world markets which can never be known in advance. In trying to find a solution for this fundamental problem of the surplus, the present bill offers no constructive suggestion. It seeks merely to increase the prices paid by the consumer, with the inevitable result of stimulating production on the part of the farmer and decreasing consumption on the part of the public. It ignores the fact that production is curbed only by decreased, not increased, prices. In the end the equalization fee and the entire machinery provided by the bill under consideration will merely aggravate conditions which are the cause of the farmer's present distress.

We must be careful in trying to help the farmer not to jeopardize the whole agricultural industry by subjecting it to the tyranny of bureaucratic regulation and control. That is what the present bill will do. But, aside from all this, no man can foresee what the effect on our economic life will be of disrupting the long-established and delicately adjusted channels of commerce. That it will be far-reaching is undeniable, nor is it beyond the range of possibility that the present bill, if enacted into law, will threaten the very basis of our national prosperity, through dislocation, the slowing up of industry, and the disruption of the farmer's home market, which absorbs 90 per cent of his products. . . .

The effect of this plan will be continuously to stimulate American production and to pile up increasing surpluses beyond the world demand. We are already overproducing. It has been claimed that the plan would only be used in the emergency of occasional surplus which unduly depresses the price. No such limitations are placed in the bill. But on the other hand the definition of surplus is the "surplus over domestic requirements" and as we have had such a surplus in most of the commodities covered in the bill for 50 years and will have for years to come it means continuous action. It is said that by the automatic increase of the equalization fee to meet the increasing losses on enlarged dumping of increasing surplus that there would be restraint on production. This can prove effective only after so great an increase in production as will greatly enlarge our exports on all the commodities except cotton. With such increased surpluses dumped from the United States on to foreign markets the world prices will be broken down and with them American prices upon which the premium is based will likewise be lowered to the point of complete disaster to American farmers. It is impossible to see how this bill can work.

Several of our foreign markets have agriculture of their own to protect and they have laws in force which may be applied to dumping and we may expect reprisals from them against dumping agricultural products which will even more diminish our foreign markets.

The bill is essentially a price-fixing bill, because in practical working the board must arrive in some way at the premium price which will be demanded from the American consumer, and it must fix these prices in the contracts at which it will authorize purchases by flour millers, packers, other manufacturers, and such cooperatives as may be used, for the board must formulate a basis upon which the board will pay losses on the export of their surplus. . . .

The main policy of this bill is an entire reversal of what has been heretofore thought to be sound. Instead of undertaking to secure a method of orderly marketing which will dispose of products at a profit, it proposes to dispose of them at a loss. It runs counter to the principle of conservation, which would require us to produce only what can be done at a profit, not to waste our soil and resources producing what is to be sold at a loss to us for the benefit of the foreign consumer. It runs counter to the well-considered principle that a healthy economic condition is best maintained through a free play of competition by undertaking to permit a legalized restraint of trade in these commodities and establish a species of monopoly under Government protection. . . . For many generations such practices have been denounced by law as repugnant to the public welfare. It can not be that they would now be found to be beneficial to agriculture.

This measure is so long and involved that it is impossible to discuss it without going into many tiresome details. Many other reasons exist why it ought not to be approved, but it is impossible to state them all without writing a book. The most decisive one is that it is not constitutional. This feature is discussed in an opinion of the Attorney General, herewith attached and made a part hereof, so that I shall not consider the details of that phase of my objections. Of course it includes some good features. Some of its provisions, intended to aid and strengthen cooperative marketing, have been borrowed from proposals that do represent the general trend of constructive thought on the agricultural problem. In this measure, however, these provisions are all completely subordinated to the main objective, which is to have the Government dispose of exportable surpluses at a loss and make some farmer taxpayers foot the bill. This is not a measure to help cooperative marketing. Its effect, on the contrary, is to eliminate the very conditions of advantage that now induce farmers to join together to regulate and improve their own business. . . .

24
The Agricultural Adjustment Act (12 May 1933)
[Stat. XLVIII, 31]

An act to relieve the existing national economic emergency by increasing agricultural purchasing power, . . . to provide for the orderly liquidation of joint-stock land banks, and for other purposes. . . .

TITLE I—AGRICULTURAL ADJUSTMENT

Declaration of Emergency

That the present acute economic emergency being in part the consequence of a severe and increasing disparity between the prices of agricultural and other commodities, which disparity has largely destroyed the purchasing power of farmers for industrial products, has broken down the orderly exchange of commodities, and has seriously impaired the agricultural assets supporting the national credit structure, it is hereby declared that these conditions in the basic industry of agriculture have affected transactions in agricultural commodities with a national public interest, have burdened and obstructed the normal current of commerce in such commodities, and render imperative the immediate enactment of title I of this Act.

Declaration of Policy

Sec. 2. It is hereby declared to be the policy of Congress—

(1) To establish and maintain such balance between the production and consumption of agricultural commodities, and such marketing conditions therefor, as will reestablish prices to farmers at a level that will give agricultural commodities a purchasing power with respect to articles that farmers buy, equivalent to the purchasing power of agricultural commodities in the base period. The base period in the case of all agricultural commodities except tobacco shall be the prewar period, August 1909–July 1914. In the case of tobacco, the base period shall be the postwar period, August 1919–July 1929.

(2) To approach such equality of purchasing power by gradual correction of the present inequalities therein at as rapid a rate as is deemed feasible in view of the current consumptive demand in domestic and foreign markets.

(3) To protect the consumers' interest by readjusting farm production at such level as will not increase the percentage of the consumers' retail expenditures for agricultural commodities, or products derived therefrom, which is returned to the farmer, above the percentage which was returned to the farmer in the prewar period, August 1909–July 1914. . . .

Sec. 6. (a) The Secretary of Agriculture is hereby authorized to enter into option contracts with the producers of cotton to sell to any such producer an amount of cotton to be agreed upon not in excess of the amount of reduction in production of cotton by such producer below the amount produced by him in the preceding crop year, in all cases where such producer agrees in writing to reduce the amount of cotton produced by him in 1933, below his production in the previous year, by not less than 30 per centum, without increase in commercial fertilization per acre.

(b) To any such producer so agreeing to reduce production the Secretary of Agriculture shall deliver a nontransferable-option contract agreeing to sell to said producer an amount, equivalent to the amount of his agreed reduction, of the cotton in the possession and control of the Secretary.

(c) The producer is to have the option to buy said cotton at the average price paid by the Secretary for the cotton procured under section 3, and is to have the right at any time up to January 1, 1934, to exercise his option, upon proof that he has complied with his contract and with all the rules and regulations of the Secretary of Agriculture with respect thereto, by taking said cotton upon payment by him of his option price and all actual carrying charges on such cotton; or the Secretary may sell such cotton for the account of such producer, paying him the excess of the market price at the date of sale over the average price above referred to after deducting all actual and necessary carrying charges: *Provided,* That in no event shall the producer be held responsible or liable for financial loss incurred in the holding of such cotton or on account of the carrying charges therein: *Provided further,* That such agreement to curtail cotton production shall contain a further provision that such cotton producer shall not use the land taken out of cotton production for the production for sale, directly or indirectly, of any other nationally produced agricultural commodity or product. . . .

PART 2—COMMODITY BENEFITS

General Powers

Sec. 8. In order to effectuate the declared policy, the Secretary of Agriculture shall have power—

(1) To provide for reduction in the acreage or reduction in the production for market, or both, of any basic agricultural

commodity, through agreements with producers or by other voluntary methods, and to provide for rental or benefit payments in connection therewith or upon that part of the production of any basic agricultural commodity required for domestic consumption, in such amounts as the Secretary deems fair and reasonable, to be paid out of any moneys available for such payments. . . .

(2) To enter into marketing agreements with processors, associations of producers, and others engaged in the handling, in the current of interstate or foreign commerce of any agricultural commodity or product thereof, after due notice and opportunity for hearing to interested parties. The making of any such agreement shall not be held to be in violation of any of the antitrust laws of the United States, and any such agreement shall be deemed to be lawful: . . .

Processing Tax

Sec. 9. (a) To obtain revenue for extraordinary expenses incurred by reason of the national economic emergency, there shall be levied processing taxes as hereinafter provided. When the Secretary of Agriculture determines that rental or benefit payments are to be made with respect to any basic agricultural commodity, he shall proclaim such determination, and a processing tax shall be in effect with respect to such commodity from the beginning of the marketing year therefor next following the date of such proclamation. The processing tax shall be levied, assessed, and collected upon the first domestic processing of the commodity, whether of domestic production or imported, and shall be paid by the processor. . . .

(b) The processing tax shall be at such rate as equals the difference between the current average farm price for the commodity and the fair exchange value of the commodity; except that if the Secretary has reason to believe that the tax at such rate will cause such reduction in the quantity of the commodity or products thereof domestically consumed as to result in the accumulation of surplus stocks of the commodity or products thereof or in the depression of the farm price of the commodity, then he shall cause an appropriate investigation to be made and afford due notice and opportunity for hearing to interested parties. If thereupon the Secretary finds that such result will occur, then the processing tax shall be at such rate as will prevent such accumulation of surplus stocks and depression of the farm price of the commodity. . . .

(c) For the purposes of part 2 of this title, the fair exchange value of a commodity shall be the price therefor that will give the commodity the same purchasing power, with respect to articles farmers buy, as such commodity had during the base period specified in section 2; . . .

(d) As used in part 2 of this title—

(1) In case of wheat, rice, and corn, the term "processing" means the milling or other processing (except cleaning and drying) of wheat, rice, or corn for market, including custom milling for toll as well as commercial milling, but shall not include the grinding or cracking thereof not in the form of flour for feed purposes only.

(2) In case of cotton, the term "processing" means the spinning, manufacturing, or other processing (except ginning) of cotton; and the term "cotton" shall not include cotton linters.

(3) In case of tobacco, the term "processing" means the manufacturing or other processing (except drying or converting into insecticides and fertilizers) of tobacco.

(4) In case of hogs, the term "processing" means the slaughter of hogs for market.

(5) In the case of any other commodity, the term "processing" means any manufacturing or other processing involving a change in the form of the commodity or its preparation for market, as defined by regulations of the Secretary of Agriculture; and in prescribing such regulations the Secretary shall give due weight to the customs of the industry.

(e) When any processing tax, or increase or decrease therein, takes effect in respect of a commodity the Secretary of Agriculture, in order to prevent pyramiding of the processing tax and profiteering in the sale of the products derived from the commodity, shall make public such information as he deems necessary regarding (1) the relationship between the processing tax and the price paid to producers of the commodity, (2) the effect of the processing tax upon prices to consumers of products of the commodity, (3) the relationship, in previous periods, between prices paid to the producers of the commodity and prices to consumers of the products thereof, and (4) the situation in foreign countries relating to prices paid to producers of the commodity and prices to consumers of the products thereof. . . .

L. *The National Recovery Administration*

The New Deal was a unique episode in American history partly because the Great Depression was very severe, partly because the Roosevelt administration immediately undertook a massive program to counteract it, and not least because the technique of the N.R.A. was unlike anything done before or since by American government.

Roosevelt hoped to dismiss fear and greed, which in his view were the principal actors in the depression, from the industrial sector by establishing a "great cooperative movement" (25). Each industry would organize and rule itself and thereby revitalize itself.

The National Industrial Recovery Act (26) established the framework under which hundreds of industry codes (27, for example) were rapidly set in operation. Each was in effect an elaborate cartel agreement of the sort that would have been illegal under the antitrust laws, whose operation had for this very reason been suspended by the N.I.R.A. That the code agreements—like any other cartel arrangements—might raise prices and wages seems plausible enough, but whether higher prices and wages, achieved in this way, would have tended to increase total incomes and national production is doubtful.

Aside from its doubtful merits on economic grounds, the N.R.A. had political implications that aroused objections. To some it seemed that the organization of industry, under public control, was the last stage but one on the road to socialism. Others, on the contrary, recognized in the spectacle of all industry cartelizing itself with the government's blessing a dismaying similarity to industrial organization under Mussolini, not much altered by the substitution of a blue eagle for the fasces. As a result, some of the fear and uneasiness that had been created by the depression was now transferred to the N.R.A.

Such suspicions might eventually have been calmed, and cartelization by fiat might have become a standard part of the repertoire of American economic policy. But the unique experiment was put to a quick and decisive end. It was demolished by the *Schechter* or "sick chicken" case (28), as it was known at the time. In this decision, the Supreme Court held unanimously that the N.I.R.A. was unconstitutional; this rebuff was the first of a series that led to the designation of the Justices as the Nine Old Men and to the protracted battle between Court and President. This epoch was one during which the great influence that the Constitution empowers the Court to exercise over economic policy became much more visible than it generally is.

The various public works programs set in motion by the New Deal (and by Title II of the N.I.R.A. [26]) fared much better. Their constitutionality was unquestionable, and their economic utility much more certain. The fundamental notion was not in the least novel, but the large programs of this sort, administered by the federal government, were. They have since become an accepted method of dealing with business recessions.

25
FRANKLIN D. ROOSEVELT (1882–1945)
Message to Congress on N.I.R.A. (17 May 1933)
[Public Papers and Addresses of F. D. Roosevelt,
(Rosenman, ed., 1938) II, 202]

Before the Special Session of the Congress adjourns, I recommend two further steps in our national campaign to put people to work.

I

My first request is that the Congress provide for the machinery necessary for a great cooperative movement throughout all industry in order to obtain wide reemployment, to shorten the working week, to pay a decent wage for the shorter week and to prevent unfair competition and disastrous overproduction.

Employers cannot do this singly or even in organized groups, because such action increases costs and thus permits cut-throat underselling by selfish competitors unwilling to join in such a public-spirited endeavor.

One of the great restrictions upon such cooperative efforts up to this time has been our anti-trust laws. They were properly designed as the means to cure the great evils of monopolistic price fixing. They should certainly be retained as a permanent assurance that the old evils of unfair competition shall never return. But the public interest will be served if, with the authority and under the guidance of Government, private industries are permitted to make agreements and codes insuring fair competition. However, it is necessary, if we thus limit the operation of anti-trust laws to their original purpose, to provide a rigorous licensing power in order to meet rare cases of non-cooperation and abuse. Such a safeguard is indispensable.

II

The other proposal gives the Executive full power to start a large program of direct employment. A careful survey convinces me that approximately $3,300,000,000 can be invested in useful and necessary public construction, and at the same time put the largest possible number of people to work.

Provision should be made to permit States, counties and municipalities to undertake useful public works, subject, however, to the most effective possible means of eliminating favoritism and wasteful expenditures on unwarranted and uneconomic projects.

We must, by prompt and vigorous action, override unnecessary obstructions which in the past have delayed the starting of public works programs. This can be accomplished by simple and direct procedure.

In carrying out this program it is imperative that the credit of the United States Government be protected and preserved. This means that at the same time we are making these vast emergency expenditures there must be provided sufficient revenue to pay interest and amortization on the cost and that the revenues so provided must be adequate and certain rather than inadequate and speculative.

Careful estimates indicate that at least $220,000,000 of additional revenue will be required to service the contemplated borrowings of the Government. This will of necessity involve some form or forms of new taxation. A number of suggestions have been made as to the nature of these taxes. I do not make a specific recommendation at this time, but I hope that the Committee on Ways and Means, of the House of Representatives, will make a careful study of revenue plans and be prepared by the beginning of the coming week to propose the taxes which they judge to be best adapted to meet the present need and which will at the same time be least burdensome to our people. At the end of that time, if no decision has been reached or if the means proposed do not seem to be sufficiently adequate or certain, it is my intention to transmit to the Congress my own recommendations in the matter.

The taxes to be imposed are for the purpose of providing re-employment for our citizens. Provision should be made for their reduction or elimination:

> First, As fast as increasing revenues from improving busi-ness become available to replace them;
> Second, Whenever the repeal of the 18th Amendment now pending before the States shall have been ratified and the repeal of the Volstead Act effected. The pre-Prohibition revenue laws would then automatically go into effect and yield enough wholly to eliminate these temporary reemployment taxes.

Finally, I stress the fact that all of these proposals are based on the gravity of the emergency and that therefore it is ur-gently necessary immediately to initiate a reemployment cam-paign if we are to avoid further hardships, to sustain business improvement and to pass on to better things.

For this reason I urge prompt action on this legislation.

26
The National Industrial Recovery Act (16 June 1933)
[Stat. XLVIII, 195]

An act to encourage national industrial recovery, to foster fair competition, and to provide for the construction of certain useful public works, and for other purposes. . . .

TITLE I—INDUSTRIAL RECOVERY

Declaration of Policy

Sec. 1. A national emergency productive of widespread un-employment and disorganization of industry, which burdens interstate and foreign commerce, affects the public welfare, and undermines the standards of living of the American people, is hereby declared to exist. It is hereby declared to be the policy of Congress to remove obstructions to the free flow of interstate and foreign commerce which tend to diminish the amount thereof; and to provide for the general welfare by promoting the organization of industry for the purpose of co-operative action among trade groups, to induce and maintain united action of labor and management under adequate governmental sanctions and supervision, to eliminate unfair competitive practices, to promote the fullest possible utilization of the present productive capacity of industries, to avoid undue restriction of production (except as may be temporarily required), to increase the consumption of industrial and agricultural products by increasing purchasing power, to reduce and relieve unemployment, to improve standards of labor, and otherwise to rehabilitate industry and to conserve natural resources.

Administrative Agencies

Sec. 2. . . . (c) This title shall cease to be in effect and any agencies established hereunder shall cease to exist at the expiration of two years after the date of enactment of this Act, or sooner if the President shall by proclamation or the Congress shall by joint resolution declare that the emergency recognized by section 1 has ended.

Codes of Fair Competition

Sec. 3. (a) Upon the application to the President by one or more trade or industrial associations or groups, the President may approve a code or codes of fair competition for the trade or industry or subdivision thereof, represented by the applicant or applicants, if the President finds (1) that such associations or groups impose no inequitable restrictions on admission to membership therein and are truly representative of such trades or industries or subdivisions thereof, and (2) that such code or codes are not designed to promote monopolies or to eliminate or oppress small enterprises and will not operate to discriminate against them, and will tend to effectuate the policy of this title: *Provided,* That such code or codes shall not permit monopolies or monopolistic practices: *Provided further,* That where such code or codes affect the services and welfare of persons engaged in other steps of the economic process, nothing in this section shall deprive such persons of the right to be heard prior to approval by the President of such code or codes. The President may, as a condition of his approval of any such code, impose such conditions (including requirements for the making of reports and the keeping of accounts) for the protection of consumers, competitors, employees, and others, and in furtherance of the public interest, and may provide such exceptions to and exemptions from the provisions of such code, as the President in his discretion deems necessary to effectuate the policy herein declared.

(b) After the President shall have approved any such code, the provisions of such code shall be the standards of fair competition for such trade or industry or subdivision thereof. Any violation of such standards in any transaction in or affecting interstate or foreign commerce shall be deemed an unfair method of competition in commerce within the meaning of the Federal Trade Commission Act, as amended; but nothing in this title shall be construed to impair the powers of the Federal Trade Commission under such Act, as amended. . . .

(d) Upon his own motion, or if complaint is made to the President that abuses inimical to the public interest and contrary to the policy herein declared are prevalent in any trade or industry or subdivision thereof, and if no code of fair competition therefor has therefore been approved by the President, the President, after such public notice and hearing as he shall specify, may prescribe and approve a code of fair competition for such trade or industry or subdivision thereof, which shall have the same effect as a code of fair competition approved by the President under subsection (a) of this section. . . .

Agreements and Licenses

Sec. 4.(a) The President is authorized to enter into agreements with, and to approve voluntary agreements between and among, persons engaged in a trade or industry, labor organizations, and trade or industrial organizations, associations, or groups, relating to any trade or industry, if in his judgment such agreements will aid in effectuating the policy of this title with respect to transactions in or affecting interstate or foreign commerce, and will be consistent with the requirements of clause (2) of subsection (a) of section 3 for a code of fair competition.

(b) Whenever the President shall find that destructive wage or price cutting or other activities contrary to the policy of this title are being practiced in any trade or industry or any subdivision thereof, and, after such public notice and hearing as he shall specify, shall find it essential to license business enterprises in order to make effective a code of fair competition or an agreement under this title or otherwise to effectuate the policy of this title, and shall publicly so announce, no person shall, after a date fixed in such announcement, engage in or carry on any business, in or affecting interstate or foreign commerce, specified in such announcement, unless he shall have first obtained a license issued pursuant to such regulations as the President shall prescribe. The President may suspend or revoke any such license, after due notice and opportunity for hearing, for violations of the terms or conditions thereof. Any order of the President suspending or revoking any such license shall be final if in accordance with law. . . .

Sec. 5. While this title is in effect . . . and for sixty days thereafter, any code, agreement, or license approved, prescribed, or issued and in effect under this title, and any action complying with the provisions thereof taken during such period, shall be exempt from the provisions of the antitrust laws of the United States.

Nothing in this Act, and no regulation thereunder, shall prevent an individual from pursuing the vocation of manual labor and selling or trading the products thereof; nor shall anything in this Act, or regulation thereunder, prevent anyone from marketing or trading the produce of his farm.

Limitations upon Application of Title

Sec. 6. (a) No trade or industrial association or group shall be eligible to receive the benefit of the provisions of this title until it files with the President a statement containing such information relating to the activities of the association or group as the President shall by regulation prescribe. . . .

Sec. 7. (a) Every code of fair competition, agreement, and license approved, prescribed, or issued under this title shall contain the following conditions: (1) that employees shall have the right to organize and bargain collectively through representatives of their own choosing, and shall be free from the interference, restraint, or coercion of employers of labor, or their agents, in the designation of such representatives or in self-organization or in other concerted activities for the purpose of collective bargaining or other mutual aid or protection; (2) that no employee and no one seeking employment shall be required as a condition of employment to join any company union or to refrain from joining, organizing, or assisting a labor organization of his own choosing; and (3) that employers shall comply with the maximum hours of labor, minimum rates of pay, and other conditions of employment, approved or prescribed by the President.

(b) The President shall, so far as practicable, afford every opportunity to employers and employees in any trade or industry or subdivision thereof with respect to which the conditions referred to in clauses (1) and (2) of subsection (a) prevail, to establish by mutual agreement, the standards as to the maximum hours of labor, minimum rates of pay, and such other conditions of employment as may be necessary in such trade or industry or subdivision thereof to effectuate the policy of this title; and the standards established in such agreements, when approved by the President, shall have the same effect as a code of fair competition, . . .

(c) Where no such mutual agreement has been approved by the President he may investigate the labor practices, policies, wages, hours of labor, and conditions of employment in such trade or industry or subdivision thereof; and upon the basis of such investigations, and after such hearings as the President finds advisable, he is authorized to prescribe a limited code of fair competition fixing such maximum hours of labor, minimum rates of pay, and other conditions of employment in the trade or industry or subdivision thereof investigated as he finds to be necessary to effectuate the policy of this title, which shall have the same effect as a code of fair competition approved by the President under subsection (a) of section 3. The President may differentiate according to experience and skill of the employees affected and according to the locality of employment; but no attempt shall be made to introduce any classification according to the nature of the work involved which might tend to set a maximum as well as a minimum wage.

(d) As used in this title, the term "person" includes any individual, partnership, association, trust, or corporation; . . .

TITLE II—PUBLIC WORKS AND CONSTRUCTION PROJECTS

Federal Emergency Administration of Public Works

Sec. 201. (a) To effectuate the purposes of this title, the President is hereby authorized to create a Federal Emergency Administration of Public Works, all the powers of which shall be exercised by a Federal Emergency Administrator of Public Works, . . . and to establish such agencies, to accept and utilize such voluntary and uncompensated services, to appoint, without regard to the civil service laws, such officers and employees, and to utilize such Federal officers and employees, and, with the consent of the State, such State and local officers and employees as he may find necessary, to prescribe their authorities, duties, responsibilities, and tenure, and, without regard to the Classification Act of 1923, as amended, to fix the compensation of any officers and employees so appointed. The President may delegate any of his functions and powers under this title to such officers, agents, and employees as he may designate or appoint.

(b) The Administrator may, without regard to the civil

service laws or the Classification Act of 1923, as amended, appoint and fix the compensation of such experts and such other officers and employees as are necessary to carry out the provisions of this title; and may make such expenditures (including expenditures for personal services and rent at the seat of government and elsewhere, for law books and books of reference, and for paper, printing and binding) as are necessary to carry out the provisions of this title. . . .

(d) After the expiration of two years after the date of the enactment of this Act, or sooner if the President shall by proclamation or the Congress shall by joint resolution declare that the emergency recognized by section 1 has ended, the President shall not make any further loans or grants or enter upon any new construction under this title, and any agencies established hereunder shall cease to exist and any of their remaining functions shall be transferred to such departments of the Government as the President shall designate: . . .

Sec. 202. The Administrator, under the direction of the President, shall prepare a comprehensive program of public works, which shall include among other things the following: (a) Construction, repair, and improvement of public highways and park ways, public buildings, and any publicly owned instrumentalities and facilities; (b) conservation and development of natural resources, including control, utilization, and purification of waters, prevention of soil or coastal erosion, development of water power, transmission of electrical energy, and construction of river and harbor improvements and flood control and also the construction of any river or drainage improvement required to perform or satisfy any obligation incurred by the United States through a treaty with a foreign Government heretofore ratified and to restore or develop for the use of any State or its citizens water taken from or denied to them by performance on the part of the United States of treaty obligations heretofore assumed: *Provided,* That no river or harbor improvements shall be carried out unless they shall have heretofore or hereafter been adopted by the Congress or are recommended by the Chief of Engineers of the United

States Army; (c) any projects of the character heretofore constructed or carried on either directly by public authority or with public aid to serve the interests of the general public; (d) construction, reconstruction, alteration, or repair under public regulation or control of low-cost housing and slum-clearance projects; (e) any project (other than those included in the foregoing classes) of any character heretofore eligible for loans under subsection (a) of section 201 of the Emergency Relief and Construction Act of 1932, as amended, and paragraph (3) of such subsection (a) shall for such purposes be held to include loans for the construction or completion of hospitals the operation of which is partly financed from public funds, and of reservoirs and pumping plants and for the construction of dry docks; and if in the opinion of the President it seems desirable, the construction of naval vessels within the terms and/or limits established by the London Naval Treaty of 1930 and of aircraft required therefor and construction of heavier-than-air aircraft and technical construction for the Army Air Corps and such Army housing projects as the President may approve, and provision of original equipment for the mechanization or motorization of such Army tactical units as he may designate: *Provided, however,* That in the event of an international agreement for the further limitation of armament, to which the United States is signatory, the President is hereby authorized and empowered to suspend, in whole or in part, any such naval or military construction or mechanization and motorization of Army units: . . .

Sec. 203. (a) With a view to increasing employment quickly (while reasonably securing any loans made by the United States) the President is authorized and empowered, through the Administrator or through such other agencies as he may designate or create, (1) to construct, finance, or aid in the construction or financing of any public-works project included in the program prepared pursuant to section 202; (2) upon such terms as the President shall prescribe, to make grants to States, municipalities, or other public bodies for the construction, repair, or improvement of any such project, but no such grant shall be in excess of 30 per centum of the cost of the labor and materials employed upon such project; (3) to acquire by purchase, or by exercise of the power of eminent domain, any real or personal property in connection with the construction of any such project, and to sell any security acquired or any property so constructed or acquired or to lease any such property with or without the privilege of purchase: *Provided,* That all moneys received from any such sale or lease or the repayment of any loan shall be used to retire obligations issued pursuant to section 209 of this Act, in addition to any other moneys required to be used for such purpose; (4) to aid in the financing of such railroad maintenance and equipment as may be approved by the Interstate Commerce Commission as desirable for the improvement of transportation facilities; . . . *Provided,* That in deciding to extend any aid or grant hereunder to any State, county, or municipality the President may consider whether action is in process or in good faith assured therein reasonably designed to bring the ordinary current expenditures thereof within the prudently estimated revenues thereof. . . .

(d) The President, in his discretion, and under such terms as he may prescribe, may extend any of the benefits of this title to any State, county, or municipality notwithstanding any constitutional or legal restriction or limitation on the right or power of such State, county, or municipality to borrow money or incur indebtedness.

Sec. 204. (a) For the purpose of providing for emergency construction of public highways and related projects, the President is authorized to make grants to the highway departments of the several States in an amount not less than $400,000,000, to be expended by such departments in accordance with the provisions of the Federal Highway Act, approved November 9, 1921, as amended and supplemented, . . .

Sec. 205. (a) Not less than $50,000,000 of the amount made available by this Act shall be allotted for (A) national forest highways, (B) national forest roads, trails, bridges, and related projects, (C) national park roads and trails in national parks owned or authorized, (D) roads on Indian reservations, and (E) roads through public lands, to be expended in the same manner as provided in paragraph (2) of section 301 of the Emergency Relief and Construction Act of 1932, in the case of appropriations allocated for such purposes, respectively, in such section 301, to remain available until expended. . . .

Sec. 206. All contracts let for construction projects and all loans and grants pursuant to this 'title shall contain such provisions as are necessary to insure (1) that no convict labor shall be employed on any such project; (2) that (except in executive, administrative, and supervisory positions), so far as practicable and feasible, no individual directly employed on any such project shall be permitted to work more than thirty hours in any one week; (3) that all employees shall be paid just and reasonable wages which shall be compensation sufficient to provide, for the hours of labor as limited, a standard of living in decency and comfort; (4) that in the employment of labor in connection with any such project, preference shall be given, where they are qualified, to ex-service men with dependents, and then in the following order: (A) to citizens of the United States and aliens who have declared their intention of becoming citizens, who are bona fide residents of the political subdivision and/or county in which the work is to be performed, and (B) to citizens of the United States and aliens who have declared their intention of becoming citizens, who are bona fide residents of the State, Territory, or district in which the work is to be performed: *Provided,* That these preferences shall apply only where such labor is available and qualified to perform the work to which the employment relates; and (5) that the maximum of human labor shall be used in lieu of machinery wherever practicable and consistent with sound economy and public advantage. . . .

Subsistence Homesteads

Sec. 208. To provide for aiding the redistribution of the overbalance of population in industrial centers $25,000,000 is hereby made available to the President, to be used by him through such agencies as he may establish and under such regulations as he may make, for making loans for and otherwise aiding in the purchase of subsistence homesteads. The moneys collected as repayment of said loans shall constitute a revolving fund to be administered as directed by the President for the purposes of this section. . . .

27

Code of Fair Competition for the Wall Paper Manu-facturing Industry (1933)
[N.R.A., *Codes of Fair Competition* (1933) I, 267]

August 22, 1933.

The President,
  The White House.

My Dear Mr. President: This is a report of the hearing on the Code of Fair Competition for the Wall Paper Manufacturing Industry in the United States, conducted in Washington on August 7th and 8th, 1933, in accordance with the provisions of the National Industrial Recovery Act.

PROVISIONS OF THIS CODE AS TO WAGES AND HOURS

Sec. II. On and after the effective date the minimum wage that shall be paid by any employer in the Wall Paper Manufacturing Industry shall be at the rate of thirty-five cents (35¢) per hour, or fourteen dollars ($14.00) per week for 40 hours of labor for males, and at the rate of thirty-two and one half cents (32½¢) per hour or thirteen dollars ($13.00) per week for 40 hours of labor for females.

Sec. III. The limit of hours of labor for all employees excepting outside salesmen, emergency repair crews, superintendents and their supervisory staff, shall be 40 hours in each week, but further provided that all such employees paid on an hourly basis shall be paid at the rate of time and a half for all hours per week over 40.

Economic Effect of the Code

The Wall Paper Manufacturing Industry is one of the relatively small manufacturing industries in the United States. In 1929 there were 56 manufacturing plants which employed approximately 4,700 workers; in 1931 there were 50 manufacturers employing approximately 3,734 workers; in 1933 there are only 36 manufacturers with a corresponding decrease in workers, which, because of lack of statistics it is impossible to estimate.

The decline in the number of workers required to produce the necessary supply of wall paper has been consistent since 1923. From 1931 until the present the decrease in employment became more marked.

By reducing the customary 50-hour week which has prevailed in this industry to the 40-hour week required by the Code, the increase in employment will be approximately 15 per cent (15%) of 1929 figures, or approximately 700 workers.

Unless the consumption of wall paper greatly increases within the near future, this particular industry does not offer a very promising field for the reemployment of workers on any large scale.

Findings

The Administrator finds that:

(a) The Code as recommended complies in all respects with the pertinent provisions of Title I of the Act, including without limitation, subsection (a) of Section 7, and subsection (b) of Section 10 thereof; and that

(b) The applicant group imposes no inequitable restrictions on admission to membership therein and is truly representative of the Wall Paper Manufacturing Industry; and that

(c) The Code as recommended is not designed to promote monopolies or to eliminate or oppress small enterprises and will not operate to discriminate against them, and will tend to effectuate the policy of Title I of the National Industrial Recovery Act.

It is recommended, therefore, that this Code be immediately adopted.

Respectfully submitted.

HUGH S. JOHNSON,
Administrator.

Code of Fair Competition for the Wall Paper Manufacturing Industry

To effectuate the policy of Title I of the National Industrial Recovery Act insofar as it is applicable to the Wall Paper Manufacturing Industry, the following provisions are established as a Code of Fair Competition for the Wall Paper Manufacturing Industry.

I—Definitions

A. The term "Wall Paper Manufacturing Industry" is defined to mean the process of printing, imprinting, or embossing upon raw paper stock a pattern and/or design in colors or otherwise, thus producing an article suitable for decoration or the embellishment of walls and/or ceilings in homes, hotels, apartments, or other buildings.

B. The term "manufacturer" shall include, but without limitation, any person, partnership, association, trust, or corporation, and all who employ labor in the conduct of any branch of the Wall Paper Manufacturing Industry as defined above.

C. The term "employees" as used in this Code, shall include all persons employed in the conduct of the operations of manufacturing wall paper.

D. The term "printing machines", as used herein, is defined to mean wall paper printing machines; or ink embossing machines producing finished wall paper that has not been printed.

E. The term "line or lines", as used herein, is defined to mean all the wall papers produced by any manufacturer during a current year.

F. The term "current year" is defined to mean the twelve

months' period succeeding June 30th of each year.

G. The term "jobs" as used herein is defined to mean all unsold wall papers which have been in a line of a manufacturer in any current year and which shall not be included in the line or lines of such manufacturer in the succeeding current year.

H. The term "effective date", as used herein, is defined as the second Monday after the approval by the President of the United States of this Code or any part thereof or addition thereto.

II—Minimum Wages

(a) On and after the effective date the minimum wage that shall be paid by any employer in the Wall Paper Manufacturing Industry shall be thirty-five cents (35¢) per hour or fourteen dollars ($14.00) per week for forty (40) hours of labor for males, and at the rate of thirty-two and one half cents (32½¢) per hour, or thirteen dollars ($13.00) per week for forty (40) hours of labor for females.

(b) The existing amounts by which wage rates in the higher-paid classes exceed wages in the lower-paid classes shall be maintained.

III—Maximum Hours

(a) The limit of hours of labor for all employees, excepting outside salesmen, emergency repair crews, superintendents, and their foremen, shall be forty (40) hours in each week; but further provided that all such excepted employees paid on an hourly basis shall be paid at the rate of time and one half for all hours per week over forty (40).

(b) Each manufacturer in this industry shall be limited to two eight-hour shifts; however, no employee shall be required to work more than one eight-hour shift in any one day.

IV

On and after the effective date employers shall not employ or have in their employ any person under the age of 16 years.

V

As required by Section 7 (a) of Title I of the National Industrial Recovery Act it is provided:

"(1) That employees shall have the right to organize and bargain collectively through representatives of their own choosing, and shall be free from the interference, restraint, or coercion of employers of labor, or their agents, in the designation of such representatives or in self-organization or in other concerted activities for the purpose of collective bargaining or other mutual aid or protection;

"(2) That no employee and no one seeking employment shall be required as a condition of employment to join any company union or to refrain from joining, organizing, or assisting a labor organization of his own choosing;

"(3) That employers shall comply with the maximum hours of labor, minimum rates of pay, and other conditions of employment approved or prescribed by the President."

VI—Standards

Nothing contained in this Section shall apply to or affect in any way contracts between members of the Wall Paper Manufacturing Industry and others in existence prior to the effective date of this Code.

(a) This Code hereby provides that all manufacturers of wall paper shall comply with Commercial Standard CS 16–29 Bureau of Standards, as adopted on May 25, 1929, at a conference of manufacturers, distributors, users of wall paper, and others interested, and approved and promulgated August 1, 1929, by the Department of Commerce.

(b) As an addition to the matter set forth in the said Commercial Standard CS 16–29, a further standard for this Industry and further regulation of the kinds and weights of raw stock to be used hereby are established, to wit: No wall paper printed on less than ten (10) ounce stock, or below the said Commercial Standard requirements in any other respect, shall bear any mark or statement that such papers conform to the said Commercial Standard CS 16–29.

(c) No wall paper shall be printed on raw stock in weight less than nine (9) ounces, except that to be marked "less than nine (9) ounce stock" on the selvage.

(d) Ungrounded goods shall be plainly marked by the manufacturer on the selvage of the Wall Paper and all manufacturers shall mark their samples with the word "ungrounded."

VII

The following shall constitute unfair methods of competition:

(a) The copying of designs and/or patterns.

(b) The selling of goods at less than cost, except jobs.

(c) Failure to maintain an adequate differential in the selling prices to the wholesaler and retailer.

(d) The making of sample books by any manufacturer for any customer and failing to include in the cost of said sample books the cost of the wall paper used therein, charged at the same rate by said manufacturer to said customer as the goods said customer has purchased for stock, and in addition any other expenses incurred in the making of said sample books. This shall not apply to one book known as Book of Selections furnished to a customer by a manufacturer with his order. No more than one sample book or Book of Selections shall be given to a customer by a manufacturer.

(e) The selling of goods as jobs by any manufacturer before the 31st day of December in any year, and at lower prices than 33⅓ per cent below the individual seller's established current minimum price of the same grade to the same buyer.

(f) The false marking or branding of products of the Industry.

(g) The making of or causing or permitting to be made or published any false, untrue, or deceptive statement by way of advertisement or otherwise, concerning the grade, quality, quantity, substance, character, nature, origin, size, or preparation of any product of the Industry.

(h) The defamation of competitors by falsely imputing to them dishonorable conduct, inability to perform contracts, questionable credit standing, or by other false representations, or in disparagement of the grade or quality of their goods.

(i) The imitation of the trade-marks, trade names, slogans, or other marks of identification of competitors.

(j) The securing of information from competitors concerning their business by false or misleading statements or representations or by false impersonations of one in authority.

(k) The payment or allowance of unearned rebates, refunds, credits, or discounts, whether in the form of money or otherwise.

(l) Deviation from the established standards of the Industry by any deceptive or false means or devices whatsoever.

(m) To make any sample allowance to any purchaser on any borders or any goods less than 30 inches in width. On 30-inch goods the sample allowance shall not be greater than an allowance of eight yards for the price of five.

VIII

No manufacturer shall sell any goods on more favorable terms than the following: 91 days net (with no dating). Discount for cash payment, 3%, 30 days; 2%, 60 days; 1%, 90 days. An additional deduction to be allowed for cash payment within discounting periods for shipments made in September, 4%; in October, 3%; in November, 2%; in December, 1%. Cash discounts and deductions to apply for cash payments only, and not to be allowed when other charges are overdue.

IX

All manufacturers shall sell their products on the basis f.o.b. own mill or mills, with no greater freight allowance than railroad freight equalization, carload rates or L.C.L. rates, as the case may be, to nearest competing operating mill to the customer being sold. No freight shall be prepaid by any manufacturer.

X

The establishment of a uniform Cost System for this Industry is recommended and shall be established as soon as possible under the direction of the Executive Committee of the Wall Paper Manufacturing Industry.

XI

With a view to keeping the President of the United States and the Administrator informed as to the observance or non-observance of this Code, and as to whether the Wall Paper Manufacturing Industry is taking appropriate steps to effectuate in all respects the declared policy of the National Industrial Recovery Act, the Executive Committee of the Wall Paper Manufacturing Industry, is hereby constituted and shall be composed of five members, chosen by a fair method of selection and approved by the Administrator. Each employer shall file with the Executive Committee statistics covering the number of employees, wage rates, employee earnings, hours of work, and such other data or information as may be from time to time required by the Administrator.

Except as otherwise provided in the National Industrial Recovery Act, all statistics, data, and information filed in accordance with the provisions of Article XI shall be confidential, and the statistics, data, and other information of one employer shall not be revealed to any other employer except for the purpose of administering or enforcing the provisions of this Code. The Executive Committee of the Wall Paper Manufacturing Industry shall have access to any and all statistics, data, and information that may be furnished in accordance with the provisions of this Code.

XII

Any employer may participate in the endeavors of the Executive Committee of the Wall Paper Manufacturing Industry relative to the revisions or additions to this Code by accepting the proper pro rata share of the costs and responsibility of creating and administering it.

XIII

This Code and all the provisions thereof are expressly made subject to the right of the President, in accordance with the provision of Clause 10 (b) of the National Industrial Recovery Act, from time to time to cancel or modify any order, approval, license, rule, or regulation, issued under Title I of said Act, and specifically to the right of the President to cancel or modify his approval of this Code or any conditions imposed by him upon his approval thereof.

XIV

Such of the provisions of this Code as are not required to be included therein by the National Industrial Recovery Act may, with the approval of the President, be modified or eliminated as changes in circumstances or experience may indicate. They shall remain in effect unless and until so modified or eliminated or until the expiration of the Act. It is contemplated that from time to time supplementary provisions to this Code or additional codes will be submitted for the approval of the President, to prevent unfair competition in price and other unfair and destructive practices and to effectuate the other purposes and policies of Title I of the National Industrial Recovery Act consistent with provisions thereof.

XV

If any provision of this Code is declared invalid or unenforceable, the remaining provisions shall nevertheless continue in full force and effect the same as if they had been separately presented for approval and approved by the President.

XVI

This Code shall be in operation on and after the effective date as to the whole Wall Paper Industry except as an exemption from or a stay of application of its provisions may be granted by the Administrator to a person applying for the same or except as provided in an Executive Order.

XVII

This Code of Fair Competition shall become effective on the second Monday after the approval of same by the President of the United States.

The undersigned do hereby certify that the foregoing is a true copy of the Code of Fair Competition for the Wall Paper Manufacturing Industry submitted to the Administrator under the National Industrial Recovery Act, as amended by authority of the Executive Committee of the Wall Paper Manufacturing Industry. . . .

28

Schechter Poultry Corp. vs. United States (1935)

[295 U.S. 495]

Mr. Chief Justice Hughes delivered the opinion of the Court.

Petitioners . . . were convicted in the District Court of the United States for the Eastern District of New York on eighteen counts of an indictment charging violations of what is known as the "Live Poultry Code," and on an additional count for conspiracy to commit such violations. By demurrer to the indictment and appropriate motions on the trial, the defendants contended (1) that the Code had been adopted pursuant to an unconstitutional delegation by Congress of legislative power; (2) that it attempted to regulate intrastate transactions which lay outside the authority of Congress; and (3) that in certain provisions it was repugnant to the due process clause of the Fifth Amendment. . . .

The defendants are slaughterhouse operators. . . . A.L.A. Schechter Poultry Corporation and Schechter Live Poultry Market are corporations conducting wholesale poultry slaughterhouse markets in Brooklyn, New York City. . . . Defendants ordinarily purchase their live poultry from commission men at the West Washington Market in New York City or at the railroad terminals serving the City, but occasionally they purchase from commission men in Philadelphia. They buy the poultry for slaughter and resale. After the poultry is trucked to their slaughterhouse markets in Brooklyn, it is there sold, usually within twenty-four hours, to retail poultry dealers and butchers who sell directly to consumers. The poultry purchased from defendants is immediately slaughtered, prior to delivery, by shochtim in defendants' employ. Defendants do not sell poultry in interstate commerce. . . .

Of the eighteen counts of the indictment upon which the defendants were convicted, aside from the count for conspiracy, two counts charged violation of the minimum wage and maximum hour provisions of the Code, and ten counts were for violation of the requirement (found in the "trade practice provisions") of "straight killing." . . . The charges in the ten counts, respectively, were that the defendants in selling to retail dealers and butchers had permitted "selections of individual chickens taken from particular coops and half coops."

Of the other six counts, one charged the sale to a butcher of an unfit chicken; two counts charged the making of sales without having the poultry inspected or approved in accordance with regulations or ordinances of the City of New York; two counts charged the making of false reports or the failure to make reports relating to the range of daily prices and volume of sales for certain periods; and the remaining count was for sales to slaughterers or dealers who were without licenses required by the ordinances and regulations of the City of New York.

First. Two preliminary points are stressed by the Government with respect to the appropriate approach to the important questions presented. We are told that the provision of the statute authorizing the adoption of codes must be viewed in the light of the grave national crisis with which Congress was confronted. Undoubtedly, the conditions to which power is addressed are always to be considered when the exercise of power is challenged. Extraordinary conditions may call for extraordinary remedies. But the argument necessarily stops short of an attempt to justify action which lies outside the sphere of constitutional authority. Extraordinary conditions do not create or enlarge constitutional power. The Constitution established a national government with powers deemed to be adequate, as they have proved to be both in war and peace, but these powers of the national government are limited by the constitutional grants. Those who act under these grants are not at liberty to transcend the imposed limits because they believe that more or different power is necessary. Such assertions of extra-constitutional authority were anticipated and precluded by the explicit terms of the Tenth Amendment,—"The powers not delegated to the United States by the Constitution, nor prohibited by it to the States, are reserved to the States respectively, or to the people."

The further point is urged that the national crisis demanded a broad and intensive cooperative effort by those engaged in trade and industry, and that this necessary cooperation was sought to be fostered by permitting them to initiate the adoption of codes. But the statutory plan is not simply one for voluntary effort. It does not seek merely to endow voluntary trade or industrial associations or groups with privileges or immunities. It involves the coercive exercise of the law-making power. The codes of fair competition, which the statute attempts to authorize, are codes of laws. If valid, they place all persons within their reach under the obligation of positive law, binding equally those who assent and those who do not assent. Violations of the provisions of the codes are punishable as crimes.

Second. The question of the delegation of legislative power. . . .

For a statement of the authorized objectives and content of the "codes of fair competition" we are referred repeatedly to the "Declaration of Policy" in section one of Title I of the Recovery Act. Thus, the approval of a code by the President is conditioned on his finding that it "will tend to effectuate the policy of this title." §3 (a). The President is authorized to impose such conditions "for the protection of consumers, competitors, employees, and others, and in furtherance of the public interest, and may provide such exceptions to and exemptions from the provisions of such code as the President in his discretion deems necessary to effectuate the policy herein declared."

Id. The "policy herein declared" is manifestly that set forth in section one. That declaration embraces a broad range of objectives. Among them we find the elimination of "unfair competitive practices." . . .

. . . We think the conclusion is inescapable that the authority sought to be conferred by §3 was not merely to deal with "unfair competitive practices" which offend against existing law, and could be the subject of judicial condemnation without further legislation, or to create administrative machinery for the application of established principles of law to particular instances of violation. Rather, the purpose is clearly disclosed to authorize new and controlling prohibitions through codes of laws which would embrace what the formulators would propose, and what the President would approve, or prescribe, as wise and beneficent measures for the government of trades and industries in order to bring about their rehabilitation, correction and development, according to the general declaration of policy in section one. Codes of laws of this sort are styled "codes of fair competition."

We find no real controversy upon this point and we must determine the validity of the Code in question in this aspect. . . .

The question, then, turns upon the authority which §3 of the Recovery Act vests in the President to approve or prescribe. If the codes have standing as penal statutes, this must be due to the effect of the executive action. But Congress cannot delegate legislative power to the President to exercise an unfettered discretion to make whatever laws he thinks may be needed or advisable for the rehabilitation and expansion of trade or industry. . . .

Accordingly we turn to the Recovery Act to ascertain what limits have been set to the exercise of the President's discretion. *First*, the President, as a condition of approval, is required to find that the trade or industrial associations or groups which propose a code, "impose no inequitable restrictions on admission to membership" and are "truly representative." That condition, however, relates only to the status of the initiators of the new laws and not to the permissible scope of such laws.

Second, the President is required to find that the code is not "designed to promote monopolies or to eliminate or oppress small enterprises and will not operate to discriminate against them." And, to this is added a proviso that the code "shall not permit monopolies or monopolistic practices." But these restrictions leave virtually untouched the field of policy envisaged by section one, and, in that wide field of legislative possibilities, the proponents of a code, refraining from monopolistic designs, may roam at will and the President may approve or disapprove their proposals as he may see fit. . . .

Nor is the breadth of the President's discretion left to the necessary implications of this limited requirement as to his findings. As already noted, the President in approving a code may impose his own conditions, adding to or taking from what is proposed, as "in his discretion" he thinks necessary "to effectuate the policy" declared by the Act. Of course, he has no less liberty when he prescribes a code of his own motion or on complaint, and he is free to prescribe one if a code has not been approved. The Act provides for the creation by the President of administrative agencies to assist him, but the action or reports of such agencies, or of his other assistants,—their recommendations and findings in relation to the making of codes—have no sanction beyond the will of the President, who may accept, modify or reject them as he pleases. Such recommendations or findings in no way limit the authority which §3 undertakes to vest in the President with no other conditions than those there specified. And this authority relates to a host of different trades and industries, thus extending the President's discretion to all the varieties of laws which he may deem to be beneficial in dealing with the vast array of commercial and industrial activities throughout the country.

Such a sweeping delegation of legislative power finds no support in the decisions upon which the Government especially relies. . . .

To summarize and conclude upon this point: Section 3 of the Recovery Act is without precedent. It supplies no standards for any trade, industry or activity. It does not undertake to prescribe rules of conduct to be applied to particular states of fact determined by appropriate administrative procedure. Instead of prescribing rules of conduct, it authorizes the making of codes to prescribe them. For that legislative undertaking, §3 sets up no standards, aside from the statement of the general aims of rehabilitation, correction and expansion described in section one. In view of the scope of that broad declaration, and of the nature of the few restrictions that are imposed, the discretion of the President in approving or prescribing codes, and thus enacting laws for the government of trade and industry throughout the country, is virtually unfettered. We think that the code-making authority thus conferred is an unconstitutional delegation of legislative power.

Third. The question of the application of the provisions of the Live Poultry Code to intrastate transactions. . . . This aspect of the case presents the question whether the particular provisions of the Live Poultry Code, which the defendants were convicted for violating and for having conspired to violate, were within the regulating power of Congress.

These provisions relate to the hours and wages of those employed by defendants in their slaughterhouses in Brooklyn and to the sales there made to retail dealers and butchers.

(1) Were these transactions *"in"* interstate commerce? Much is made of the fact that almost all the poultry coming to New York is sent there from other States. But the code provisions, as here applied, do not concern the transportation of the poultry from other States to New York, or the transactions of the commission men or others to whom it is consigned, or the sales made by such consignees to defendants. When defendants had made their purchases, whether at the West Washington Market in New York City or at the railroad terminals serving the City, or elsewhere, the poultry was trucked to their slaughterhouses in Brooklyn for local disposition. The interstate transactions in relation to that poultry then ended. Defendants held the poultry at their slaughterhouse markets for slaughter and local sale to retail dealers and butchers who in turn sold directly to consumers. Neither the slaughtering nor the sales by defendants were transactions in interstate commerce. . . .

The undisputed facts thus afford no warrant for the argument that the poultry handled by defendants at their slaughterhouse markets was in a *"current"* or *"flow"* of interstate commerce and was thus subject to congressional regulation. The mere fact that there may be a constant flow of commodities into a State does not mean that the flow continues after the property has arrived and has become commingled with the mass of property within the State and is there held solely for local disposition and use. So far as the poultry here in question is concerned, the flow in interstate commerce had ceased. The poultry had come to a permanent rest within the State. It was not held, used, or sold by defendants in relation to any further transactions in interstate commerce and was not destined for transportation to other States. Hence, decisions which deal with a stream of interstate commerce—where goods come to rest within a State temporarily and are later to go forward in interstate commerce—and with the regulations of transactions involved in that practical continuity of movement, are not applicable here. . . .

(2) Did the defendants' transactions directly *"affect"* interstate commerce so as to be subject to federal regulation? The power of Congress extends not only to the regulation of transactions which are part of interstate commerce, but to the protection of that commerce from injury. . . .

In determining how far the federal government may go in controlling intrastate transactions upon the ground that they "affect" interstate commerce, there is a necessary and well-established distinction between direct and indirect effects. The precise line can be drawn only as individual cases arise, but the distinction is clear in principle. Direct effects are illustrated by the railroad cases we have cited, as *e.g.*, the effect of failure to use prescribed safety appliances on railroads which are the highways of both interstate and intrastate commerce, injury to an employee engaged in interstate transportation by the negligence of an employee engaged in an intrastate movement, the fixing of rates for intrastate transportation which unjustly discriminate against interstate commerce. But where the effect of intrastate transactions upon interstate commerce is merely indirect, such transactions remain within the domain of state power. If the commerce clause were construed to reach all enterprises and transactions which could be said to have an indirect effect upon interstate commerce, the federal authority would embrace practically all the activities of the people and the authority of the State over its domestic concerns would exist only by sufferance of the federal government. Indeed, on such a theory, even the development of the State's commercial facilities would be subject to federal control. . . .

The distinction between direct and indirect effects has been clearly recognized in the application of the Anti-Trust Act. Where a combination or conspiracy is formed, with the intent to restrain interstate commerce or to monopolize any part of it, the violation of the statute is clear. . . . But where that intent is absent, and the objectives are limited to intrastate activities, the fact that there may be an indirect effect upon interstate commerce does not subject the parties to the federal statute, notwithstanding its broad provisions. . . .

While these decisions related to the application of the federal statute, and not to its constitutional validity, the distinction between direct and indirect effects of intrastate transactions upon interstate commerce must be recognized as a fundamental one, essential to the maintenance of our constitutional system. Otherwise, as we have said, there would be virtually no limit to the federal power and for all practical purposes we should have a completely centralized government. We must consider the provisions here in question in the light of this distinction. . . .

The question of chief importance relates to the provisions of the Code as to the hours and wages of those employed in defendants' slaughterhouse markets. It is plain that these requirements are imposed in order to govern the details of defendants' management of their local business. The persons employed in slaughtering and selling in local trade are not employed in interstate commerce. Their hours and wages have no direct relation to interstate commerce. The question of how many hours these employees should work and what they should be paid differs in no essential respect from similar questions in other local businesses which handle commodities brought into a State and there dealt in as a part of its internal commerce. This appears from an examination of the considerations urged by the Government with respect to conditions in the poultry trade. Thus, the Government argues that hours and wages affect prices; that slaughterhouse men sell at a small margin above operating costs; that labor represents 50 to 60 per cent of these costs; that a slaughterhouse operator paying lower wages or reducing his cost by exacting long hours of work, translates his saving into lower prices; that this results in demands for a cheaper grade of goods; and that the cutting of prices brings about demoralization of the price structure. Similar conditions may be adduced in relation to other businesses. The argument of the Government proves too much. If the federal government may determine the wages and hours of employees in the internal commerce of a State, because of their relation to cost and prices and their indirect effect upon interstate commerce, it would seem that a similar control might be exerted over other elements of cost, also affecting prices, such as the number of employees, rents, advertising, methods of doing business, etc. All the processes of production and distribution that enter into cost could likewise be controlled. If the cost of doing an intrastate business is in itself the permitted object of federal control, the extent of the regulation of cost would be a question of discretion and not of power.

The Government also makes the point that efforts to enact state legislation establishing high labor standards have been impeded by the belief that unless similar action is taken generally, commerce will be diverted from the States adopting such standards, and that this fear of diversion has led to demands for federal legislation on the subject of wages and hours. The apparent implication is that the federal authority under the commerce clause should be deemed to extend to the establishment of rules to govern wages and hours in intrastate trade and industry generally throughout the country, thus overriding the authority of the States to deal with domestic problems arising from labor conditions in their internal commerce.

It is not the province of the Court to consider the economic advantages or disadvantages of such a centralized system. It is sufficient to say that the Federal Constitution does not provide for it. Our growth and development have called for wide use of the commerce power of the federal government in its control over the expanded activities of interstate commerce, and in protecting that commerce from burdens, interferences, and conspiracies to restrain and monopolize it. But the authority of the federal government may not be pushed to such an extreme as to destroy the distinction, which the commerce clause itself establishes, between commerce "among the several States" and the internal concerns of a State. The same answer must be made to the contention that is based upon the serious economic situation which led to the passage of the Recovery Act,—the fall in prices, the decline in wages and employment, and the curtailment of the market for commodities. Stress is laid upon the great importance of maintaining wage distributions which would provide the necessary stimulus in starting "the cumulative forces making for expanding commercial activity." Without in any way disparaging this motive, it is enough to say that the recuperative efforts of the federal government must be made in a manner consistent with the authority granted by the Constitution.

We are of the opinion that the attempt through the provisions of the Code to fix the hours and wages of employees of defendants in their intrastate business was not a valid exercise of federal power. . . .

On both the grounds we have discussed, the attempted delegation of legislative power, and the attempted regulation of intrastate transactions which affect interstate commerce only indirectly, we hold the code provisions here in question to be invalid and that the judgment of conviction must be reversed.

M. Regulation of the Financial Market

Caveat emptor, the legal doctrine that holds the buyer responsible for judging the merits of what he buys, is a mere convention. It operated in Anglo-American law for only a short time, and it has been steadily superseded by the opposite convention that makes the seller more nearly responsible for giving the buyer what he really wants and liable for some losses arising from hidden defects in the goods he sells. The displacement of *caveat emptor* has meant that losses due to accidental faults no longer fall on the unlucky buyer alone but are distributed instead among all buyers, each of whom pays a small insurance premium in the form of slightly higher prices to cover the costs that the seller encounters as a result of his increased liability.

This shift is usually explained as a response to the increasing complexity of goods: a medieval housewife could detect a worm in the apple more easily than a modern motorist can discover an unbalanced crankshaft. This assumption of the buyer's incapacity to judge has also been used to justify proposals that would require the seller clearly and accurately to label the contents of his goods. On this account, a variety of systems have grown up under which government certifies the quality of goods and services by licensing doctors and lawyers, or inspecting meat, or condemning adulterated food, or censoring certain types of misleading advertisements.

In no case, however, is the modern American less able to judge the true merits of a commodity—or so it has been said— than when he sets out to buy securities. The operations of the money market are so abstract and so esoteric that even such sophisticated men as the Senators investigating Wall Street in 1932 were obviously awed by the mystique of "bear raids" and the sinister practice of "selling short," and their investigation lent weight to the long-standing complaint that small, private investors were at the mercy of the professionals. This complaint was undoubtedly reinforced by the accurate observation that no other branch of commerce is intrinsically so fertile an environment for fraud.

Such beliefs, buttressed by the impression that the great crash of 1929 was due in part to questionable practices in the stock market, led to the passage in 1933 and 1934 of the laws establishing the Securities and Exchange Commission. These statutes established certain rules of procedure that have resulted in a diminution of fraud and of deliberate manipulation of stock prices. The Commission's opinion in an early case (29) suggests the range and power of its supervisory activities. Curiously enough, the operations of the SEC have not displaced from the securities market *caveat emptor* in its most important sense. The buyer, although protected against certain flagrant abuses, must still decide for himself what constitutes a good investment, and the results of his errors are still borne directly by himself. In the same way, a licensed doctor may prove to be insufficiently skilled, or inspected meat insufficiently tender. In short, no system of public inspection or approval lifts from the individual the entire burden of choice.

29

Securities and Exchange Commission, Findings and Opinion in the Matter of National Educators Mutual Association, Inc. (1935)

[1 S.E.C. 208]

This is a proceeding to determine whether a stop order shall issue pursuant to Section 8 (d) of the Securities Act of

1933, suspending the effectiveness of the registration statement filed May 27, 1935, on Form A-1 by National Educators Mutual Association, Inc., hereinafter called the "registrant." The contention is that the registration statement contains untrue statements of material facts, and omits to state material facts required to be stated and necessary to make the statements therein not misleading with regard to Items 19, 23, 29, 37, 38, 54, 55, and Exhibits "F" and "G". This contention extends also to the prospectus insofar as it reflects the information contained in these items. A further contention is that the consent of various persons to the use of their names in the registration statement, as required by Section 7 of the Act, has not been filed.

After confirmed telegraphic notice, as prescribed by Section 8 (d) hearings were held on June 27 and 28, 1935, before a trial examiner of the Commission, in Washington, D.C., at which the Commission and the registrant were represented by counsel. Evidence was taken and the trial examiner made his report containing findings of fact. These findings, however, are merely advisory and are not binding upon the Commission. (*In the matter of Continental Distillers and Importers Corporation,* 1 S.E.C. 54, [1935]). Counsel for the registrant and counsel for the Commission advised the Commission that it was not their intention to file briefs or exceptions to such report.

In the course of the hearing the registrant announced that it consented to the entry of a stop order and admitted by a written stipulation, which was made part of the record, that the numerous deficiencies charged existed in the registration statement and prospectus, and further admitted that in addition to these, other deficiencies also existed. Findings will thus cover not only those deficiencies put in issue by the Commission's notice, but also those covered by the admissions of the registrant. Despite the registrant's consent to the issuance of a stop order, the nature of this case, in essence, an enterprise to deal in an irresponsible fashion with the small savings of city and county school teachers, makes it not only desirable but imperative to file these findings and this opinion, so that the untruthfulness and the unfairness of the registrant's officers should be a matter of public record. (*Cf. In the matter of Big Wedge Gold Mining Company*, 1 S.E.C. 98, [1935]).

The registrant was incorporated under the laws of the State of Tennessee on October 31, 1932. Its present officers are: President, F. L. Browning of Nashville, Tenn., described as past president State Teachers Association; Executive Vice President, Charles G. Pfab, also of Nashville; Secretary-Treasurer, R. O. Smith of Maryville, Tenn., described as superintendent of city schools; Assistant Secretary-Treasurer, Neal B. Spahr of Knoxville, Tenn.; Director, F. S. Elliott of Memphis, Tenn., described as president of West Tennessee Education Association; Director, Arthur L. Rankin of Chattanooga, Tenn., described as superintendent. These names and these descriptions are carried on the first page of the prospectus. In addition there is set forth upon the same page of the prospectus a list of 31 "advisory directors", all residents of Tennessee, and with few exceptions, all having designations such as "Dean", "Principal", "Superintendent", etc. Obviously, this array of names—one hopes innocently lent—was intended to give an air of respectability and educational "mutuality" to an enterprise that fortunately for the protection of the investing school teachers of Tennessee and other states sought to register under the Securities Act of 1933.

The authorized capital stock of the registrant consists of 25,000 shares of common stock, no par value, "12,000 shares of which have been issued and are outstanding, being paid in at the price of 10 cents per share."

Since the organization of the registrant its principal business appears to have been the solicitation of subscriptions for so-called Endowment Bonds which were sold in units described as "5 annual payment 12-year Endowment Bond with 5 shares Bonus stock." As of the date of hearing, the registrant had received subscriptions for approximately 1,000 of these "bonds" from residents of Tennessee. As of April 30, 1935, the date of the balance sheet, the registrant had received $53,-272.61 on account of these subscriptions, of which sum $35,-943.58 or 70 per cent was disbursed for "sales expense." According to the evidence the purchaser of the foregoing units is to pay $750 in 5 annual installments, or the equivalent thereof in monthly, quarterly, or semiannual payments, and will receive at the end of 12 years $1,000 in cash and 5 shares of the no par common stock of a "stated" value of $50 each. This was alleged to be the stated value despite the fact that shares of the same class, issued to the organizers of the company, were paid in at the price of 10 cents per share.[1]

The registration statement before us covers a new offering of units, each consisting of a "5 annual payment, 10-year endowment bond, with 5 shares of stock." Under the terms of the offering the purchaser of a unit is to pay the sum of $750 in cash in annual installments of $150 each. In return for the $750 paid in over a period of 5 years, the company agrees to pay the investor at the end of 10 years $750 in cash and five shares of stock, as previously issued, which stock has a "stated" value of $50 per share. The registrant proposes to issue 1,000 such "bonds." The face and back of the bond contain the figures "$1,000" prominently displayed and proclaim in large letters that the registrant "will pay the sum of One Thousand ($1,000.00) Dollars," but underneath, in much smaller type, appears the statement, in parentheses "(Consisting of $750 cash and $250 stock)." The registrant has admitted that this use of the words and figures, "one thousand dollars" is incorrect. We find it untrue and misleading. The fact is that the principal amount of the "bond," if it can even be called a bond,[2] is but seven hundred and fifty dollars.

Equally misleading is the whole contract attached to this so-called "bond." A full page, for example, sets forth the "Guaranteed Cash Surrender Value" of the "bond." In bold letters are the words—"At end of the Second Bond Year. * * *

[1] Although it was claimed by the registrant that the stated value of this stock is $50 per share, the balance sheet carries the capital stock liability on the basis of 10 cents per share. The registrant has now stipulated that the stated value of these shares is 10 cents.

[2] The registrant itself admitted that this use of the word "bond" is incorrect.

$313.60." In fine print there follows—"consisting of five shares of the Capital Stock of the National Educators Mutual Association, Inc., herein valued at $50 per share and $63.60 in cash." And so on until the end of the tenth bond year. This fine and calculated language is said by these gentlemen to apprise the unsuspecting school teacher that after an investment of $300 in hard cash the school teacher is "guaranteed" $63.60 and five shares of stock for which the promoters of this scheme have paid a mere 50 cents. We find the contrary to be the case. The Supreme Court of the United States has upheld the action of a state securities commission in debarring a contract as fraudulent whose terms were less scandalous than these. *Investors' Syndicate* v. *McMullen*, 274 U.S. 717 (1927); *cf. Porter* v. *Investors' Syndicate*, 286 U.S. 461 (1932), *aff'd on rehearing*, 287 U.S. 346 (1932).

The expected gross proceeds of the issue amount to $750,-000, of which sum $150,000 will constitute selling expenses. Thus, disregarding the first payment as constituting "selling expense," it will be seen that the registrant is to receive 4 payments of $150 each, which, compounded annually at, say, 6 per cent—a yield far too high to comport with the conservatism that should attend an enterprise of this nature—would yield approximately $930 if, *but only if*, the registrant has no expenses, suffers no losses and pays no salaries whatsoever during that entire period. But even if this unusual result could be achieved the value of a share would only be $36, assuming that there were, even though such is not the case, no other shares entitled to participate in these profits. In view of the fact that this same class of stock was sold to the promoters at 10 cents a share, and in view of the normal probabilities of operation, our finding is that attributing a "stated value" of $50 a share to the common stock in the fashion in which it has been done by this registrant is highly misleading.

According to the evidence, Charles G. Pfab, an officer and director, controls the registrant. He was also the promoter of the Company and acted as underwriter with respect to the previous issue of "12-year endowment bonds." He will also act as underwriter for the present issue, although the registration statement and prospectus fail to reveal such fact, and to him will go the "selling expense," now increased to twice the previous rate, and constituting 20 per cent of the offering price. An examination of this entire scheme tends to indicate that Mr. Pfab and his associates are to obtain the use of investors' money for 10 years, at the end of which time they agree to repay the principal. The sole compensation to the bondholders for the use of their money is the stock which will allow them to share less than equally with Mr. Pfab and his associates the amounts that their money may earn.

The name of the registrant deserves special attention. The record discloses that the name, "National Educators Mutual Association, Inc.," was adopted in 1930. According to the testimony of Pfab, the registrant now proposes to sell its securities for the first time in states other than Tennessee, in which it was incorporated. By the registrant's own admission, the "name of the company has the capacity of being misleading in that it tends to create the impression in the minds of persons who are asked to purchase the securities registered—that it is connected with the National Education Association." This latter association is a voluntary organization of persons actively engaged in educational work, with a membership of 187,000 in January 1935. Our finding is that the particular combination of words chosen for the name of the registrant is misleading and was used primarily for the purpose of creating in the minds of the public the erroneous impression that it is affiliated with the National Education Association. (*Cf. Federal Trade Commission* v. *Civil Service Training Bureau, Inc.*, C.C.A. 6th, June 29, 1935.)

The inclusion of the word "Mutual" in the name of the registrant is subject to the same criticism. Very generally speaking, mutual benefit associations are either purely voluntarily aggregations of individuals or bodies corporate, formed and organized, not to return a profit to a few but, aside from fraternal objects, for the purpose of rendering financial aid or other assistance to all their members, or certain designated beneficiaries of the latter, when visited by sickness, death, or other misfortunes specifically agreed upon. They are founded

upon the principle of entire mutuality in relation to burdens
as well as benefits. According to the evidence, the registrant
was organized solely for business purposes and the pecuniary
profit of its stockholders. It does not possess the characteristics
of a mutual company. Our finding is that the use of the word
"mutual" in the title of the registrant is incorrect and misleading.

The disastrous financial history of the registrant is concealed
rather than revealed by the form in which its balance sheet
and profit and loss statements were submitted. Under Item 55
of the registration statement, in the profit and loss statements
for the years ending December 31, 1933, and December 31,
1934, and for the period ending April 30, 1935, certified by
Dahlberg and Co., Certified Public Accountants of Nashville,
Tenn., the registrant shows under "miscellaneous other income" an item entitled "Contributed by Sales Agent" the
amounts, $583.56, $3,042.36, $1,964.86. Suffice it to say that
Charles G. Pfab acted as sales agent and made these contributions. The registrant admitted that if it had not been for
this claimed statement of income, the company would have
shown a net loss in its profit and loss statement. Pfab testified
that since its organization, the registrant has operated at a
loss, and that the amount of such loss is equal to the amount
donated by Pfab. In order to present an attractive security to
the public, it was desirable that the financial condition of the
company be presented in a favorable light. Sound accounting
theory and practice require that no income could be considered
as having been realized by reason of the contributions, and
accordingly, the amount of same should not have appeared in
the profit and loss statement at all. Our finding is, and the
registrant admits, that the total amount of the donations aggregating $5,542.63, should have been reflected on the balance
sheet as "Donated surplus," and that a corresponding amount,
representing the loss resulting from the company's operations,
should have been shown on the balance sheet as "Earned Surplus–Deficit." As we have had occasion to state before, "We
deem it very important that earnings should not be misrepre-
sented." (In the matter of General Income Shares, Inc., 1

S.E.C. 110, [1935]). This device adopted by the registrant to conceal its losses, sponsored by an accountant that represents itself as having not only independence but also integrity and ability, seems especially reprehensible since a purely non-existent income was "created." In substance there was nothing more than a cancellation of an indebtedness, which even for income-tax purposes is not regarded as income.[3] Including it as such was highly misleading.

With respect to Items 1, 3, 11, 14, 15, 19, 20, 23, 27, 29, 31, 32, 33, 34, 36, 37, 38, 39, 41, 42, 43, 44, 45, 47, 51, 52, 53, 54, 55, and Exhibits "B", "F", and "G", we adopt the trial examiner's findings since they are in full accord with the evidence adduced at the hearing. Our finding is that these items contain untrue statements of material facts, or omit to state material facts required to be stated therein and necessary to make the statements therein not misleading.

The deficiencies in the prospectus need not be specifically discussed, except as noted hereafter, since they only reflect those heretofore noted in the registration statement.

The registrant, since this hearing was held, has filed amendments seeking to correct some of the glaring misstatements contained in the registration statement. Though we do not pass upon these amendments at this time, the fact that this registrant has attempted to cure the deficiencies leading to this stop order proceeding by amendments filed since the hearing, makes it appropriate to set forth the considerations that under the Act justify the Commission in lifting a stop order once entered. Obviously, such action should not be lightly done nor without complete assurance that the registration statement and prospectus are now free from misrepresentation and ingenuous misstatement. As we have said before, our powers do not extend to preventing the public offering of a security if the truth concerning it be told, but the truth, under the Congressional mandate embodied in the Act, means the full truth. (*Cf.*

[3] See Treas. Reg. 86, Art. 22 (a)—14; *United States v. Oregon-Washington R. & Nav. Co.*, 251 F. 211 (C.C.A. 2d, 1918); *Commissioner v. Auto Strop Safety Razor Co.*, 74 F. (2d) 226 (C.C.A. 2d, 1934).

In the matter of Plymouth Consolidated Gold Mines, Inc.,
1 S.E.C. 139, [1935]). The registration statement seeks to
ascertain certain very definite particulars of a registrant. In
many instances, answers to these may be technically adequate
when viewed item by item. The combination of these items,
especially those required to be set forth in the prospectus,
generally reveal the character of the offering being made and
the nature of the security the investor is being solicited to buy.
But it may frequently be true that the cumulative effect of
these individual items is carefully and intentionally concealed
by their segregation in the prospectus, with the result that the
impression left upon the reader by the prospectus is fundamen-
tally untrue and misleading. The challenge of the Commission
can thus under the Act be not only to individual items in the
registration statement and prospectus as such, but upon the
broad basis that the general effect of the prospectus as an entirety is to create an untrue and misleading picture in the
minds of prospective investors. Frequently the prospectus,
which is and should be a selling document, attempts to summarize in broad terms the nature of the offering. If this summarization is untrue, it can undoubtedly be challenged by the
Commission. But even where there is no such summarization,
the circumstances of a particular offering [may] well be such
as to make the absence of statements setting forth in simple
language the consequences of certain features of the financial
structure of the registrant have the effect of portraying an
essentially inadequate and misleading picture to the investor.

These considerations have particular bearing in this instance.
The general statement of the nature of this particular enterprise contained in the prospectus and set forth in the footnote
is obviously far from the fact.[4] The cynically minded might

[4] "For many years a great deal of thought has been given by the
educators to the situation and the needs of the teachers for a service
to them such as this Association now offers. Many authorities have
been consulted and no little time and expense devoted to a study
of the matters involved.

"It is evident to most observers that members of the teaching
profession, devoting their whole time in the service to the public's
interest, do not have the opportunities available to persons of other

well read certain paragraphs of this statement as indicating that educators or school teachers are unused to financial transactions and thus reach the conclusion which seems to be the hope of this enterprise that they are easily duped. But it is the avowed belief of the gentlemen who conduct this enterprise that the school teachers to whom they are proposing to sell these "bonds" have little knowledge of the niceties of finance and investment. How much more reprehensible does their con-

---

occupations to come in contact with nor study those fields for safely accumulating their individual shares in worldly goods.

"Proceeding with that understanding and with the thought in mind that what an educator has as capital assets is largely education and time, converted into terms of service, which is devoted to the public's interest in exchange for a compensation that, during his or her lifetime, must produce the desired financial reward. Furthermore, that the average of income derived therefrom and the accumulation of savings thereby effected are not liable to provide the desired estate, much less one that is comparable to that so gained and obtained by others engaged in other business activities.

"Keeping in mind this fact, which is accepted by every authority of finance and economics, that life insurance is the first basis upon which a sizable estate can be created with certainty, by those whose means will not otherwise provide for one, this Association was organized, first, to finance a Life Insurance Company as its ultimate objective, and to render service primarily for the educator's needs.

"Second. To provide a means whereby savings from salary or income may be invested in a class and character of security that by its nature would encourage the ultimate of thrift in the individual over the productive period of his or her service years to the end that these savings may be invested with safety and set to work creating the largest possible secondary estate.

"Third. To provide means whereby teachers may be able to borrow money to further their education, also to advance money against their salaries and to discount school salary warrants.

"To that end and for that purpose, the founders developed their plans and created this corporation and will establish an advisory board of directors from among the leading educators in the States in which this Association will operate. In this manner the teachers of the various States in which this Association will operate will be in close touch with the directorate of the Association for the benefits such contract may afford them in consulting and advisory service."

duct then become in the light of such a belief! How much
more important does it then devolve upon them to state frankly
that they are in essence asking school teachers to put their
savings in their control and for their management of these savings these school teachers are to give them more than half of
the profits that may enure to the enterprise. For, in essence,
in this "mutual" enterprise profits go to promoters and advisors
in the ratio of approximately 60 per cent and to the investing
"bondholders" in the ratio of approximately 40 per cent! No
array of locally prominent names should be permitted to conceal these facts;[5] nor, we hope, will any future prospect be
left unaware of the danger of entrusting the small savings derived from school teaching in the hands of men who upon this
record and by their own admissions have demonstrated untruthfulness and misfeasance in positions of trust and confidence.

A stop order in accordance with these findings and opinion,
suspending the effectiveness of the registration statement, will
issue.

[5] Three thousand shares of stock were reserved for distribution
as bonus stock to the officers, directors, and "advisory directors"
of the registrant. One hundred shares was to be given "for each
bond purchased and is issued for the payment of the bond and
services rendered to the Association such as attending meetings,
keeping the bondholders advised as to the conditions of the Association, and assisting the salesmen in selling."

For Product Safety Concerns and Information please contact our
EU representative GPSR@taylorandfrancis.com Taylor & Francis
Verlag GmbH, Kaufingerstraße 24, 80331 München, Germany